D0613062

TROUBLESOME PEOPLE

Enemies of War: 1916-1986

By the same author
Fortune's Hostages
Sidney Bernstein
Freya Stark
The Letters of Freya Stark:
Volume VII (Some Talk of Alexander 1952–59)
Volume VIII (Traveller's Epilogue 1960–80) (ed.)

TROUBLESOME PEOPLE

Enemies of War: 1916-1986

BY

CAROLINE MOOREHEAD

HAMISH HAMILTON · LONDON

First published in Great Britain in 1987
by Hamish Hamilton Ltd
27 Wrights Lane, London W8 5TZ

© 1987 Caroline Moorehead

All rights reserved.

British Library of Cataloguing in Publication Data
Moorehead, Caroline
   Troublesome people : enemies of war
   1916–1986.
   1. Pacifism——History——20th century
   I. Title
   327.1'72'0904   JX1950

ISBN 0-241-12105-1

Printed in Great Britain by
Butler & Tanner, Frome, Somerset

After all, we have to admit that it is always the troublesome people who force us to remedy the abuses that we lazily let slide.

Bernard Shaw, on conscientious objectors, in
What I Really Wrote about the War.

For my father
1910–1983

Acknowledgements

This book would not have been possible without the help and kindness of enormous numbers of people who either are or once were pacifists. I would like to thank them, and others:

Jim Adler, Marit von Ahlefeld, Dr. Tatsuicho Akizuki, Pat Arrowsmith, John Aucrum, Virginia Barrow, Meg Beresford, Dorothy Bing, Michael Biggs, Richard Boardman, Jim Bristol, Tom and Maisie Carlisle, April Carter, Lord Archibald, Fenner Brockway, Steven Brown, Volkmar Diele, Polly Duncan, Barbara Eggleston, Harry Everett, John Ferguson, the late Rev. Patrick Figgis, Valerie Flassali, Roger Franklin, Uschi Fuchs, Dr. Kenneth Greer, Ursula Hagedorn, Denis Hayes, Mark Hayler, William Heard, Ed Hedemann, Bill Hetherington, Taeko Hirano, Dorothy Hogg, Ferdi Hülser, Jean and Jill Hutchinson, Ronald Huzzard, John Hyatt, Storm Jameson, Carla Johnston, the Jonah Community in Baltimore, Chris Judge Smith, Cornelia Junghaus, Gunter and Monica Kahl, Jorg Kammler, Jenz Kasnak, Yoshitaka Kawamoto, John Keegan, Randy Kehler, Msgn. Bruce Kent, Werner Kratschell, Prof. Saburo Kugai, Yasuko Kusachi, Joan Layton, Lord Macleod of Fuinary, Ron Mallone, Zen Matsutani, Muriel McMillan, Jan Melichar, Gerda Meyer, Eva Michls, Ted Milligan, Harry Mister, Hilda Morris, the late Richard Murry, Doris Nicholls, Nikkyo Niwano, Canon Paul Ostreicher, Nora Page, Frances Partridge, Amy Pastan, Katherine Perry, Basil Priestley, Philip Radley, Michael Randle, Chip Reynolds, Andrew Rigby, Ingrid von Rosenberg, Joyce Runham Brown, Sydney Russell, Bayard Rustin, Roger Ruston, Gyoto Sato, Janet Savelli, Karl Senge, Anthony Sheil, Prof. Naomi Shono, Michael Simmons, Zohara Simmons, Tony Smythe, Pam Solo, Myrtle Solomon, the Rev. Lord Donald Soper, Christopher Sinclair-Stevenson, Jeremy Swift, Ishiguro Tachibana, Hamish Walker, Nicholas Walter, Wolfgang and Helga Weber Zucht, the late Lylie Valentine, Roger Williamson, Canon Gordon

Wilson, Arthur Windsor, Gerald Wingate, Edith Wynner, Senji Yagamuchi, and the staff of the Imperial War Museum, Department of Sound Records.

I am grateful to Muriel McMillan, for letting me quote from her husband's letters; to Frances Partridge, for letting me use extracts from her diaries which appeared in *A Pacifist's War* (The Hogarth Press; 1978); to Catherine Reilly, for permission to quote from Margaret Sackville's poem *A Memory* (*Scars upon My Heart: Women's Poetry and Verse of the First World War*: 1981); to George Sassoon, for permission to use some lines from Siegfried Sassoon's *Aftermath* (*Collected Poems: 1908-1956*; 1961); and to the CBCO, for the information contained in their booklet *Troublesome People* on COs in the 1914–18 war.

I would most particularly like to thank David Cheshire, who gave me the idea for this book, and Teddy Hodgkin, who read and worked on the manuscript and made many essential suggestions.

Illustrations

For kind permission to reproduce the pictures in this book, grateful thanks must go to the following:

The Peace Pledge Union (1st World War force feeding suit); the Library Committee of the Religious Society of Friends (G. P. Micklewright's 1st World War CO cartoons, the arrest of Fenner Brockway, banquet for 17 ex-prisoner MPs, Clifford Allen at the time of the NCF's foundation, Gandhi, 1931); the Central Board for Conscientious Objectors (1st World War COs sent to France); the Women's International League for Peace and Freedom (Women's Peace Conference, The Hague, 1915); the Sport and General Press Agency (Bertrand Russell, 1910); Sydney Russell (George Lansbury); Diana Hargrave of the Kibbo Kift Foundation (Kibbo Kift rally); Bayard Rustin (Bayard Rustin and Muriel Lester); the BBC Hulton Picture Library (2nd World War woman prisoner in Holloway); John F. Riley (2nd World War COs on the land); the Associated Press (Martin Niemöller, the Mississippi march, 1966, draft burning in Milwaukee, 1968, pacifist aboard Polaris submarine *Ethan Allen*, 1960); Duncan Baxter of the *Sunday Times* (Greenham Common sitdown, 1980); Brian Harris of *The Times* (CND 'Mutants', 1983).

If, despite our researches, there is anyone who is not credited, we hope you will accept our apologies.

Contents

Foreword

'Travels among the war resisters' might have been another sub-title for this book. It is not a history of 20th century pacifists, nor a comprehensive account of the peace movement since the First World War. Rather, by talking to pacifists in the countries where conscientious opposition to war has been most active this cen-tury, and where the debate about pacifism has been sharpest — Britain, the United States, West Germany, Japan — I have tried to draw a picture of what modern pacifists are actually like; to give an idea of their style, their diversity, their origins and their eloquence; to show how and where their feelings about war and peace have fitted in with their other beliefs; to demonstrate how varied and above all how very numerous they have been and are today. More than anything else, perhaps, I wanted to show how, for all the threads that link pacifists to their roots and to their mentors, for all the contacts that bind them to each other all over the world, pacifism is basically the most lonely of beliefs, held for the most part in private, and sustained in isolation, often in the face of powerful opposition.

I wanted, also, to show that of all modern movements pacifism ranks with the battle for women's suffrage as the one most ten-aciously, most lastingly and most universally held; and that it has pushed people to the most remarkable feats of endurance. To profess this faith, people have fasted, marched, survived long winters of extreme discomfort protesting at the gates of military bases, and been arrested more times than it is possible to record. Some have risked the death penalty rather than alter their views; some have indeed died for it. A few, their health and spirit broken by punishment, have gone mad. There is a stubborn-ness, an obduracy, about pacifism that can be infuriating; it can also be heroic, admirable.

Nowhere have I tried to define the term 'pacifist': pacifism has meant different things to different people at different times. Not all the people in this book would refer to themselves as 'pacifists', but all would see themselves as belonging to some kind of pacifist tradition, and it is as followers of that tradition, whatever the form it has taken for them, that they find a place here. This is particularly true, perhaps, in the United States, where pacifism — though not always regarded as such — has been at the heart of one of the greatest achievements of this century: the civil rights movement. Behind the tactics of non-violence lies the clearest pacifist philosophy.

Pacifist belief relies on a notion of personal morality. Conscientious objectors, who embody this sense of responsibility, form a crucial element in pacifist ideology, though they became important only with the advent of conscription in Europe at the end of the 18th century.

The exact point where pacifist rejection of war begins has varied from century to century and group to group and continues to vary today. At its most extreme, pacifism can mean complete dissociation from society and all its violent tenets, like the Huttrite communities of the 16th century; it can mean refusing to kill animals as well as men, and rejecting, like the Anabaptists, the whole structure of government, along with the machinery of war, as basically violent in character; it can mean absolute non-violence for oneself, but no strictures on those who have not seen the light (some Buddhists); it can mean the refusal to condone or be involved in one war, but not all wars, as in the case of American pacifists in the war between the states. In between come those who protest against war, in whatever form it appears, but not against self-defence; and those who refuse to fight, not because they are against fighting, but because they do not believe that the state has any right to order them to do so. Most common in the 20th century Western world have been those who have opposed war from rationalist, humanitarian reasons, rather than purely religious ones, men rejecting not government itself, but only the use by governments of what they consider unnecessary violence, and who have tried at the same time to integrate pacifism into the order of the world. Such people often see themselves as disciples of the great teachers of non-violence, Thoreau, Garrison, Tolstoy and Gandhi, all of whom argued that the techniques of non-resistance are ultimately more effective than, as well as ethically superior to, violence. It is the very diversity of these beliefs and the complexity of their origins that has made the task of the Tribunals set up to pass judgment on those who hold them during times of war so very hard.

Pacifism, in the narrow sense of the rejection of war by an individual, is rather less than 2,000 years old. Before the Christians, as Peter Brock shows in *Pacifism in Europe to 1914*, there is no record of a soldier refusing to take part in war on grounds of conscience; and right up until the early 18th century Western pacifism was a concern only of those who belonged firmly inside the Christian teachings.

Though a number of sayings have been attributed to Jesus which collectively suggest rejection of violence — 'all they that take the sword shall perish with the sword'; 'blessed are the peacemakers: for they shall be called the children of God' — no pronouncement is in fact to be found in the Gospels concerning the rightness or wrongness of military service. Christian scholars agree that Jesus preached a philosophy of non-violence; where they disagree is over what precisely it meant and whether it was intended to cover all circumstances and all times.

Many of the early church fathers condemned war, and two of them, Tertullian and Origen, stated unequivocally that Christ's words were incompatible with war. By the 4th century, though official church sayings continued to be anti-military in tone, soldiering had become an accepted profession for Christians, Constantine having accommodated the Church to the necessities of warfare. It was under the sign of the cross that his army defeated that of his imperial rival, Maxentius, and a Christian emperor was to become the protector of the persecuted sect: at a price. In 314, two years after Constantine's victory at the Milvian Bridge outside Rome, a Church synod in Arles declared: 'Concerning those who lay down their arms in time of peace: let them be excluded from communion.' Those with conscientious scruples were to be tolerated in time of war but not in time of peace. Soon, they acquired a patron saint, in the form of St. Maximilianus. Early in the 5th century, St. Augustine of Hippo produced his theory of a Just War — that a war fought for a just cause, with a right intention, declared by lawful authority, conducted within certain strict moral limits and only in the very last resort, could be justified — which, alongside the notion of the Holy War, was to become medieval Christianity's stand on war and peace. With the barbarian invasions, pacifism among the Christians vanished, and reappeared only later and then among more obscure sects and not in the mainstream of the Roman Catholic and Orthodox Churches.

The first people to reawaken pacifism in the medieval world were the Cathars, followers of the 3rd century prophet Mani, born in Mesopotamia, who saw the world as the scene of permanent combat between the power of good and the equally strong power of evil. Cathars ate no meat and shed no blood: they repudiated the material world as coming from Satan, and celebrated only the kingdom of the spirit. Manichaeism flourished for a time in the Balkans, emerging also in Italy, and later in France where, known as Albigensians, its numerous supporters were eventually crushed by Simon de Montfort. The 15th century saw the Waldensians in Lyons, preaching Christian obedience and the literal following of the Sermon on the Mount, and a number of Bohemian sects rejecting non-violence; the 16th, the Anabaptists, born in Zurich as an extension of the Reformation, who repudiated the state and all its laws and turned instead to higher dictates. The Anabaptists, too, moved and took new roots and new positions. In north-west Germany and the Netherlands, they were influenced by a former Catholic priest called Menno Simons, founder of the Mennonites, who announced his desire to build up a new congregation of Christians 'without spot or wrinkle'.

In England, there were also the Quakers. George Fox, a Leicestershire shoemaker, preached the need to return to what he saw as the spiritual teachings of Christ. Fox repudiated 'carnal weapons', and by 1652 was writing, 'The peacemaker hath the Kingdom and is in it'. Persecuted, condemned as traitors and reviled, it was not until the end of the 17th century that the Quakers emerged as an organized body, with regular yearly meetings, all subscribing to the belief that peace and persuasion were better politics, and had more force, than war and the use of weapons. A peace document, originally worded by Fox, is still the basis of a leaflet used by Quakers when explaining their principles about warfare. 'We utterly deny all outward wars and strife, and fighting with outward weapons, for any end, or under any pretence whatever . . . the spirit of Christ, which leads us unto all Truth, will never move us to fight and war against any man . . .'

It was in America that the struggle for freedom of conscience, later to provide the roots for non-violent disobedience, took shape, chiefly in New England and Pennsylvania, where in the 17th century religious pacifists won the right to refuse to bear arms. Asserting that the state had no authority over matters of conscience, and taking literally the New Testament words 'resist not evil', many of the peace Churches, the Mennonites, Brethren and Amish, withdrew to a large extent from the world, becoming known in the process as the 'non-resistants'.

The Quakers, refusing to see their meetings as little islands to be preserved from the wickedness of the world, took a different view and argued that, on the contrary, it would be their vision, one of goodness and peace, that would conquer. When the Society of Friends established the government of Pennsylvania, they planned that civil authority should flow from their own direct understanding of what was right, their 'inner light'. Nothing that could be construed as support for state violence in any of its forms was to be endorsed: the Friends would pay no war taxes, give no fees to others to take their place as soldiers, and they would serve the war machine in no alternative capacity. The Great Law, introduced by William Penn in 1682, at a moment when in Britain over a hundred crimes were still punishable by death, made murder and treason the only two capital offences. During both the Revolution and the Civil War, Quakers were repeatedly imprisoned, fined, and their property confiscated. They were little liked. In 1660 a report in Virginia had referred to them as an 'unreasonable and turbulent sort of people' — not militant, but they could be fiercely and provocatively stubborn.

Right up until the 20th century, however, direct action of a pacifist nature was seen, not as something that might become an organized mass movement towards social change, but as an individual's testimony, a gesture of personal creed. Individuals, not groups, are remembered and honoured for their stands. John Woolman, one of the most significant figures in the early history of non-violence, castigated fellow Quakers who were also slave-holders in the South, and refused to pay his taxes in support of the war against the French or of that against the Indians, observing that 'to refuse the active payment of a Tax which our society generally paid, was exceedingly disagreeable; but to do a thing contrary to my conscience appeared yet more dreadful'. William Lloyd Garrison spoke out firmly for the need to 'assail iniquity' — in his case, the death penalty, slavery and warfare — but only with words. Henry David Thoreau, the philosopher-naturalist, is best loved of all American civil libertarians. For some years he had refused to pay his poll tax, though he paid other taxes, like the highway tax, insisting that the poll tax went directly to support a government which sanctioned slavery, of which he did not approve. In 1846, he was arrested as he was on his way to the shoemaker to collect a shoe that had just been mended. His friend Ralph Waldo Emerson is said to have visited him in his cell and asked: 'Henry, why are you here?' 'Why,' Thoreau replied, 'are you *not* here?'

The result of his one night in captivity is possibly the best known of all American pacifist texts and the most widely quoted, for in it Thoreau defines the exact nature of the division that every pacifist faces when he feels that he can no longer serve his government in war and violence. 'The authority of government,' writes Thoreau, '. . . is still an impure one: to be strictly just, it must have the sanction and consent of the governed . . . There will never be a really free and enlightened State, until the State comes to recognize the individual as a higher and independent Power, from which all its own power and authority are derived, and treats him accordingly.'

Throughout the 18th and 19th centuries, Europe produced a growing number of protesters against war. Philosophers and statesmen drew up visions of a united Europe, in which war would be seen as a crime against humanity, and wrote a series of carefully argued peace plans to give substance to their dreams. From 1815 on, peace societies sprang up in most states, some radical and socialist, seeing peace as part of a new order, others conservative, seeing it as a preserver of the old one. The Peace Society, founded in London in 1816, drew together pacifists from across the whole spectrum of religious and moral belief, allying a call for peace to other reforms, such as the abolition of slavery and penal reform. In New York, the previous year, David Low Dodge, a merchant and keen peace pamphleteer, had founded a similar American society. Both were 'principled against all wars, under any pretence'. By 1825, however, when there were 25 pacifist societies in Britain alone and more than 30 in the United States, the realization had spread that something more was needed: that it was no longer enough to appeal simply to morality. A peace programme was drawn up by the British Peace Society, calling for the settlement of international disputes by arbitration, and expressing support for the 'policeman but not the soldier'.

From the early 1840s on, Europe saw many international peace congresses and late in the century a 'great peace crusade' was launched in Western Europe, which put forward a phased programme of disarmament and the building up of anti-militaristic international laws. Individual men and women continued to speak out against war: men like Jean de Triac, a Catholic writer, who described war as *'meurtre en grand'*. By the end of the century, anti-militarism was written into the manifestos of the nascent socialist parties all the way from the Balkans to France.

It was also towards the end of the century that pacifism acquired one of its most eloquent spokesmen. In 1857 Tolstoy had watched a man being guillotined in Paris and had been revolted; once an enthusiastic soldier, his 'conversion' to total pacifism took place in the late 1870s, when he began equating war and capital punishment with murder, and in *A Confession* he wrote of 'non-resistance to evil'. Tolstoy's pacifism was based on the need for personal responsibility; he saw it as an ethical imperative, expressed most purely and most simply in the teaching of Christ. The state itself, he maintained, was the greatest obstacle to the law of love. 'Government is violence,' he wrote to a Hungarian admirer, 'Christianity is meekness, non-resistance, love. And therefore, government cannot be Christian, and a man who wishes to be a Christian must not serve government' — nor swear official oaths, collaborate with the police, or perform military service. To resist war was to liberate mankind from its shadow. 'Universal military service,' declared Tolstoy in *The Kingdom of God is Within You*, 'is the last stage of violence that governments need for the maintenance of the whole structure . . . and its removal would bring down the whole building.' In this, he was anticipating the arguments of the most persuasive of the 20th century pacifists.

If Tolstoy's doctrine of social protest by withdrawal was hard to follow, his influence over later pacifists was immense, largely because of his realization that pacifism had to emerge from its Christian roots. It was, he believed 'universal to all mankind', precisely because its origins lay in an ethical principle 'intelligible and common to all men, of whatever religion or nation, whether Catholic, Mohammedan, Buddhist, Confucian, whether Spanish or Japanese', and that the day had to be sought when 'of wars and armies as there are now, there will remain only the recollection'. Soon after it was published, Gandhi read *The Kingdom of God is Within You*. 'Russia gave me in Tolstoy,' he was to write, many years later, 'a teacher who furnished a reasoned basis for my non-violence.'

This is a book about the lives of individual pacifists. It is the story of a number of 'troublesome people' who, each in their own way, have found war unacceptable, and tried to push the world a little in the direction of peace. As part of a mass movement they have been singularly unsuccessful. But they have been necessary, as custodians of individual freedom, and their refusal to conform has proved subtly threatening to the states whose citizens they are; and they may become more so, as the machinery of war becomes more lethal. It is as single witnesses that their ideas stand out, and shine as brightly, and in much the same way, as they did in 1846, when Thoreau chose to go to prison rather than support his country's war against Mexico.

PART ONE

1

1916: a faith defined

January 5, 1916, was a Wednesday. By early afternoon Members of Parliament were gathering in the corridors and lobbies of the House of Commons; the turn-out was unusually large, men in uniform, hurriedly returned from the front, mingling with those in frock coats. There was an air of expectation, almost eagerness, as before a contest. When the House sat, at 2.45, a first few items of business were rapidly dealt with: the Mediterranean Expeditionary Force, the casualties on the Western Front, Exchequer bonds, lunacy institutions and enemy companies in England, all dispatched in no more than a few sentences each.

Shortly after three o'clock, the Prime Minister, Herbert Asquith, rose to speak. This was the moment the members had been waiting for; with varying degrees of approval or hostility, most of them had seen it coming. Asquith's motion was short: 'That leave be given to bring in a Bill to make provision with respect to Military Service in connection with the present war.' If the words were designed to sound mild, uncontroversial, there was no one present who did not know precisely what they meant: a call to permit the introduction of military conscription, for the first time in the history of the country.

Asquith spoke, to a largely silent audience, for less than an hour. He talked about the failure of the Derby Scheme, the last passionate call for single men to attest their willingness to serve; he mentioned casualties in France, the Gallipoli campaign, the importance of rapid victory; he spoke about the need to think very clearly about men who could reasonably ask for exemption from the army, whether on grounds of work, or domestic circumstances or religious scruples, and here he reminded the House of the example of Pitt, who had exempted Quakers from the war against Napoleon; he mentioned his 'pledge' to married men that they would not have to serve before all single ones were at least accounted for. Conscription was not what he himself

3

wished for, he insisted, but what was to be done? 'I should,' he concluded at last, 'have been very glad myself if it could have been done without; no one would have been more glad than I . . .'

Then Asquith sat down, leaving it to Andrew Bonar Law, Secretary of State for the Colonies, and Walter Long, President of the Local Government Board, to conduct the bitter battle in the Commons through to victory. And bitter it soon was. The fact that conscription, never before needed in Britain, could have been foreseen by anyone with his eye on the progress of the war made it no more palatable than if it had come as a complete surprise.

In the afternoons and long evenings that followed, there was vehement debate in Parliament about the nature of liberty and freedom, and much was heard of the fact that Britain had never before known such coercion and could not now surely tolerate it. But there was also relief and warm acceptance: some spoke of the vital importance of full manpower for a final push at the Front; others of a 'slackers' charter', and how disgraceful it was that so many cowardly young men were hanging back; while others again wondered what use were the British traditions of liberty to a country soon to be overrun by the Huns. J. H. Thomas, a railwaymen's member, declared that, for his part, he thought the move for conscription was all a huge conspiracy; he was sure the unions, fearing that conscription might be used to deprive them of hard-won rights, would never stand for it.

Outside the Chamber itself, along the corridors, in the tea rooms and lobbies, day after day, emissaries from the anti-conscription bodies, who like the Parliamentarians had seen this moment coming, gathered and talked and plotted, attempting to put steel into the hearts of the few MPs in the House who had spoken against conscription: men like Arthur Ponsonby and Charles Trevelyan of the Union for Democratic Control, others like Philip Snowden and Ramsay MacDonald, pacifist and internationally-minded socialists of the Independent Labour Party (ILP) and T. E. Harvey who spoke for the Quakers.

But increasingly, as the days passed, the chief concern of these dedicated pacifists was no longer how to prevent the Bill becoming law, which now seemed inevitable, but how to make sure that it contained decent provisions for exemption for those whose consciences forbade them to fight. This little band was remarkably tenacious, returning again and again to the need for safeguards, but, as opinion in the House swung solidly behind conscription, they were not popular. 'How hot and hostile,' John Graham, a Manchester Quaker, was to write soon after the war, 'was the atmosphere in which this group, sitting close together on a bench below the gangway, fought the good fight.'

In the end, they achieved very little. On its third reading, on January 24, the Military Service Act (2) was approved by 383, with only 36 against and some 30 of those Liberals. The Labour Members had objected, but now capitulated. The 60 Irish Nationalists, after being promised that conscription would not apply to Ireland, abstained. In the House of Lords, there were no amendments, the Bishop of London commenting only that he personally thought very little indeed of conscience until it was 'educated'. As from March 2, so the new law decreed, all single men between the ages of 18 and 41, residents of Great Britain, were liable to be called up. Exemptions were to be granted — for reasons of health, the demands of home or business, or for work of national importance, and even for conscience, 'on the grounds of a conscientious objection to bearing arms' — an amendment having been introduced to avoid further defections. Provided, that was, that one of the Tribunals before which the cases would be heard was convinced that the plea was genuine.

At the end, after the debates and the bitterness, the arguing and the passion, there was only one resignation. Before leaving the Cabinet, Sir John Simon, the Liberal Home Secretary, rose to ask: 'Does anybody really suppose that once the principle of compulsion is conceded you are going to stop here? . . . The real issue is whether we are to begin an immense change in the fundamental nature of our society.' His question, like a faint and distant ghost, has hung over every pacifist debate this century.

In the press, once the Bill was through, there was strangely little comment, either of approval or condemnation. There was not even much jubilation in Lord Northcliffe's newspapers, *The Times* and the *Daily Mail*, despite his enthusiasm for conscription. Elsewhere, however, the reaction was sharp and immediate. When the unions were canvassed, opposition to the Bill was found to stand at 2,121,000 against and 541,000 for; as J. H. Thomas had warned, miners, railwaymen, locomotive engineers and firemen, transport workers and dockers, all spoke out against what they declared to be servitude.

Though clamorous, their protest was not to endure. Quite soon, on the promise of exemption in the case of necessary work, the union opposition died away. But while the government settled down to devise the machinery to implement conscription — a problem, as rapidly became apparent, made almost insurmountable by the speed with which the Act had been passed and the consequent woolliness of its wording — a meeting of the more dedicated opponents to conscription gathered in Devonshire House, the Quaker headquarters, in Bishopsgate. It gave some indication of how very strong resistance was going to be.

The meeting had been called by the No-Conscription Fellowship (NCF), an organization founded early in the war after Fenner Brockway, the young editor of the *Labour Leader*, had called on readers 'who are not prepared to take the part of a *combatant*' to band themselves together 'so that we may know our strength'. So widespread and immediate had been the response to the letter that his wife Lilla had suggested he write to the newspaper outlining the idea that, by the time the Military Service Act was passed at the end of January 1916, some 2,000 young men of military age, representing 198 branches already efficiently organized around the country, bound by a common determination to 'refuse from conscientious motives to bear arms', were ready to converge on the meeting in London, to show their disapproval of the new act and to agree on ways of making good their threat of resistance to it.

In its own way, the gathering at Devonshire House, which lasted two days, was as momentous an occasion as the earlier debate in the House of Commons. In less than 48 hours the machinery of resistance, every bit as elaborate but in many ways more efficient than the one it opposed, had been laid down. It was to form the backbone of a network that was to unite hundreds of young men in prison and detained in military barracks up and down the country, many of them alone and all

6

of them under pressure, for most of the three remaining years of war.

Some of the quality of this meeting had to do with the calibre of its leaders. Fenner Brockway, by this time honorary secretary of the association he had brought into existence, had been joined by James Hindle Hudson, a teacher and later a Labour MP, C. H. Norman, writer of eloquent ILP pamphlets, a scholarly-looking man with a thin and disapproving nose, and one of the first people to be inhumanly treated by the military authorities, and the Rev. Leyton Bishops, later general secretary of the Fellowship of Reconciliation. Round the nucleus of these men had gathered other prominent dissenters, whose strength lay as much in their intellect as in the diversity of their pacifist convictions, whether religious, humanist or socialist. Bertrand Russell, prominent mathematician and Fellow of Trinity College, Cambridge, was one of them; Dr. Albert Salter, distinguished bacteriologist, author of *The Religion of a CO*, a pamphlet whose stirring profession of Christian pacifism had provoked enormous controversy in 1915, was another. 'Look! Christ in khaki, out in France thrusting His bayonet into the body of a German workman,' Salter had written, a bald, benign man too phlegmatic in appearance to seem capable of such lively passion. 'See! The Son of God with a machine gun, ambushing a column of German infantry . . . Hark! The Man of Sorrows in a cavalry charge, cutting, hacking, thrusting, crushing, cheering. No! No! That picture is an impossible one and we all know it.' Then there was Edward Grubb, Quaker campaigner and former organizing secretary of the Howard League for Penal Reform, white-haired and eminent, and Clifford Allen, the NCF chairman, a young man already widely seen as the hero of the war resisters. It was Allen, pale and quizzical, with a surprisingly deep voice and invariable Gladstone collar and large black tie, who most inspired the gathering. In appearance, he was rather like a wading bird, alert and deliberate, his pointed chin high, his head tilted a little to the left. In her diary that evening, Beatrice Webb, who had been watching the proceedings from the gallery that fringed the bare, circular hall, noted: 'The Chairman was a monument of Christian patience and lucid speech — his spiritual countenance, fine gentle voice and quiet manner serving him well as the president

7

of a gathering of would-be-martyrs for the sacred cause of peace.'

Beatrice Webb approved of their leaders, who in photographs, seated formally at tables or standing grouped outside courtrooms, seemed the epitome of Edwardian respectability with their large-brimmed hats and drooping moustaches, like gatherings of obscure literary societies or reunions of country clergymen, but she was not altogether as admiring of the younger pacifists in the audience. 'Among the 2,000,' she went on to record, 'were many diverse types. The intellectual pietist, slender in figure, delicate in feature and complexion, benevolent in expression, was the dominant type. These youths were saliently conscious of their own righteousness. That they are superior alike in heart and intelligence to the "average" sensual man is an undoubted fact: ought one to quarrel with them for being aware of it? And yet the constant expression, in word and manner, of the sentiment avowed by one of them, "We are the people whose eyes and ears are open", was unpleasing . . . Here and there were misguided youths who had been swept into the movement because "conscientious objection" might save them from the terrors and discomforts of fighting — pasty-faced boys, who looked dazed at the amount of heroism being expected from them.'

Outside the building, along the streets, drawn by the promise of a fight, pro-conscription hecklers had been joined by a small group of sailors, some of whom managed to scramble over a gate and get inside the hall. As the ultra-nationalist *Daily Mail* later described the scene, they found 'only mild-faced creatures, mostly thinnish and large-eyed — with rakish, untrimmed hair, no hats and in many cases thin apostolic beards. Their anger melted and they retreated as though they had stumbled unwittingly into a woman's room.' (The *Tribunal*, the paper of the war resisters, reported the encounter as friendly, saying that the sailors left after talking pleasantly to the stewards.) In those early days their distaste was still confined to crude mockery; the vitriol came later.

Philip Snowden, Clifford Allen and Fenner Brockway each rose to speak. To prevent further enraging the crowd outside, whose barracking could plainly be heard throughout the hall, the decision was made not to applaud. As each speaker finished talking, delegates stood and silently waved handkerchiefs or pieces of paper. Sixty-two resolutions had been sent in from the branches and it soon became plain that their tone was militant. As the hours passed the men voted to reject service in any specially created non-combatant corps — a possibility mooted in Parliament — and to refuse all alternative work that might directly or indirectly lead to 'more efficient organizing of the country for war', though in the end the exact form of their protest was left up to them.

On the second day, Fenner Brockway read out the names of 15 NCF members already arrested by the military as conscientious objectors. After each name he paused; the 2,000 men sitting in the rows of seats before him rose and waved their white pieces of paper and their white handkerchiefs in silence. At the end of the day Allen read out the agreed pledge: 'We, representing thousands of men who cannot participate in warfare and are subject to the Military Service Act' — he spoke very clearly, his voice sounding through an absolutely still hall — 'unite in comradeship with those of our number who are already suffering for conscience's sake in prison or the hands of the military. We appreciate the spirit of sacrifice which actuates those who are suffering on the battlefield, and in that spirit we renew our determination, whatever the penalties awaiting us, to undertake no service which for us is wrong . . .' Coming away from what he called 'two delicious days and nights of conference', Bertrand Russell wrote to Lady Ottoline Morrell: 'The spirit of the young men was magnificent. They would not listen to even the faintest hint of compromise . . . Most of them will be arrested within the next few days and taken to camp. What will happen there, no one knows.'

It was perfectly true. No one, in the spring of 1916, had any idea at all about what was going to happen. The government, the Military Service Act now finally carried and in force, was counting on an orderly progression towards full conscription. What neither they, nor anyone else, could have expected was the extraordinary vehemence of the protest which was to follow, nor the lengths to which men, once they decided that their conscience set them against the war, were prepared to go to to protect that belief. And as public attitudes hardened against these

9

men, as their treatment soon became indistinguishable from torture, so that eventually 69 were dead and 39 more went mad, so determination grew among all conscientious objectors to stand firm.

The point was, there was a great deal more at stake here than a simple protest against warfare. As Sir John Simon had perceived, the fundamental nature of British society was about to be questioned. What was at issue was nothing less than man's individual sense of responsibility and his relationship with the state. Few of the 16,000 men who now began to come forward to declare their own particular stand against the war had ever heard of Tolstoy, or read Thoreau, or were indeed even particularly believing Christians. Yet, coming from a dozen viewpoints and a dozen backgrounds in a country solidly dedicated to pursuing a war, in which not to volunteer was to be branded a coward, these hundreds, soon thousands, of objectors seem to have reached the same point, and, having reached it, found the strength with which to hold on to it. Nor were they alone. Protest, tough, united, unbreakable, was to occur everywhere, all across Europe and, after 1917, in the United States, with men standing out for their personal conviction that war was wrong. But it was in Britain, because of the nature of the British constitution, and because it was the country in which the dilemma was first and most clearly expressed, that the debate took shape. In the remaining years of the war, on both sides of the Atlantic, arguments strengthened, so that, by 1919, it was never going to be quite so easy to ignore a man's right to follow his conscience in time of war — a fact of immense importance in what was to become a century of almost unceasing warfare. Persecuted, reviled, mocked, the Anglo-Saxon conscientious objectors of the First War nonetheless laid down the foundation for all later war protest, whatever and wherever the war; and it is their stand that continues to be felt in the trials and sentences of modern war protesters.

Of course, there were many roots and precedents to draw from, if people cared to seek them. And an increasing number now did, to reassure themselves about the legality and morality of their protest. If socialists, they turned back to the 19th century peace movements which had branded war as a crime against humanity and to Thoreau, who wrote with eloquence about man's conscience after his night in jail for refusing to pay his taxes towards the war with Mexico; if Christians, they either returned to the Sermon on the Mount, St. Matthew and the first pacifist teachings of Tertullian, Cyprian and Origen, or subscribed to St. Augustine of Hippo's theory of a 'just war', or even followed Erasmus and the Catholic humanists in arguing for peace on largely secular grounds rather than as a strict interpretation of the Gospels. Utopians, radical humanitarians, anarchists or those who believed in policemen but not soldiers, were now busy re-examining the foundations for those beliefs.

Even so, none of this was quite the point, even if the very diversity of their responses, and the varied origins of their pacifist convictions, were soon to make the task of the Tribunals set up to judge them so very hard. 'Absolutists', those who refused not only to bear arms but to have any truck at all with the war, and 'alternativists', who would work to help the war, provided they did not have to bear arms, shared one fundamental conviction, and that was their right to the 'element of personal responsibility', an individual's moral decision to withhold co-operation in the process of waging war. By opposing conscription they were rejecting the war; by refusing to have their conscience overruled they were challenging the generally accepted authority of the state. This was new; and, soon, very threatening.

Something of the Englishman's profound sense of outrage, confronted by this new weapon of coercion, is to be found in the words of Bertrand Russell, delivered from the dock, less than two months later, after being arrested under the Defence of the Realm Act for publishing a pamphlet supposed to be an incitement to resistance. 'It is not only I that am in the dock; it is the whole tradition of British liberty which our forefathers built up with great trouble and with great sacrifice. Other nations may surpass us in other respects, but that tradition has been the supreme good that we in this country have preserved more than anything else, and for that liberty of the individual I stand.' Better than anyone, perhaps, Russell, too old at 44 to be conscripted but not too old to go to jail for his opposition to the war, understood and expressed just what was at stake for the conscientious objectors of the First War. 'To stand out against a war,' he was to write, many years after it was all over, 'when it

11

comes, a man must have within himself some passion so strong and indestructible that mass hysteria cannot touch it . . .'

At the outbreak of war, so enthusiastic had been the response to calls for volunteers, that a soldier had to be 5 feet 8 inches tall to hope for a place in the army. In 1914 Britain had not known a major war for 100 years, while on the Continent the last war between the great powers now lay well over 40 years in the past. A young man did not expect to be personally involved in a war. As an Englishman it was still perfectly possible to see it as a far-away affair, of comradely forced marches and triumphant battles, fought by small bands of trained professionals and quickly over. Those tall and privileged enough to serve, like the young poet Julian Grenfell, considered themselves fortunate: 'Isn't it luck for me to have been born so as to be just the right age and just in the right place,' he wrote in a letter, 'not too high up to be worried — and to enjoy it to the most!'

By October 1914, after the Battle of the Marne, when the mobile war had turned into trench warfare and no one any longer expected the conflict to be over quite so quickly, a volunteer only needed to reach the height of 5 feet 5 inches to be accepted as a soldier. And after the second battle of Ypres, in May 1915, when the Germans used poison gas for the first time and 30,000 more British men were dead, the height came down again, to 5 feet 3 inches. But still the volunteers kept on coming, though there were not enough uniforms for them to wear or guns for them to train with. And they kept dying too, for between April and December 1915, 252,000 men, allied troops from Britain, Australia and New Zealand, became casualties at Gallipoli. Between the day when war was declared and the introduction of conscription, 18 months later, 2,675,149 men in Britain had volunteered to serve, some at least presumably attracted by Julian Grenfell's 'big picnic without the objectlessness of a picnic'. Except that by January 1916 the volunteers were finally beginning to dry up.

If what was now clearly a stalemate on the Western Front was going to be broken — by 1915 trenches and barbed wire stretched virtually the entire way from the shores of Flanders to Switzerland — it was now apparent that warfare was going to have to cease to be a distant, purely military affair and depend instead on mobilization and full control of the nation's resources. And even though newspapers continued to portray the war as glorious, a time of honour and sacrifice and moral certainties, and though censors dressed up casualty figures to look more like victories than defeats, there was really no longer any escaping the fact that the fighting was a murderous affair; and that Julian Grenfell was only one of the many thousand young Englishmen now dead.

The trenches, as men returned from the front were able to report, were not the oases of comfort as described by some of the newspapers, but squalid, smelly, cold, cramped, always wet and often flooded so that high boots were now articles of regular uniform. Furthermore they were infested with lice and extremely large rats which fed on the corpses. In one stretch of enclosed trench a cat had been shut up overnight to cope with the rat crisis: the next morning the soldiers found nothing, the cat, bones and fur having all been devoured. All along the Front there was a smell of rotting flesh from bodies and dead horses. By early 1916, too, atrocity rumours — the Canadian soldier crucified at Ypres, the Germans rendering corpses into fats for nitroglycerine, candles and industrial lubricants — were going around. Even the ubiquitous Field Service Post Card, with its few bald printed options — 'I am quite well; I have been admitted into hospital sick and am going on well wounded and hope to be discharged' — could not quite disguise the fact that modern warfare was not much fun.

In Britain, the women poets were now writing of sorrow. 'Silence which might be felt, no pity in the silence,' said Margaret Sackville in *A Memory*.

> Horrible, soft like blood, down all the blood-stained ways;
> In the middle of the street two corpses lie unburied,
> And a bayoneted woman stares in the market place . . .
> Who shall deliver us from the memory of these dead?

Not so heroic, then, but pointless and very bloody: why volunteer to die in such confusion?

Much of the subsequent fiasco of the Conscription Act has been blamed on the speed with which it was hustled through Parliament, with no time given to consideration of how in practice it was going to work. Asquith, unnerved by what he feared would be massed opposition to it, felt that only once he could demonstrate that volunteers were really exhausted would Parliament authorize the use of compulsory powers. To him as to all the others who took pride in the fact that Britain had seen no form of military compulsion since Charles II outlawed impressment and the feudal levy in 1660, and that the great Victorian imperial conquests had easily been sustained by volunteers, conscription could only be abhorrent. As Lord Salisbury had put it, with considerable satisfaction, the Boer War had been waged by soldiers, not coerced to fight, but drawn by the 'emoluments and the honours of a great and splendid vocation'. The voluntary principle was the glory of the British nation.

In 1908 Herbert Asquith had succeeded Campbell-Bannerman as Prime Minister. Seven years later, a coalition government including Conservatives, with Asquith still Prime Minister, took over and committed conscriptionists were brought for the first time into power just at the very moment when the flow of volunteers was beginning to dry up. The country was divided: on one side, the advocates of conscription inside and outside Parliament, men like Lord Curzon, former Viceroy of India, and Lord Milner, former High Commissioner in South Africa, spurred on by Northcliffe's newspapers; and on the other some Liberals, organized Labour, the Independent Labour Party and a growing number of religious bodies. It was against this background that, in August 1915, a new Act had been passed to empower the local Government Board to compile a register of all men and women between the ages of 15 and 65 (accompanied by a placatory pledge that this would not be used for military purposes). When, in due course, the register revealed that 2,179,231 single men of military age were still not in the forces, the next step, by which the 17th Earl of Derby became Director-General of Recruiting, charged with launching a great push for volunteers, was inevitable. For a while, it had seemed that Derby, the popular, bluff friend of George V, might succeed: long queues of men were to be seen forming at the recruiting office. But not enough of them. With the Gallipoli campaign a disaster, with the news that British casualties had now reached 528,227 killed, wounded or missing, and with the decision to use every

14

last man to break the stalemate in the trenches of the Western Front, conscription had become unavoidable.

What there was not, then, was support, or even a very great deal of public understanding, for the men of military age who now, in the early spring of 1916, decided to face arrest rather than be conscripted. The fact that they were such a very mixed lot, belonging to no clear class, religion or party, only added to the general confusion. Yet there was a pattern, and a set of organizations, to link them; and to understand these men and ideas it is important to know something of the various anti-war currents of the years before 1914 and to see how each had reacted when faced with the reality of war.

Before 1914, foreign affairs, like the waging of the war later on, was seen as something best left to the professionals, to the diplomats and the soldiers. In any case most members of the Labour Party, the group most internationally minded and concerned about war, did not really believe a war would come, placing their faith in the strength of the European Labour Movement and taking heart from International Socialist meetings, their repeated slogans, 'War against war', and the reiterated assertions by European socialist leaders like Jean Jaurés in France and the Belgian Emil Vandervelde that workers everywhere were determined to remain at peace.

Apart from Keir Hardie, the much-loved Scottish leader of the ILP, and first chairman of the Parliamentary Labour Party, few people in England seriously expected a European war, though during the winter of 1913-14 the ILP did run a campaign against militarism, arguing that the 'militarists' and arms manufacturers were trying to drive Europe into war. The outbreak of war on August 4, 1914, found the British Labour movement divided over the war, opposed to it in principle, but swept along by the patriotic tide. The German invasion of Belgium swung most remaining members of the Labour Party to the pro-war side, and Ramsay MacDonald resigned as chairman, though he and Keir Hardie together continued to denounce the war on political grounds, blaming its outbreak on secret diplomacy and what they declared to be a false doctrine of the balance of power, while George Lansbury, champion of women's suffrage, editor of the *Daily Herald* and later best known and most respected of the Labour pacifists, told his readers: 'War is hell.' 'All forms of militarism belong to the past,' said Hardie. 'It comes down to us as a relic of the days when kings and nobles ruled as well as reigned, and when the workers were voteless, voiceless serfs. Militarism and Democracy cannot be blended.' Not long before he died, in September 1915, Hardie was still calling on members to resist the nationalist hysteria, though his tone had become very gloomy: 'Our demonstrations and speeches and resolutions are all alike futile. We have no means of hitting the warmongers. We simply do not count.'

Hitting the warmongers, perhaps not; inspiring those ready to be swayed, certainly. Fenner Brockway was the son of nonconformist missionaries, living in a settlement in what was then slum land in Islington, when as a journalist, a serious figure with a rather long face and smooth black hair, he was sent to interview him. 'Young man,' said Keir Hardie, 'if you put away your notebook and your pencil I'll talk to you.' Brockway, now in his nineties and still active on platforms at pacifist gatherings, remembers the occasion well. 'I think that instinctively I was a pacifist in my teenage years — but it was Keir Hardie who made me a specific one. I went to see him a young liberal and I left a young socialist. He emphasized the anti-militaristic attitude a socialist should have: it was unthinkable to him that workers should kill fellow workers in war.' Faith in pacifism, thus acquired and then held with incredible tenacity, has marked many of the staunchest political conscientious objectors.

The shooting of Jean Jaurés, by pro-war French patriots in a Paris café on July 31, 1914 after the great socialist street meetings in the capital to protest against the possibility of war, came as a blow to those in England who had seen in him the only man in Europe who might have given direction to a strong European peace party. Nonetheless Philip Morrell, Liberal MP and later to be a devoted crusader on behalf of conscientious objectors, did his best to rouse some anti-war feeling in the House of Commons, and soon a peace party of some 40 MPs had formed, with the five ILP members now led by Ramsay MacDonald, a few Labour, and 25 Liberals. The Bedford Square house of Philip and Ottoline Morrell became a meeting place for parliamentary pacifists, and in the evenings men like Arthur Ponsonby, son of Queen Victoria's private secretary and at one time her page of honour, Bertrand Russell, Duncan Grant, the painter, and Norman Angell, founder of the Neutrality League, and later winner of the Nobel prize for peace, met and debated what concrete form their views might take.

It was in the course of these meetings, early in September, that Charles Trevelyan, the Liberal MP who had resigned his post as Parliamentary Secretary at the Board of Education at the outbreak of war, suggested that they found a Union for Democratic Control (UDC), not precisely a pacifist body, but in order to condemn the 'secret diplomacy' that had led Britain into the war, and to oppose what they saw as 'Prussianism in Britain'. This small coalition of Liberal and ILP critics of war now called for negotiated peace; what they envisaged was some form of international police force, subject to civilian authority, and reduction in the power of the 'war traders' of Europe, the nine leading armament manufacturers. In November, the UDC published its manifesto and by its first birthday it had set up nearly 100 branches under the energetic secretaryship of Edmund Dene Morel.

Shortly after conscription was introduced Philip Snowden, a member of the ILP and particularly interested in foreign affairs, made a speech in Parliament on behalf of the anti-war group and in favour of a negotiated peace. Its reception was largely hostile. Charles Stanton, a pro-war trade unionist and Labour MP for Merthyr Tydvil rose to say that it was painful to have to 'listen to the croakings and bleatings of these frightened lambs . . . breathing treachery'. The 'pro-Germans', as the UDC members — and indeed all those opposing the war — were now becoming known, were much disliked. In her memoirs, written many years later, Lady Ottoline Morrell recalled: 'We and our friends seemed like a wretched little shivery humiliated group of people who alone remained sober, but despised, disgraced.'

Those of them like Duncan Grant and Lytton Strachey who belonged among the Bloomsbury group faced up to their isolation, however, with panache, their customary endless conversations, and not without a little fun. If the fashionable set now kept away from the 'pro-Germans', many old friends continued to turn up for Lady Ottoline's Thursday evenings in Bedford Square, where the parties were very gay, with much dressing up in Persian and Turkish costumes, while Philip Morrell played the pianola and the guests danced, 'following the rhythm' as the spirit moved them. From Ashenam, Virginia Woolf's house in Sussex, she and Vanessa, Clive Bell and Duncan Grant would walk across the Downs discussing Lytton Strachey's sacking from the *Spectator* for his anti-war views, and whether Clive Bell should agree to serve on a committee to recommend safeguards for conscientious objectors.

Pacifism had come to Bloomsbury through Goldsworthy Lowes Dickinson, fellow of King's College and member of the Cambridge Apostles society, who believed that the 'pursuit of all that is lovely in nature' was becoming more and more difficult throughout the world, because modern governments and modern industrialists were spreading 'ugliness, meanness and insincerity'; and through Leonard Woolf, who was convinced that socialism was the only answer to the world's ills. How could this war, which was horrible, unnecessary and fundamentally about nothing, be reconciled with reason or with the love of art and beauty? 'To me,' wrote Lowes Dickinson, 'the worst kind of disillusionment was that connected with universities and historians . . . Abroad was heard only the sound of guns, at home only the ceaseless patter of a propaganda utterly indifferent to truth'. As Bertrand Russell was to write later, echoing almost precisely the same feelings of disillusion and regret: 'As a lover of truth, the national propaganda of all the belligerent nations sickened me. As a lover of civilization, the return to barbarism appalled me. As a man of thwarted parental feeling, the massacre of the young wrung my heart. I hardly supposed that much good would come of opposing the war, but I felt that for the honour of human nature those who were not swept off their feet should show that they stood firm.'

It was not always easy. Bloomsbury's apparent refusal to treat the war seriously provoked not only the indignation of the most conservative war supporters but caused rifts with former friends. As Vanessa Bell and Virginia Woolf settled down to continue writing and painting as best they could, as E. M. Forster went to Alexandria to work with the newly-formed Wounded and Missing Bureau of the Red Cross (from where he wrote home in characteristically Bloomsbury tones: 'It is a damned bore . . . but one has to see it through, and see it through with the knowledge that whichever side wins, civilization in Europe will be pipped for the next 30 years . . .'), so it was left to H. G. Wells to pour scorn on what he considered the inexcusable irreverence of the 'Genteel Whigs': 'It was of course natural and inevitable that the German onslaught upon Belgium and civilization generally should strike these recluse minds not as monstrous ugly wickedness to be resisted and overcome at any price, but merely as a nerve-wracking experience. Guns were going off on both sides. The Genteel Whig was chiefly conscious of a repulsive vast excitement all about him in which many people did inelegant and irrational things.'

His attack was not wholly fair, for some of those who gathered at Garsington and Ashenam were extremely active in their pursuit of what they now believed to be right, many contributing passionately argued articles against the war to Lansbury's *Daily Herald*. Bertrand Russell had started out the war as a much-respected philosopher, Fellow of the Royal Society, co-author with A. N. Whitehead of *Principia Mathematica*, the holder of a fellowship at Trinity College, Cambridge, and a supporter of the Liberal Party which he trusted not to lead Britain into a war so absurd as to be inconceivable. When it became apparent that Britain was nonetheless heading at some speed towards war, Russell, feeling outraged by the Liberals' betrayal, plunged hastily into a campaign to keep the country neutral. Convinced that, once the war came, it was likely to be over very soon, he concentrated on how to avoid equally insane outbreaks of fighting in the future, but when it became obvious that hostilities were going to be prolonged he turned to opposing the Military Service Act and to supporting the conscientious objectors.

If at first he complained that Clifford Allen was just like a 'dissenting parson', he soon recognized that the serious, frail and even-tempered young man was in fact a born leader, with a rare ability to create harmony among a collection of very dissimilar followers. By keeping the statement of NCF faith so direct — an objection to fighting because human life was held to be sacred, and the importance, whatever the consequences, of obeying 'conscientious convictions rather than the commands of government' — Allen was able to recruit and retain members as easily among the religious pacifists as among anarchists and socialists.

Because of his age, Russell could only be an associate of the NCF, but as a member of the Political Committee, along with the writer H. N. Brailsford, he could work for repeal of the new Act and stand by in order to take the place of National Committee Members should they be arrested — as indeed many soon were. In the first rushed and optimistic weeks that followed the passing of the Conscription Act, Russell was active with others like Allen and Catherine Marshall, a tall, smartly dressed young woman given to wearing blue velvet dresses, one of the moving spirits in the non-militant National Union of Women's Suffrage societies and the British Section of the League for Peace and Freedom, and now to become the most efficient advocate for the conscientious objectors, in setting up an organization for the NCF so efficient and so dispersed that it could not easily be destroyed by sudden attack. Catherine Marshall, whose appearance, when flustered, could be deceptively scatty, wispy hair flying out from her bun, was a master of organization: within what seemed like hours of the Bill becoming law she had started the nucleus of an impressive record department, keeping tags on the status, experience and whereabouts of every conscientious objector in the country and using this material, through the various departments of the NCF, as the basis for speeches, articles, over a million copies of various pamphlets, as well as a weekly journal called the *Tribunal*. During the early spring of 1916 the NCF and its busy members were still full of hope; the Act, they thought, could never be enforced once it was plain that 10,000 young men were going to refuse to fight. 'I really believe,' Bertrand Russell wrote to Lady Ottoline, 'they will defeat the government and wreck conscription, when it is found that they won't yield.'

And they had other, very enthusiastic and completely dedicated support to draw on, in the form of many young Quakers. The Society of Friends was in fact currently in a healthy state of renewal, stimulated by the Young Friends Movement, eager to draw the Society away from its earlier 'parochialism and exclusiveness' and towards a 'fellowship of service', its plans hatched out in long pre-war sessions of summer schools and tramps over Yorkshire moors.

The Yearly Meeting of 1915 was particularly well attended. Quakers are taught simply that 'conscientious conviction always arises from the light of God in a man's heart'. But the younger anti-war Friends, in the shape of the Friends Service Committee, now managed to push the Society towards a firmer pacifist position, uncompromisingly opposed to war, and even taking a strong position against any form of alternative service. The stand was pleasingly clear, but not unexpected. At the Meeting for Sufferings of November 1914 a Declaration on the War had been drawn up for circulation to all Meetings of Friends. 'All war,' it read 'is utterly incompatible with the plain precepts of our Divine Lord and Lawgiver . . . It is a solemn thing to stand forth to the nation as the advocates of inviolable peace; and our testimony loses its efficacy in proportion to the want of consistency in any among us.'

The Young Quaker, however, now faced with conscription, had to choose for himself. He could volunteer and become a soldier — and in due course a third of those eligible to fight did so; he could join one of the ancillary bodies like the Red Cross or the Friends Ambulance Unit, or he could, once it was set up, offer to take part in alternative war work, whether for distressed enemy aliens at home or with the Friends' War Victims Relief Committee abroad. Or he could refuse all dealings with the machinery of war, and this many now did, going to join the gathering ranks of NCF members.

They were not of course the only religious believers to oppose war. The crowds which had gathered in Trafalgar Square as peace hung in the balance had contained large numbers of people who felt passionately that war itself was un-Christian. The Minister of the Presbyterian Church in Crouch End was a man called Richard Roberts. On the first Sunday after the outbreak of fighting he was appalled to see that a small group of young Germans, regular attenders at his services, had vanished from his congregation. Resolving that as a Christian minister he could take no part in the war, he and Henry Hodgkin, a former missionary in China, both distressed by the 'confused utterances of the Christian Churches', now gathered round them anyone who was 'seeking a new order based on Christian principles'. In January 1915, 150 of them met in a hall in Cambridge and formed the Fellowship of Reconciliation (FOR).

The intentions of the new body, which by the time conscription came in was established in William Morris's old rooms in Red Lion Square in Bloomsbury, was to unite all Christian pacifists; but there was something too meek about their goal of 'a world order based on love' to inspire much vigorous support.

More absolute and, in the end, more numerous were all those young men who believed they owed allegiance to no earthly ruler and thus could not become involved in the affairs of this world and certainly not of its wars. Between them, the Plymouth Brethren, Jehovah's Witnesses, Muggletonians, Peculiar People, Dependent Cocklers and many others, who believed in literal biblicism and the Apocalypse, by the end of the war out-numbered Quakers and socialists among the more extreme con-scientious objectors. The Christadelphians alone, who opposed not armies as such but the armies of *this* world, provided 1,716 absolute refusers.

No account of these early pacifists would be complete without reference to the women — those for, as well as those against, the war. On both sides of the Atlantic, spurred on by tenacious and often very brave women in the European countries at war, they fought committed battles, either to bring their men into the war, or to keep them out of it. If they never had to face up to the misery of the trenches, there was nonetheless something admir-able about this tough, articulate, and absolutely single-minded band of women in their long skirts and respectable hats, heck-ling, marching, running committees and drafting resolutions.

By the time war broke out the battle for the female vote in Britain was just nine years old. Under the impassioned leader-ship of Emmeline Pankhurst and her daughter Christabel, the Women's Social and Political Union had progressed from public speaking, through the breaking of window panes and on up to large-scale arson. At first, the women's suffrage move-ments were fairly open to talking about peace, and about how women could influence the policy-makers to halt the fighting. However, as casualties mounted, and atrocity stories came back from Belgium and the trenches, the mood of many suffragettes shifted towards halting all suffrage and pacifist activity until the end of the war, and to helping to support it instead. After Millicent Garrett Fawcett told a meeting of the National Union of Suffrage Societies that until the Germans had been driven from Belgium and France she personally believed that it was 'akin to treason to talk of peace', the break between the peace and war factions of the women was unavoidable.

While many previously militant women now settled down to run canteens, and hand out white feathers to those they saw as shirkers, and Baroness Orczy founded the Women of England's Active Service League ('Your hour has come! . . . Together we have laughed and cried over that dauntless Englishman, the Scarlet Pimpernel . . . now we shall form ourselves into an Active Service League . . . influencing our men to offer them-selves at once to the nearest recruiting officer'), Mrs. Pankhurst embarked on a countrywide drive to make women support the war. Like Mrs. Fawcett, when asked about negotiated peace she spoke of 'cowardly treason'.

In June 1915, on a day of heavy rain, Mrs. Pankhurst led a two-mile procession from Whitehall, down the Mall, up Picca-dilly and to Trafalgar Square to recruit women for the muni-tions factories. The march set out at three o'clock, with 90 bands playing the 'Marseillaise'. At its head walked a girl in white, carrying a Union Jack. Behind her strode orderly phalanxes of women in colour groups: the first hundred white, the next blue, the third in red, officered by marshals in red sashes with assist-ants in blue, bearing the flags of the allies and banners with huge embroidered mottoes: 'For Men must fight and Women must work' and 'Let none be Kaiser's Cats' Paws'. The rain con-tinued to pour down, but happily there was enough wind to keep the flags flapping.

Behind the colours came a great floral wagon, then girls dressed in national costumes of the countries at war on the British side. All along the route, at convenient points, had been set up little tables to act as recruitment centres for women wish-ing to enlist for war work. At the end of the day, on a podium, standing between Winston Churchill and Lloyd George, Mrs. Pankhurst called for three cheers for the Army and the Navy. The shouting was tremendous. As the *Daily Express* noted approvingly next morning: 'A wonderful procession it was. It was artistic and essentially feminine, and yet gave an over-whelming impression of orderliness and strength . . .'

The newspapers were never as kind, by contrast, to the

other band of energetic women, the internationally minded who by now, the schism with their pro-war former colleagues total, had formed themselves into active committees pursuing the cause of peace on both sides of the Atlantic. 'Peacettes' was how the reporters invariably referred to them. What seems impressive now is that so very many were prepared to embark on a scheme of such improbable success and certain unpopularity, and that having decided to do so they should be so skilful in their arrangements.

The peacettes wherever they were to be found were remarkably alike, despite the enormous differences in nationality and background. They were of much the same age, nearly all being in their thirties or early forties; they had excellent constitutions since almost all were destined to live to a very great age, and they possessed great fortitude, travelling backwards and forwards across the Atlantic and up and down Europe at war in appalling and often frightening conditions, with nowhere to stay, little to eat, and frequently having to unpin their buns to be searched for concealed weapons at frontiers. Many were exceedingly strong characters, preferring to lead than to be led.

These women peacemakers saw their roots not only in the suffrage movements, but more importantly perhaps in the great pre-war international peace conferences like those held in The Hague in 1899 and 1907. By 1914 most women's organizations in America, where much of this new impetus for peace-making now took place, had resolutions on their books committing them to peace and arbitration. Three weeks after war had been declared in Europe a prominent suffragette called Fanny Garrison Villard had had no difficulty at all in finding 3,000 women to lead down Fifth Avenue, in a march against the war. They were dressed in black, bearing flags of the countries involved and marching to the beat of muffled drums. In January 1915, a vast convention of women packed the Grand Ballroom of the New Willard Hotel in Washington to proclaim a 'programme for constructive peace' under the aegis of a new 'Women's Peace Party'. The chair was taken by Jane Addams, one of the great names in the American women's movement, a somewhat controversial and autocratic woman, a pioneer socialist who had visited Tolstoy in 1896 and ran a settlement called Hull House for poor immigrants in Chicago (likened by some of the feminists to a convent school). Born in Illinois in 1860, she had grown up convinced that the 'nurturing and protective function' in women created in them a more developed sense of moral obligation than it did in men.

One frequent European visitor to America was Rosika Schwimmer, founder at the age of 26 of the Hungarian Association of Working Women, who was to prove one of the most dynamic and formidable of all the peace women. She was eloquent, tough and indefatigable, producing opinions and pamphlets on everything from state child care to home economics and marriage in both Hungarian and German, writing short stories and a novel and delivering innumerable lectures. She wore brightly-coloured, loose-fitting dresses and no corset, as was only proper for a follower of the dress reform movement, and a pince-nez, and she spoke nine languages fluently, making audiences laugh with her heavy-handed jokes about men. She referred to herself as a 'very, very radical feminist'. Photographs show a plump, stern face with heavy black eyebrows and rather frizzy wild black hair, under immense, plumed hats.

By 1915 Rosika Schwimmer had been declared an enemy 'alien' in England (with her deep, slightly throaty voice she made the word sound a bit like 'lion') but had nonetheless already made several trips across the Atlantic trying to set up a delegation of prominent British personalities to carry a mediation plan to President Wilson, begging him to call immediately for an end to all hostilities. Wilson, she said, was 'a great force for peace'. It was up to him to call the Neutral Conference: 'If you do not help us end the war in Europe before the militants end it,' she warned, frowning sternly over her pince-nez, 'you too will be drawn in.'

By now the decision had been made to hold a new peace conference at The Hague and, early in April, 47 American women, led by Jane Addams and branded 'both silly and base' by ex-President Theodore Roosevelt, set sail on the Dutch ship *Noordam*, ballasted by wheat, but in some danger since the Germans were regularly sinking ships and they could not carry the American flag, their mission not being official.

In Britain 180 women had applied for passports to go as delegates. In the end, only 25 were issued, and when these women reached Tilbury they found that the North Sea had been closed to shipping. Three British delegates, already outside the country, finally reached The Hague. Northcliffe's newspapers made much of the ridiculousness of their plight.

The conference, however, was a success. One thousand one hundred and thirty-six women gathered in the largest hall they could find in The Hague, the Direntium, a Moorish-looking building in the Zoological Gardens ('Peacettes at Dutch Zoo', wrote the *Daily Express*), which had ornate balconies and boxes and great twirling balustrades. On the platform, dwarfed by vast potted palms and wearing an assortment of hats, feathers and mantillas, sat a row of rather stern and certainly, in the official photographs, unsmiling women. By the fourth day, 20 resolutions had been agreed on and the decision was made to despatch a number of delegates, bearing these resolutions, as unofficial peace emissaries to the heads of state of both belligerent and neutral countries. ('The sitting,' concluded the *Daily Express*, 'was remarkable for its extreme dullness . . . the most noteworthy feature of the first day's proceedings was the enthusiasm displayed by the delegates at the promise which was made to treat them to an excursion to the tulip fields at Haarlem.') In the eyes of reporters, women pacifists have rarely ever been anything other than absurd.

Between May and August Rosika Schwimmer, Jane Addams and 11 other delegates split into two parties and, rehearsing their speeches as they went, visited 14 capitals, including Washington. In Rome they saw the Pope. It was a frustrating experience. Often with individual leaders, who turned on great charm for their lady visitors, the peace emissaries appeared to be on the edge of success, with first Sweden, then America, seeming to promise to take an initiative in setting up a conference. However, feelings about the war itself were changing. The growing casualties, then the sinking of the *Lusitania* in May, with more than 1000 dead, including 38 babies, and 100 Americans, which produced strong protests from President Wilson and violent riots in England, somewhat weakened their appeal.

Support fell away further after an unfortunate remark made by Jane Addams after her return to New York on the *St. Louis* on July 5. A large public meeting had been laid on in her honour at

Carnegie Hall. She spoke quietly, of what she called an 'old man's war in Europe' in which the young were dying, and then declared that before men would engage in bayonet charges — they were given 'rum in England and absinthe in France . . . that they have to give them dope before the bayonet charge is possible.' Her words may have moved her listeners, but the newspapers chose to interpret them differently, as a slur upon the courage of warriors. '"Troops drink crazed," says Miss Addams,' read one headline. 'Jane Addams is a silly, vain, impertinent old maid,' added the *New York Times*. Opponents of the peace movement and of the suffragettes made much of it.

Most of the women now turned back to their own national organisations, of which 12 had been formed to run the international women's peace movement born at The Hague. Jane Addams had agreed to become its chairman, Rosika Schwimmer one of the vice-chairmen. She was by now one of the only women left who still hoped for international intervention. During the autumn of 1915 she prevailed on Henry Ford to back a conference of neutrals and to send delegates across the Atlantic in a 'peace ship' modelled on President Wilson's 'Christmas ship' with his presents to the orphans in Europe.

Early in December the *Oscar II* set out, with almost as many journalists as delegates on board, not least because many of the better-known feminist pacifists had shunned the mission after a particularly virulent campaign against it in the press. Just the same, there was a noisy send-off at Hoboken docks, with orchestras and much waving of flags.

Hardly surprisingly, perhaps, given that it was mid-winter, the crossing was not very agreeable, with the women crammed three and four to a cabin. They became increasingly fractious. The journalists were judged to have behaved appallingly, refusing to take the high-minded discussions seriously, and sending off 'insolence and scandal mongering' stories instead. Henry Ford, who had agreed to make the crossing with them, so that he could 'get the boys out of the trenches by Christmas', was apparently somewhat baffled by the confusion and prevailing tone of acrimony; he refused to discuss tactics and would talk only of his new tractor. When the *Oscar II* (or 'Oscatwo', as the American newspapers insisted on referring to it) docked in Norway, Ford hurried back home, leaving the ladies to be fêted

27

over Christmas in the Grand Palace Hotel in Stockholm, where the orchestra in the scented winter garden played 'The Stars and Stripes Forever' in their honour.

The conference did take place, and it did become something of a forum for the peace groups in Europe, but in the end it was very little heeded, even if Rosika Schwimmer, endlessly optimistic, went on believing all her life that it had been one of the few sane and generous actions in a sea of madness. Henry Ford, it was said, had become so embarrassed by it all that it could not even be mentioned in his presence. The pacifist fervour of the international women, from now on, as Europe closed itself against them and contacts became ever harder to maintain with countries at war, would have to express itself largely on their own home fronts.

These, then, were the people lined up against the war with Russell's 'passion so strong and indestructible that mass hysteria cannot touch it'. What, now that conscription faced them, would become of them all?

2

The conscientious objectors

Dorothy Bing was having breakfast when a policeman came with a summons for her brother Harold. She was just 16, in her third year at Selhurst Grammar School in South London, to which, the mortgage paid off, her parents had decided they could at last afford to send her. Harold was two and a half years older, but looked so much younger, so like a still-small adolescent boy, that at the door the policeman paused to check he had the right name. When he found that he had, he produced some handcuffs and led the boy off to Kingston, to the military barracks.

The Bings had been expecting the morning summons for some weeks. They were a pacifist household; Harold's father called himself a Tolstoyan. While in exile in England, Chertkov, Tolstoy's disciple and confidant, had been to their small, comfortable, red brick, terraced house in what was then the market town of Croydon, surrounded by fields and woods. On August 3, 1914, father and son had walked 11 miles from home to Trafalgar Square to hear Keir Hardie and George Lansbury speak from the foot of Nelson's column against the war.

Harold Bing had never had any doubts about his own views on war. A photograph taken in the early summer of 1915 shows a good-looking boy in a scholar's gown; he has a straight nose and a wide and rather sensual mouth, somewhat at odds with his severe, even forbidding expression. That summer, Harold left Croydon Borough Secondary School and worked in an insurance office, waiting to be called up. 'Through that year,' remembered Dorothy Bing early in 1985, by then a retired school teacher well into her eighties, a kindly, large woman with very precise gestures, 'it gradually dawned on me that Harold would take the conscientious objector stand. I spent the whole of one night awake thinking. I just could not imagine Jesus Christ taking up a bayonet or dropping a bomb. I worried and worried. It took me all night but then I concluded that he was doing the right thing. When he told mother, she was surprised. Father was pleased, though he had never preached pacifism to us.'

Harold Bing died in 1975 and the rest of the family are dead. Dorothy Bing still lives in Alton Road, at the end of the row of terraced houses, now engulfed in many miles of suburb. In 1916, when Harold was making his decision to protest, she was still collecting the milk every morning from a farmer at the end of the road in a wooden pail. It was village, not city, life.

At Kingston Barracks, Harold Bing was ordered to put on a uniform. He refused. The sergeant told him that he was the scum of the earth; he called him a 'worm', one of the 'white feather crew'. At his Tribunal hearing a few days later the chairman asked him how old he was. '18.' 'Oh, in that case you're not old enough to have a conscience. Case dismissed.' He was given a month to reconsider his attitude before his appeal.

Somewhere around his 19th birthday Harold Bing was sentenced to six months' hard labour for his absolute 'intransigence'. Offered alternative work, involving no weapons and no killing, he refused. The whole family went to hear the court martial, held in Winchester; they found the prisoner surprisingly impassive, almost wooden. 'My father commented on it afterwards,' says Dorothy Bing. 'He used to say: "you would hardly know the boy. He's like a block of wood."'

Up until now Dorothy's parents had insisted that she was too young to work for any of the anti-war movements, but when Harold was sent to serve his first sentence she was allowed to join the Croydon branch of the NCF and work as its secretary, while her father became its chairman. After school, when the Tribunals of local conscientious objectors were scheduled to be heard in Kingston, she would take her bicycle and carry fruit and cake and messages to those in the dock. At Christmas, a group of them went up to Wormwood Scrubs, where Harold was being held, and sang carols outside the prison gates.

But what she remembers most vividly is the extraordinary isolation of being a conscientious objector's sister. The Bings were asked to leave the Unitarian Church, where they had been regular attenders for many years. At the request of the minister, Dorothy stopped teaching Sunday School. Then her mother's sisters wrote to say they would not be speaking to the family again. 'You see, if you met somebody and said: "my brother is a conscientious objector", they looked aghast. It was the last thing anybody did in respectable society. You just didn't go to prison.' Until her mother's death, many years after the war was over, her sisters behaved as if she no longer existed.

On paper the Tribunals were intended to be fair. Their task, so those who were appointed to serve on them were told, was to give every consideration 'to the man whose objection generally rests on religious or moral convictions'. By the end of March 1916, the system for enforcing the Conscription Bill was complete, with some 2,000 Tribunals around the country ready to hear precisely why it was that this fine body of unmarried men wished not to fight.

It is possible that the Tribunals were doomed long before they summoned their first conscientious objector. Planned as independent, judicial bodies, with fair-minded citizens as members, they were for the most part the same Tribunals as had been set up by the Derby scheme to secure men for the army. Not surprisingly, they found it hard to change their approach. Little effort had gone into finding people with religious or socialist sympathies to serve on them, so that the eight or nine members were almost without exception elderly local businessmen, former civil servants and policemen, clergymen and the owners of larger shops, all members of the middle classes and to a man firmly behind the country and its commitment to war. The few women, wrote John Graham after the war, were almost always considerably harder on conscientious objectors than the men. Stipendiary magistrates or county court judges were appointed as chairmen, and the final verdict, often after a few clearly audible words of disparagement from the military emissary from the War Office seconded to each Tribunal, in full military khaki uniform, was left to them.

From the beginning, there was considerable muddle. The machinery for the new Act was built around the military register, which even the director of recruiting, Major Auckland Geddes, had admitted contained numerous errors. Responsibility was shared between the War Office, which was in charge of call-up, the Local Government Board, which dealt with exemptions, and the Home Office and Board of Trade, which handled alternative work schemes. What was more, no one had worked out who precisely was going to be eligible for exemption, nor whether in fact it applied at all to men with political and moral objections to war, or only to those with religious convictions, as Kitchener and Colonel Wyndham Childs, director of Personal Services at the War Office, were insisting. Tribunals had been told that exemption would be 'the minimum required to meet the conscientious scruples of the applicant'. Did that mean only exemption from combatant service? Or could absolute exemption also be granted? Most Tribunals, at least at first, decided to take no risks. As a matter of policy, whatever the plea, they would grant no absolute exemptions at all. Confused by arguments few could really follow, horrified by the numbers of young men who now started appearing before them, they simply said no. For many of them, in any case, the matter was really perfectly simple: they had been told that their duty was to 'protect the nation by obtaining as many men as possible for the Army', and so they would. And if applicants foolishly persisted in refusing an offer of alternative work — in the cases where they were fortunate enough to be offered it — well then, arrest, court martial and imprisonment were precisely what they deserved.

And so the hearings began. Some men came of their own free will; others were rounded up in improbable places — playing in orchestras, teaching in schools, in studios and banks and offices and farmhouses. Because there were now so many to be processed, on so very many different appeals, of which conscience was only one — and, of course, a very small one, affecting less than ten per cent of all applicants — hearings were kept short, seldom lasting more than five minutes and often very much less. They were held in public, and applicants were allowed to be represented by a friend or a solicitor.

By late March 75 letters a day were reaching Philip Snowden's desk in the House of Commons describing offensive and dismissive Tribunals, chairmen who froze out inarticulate young farm labourers with their icy courtesy and byzantine questions, and others who thought that Thoreau was the name of an American president. 'Do you ever wash yourself?' one chairman was reported to have asked a young religious protester. 'You don't look as if you do. Yours is a case of an unhealthy mind in an unwholesome body.' Another was told:

'You are nothing but a shivering mass of fat.' Before the Tribunal in Wigton, one young man, too terrified to speak, or possibly even dumb, for no one bothered to find out, was represented by his father: on learning that the boy himself was not to speak, the chairman dismissed the case and directed him to join the army. Before Springhead Tribunal, one brother lost his case; the second brother's was not even heard, on the grounds that there was no point. Day after day, in the House of Commons, Philip Snowden rose to chronicle the abuses, and even produced a pamphlet entitled *British Prussianism: the Scandal of the Tribunals*; day after day, the more popular newspapers continued to mock and ridicule the 'conchies', the 'won't-fight-funks'.

None of this had much effect. Eva Gore-Booth, an active pre-war suffragette, was one of the many NCF supporters who now offered to act as a witness of the Tribunals. Sitting in what she described as an 'ugly, airless room with its hot looking glass roof' she noted that the destruction of the ordinary domestic life of the country was such that it was 'like walking down a street looking at the remains of the shops after a Zeppelin raid' in that one small business after another was being picked off by the Tribunal. 'One man particularly,' she reported 'it was impossible to get out of one's head. He was a working man whose two sons had started a little tailoring business three years ago. One of them was already at the war, and the old man had come to claim redemption for the remaining son . . . He had brought with him a solicitor, who explained that if his son had to go the business would have to be shut up, and the old man and his wife of sixty-eight would have to go to the workhouse . . . There was a moment's pause. Then the Military Representative looked up and said decidedly: "We want that man . . ." The old man, who had stood all through the proceedings, turned and groped out of the room.'

It was hardly surprising, then, that the Tribunals found little sympathy for the conscientious objectors, who stood to quote Matthew V.9 ('Blessed are the meek, for they shall inherit the earth'); who spoke of the brotherhood of man; who, like James Strachey or David Garnett, argued that war was ugly and irrational; or who, like Francis Meynell, a Roman Catholic, protested that to be waged at all a Just War must fulfil St. Thomas Aquinas's conditions and that this one did not. Nor that they

33

were impatient with the men who said nothing at all, mystified by the severity of the questioning and the speed with which they were marched in and out of their hearing. One survey, carried out later, revealed that 2,870 men out of a sample of 3,701 who appeared before a Tribunal had never got beyond elementary schooling.

Watching from her seat in the gallery, Eva Gore-Booth observed that there were three types of conscientious objector: 'the nervous young man who had no fluency, but whose sincerity broke through the strain of his uneasy manner . . . the other, quiet and determined; and lastly, the straight-looking young man with the pleasant face, who knew so well how to hold his end up in that rather one-sided debate . . . Two things they all had in common, they were sincere, and they were all dismissed as impostors by the Tribunal.'

Rapidly aware of how very badly matters were going for the conscientious objectors, the NCF and the Quakers began coaching all those young men awaiting their Tribunals and wishing to present a case of conscience on how to handle the questioning. What would probably happen, the applicant was told, was that he would be asked what he would do if a criminal assaulted his mother. ('Interpose my body between them' had been Lytton Strachey's widely quoted reply.) Here he had to be particularly careful. If he said he would interfere, hit back, then he was obviously a man for the war. If he said he wouldn't, well then, he was a liar and a humbug. The proper answer was a carefully phrased statement about the difference between a policeman and a soldier, between organized violence in war and the use of necessary restraint in peace time. Long answers were to be avoided; so were witticisms.

Early in March, the verdicts started appearing. The *Tribunal*, the NCF's weekly paper, kept a tag of them. Quakers, it was soon found, were receiving at least partial exemption, though they themselves had requested no preferential treatment and pointed out it was in any case absurd to favour them since each Quaker had been instructed that it was only a matter for his own individual conscience. Socialists were virtually doomed to refusal of exemption of any kind.

It was not, in fact, until June 1916 that anything approaching proper guidelines were circulated to the Tribunals. By then, for a great number of conscientious objectors, it was too late. Hundreds were in jail, serving the first of what were to be repeated sentences of 'cat and mouse', as they were known when established to deal with the suffragettes in 1913, arrest, sentence, rearrest, often hard labour and solitary confinement, for refusing to accept any form of alternative service, or, having been refused even the possibility of it, in turn refusing to become a conscript soldier.

One of the imprisoned, unyielding men was Mark Hayler, who, well into his nineties, is still living in Croydon, not far from the house in which he grew up and from which, in May 1916, he left to attend his first military Tribunal. Apart from his belief in pacifism, Hayler has been a lifelong supporter of the temperance cause: the room in which he has spent much of his time since his retirement is a small bow-windowed front sitting room, in which walls, tables, bookshelves, a Victorian desk, the mantelpiece and even the floor are piled up high with tracts and pamphlets and speeches, crumpled and faded but preserved.

When war broke out Mark Hayler had been working in a boys' reformatory school in Liverpool as secretary to the Board of Governors. He was a short, somewhat obstinate man with strong views and a keen sense of what was fair. His background was Quaker, an ancestor having been with Penn in America, and his father, like himself a keen supporter of the temperance movement, saw himself as a social reformer. 'We were all conscientious objectors,' says Hayler now. 'My four sisters as well as my four brothers. It seemed to us too ridiculous for words, war. Not really a religious feeling though, more I should say a moral point of view.'

Seeing the war approaching, and certain already of his own position, Hayler had spent the early months of 1914 joining forces with other Liverpool pacifists, holding meetings at the gasworks in Warrington. At 26, he was older than many of the young men who came to listen and explore their own doubts about war. He felt himself to be a bit of a leader. 'We had a lot of silly ideas in those days. We talked of going off to Scotland and living out of sight and sound of the authorities.' After the January 1916 debate on conscription he felt he had to tell his employer that he was a pacifist. 'I don't care what you do or

35

think,' he was told, 'but I won't have anyone arrested on these premises.'

Before the Earlestown local Tribunal, on March 3, 1916, he asked for total exemption: 'I have long been of the opinion,' he told its members, 'that war is totally wrong. I have worked and striven towards what I consider the highest brotherhood of man and my conscience would not permit me to undertake any duty under the Military and Naval authorities. If, for holding these views, which I thoroughly believe to be the right attitude towards life, I am called upon to suffer, I am prepared to face the consequences of my actions.' He was given leave to appeal; but the appeal was dismissed, and he was summoned to the army.

Hayler did nothing. A few days later he heard that soldiers were watching the station. He collected his bicycle and set off to ride to London, home. He reached the house in Croydon on Good Friday. A few days later the police came to get him. Hayler was the first conscientious objector to be arrested in Croydon. The policeman, who knew the family well, was friendly, but puzzled. He agreed to let Hayler present himself the following morning at the local police station.

Next morning, Hayler and his father went to court; the public gallery was crowded with friends but the magistrate was not sympathetic. Hayler was remanded to the cells to wait for a military escort to come to fetch him from Aldershot. The first night, in barracks, was spent sitting alone on a chair in the corner of the guardroom.

Hayler's position, in his own mind, was extremely clear. He was a civilian, not a soldier, and he would take no military order, neither the next morning, when ordered to put on a uniform, nor the day after, when told to sweep out the guardroom, nor on any one of the many dozen occasions in the years that followed. The first prison sentence, for disobeying orders, was spent in Wandsworth, the vast South London prison which even in the 1980s manages to look like a fortress, the streets around as ill-lit and untended as they must have been at the beginning of the century.

Hayler's stay in Wandsworth was instructive. On arriving, he asked to see the Governor; after several refusals, he was summoned to his office. The Governor was Colonel Brooke, later to become notorious for his treatment of conscientious objectors, who seemed to regard it as his mission in life to break their wills. He was not interested in anything his new prisoner might have to say. 'I've got a lot of men like you down below. They're in irons.' Hayler later heard from one of the warders that his mother had come to see him, bringing a rose from the garden, but that she had been turned away. An early arrival, he was there when other conscientious objectors began to be brought in. 'You could see the thing was growing. It made me more determined than ever.'

Three months later, Hayler was handed a suit of civilian clothes, a scarf and a cap, and a train pass to Norwood Junction. He arrived home to find a telegram telling him to report back to his regiment in Aldershot. It was only a matter of days before the police came for him again. This time they were rather less affable. In Aldershot, despite his continued protests that he was and intended to remain a civilian, he was informed that he was now a private soldier in the 12th battalion of the Queen's Regiment and that he was about to be court-martialled for failing to obey an order to sweep the floor. So as not to contaminate other soldiers, he was kept in a tent pitched on the grass in the grounds, with two men detailed to guard him, at a distance. By this time he had been kept hanging around guardrooms for nearly five weeks, bullied, underfed, left for hours without clothes after refusing a uniform, and 'talked to as to some lunatic unfit to be at large'. 'I can truly say,' Hayler declared to the court, 'that I hate no man, be he German, Austrian, Turk, Bulgar or those who have reviled me for not taking up arms at the present time.'

Mark Hayler does not believe himself to be an especially courageous man. But there is something very brave and dignified about his testimony, delivered before formidable military figures in uniforms, sitting on a raised dais, with the full confidence of their position and their class behind them while he stood before them, dishevelled, dirty and hungry, an outcast. The words, typed out carefully to keep and remember nearly 70 years ago, now faint and yellowing on crumbling paper stuffed into several loose boxes in the archives of the Imperial War Museum, can almost be heard sounding out, in the echoing surroundings of a military court room: 'For refusing to be a soldier

I am told I may have to forfeit my life. I cannot understand it, I thought the days of religious persecution were over, and that an Englishman could hold and express his religious convictions, none daring to make him afraid . . .' This time his sentence was read out before the entire battalion, assembled, at attention, on the parade ground: 12 months' hard labour in the civil prison of Winchester. The emphasis, remembers Hayler, was put strongly on the word 'hard'. As he was led away, he heard the commanding officer turn his horse and set off down the ranks for an inspection of the men.

Hayler and two other conscientious objectors arrived at Winchester Prison on foot, marched there under escort from the station. A soldier rang the bell, and Hayler could hear, on the other side of the heavy wooden door, the jingle of keys, 'keys of slavery, drudgery, confinement and a living tomb'. Soon he was allocated his own cell, and given an enormous suit of prison clothes to wear, great long trousers that drooped around his ankles, an immense hat and shoes that rattled round his feet like clogs. Two men would have fitted inside them comfortably. If he stood on his stool he could just see out of the window into the lane, Winchester prison being then a little way from the city centre, and over the roofs of some nearby cottages. On the days he was allowed into chapel, he would look out for the 50 or so women prisoners, the 'lady criminals' as he calls them, in their light grey dresses, aprons and caps, though they were kept screened off behind a curtain and wooden partition. He thought they looked miserable.

Mark Hayler's letters from prison were some of those read out by the Croydon No-Conscription Fellowship on the evenings in 1916 when families with conscientious objectors in prison or awaiting their Tribunals would meet. These evenings, held in the Meeting House of the local Society of Friends, did a great deal, says Dorothy Bing, to relieve the frightening feelings of isolation and of having been ostracized by families and neighbours that many women were now experiencing, as well as soothing their anxiety about money. Nearly 70 years after the First War ended, people who were children at the time, with conscientious objector fathers in prison, still remember their mothers' desperate measures to find food, and the occasional anonymous donation of money slipped through the letter box that kept many of them going. At every gathering people would bring food, play the piano and sing; sometimes a phrenologist 'read bumps'. Invariably, at some point, everyone would gather to hear the news from inside prison.

One of the main disagreements in the NCF leadership, from the very beginning, was over the question of just how far could and should men carry their protest against conscription. How, in fact, did one draw a line between what constituted sufficiently strong pressure on the government and what would break the spirit — and the health — of the men involved. The founder members, in long discussions held around the time that the Bill was going through Parliament, were divided on this. Bertrand Russell agreed with Clifford Allen that refusal to fight was all part of a larger movement leading to the eventual overthrow of the military machine and thus the ending of the war, but a majority questioned whether it was right to force men into doing things beyond their capacity to endure them. In the ranks of the NCF membership there was considerable doubt about how much courage could be expected in the face of extreme deprivation or ill-treatment.

The position, at this stage, was still straightforward. If a man, offered alternative work in the Services or the general war effort rejected it, or if, having been refused even that kind of exemption, he persisted in refusing to have any truck with the military, then he was arrested and sent to a military barracks. There, he would be treated as any other soldier guilty of insubordination and sooner or later court-martialled on a technicality — for refusing to wear a uniform or obey an order. The court martial would result in a prison sentence, to be served in a civilian prison so as not to infect other soldiers with the conscientious objector heresy. When that sentence was served, the prisoner would be released, then instantly called up again, on the 'cat-and-mouse' principle. On July 26 Lloyd George, then Secretary for War, summed up the intense hostility that many in the House of Commons now felt for these 'absolutists'. With 'that kind of man,' he declared, 'I, personally, have absolutely no sympathy whatsoever . . . I shall only consider the best means of making the path of that class as hard as possible.' Previous upholders of 'the proper exemption to meet the case' were not heard to raise much objection.

By the late summer of 1916 many hundreds of men were in jail. Winchester, Wormwood Scrubs, Lewes, Pentonville, Maidstone and Wandsworth now became the main conscientious objector prisons, particularly after they had been partially or wholly emptied as former prisoners went to join the forces. Wormwood Scrubs later was remembered for its unpleasantness; Maidstone for making escapees wear chains and a harlequin sort of dress, alternative patches of khaki and black, instead of the regular knee breeches and stockings.

Nearly all conscientious objectors found themselves sentenced to the 'third division', with hard labour. Their first 28 days were spent in solitary confinement, the first 14 without a mattress. All conversation with other prisoners was forbidden. They were allowed no pencil, no paper and no newspapers. Those who also refused prison work were punished with what was called 'close confinement' for up to 14 days — with nothing at all in their cell except for a Bible, a hymn book and an instruction book. Diet number one — bread and water — was alternated with diet number two: bread, porridge, peas and gruel.

Those who agreed to work were only marginally better off. The minimum task of mailbag sewing was 70 feet a day. The stiff canvas bags were sewn with enormous needles that looked like skewers, and they had to be pressed through the canvas by a lead knob strapped to the palm. In the early days of a sentence it took an inexperienced prisoner at least ten hours to do 30 feet and he very rarely reached his quota in much under three weeks. Some of them, frail men used to teaching or clerical work, never reached it at all. Work then simply went on longer, and continued on Sundays.

Looking out of the window was a punishable offence and the punishment was savage: three days in a basement cell on bread and water. Books were heavily rationed, as one man later remembered: 'First month: *Tomorrow in the Far East*, (a short book). Feb. 2-9: *Mirage of Life* (very short book). Feb. 9–Mar. 13: Nil. Mar. 13–Apr. 13: Southey's *Life of Nelson*. Apr. 13–May 25: Nil. May 25: *Sartor Resartus*.' The prisons were frequently very cold, very damp and always dirty. There was very little sanitation and there was never enough to eat. Many prisoners fell ill, complaining that they were getting headaches, losing their memories and, in the incessant silence, beginning to believe that they were going mad. What was surprising was the extraordinary tenacity of this strange mixed collection of men who, once they had determined on their course, very rarely indeed abandoned it for softer alternatives.

By mid-1916 it was beginning to look as if, far from being over rapidly, the war was going to last for ever. Progress on the Western Front was at a complete standstill. The imprisoned men could have been forgiven for imagining their punishment would never end. What made their stubbornness all the more extraordinary was that no two were quite alike. An analysis of 817 conscientious objectors scattered in prisons throughout the country revealed 14 to be bootmakers, 27 engineers and mechanics, 17 farmers and farm labourers, 2 policemen, 14 post office employees, 6 chartered accountants and 53 teachers. Not one of these men, before 1916, could ever have pictured himself sewing a mail bag in a prison cell.

Few of them, certainly, found it easy. As the war dragged on, as warders and those dealing with the conscientious objectors began to lose members of their own families at the front and consequently became increasingly unfriendly, and as the numbers, far from diminishing, increased again, conscription having been extended in the summer of 1916 to include married men, news of heroes and martyrs to the cause began to seep out. Reports reaching Philip Snowden told of men stripped naked not for hours, but for weeks, long before they even got to their first court martial; of others being beaten up, threatened, kept in the dark, semi-starved. Because some of these men were articulate, used to expressing themselves and getting their voices heard, their stories quickly began to be known. There was George Frederick Dutch, in 'business' since the age of 13. Before he died, he recorded his story; the tape is in the Imperial War Museum.

Dutch refused to put on uniform and found himself relegated to a tent on a cliff within the grounds of Dover barracks. It was November. The soldiers were ordered to roll up the tent walls and not to go near him again. 'Well, I didn't dress and I didn't go down . . . I think it must have been at least ten days and nights . . . just my singlet and pants and socks. Just sitting like that in the tent and before I'd been there many hours I was frozen right through with exposure . . .' Dutch would certainly have died had the camp doctor not appeared at the tent one day and asked him whether he could speak. Dutch shook his head. Could he stand? Walk? Dutch could do neither. He was carried down to the medical tent and given brandy.

On the tape, in the Imperial War Museum archives, his voice is clear, slow: 'I've never felt I wanted to be a soldier . . . I never wanted to kill people . . . Oh, we took our Bible seriously. We went to Sunday School and we read the Sermon on the Mount. We were as clear as daylight. I mean it was obvious that war and anything connected was completely opposed to the Christian gospel. The Church has squared it. The Church is always prepared . . . to square circles, if necessary.' There is surprise in his tone, a note of disappointment, betrayal. Like others, he fell further back within his own mind and beliefs and found his certainty there.

In time Dutch wound up in Wandsworth, where he encountered Mark Hayler, Harold Bing and many others. 'We tame lions here,' the sergeant told him, before putting him on 27 days' bread and water in a filthy underground cell with two pots, one for urine and one for water, which the warders took great delight in muddling up. In Wandsworth he met Eric Chappelow, a poet, friend of much of the literary establishment, a man neither brave nor at all certain how much he could endure and who wrote repeatedly to friends about his fears and his terrible sense of isolation. Chappelow, who like Dutch refused to put on a uniform, appeared at his court martial in a prison blanket, having spent many weeks without clothes. Newspaper photographers made much of the occasion.

Wandsworth was also the prison where C. H. Norman, the ILP pamphleteer, not an easy man, certainly, but hardly deserving of torture, spent most of his first three weeks in a straitjacket several sizes too small for him, on hunger strike and repeatedly fainting from the tight bindings; and where a man called Roberts became obsessed with pubic hair and eventually went mad, shouting and yelling until the warders, enraged by being unable to get at him quickly because he had piled his furniture against the cell door, savagely beat him up. Roberts later died.

On Monday, June 5, 1916, Bertrand Russell was tried under the Defence of the Realm Act, DORA, first enacted in August 1914 and a much-hated weapon and symbol of censorship and restriction, for his pamphlet about Ernest Everett, the anti-monarchist teacher whose plea for exemption from the army had been dismissed. He was fined, and Trinity College wrote to tell him that he had been sacked from his lectureship. In the court, he tried to read out a statement and was stopped. His words, later reprinted in full in the *Tribunal*, went: 'The persecution which conscientious objectors have endured has enormously increased their moral weight. It illustrates the power of that better way of passive resistance, which pacifists believe to be stronger than all the armies and navies of the world. Men inspired by faith and freed from the domination of fear are inconquerable.'

June 5 was also the day that the NCF offices were raided by police, marking the start of over three years of conflict between the NCF and the authorities. This was to be a battle no one could exactly win, though both sides were to become increasingly adept at subterfuge.

Bringing out the *Tribunal*, the organization's weekly paper describing the trials and fates of conscientious objectors up and down the country, became a game demanding ever-increasing nimbleness. Early in the NCF's life plans had been drawn up to give every visible editor an invisible double, usually in the form of a woman or someone beyond the age of call up, so that as the younger men went off to serve their prison sentences the *Tribunal* would continue to be published. Even so, the paper held on only by extraordinary feats of ingenuity, often master-minded by the seemingly indefatigable Catherine Marshall, who parried DORA's press restrictions with brilliance. One week the last page was given over to a poster urging the public to call for an end to the war. Immediately, police raided the printing works, destroying £500 worth of plant and machinery and carrying off all books and invoices. Three detectives then visited the publisher's office at 5 York Buildings, but could not get Miss Jean Beauchamp, the publisher, to reveal the name of the editor.

With one week's delay, the *Tribunal* was back, printed on a small secret hand press in a back street. Miss Beauchamp was constantly visited by police. After detectives took to keeping a permanent watch on the York Buildings offices, the copy was smuggled out of the building by an old woman with a baby who apparently visited the office every couple of days looking for charity and left with bundles of papers hidden under blankets in the pram. From her house, they were taken off to other printers, scattered and secret. From there, they were collected and posted in six different boxes.

By 1917 virtually every founder member of the NCF and every editor of the *Tribunal* was, had been, or was about to be jailed, either because they refused to join the army, or because of a clause added to DORA by which all publications dealing with the war had to pass official censorship before appearing. Because so much of the determination of the conscientious objectors came from the *Tribunal*, most of its editors seemed to feel it their mission to hold out as rebelliously and uncompromisingly as possible. The majority experienced exceedingly unpleasant years of arrest, rearrest, solitary confinement and bread and water. Their position was not always made easier by an underlying note of dissension within NCF thinking, both over tactics and the advisability of total confrontation with the authorities, and because of a mild sort of bickering that seemed to go on between Bertrand Russell and Catherine Marshall who, though energetic and tenacious, was also ground down by the incessant work.

Fenner Brockway was sent to Pentonville Prison in July 1916 after the National Committee of the NCF was taken to court for a leaflet they put out against the Conscription Act. He went in a horse-drawn Black Maria, locked in what seemed to him to be a minute darkened box. It was the first of a repeated series of sentences; by 1919 Brockway had spent 28 months in prison, the last eight of them in solitary confinement. Pentonville was, he said, talking some 70 years later of his First World War experiences, the dirtiest of all the prisons he served time in. He had a cell overlooking some hollyhocks on the ground floor. Just after his arrival he heard steps in the courtyard and looked out to see Sir Roger Casement staring at the sky. Casement was hanged next morning.

After Pentonville came Wormwood Scrubs and later Walton Jail in Liverpool. 'The silence rule was in operation. You could only speak if you were addressing a warder. But it was more than human nature could stand. We learned morse code and tapped messages on the hot water pipes that connected the cells. We used it like a telephone.' In time, morse conversation was ringing round every band of imprisoned conscientious objectors in the country. In Walton, Fenner Brockway produced a prison newspaper on lavatory paper, with news, cartoons, letters. It was this way that the inmates learned, much later in the war, about the Russian Revolution.

After a while the conscientious objectors became astonishingly imaginative, passing on to each other tips about survival and how to cope with the paralyzing loneliness of solitary confinement, during their frequent but brief moments of freedom in between sentences. In Maidstone Jail, Clifford Allen played chess with a man five cells away, by whispering moves when emptying slops, and marking them up by scratching them on the walls. Games lasted as much as 34 days, and on one occasion over half the prison population took part in a tournament. Everywhere, fearing for their sanity, men were full of inventiveness: one kept sane by making lists, another practised his piano playing on his knees, while a third, a composer and music teacher before his arrest, made up a string quartet in his head and smuggled what bits of it he could out on scraps of lavatory paper.

A few, of course, escaped from jail altogether (though most often they came back) either when on transit or between sentences, just vanishing and failing to report again. The offence of harbouring a man on the run was a fine of £20 a day or imprisonment: Catherine Marshall, who proved remarkably clever at avoiding both, calculated at one point that she was liable to 2,000 years in prison.

The NCF members, meanwhile — those still free, or, being women, more likely to remain free — were continually trying to think up ways of maintaining morale among those in prison. Men about to go to jail for a first sentence were given packets of leads for writing which could be hidden on the soles of the feet with a bit of plaster, positioned along the arch in such a way that they couldn't be seen on arrival during the compulsory first prison bath. Prisoners having completed their sentences would carry messages from those inside out to the waiting NCF women. One day, a message came asking what the current NCF policy was about defying prison rules. The answer was to be transmitted in the form of a colour signal, hung from a certain tree on a certain day. Catherine Marshall went to inspect the tree and found that it was not climbable. So she sent out a party of children with kites of the agreed colour, and the message was then circulated around the jail on the water pipes, by morse.

Both Fenner Brockway and Clifford Allen were to write of the exhilaration of what they were doing. 'I cannot describe to you the wonderful sense of comradeship there is among the COs in prison,' wrote Brockway, after several months in solitary confinement. 'We are not allowed to speak to each other, but the unity we feel does not need expression in speech.' From Maidstone, Clifford Allen reported that he was flooded with ideas, but that periods of great mental satisfaction alternated with 'intense mental and spiritual torture . . .'

It was the silence, in the end, that became unendurable. 'One hundred and ninety-five days of stitching,' wrote Allen, 'each of twenty-three hours and fifty minutes of silence. I think the greatest torture of enforced and perpetual silence is the never-ceasing consciousness of thinking in which it results.' In Walton Jail, Fenner Brockway became one of the first conscientious objectors to mutiny against it. One day five of the men asked to see the Governor and informed him that henceforth they intended to speak, loudly, openly, and whenever they wanted to. All 60 conscientious objectors in the prison followed their example.

For ten days the rebellion persisted. Brockway remembers it as a period of exuberance, cut into the long months of enforced solitude and silence, when the men exercised and talked at the same time, when evenings were filled with concerts conducted through the cell bars, with the Welsh prisoners in particular giving very fine renderings of hymns. And then the five ringleaders were deported. Fenner Brockway was sent to Lincoln Prison, with three months on bread and water and eight months in solitary confinement. 'My mind,' he remembers, 'was saved by the Sinn Feiners, whose leaders were being held, under fairly relaxed conditions, in the same prison. One day I heard steps outside my cell. I got on to my stool and saw through the slit one of the trusties. He posted a very small package in to me, containing a pencil stub and a scrap of paper, and a message. It came from De Valera and said: "Tell us what you want and we'll get it for you."'

From then on, each day when he went out to the yard for his 40 minutes' solitary exercise, Brockway found copies of the *Manchester Guardian* and the *Labour Leader*, and sometimes the *Nation*, the *Economist* and the *Observer*, waiting hidden for him down one of the drains.

There is no episode in the treatment of conscientious objectors by the British in World War One more shaming than the story of the 50 men sent, in May 1916, in four separate batches to France. It is one of stealth, confusion and vindictiveness. No one has ever agreed on whether the death sentence passed on 30 of them would actually have been carried out had it not been for the speed with which the news of their plight reached the NCF offices in London, or whether it was all just a tactic, a last rattle of military might considered necessary as a warning now the Conscription Act was about to be extended to married men. What was certainly true was that a strong feeling did exist in the army and among a number of high-ranking soldiers that conscientious objectors were traitors and deserved to be shot and that if a number of exemplary death sentences could be carried out this pernicious growth could at least be checked. By taking them to France, to the front, they could after all be shot legitimately, for disobeying an order while on active service. It is equally true however that a directive had already gone out to General Sir Douglas Haig, Commander-in-Chief of the British Expeditionary Forces, saying that no death penalty was to be passed on any conscientious objector. That decree had not been made public.

The first rumour that something peculiar was happening came when, towards the end of the first week in May 1916, a man working on the railways on the south-western outskirts of London brought into the NCF offices a note scribbled on a piece of paper and evidently thrown from the window of a train. The note said that 17 absolutist conscientious objectors, who had been placed in irons for refusing to carry stones from the beach, suspecting they were to be used to build an access road to a military camp, had been moved from Landguard Fort, in

Harwich, built originally by French prisoners during the Napoleonic wars, and were in the process of being shipped to France. Before Catherine Marshall could get in touch with Asquith the men were on their way across the Channel to Le Havre.

For the first three days a somewhat uneasy tranquillity surrounded them. Technically no longer prisoners, but soldiers, they were released; carefully watched but no longer guarded, they strolled along the sea shore. A few played football with some Frenchmen. But on May 10 they, together with the company with which they were billeted in Cinder City, were rapidly formed up and marched on to the parade ground where, a few minutes later, they were as rapidly ordered to march off again. The 17 men, dotted around the parade ground, rooted to the spot and refusing to obey an order, stayed put.

From that moment on every tactic that could be dreamt up by an imaginative — and, usually, sadistic — officer or NCO was used to persuade, coerce, bully and threaten the men into obedience. The conscientious objectors' total uncooperativeness only increased their fury. As the days passed the brutality increased. Many men left records of what happened to them in France, often written on paybooks they turned into diaries, but the strange story of 14 New Zealand conscientious objectors who improbably found themselves at the French front is perhaps the best chronicled. The articulacy of the men involved, the outrage they felt at what was now happening to them, and the particular cruelty with which they were treated kept the events vivid in their minds all their lives. Though all of them are now dead, as are the 30 British men sentenced to death, the books, letters and diaries they left give a very complete picture.

In 1915 a national register had been taken in New Zealand requiring all men of military age to say whether or not they were willing to undertake military service. Unexpectedly many — 33,700 out of 196,000 — said that they were not. In 1916, the government introduced conscription.

Archibald Baxter was one of the 14 young conscientious objectors arrested even before a Tribunal had heard his views and, after many weeks in jail, taken in the middle of one night and put on board a ship bound for Europe. The men were crammed several to each very small cabin; as a random piece of additional cruelty the portholes were sealed shut. Most of them were very sick. Those who refused to wear khaki were hauled up on deck and stripped, and their own clothes were thrown overboard; no onlooker moved to protest. When they took off the uniforms into which they had been forcibly put they were beaten with hose pipes and left naked. When the ship docked in England, they were shackled with heavy chains and marched to Sling Camp on Salisbury Plain.

In due course, perhaps because the authorities had very little idea what to do with them, the 17 were sent on again, this time to France, to a military camp in Dunkirk, on a low-lying swampy stretch of the coastline. Those who continued to refuse orders were put in solitary confinement. One warder took particular pleasure in tormenting his captives; he had them stripped, beaten, doused, then subjected to the 'shot drill', an hour-long rhythmic ritual involving shifting a bag filled with 30 pounds of sand from one point to another while wearing handcuffs. Later, several of the New Zealanders described what happened to a young man called Mark Briggs.

Briggs's objection to war was absolute: he would not even walk if told to do so by a soldier. And so a sergeant in the military police had a cable of wire looped around Briggs's chest, harnessed three soldiers to the wire and ordered them to drag him for a mile across the wooden duck boards. The batons across the boards were jagged and full of loose nails; Briggs lost his clothes, caught in the snags and torn off him. A wound in his back opened, bled and soon filled with dirt.

When this sorry little group, three heaving young soldiers and the filthy, almost naked body of a nearly unconscious man, reached a shell crater, they simply went through it and on up the other side. Archibald Baxter, who died in 1970 at the age of 88, left his own account of the event. When Briggs was pulled out of the last shell hole 'they took him by the shoulders and tipped him head over heels back into the water. Just as he had managed to get his head above water and was trying to get his breath, Booth [the sergeant] fired a handful of muck into his mouth.' The conchies were, of course, stubborn, and in their stubbornness maddeningly superior; but it is impossible now not to wonder at the brutality that stirred in Booth and his men.

Baxter himself did not fare so very well either. After he had refused to help in the cook house, the sergeant led him aside. It is the tone of almost casual reporting, as if he were describing a day at the races, that makes the episode so real:

'"Right-Oh," he said. "Come along. I've got my orders." He took me over to the poles, which were willow stumps six to eight inches in diameter and twice the height of a man, and placed me against one of them. It was inclined forward out of perpendicular. Almost always afterwards he picked the same one for me. I stood with my back to it and he tied me to it by the ankles, knees and wrists. He was an expert at the job, and he knew how to pull and strain at the ropes, till they cut into the flesh and completely stopped the blood circulating. When I was taken off my hands were always black with congealed blood. . . . Earlier in the war, men undergoing this form of punishment were tied with their arms outstretched. Hence the name of crucifixion. Later, they were more often tied to a single upright, probably to avoid the likeness to a cross. But the name stuck.'

Baxter was repeatedly threatened with the firing squad. What made it especially hard for this small group of New Zealanders was that they were so far from home, that their families had no idea where they were, and, that unlike the British conscientious objectors, they felt they had no support for their stand. It was only too easy for them to believe the officer who told them: 'Whatever happens to you you will be reported as having died or been killed on active service and these people in New Zealand will never know that you had not taken it on.' To die for the pacifist cause, but deemed to have betrayed it: that was bitter indeed.

In the end, Baxter was simply cast out of the camp, like a stray dog; given no military number, he was entitled to no rations. He scavenged. Shipped at last back to England, he was put in a mental asylum. Finally, returned to New Zealand, he was brought once more before an enraged Tribunal chairman who, hearing his story, roared out: 'What *are* you?' Baxter has all of Mark Hayler's dignified eloquence. '"A man! What do you take me for?" I replied.'

The British conscientious objectors in France were subjected to the same round of punishments, whether crucifixion, or on Field Punishment Number 1, tied to a wheel or a gun carriage, starved or stowed away in pits. When they were together they kept their morale up by singing, sometimes the 'Red Flag', sometimes hymns, and particularly 'Simply trusting every day'. They also talked. Debates, wrote H. E. Marten later, a slight boyish figure from Pinner, with a crew cut and small round wire spectacles, varied from 'the existence of a personal Devil, to one on the merits of Esperanto, from the doctrines of Marx and the Tolstoyan philosophy to vaccination'. One can picture them: a small, isolated band of rebels, hanging on to their courage with defiantly high-minded talk as if, when all else seemed to be slipping away, intellect and reason might sustain them. It was not only talk. One man was an acrobat and would occasionally do tricks, and when the conscientious objectors were taken out to the hills for rare moments of exercise they would 'run and jump' as they looked out across the Channel, to the cliffs of Dover.

Meanwhile, in London, frantic attempts were being made to retrieve them. Three additional parties of men, 16 from Richmond Castle in Yorkshire — where six former cells today still have records on the conscientious objectors, and their sentences, etched on the walls — eight from Kinmel Park, Abergele, and nine from Seaford in Sussex (though not all of these last were actually conscientious objectors), were by now known to be in France and events seemed to be moving ominously towards some sort of crisis. Catherine Marshall and Bertrand Russell believed that they had managed to secure a promise from Asquith that the men would not be shot, but deputations to Members of Parliament were kept up. Even Emmeline Pankhurst was persuaded by the mothers of nine of the prisoners in France to call on Brigadier-General Childs with pleas for clemency. She came away reassured but not impressed. The Brigadier-General, she reported, was the 'most extraordinarily cadaverous looking man I had ever beheld, his shaven head fleshless as a skull'.

Even so, no one was happy about what was going on. Repeated questioning in the House of Commons revealed considerable ambiguity on the part of the military, and even Harold Tennant seemed to be admitting that the elected civil authority was not entirely in command of its military side. Rumours began spreading that 16 were already dead. Day after day Philip Morrell and Philip Snowden pestered ministers for guarantees that the men were safe, while churchmen and some of the more Liberal newspapers kept up a persistent rumble of enquiry. Nothing was made any easier by the fact that for a while at least, until a standard printed postcard got through, no one had any firm idea of where the men were actually being held, so only then were representatives of the NCF and the Fellowship of Reconciliation able to set off for France in pursuit of them.

In the camps along the French coast, the conscientious objectors themselves had no reason at all to believe that they were going to survive. Every step they took seemed to be heading inexorably towards the death sentence. They were promised it repeatedly: they saw deserters shot; why should they be spared? 'Do not be downhearted if the worst comes to the worst' wrote Stuart Bevis to his mother. Bevis was the assistant manager of a pipe factory in London, fluent in both German and French, and, at 36, somewhat older than the others. 'Many have died cheerfully before for a worse cause.'

On Monday, June 6, the various courts martial for insubordination and refusal to obey orders completed, the first batch of men were informed that their sentences were now going to be announced. They were locked into a hut to wait. To dispel the tension, they played leap-frog, then marbles with some asbestos chips they had knocked from the walls.

Much military thought must have gone into the stage managing of this occasion, the one last chance for a military *coup de théâtre* against all objectors, everywhere. All available soldiers, some 3,000 men altogether, had been assembled in formation along three sides of the parade ground of the military camp at Henriville. Their sheer number, the massed blur of their uniforms, the sheen on their many boots, only served to highlight the fact that the objectors were very few and very vulnerable. John Forster, from Cambridge, a man friends later remembered as 'rather jolly', was the first to go. His charge was disobedience while undergoing Field Punishment. Lingering over the name, the regiment, the details, the Adjutant paused. 'Sentenced to death by being shot.' A man called Evans, standing just behind, later recorded that he could see his own name among the papers in the Adjutant's hand. At the top, in red letters, was the word 'Death'. The Adjutant paused again.

'Confirmed by General Sir Douglas Haig.' A still longer pause. Then, almost with regret, or so it seemed to the assembled men: 'Commuted to ten years' penal servitude.' 'As I stood listening to the sentences of the rest of our own party,' wrote one of the men later, and his words, though sadly not his name, are faithfully reprinted in the NCF's published account of the incident, 'the feeling of joy and triumph surged up within me, and I felt proud to have the privilege of being one of that small company of COs testifying to a truth which the world had not yet grasped, but which it would one day treasure as a most precious inheritance.'

In all, 30 men were sentenced to be shot, then had the death penalty commuted. They were shipped back to England. As if to underline their impotence in the whole affair, the War Office in London continued saying that the men were in no kind of danger, even after Harold Tennant was forced to admit in the House of Commons that he didn't know whether or not the sentences had actually been carried out. Asquith, accused of having misled the House, rose on June 29 to pledge that such a thing would never happen again.

It is quite possible that the fiasco of the conscientious objector episode in France provided the final proof that nothing that was currently being done to coerce the protesters was having any effect. On the contrary, not only were a disproportionate number of other men being detailed to guard and escort them, but the whole subject was acquiring something of a bad smell. Furthermore, attitudes towards these men were softening. The extreme hostility of much of the newspaper world was being mitigated by the stories of brutality that were emerging, while in the House of Commons Philip Snowden's unceasing work on their behalf was finally winning converts to their cause. Even Harold Tennant, not normally sympathetic towards them, rose one day in the House of Commons to admit that 'while the conscientious objector has not made my path easier . . . I'm afraid I cannot, for my part, withhold my − I do not want to use too strong a word − but certainly my respect for persons who on religious grounds will undergo privation and even persecution rather than do violence to their conscience'.

More important for the absolutist conscientious objectors themselves, Brigadier-General Wyndham Childs was turning out to be a fair man. Childs was an unusual figure. As a young

law student in Liskeard he had volunteered for service in the
Boer War, where his job had largely been that of quelling rioters
and mutineers. The Adjutant-General, Sir Nevil Macready,
had met Childs in South Africa and been impressed by his effi-
ciency; in 1916, having succeeded Lord Derby and looking for
someone able to take responsibility for objectors who, he continued to insist, were 'soldiers', he turned to his former South
African subordinate.

As a trained lawyer, Childs was obsessive about legal correct-
ness; but as a soldier he hated all forms of indiscipline and independence of action. As he was to write in his memoirs, ten years
after the war, he simply could not make himself 'recognise the
right of any person to refuse to render *some* form of service to his
country'. The result, inevitably, was a certain inconsistency in
his thinking: throughout the war he was able both to keep up
enduring hostility towards the NCF and all its work, maintaining that everything it stood for smacked of sedition, while personally feeling some sympathy for the individual conscientious
objectors. Childs was tough, intransigent and narrow-minded;
but he could also be charming and would go to great lengths if
he suspected something illegal was going on.

As their junior, Childs had readily accepted Kitchener's and
Macready's directive that any conscientious objector subject to
military law must receive the same protection against ill-
treatment as any other man in uniform. As reports began
reaching his desk in the War Office of treatment that even he
could see was considerably closer to brutality than bullying,
Childs began to intervene. He started by sending notes to
district commanders, saying that in no circumstances was
'physical coercion' to be used to force men to become soldiers.
When the brutality persisted, he acted. Surprisingly rapidly, a
brigadier-general (who had dispatched five of the conscientious
objectors to France), a lieutenant-colonel and a major commanding a battalion were all removed from their positions. His
point, Childs would say, was not only that such brutality was
legally and morally indefensible, but that it made it so much
easier for the public to feel sympathy for the conscientious
objectors.

What must have irked Childs was the fact that so very much
public attention seemed to be devoted to what was a very small

band of men. While some 1,200 absolutists were tying up a great deal of debate and attention, the 9,000 alternativists, men who had agreed from the start to accept some form of service towards the war, provided it would not involve the shedding of blood, were, with a greater or lesser degree of success but in any case largely unnoticed, getting on with their war. About half had joined the Non-Combatant Corps (the No-Courage Corps, as the press liked to call it), where they wore khaki uniforms and trained in drill squads but bore no arms, working instead as road-builders and general dogs-bodies though not as loaders of shells, an objection that caused many bitter misunderstandings.

The rest were pursuing civilian work. In January 1916, when the Conscription Bill was being drafted, a clause had been inserted about 'work of national importance'. At first no one had any idea what this might be; the Tribunals, it was thought, would sort it all out. It was not in fact until the middle of April, two months later, when the Tribunals had shown themselves very inept at devising 'equality of sacrifice' on the civilian front, that the Hon. T. H. W. Pelham, an assistant secretary at the Board of Trade, was asked to compose and circulate to the Tribunals a list of occupations that his newly-formed Committee on Work of National Importance actually considered helpful. Farms, the Committee instructed, were definitely of national importance, and so were the Red Cross, the YMCA, hospitals, mines and lunatic asylums.

After May 1916 over 4,000 men who had applied to the Tribunals for at least partial exemption were scattered around the country, driving ambulances, chopping wood, clearing out wards, making tea and sowing crops. For the most part, the scheme prospered, despite a rather petty ruling that the men had to be sent a certain distance from their own homes (to increase the sacrifice). More than half the men were over 30, and most of them were married. One thousand four hundred were Christadelphians who, as a body, had announced that, while nothing at all could ever persuade them to fight, they saw no reason not to help at home. Problems occurred mainly on the farms, where over a quarter of the men eventually made their way: farmers, understandably, were extremely suspicious of these pallid clerks and school teachers who appeared at their gates, while in turn the pale city men, accustomed to ledgers and warm offices and school rooms, found the manual work extremely tough.

In the summer of 1916, stock was taken of the small, secondary, home war: the battle against the conchies. No one could be said to be winning. The moment had come for a new tactic by the authorities, for the absolutists at least, the alternativists being seemingly under control. The government had been wrong about the impact of conscription. Neither the notorious 'cat-and-mouse' technique, the Prisoners' Temporarily Discharged for Ill Health Act, which allowed for repeated sentences, nor the ill-treatment in prisons and barracks, seemed to be having the slightest effect on morale and determination.

Those back from France were facing ten years of penal servitude. Those arrested early in the war were already well into second sentences in the third division, on bread and water, and in solitary confinement. The treatment was beginning to produce its casualties. As Fenner Brockway was to report from Walton Jail, one man in six was in hospital, one in six of the rest was suffering from serious loss of weight, and three had fainted in chapel. In jails up and down the country men were confused, sleepless, excruciatingly lonely and starved.

3

War and protest

Towards the middle of the summer of 1916, as the conscientious objectors were being shipped back to penal servitude in Britain, as Asquith promised in the House of Commons that such brutality and confusion would never re-occur and as the Battle of the Somme began in earnest on the Western Front, so a new policy for absolutists came into force. A Central Tribunal was appointed by the War Office to review the cases of all imprisoned conscientious objectors. Those they agreed were genuine would be released from prison provided they accepted to undertake 'work of national importance' under the control of a new civilian committee, which was given the name of its chairman, William Brace, Under-Secretary at the Home Office. Any man who refused, or whose plea of conscience again failed to satisfy the Tribunal, would be returned to complete his sentence in jail.

Though leading members of the NCF objected that this would be no different from any other previous 'alternative' form of work, and Clifford Allen wrote from his prison cell to say that those who accepted it would be nothing other than 'slaves playing with liberty', and therefore cease to 'count in the struggle', many of the men, shut up and increasingly desperate in Wandsworth or Wormwood Scrubs, were willing to go along with it. In the weeks following July 27, when the Central Tribunal sat to hear its first cases, 4,378 men were declared on re-examination to possess a 'genuine' objection to the war. (Two hundred and sixty-seven applications were turned down; 692 men refused even to appear before the Tribunal.)

The Brace Committee might have worked; indeed, it nearly did, except for the fact that, like the Pelham Committee before it, it suffered acutely from lack of clarity of purpose. The absolutists had been told that they were going to be given 'work of national importance'; many, in fact, looked forward to it, believing that their professional skills, as teachers, doctors, clerks or craftsmen, could certainly be of benefit to the country. The Brace committee, on the other hand, along with a large section of the public, were still obsessed with the need for 'equality of sacrifice'. As *The Times* saw it, what was required was a 'form of arduous and unremunerative public service'. From the start, the scheme was bedevilled by a spirit of punishment and retribution.

The first absolutists' settlement was at Dyce, five miles from Aberdeen. Here, on a hillside, late in August, 250 men, victims of early Tribunal intolerance, arrived to work in the granite quarries. They were given eight pence a day and food. For nine and a half to ten hours every day except Sunday they were expected to transfer stones in barrows from the mines to the crushing machines and from there in trucks to the roads where they were needed for repairs.

There were no proper buildings at Dyce. Men, thin and sickly after months of malnutrition and insufficient exercise in prison, returned after exhausting days in the mines to a row of dilapidated tents, long since thrown out by the army as unusable. Soon, the settlement turned into a field of mud; clothes and blankets, quickly damp in the persistent Scottish rain, never dried. Early in September, a man called Walter Roberts caught influenza. A few days later he died. His fellow workers, dejected and sodden in the unceasing wet, took refuge in nearby barns, until herded back to work by their warders. In the *Tribunal*, hailing Roberts as the first martyr to the cause, Fenner Brockway wrote: 'To all of us, his life and death must be an inspiration.'

Ramsay MacDonald, old opponent of the war and a crusader for decency towards the conscientious objectors during the many debates in the Commons, paid a visit to Dyce. Returning to London, he described a scene of misery and absurdity. 'It had been raining,' he told the House on October 19, 'raining, raining for days. The roads from the station to the village were simply huge, swaying masses of mud . . . In the tents there was mud . . . There they are, with barrows and shovels, trying to do navvies' work. They could not do it. There is confusion. There is no order . . . They were soft of muscle, their hands were blistered, their backs were sore . . . My point is that this was not national work. It was not useful work . . . These men simply felt that they were being punished, and that they were asked to do this because the state wished to punish them . . . It is sheer folly.

It is waste. If you are going to punish these men, punish them honestly.' Members of Parliament were not impressed. 'We can ill afford in this country,' said one, 'to coddle and canoodle these people.'

There were some, of course, who felt this attitude to be perfectly correct. Worse things were indeed happening at the front, where between July and October the Battle of the Somme had cost more than 400,000 casualties. It is very easy to see how people, hearing of their sons' deaths in France, found discussions about the treatment of conscientious objectors irrelevant and even offensive. But this was not exactly the point. The issue remained precisely the same as it had been the moment Asquith introduced conscription: a matter of moral liberty, of the relationship between any one man and the state in which he lived. That argument did not depend on events.

No scheme, however, no imaginative change of plans, was more calculated to provoke rage on the part of those already maddened by the conscientious objector debate, than the fiasco of Dartmoor Prison. By the late autumn of 1916, Dyce, finally deemed totally unsuitable, was abandoned. Strikers, and men considered to have abused their privileges (often for very trivial misdemeanours, like being three minutes late for work, or persisting in putting out 'peace propaganda') were returned to prison, while the others were sent off to make manure from bones and carcasses of animals at Bloxburn, near Edinburgh (where the stench was so appalling, and the men, allowed no baths, smelt so disgusting, that no local inhabitant would go near them), or to build roads in the Highlands. In December, Lloyd George became Prime Minister. His new War Cabinet, consisting of men more committed than before to an energetic continuation of the war, included two of the most passionate champions of compulsory military service, Lord Curzon and Lord Milner. In this new mood of discipline, a Code of Rules was drawn up for the absolutist conscientious objectors whose cases had been reviewed by the Brace Committee, with detailed guidelines about hours of work, and pay, and behaviour. To house all these men and put the rules into effect, Dartmoor Prison was taken over; and, as a sop to everyone's susceptibilities, renamed Princetown Work Centre.

The winter of 1916–17 was exceptionally cold. On the moors,

deep snow lay beyond its usual time, while a freezing wind blew almost continually across the open hillsides. During the early spring months 900 men arrived in groups to begin their work of national importance. Among them was Mark Hayler, twice arrested, twice imprisoned, twice released and now re-arrested and offered what seemed to him an acceptable and far more humane way of passing his days. In his batch were some Tolstoyans, a few socialists, a number of Quakers and a few anarchists who, on the journey to the prison, told the men they were with that they fully intended either to escape or to create havoc. 'So you see,' said Hayler later, 'Dartmoor was not a place where the angels flapped their wings.' The very disparateness of these men, the uneasy mix of their pasts and their beliefs, in the conditions in which they were now put, was enough to make certain that the work centre, like all its predecessors, was doomed.

Dartmoor Prison had been built at the beginning of the 19th century to house 10,000 French prisoners from the Napoleonic wars, then confined to six hulks in Plymouth harbour, amid growing fears of a mutiny or epidemic. They built the prison themselves, five rectangular granite buildings fanned out like the spokes of a wheel, on a desolate spot on the top of the moor, not enclosed in folds like the other villages, so that the houses built up around to house warders had a bleak and random air. By 1812 the French prisoners had been joined by Americans; 11,000 men slept on tiers of hammocks, slung from cast-iron pillars. There was no heating. The Gothic fancy of the age had made the outer walls castellated and turreted, and over the main gate, on top of three blocks of granite archway, were engraved, a little smugly perhaps, the words *Parcere Subjectis*, Spare the Humbled. By 1850 the French and the Americans were gone, but by now Dartmoor had reopened as the first British penal settlement to house British convicts, the colonies, apart from Australia, having grown sick of absorbing British felons.

The prison is not very different today. An additional perimeter wall has been built and many of the prison blocks have been repointed, to give the stone a newish air; and the train, which once brought day trippers all the way from Plymouth to Yeovil on the sixpenny 'Woolworth special', and during the

First War was used to bring conscientious objectors to Prince-town, has gone. But it is still possible to imagine the men, in the cold spring of 1917, getting off the train after a ride up from the coast, through forests and then across open moorland, trudging past the Duchy Hotel, its gaudily painted dining room famous for the teas taken there by George V while on hunting trips, then up the hill past forge and smithy and village shop, with Victorian cottage houses on either side, and then a final sharp right turn and through the great wooden gates and into the prison. In deference to the new approach, locks had been removed from the cell doors, and the warders rechristened 'Instructors'; but, still, it was a prison, and the Code of Rules was very much to be obeyed, especially after the former deputy director of Wormwood Scrubs was brought in to run the place. The men, hanging around the exercise yard that looks far out across the deserted moorland, must have longed for home.

About 200 of Princetown's conscientious objectors were put to work inside the walls. The rest were sent out on to the moors, to the farm or to the quarry, a compact hole in the hillside some quarter of a mile from the prison gates; they were told to crush oats on antiquated machinery or cart granite for ten hours a day. The clearest monument to the futility of their work can still be seen very plainly today: if you leave the prison behind you and walk down the narrow road leading to the moor, you come across, in the middle of the turbulence of the landscape, where vast granite boulders appear to tumble over each other, a perfect field. It is rectangular, perhaps three or four acres in size, and bordered by a neat, seven-foot-tall drystone wall. The grass within grows green and lush; there are no boulders, no stones, nothing. From afar, you would think it a joke of nature, a curious, abandoned experiment. The local people still refer to this pure patch of moor as 'Conchies' Field', for it was here that the men were marched every day, under the eyes of the warders on their ponies, to work on clearing stones and building walls. Nothing was ever done with the field; it was simply designated, cleared, and then left.

Mark Hayler spent a year on the moors, and was then moved to work in the prison hospital, a building barely four years old in 1917 and, after the freezing bleakness of the cell blocks, cosy beyond belief. 'I have a fine room to sleep in,' he wrote to his mother, 'spring mattress and an armchair and an ordinary chair . . . I am naturally feeling much happier.' Less exhausted by perpetual manual labour, Hayler was able to make friends with some of the other conscientious objectors and with them he was soon printing notes and news on an old prison hand press and arranging for concerts in the enormous prison chapel, a great gaunt central building, not unlike a prison block from the outside, now seldom used. He was also able to get back to his temperance work, conducting a favourable poll on the prohibition of liquor traffic one Saturday night. His scrapbook, kept with his other papers in the Imperial War Museum, contains fragments of absurd prison rules ('Lying about naked on the moors is forbidden'), cartoons of the time ('No Combatant Corps Coat of Arms', a picture of two rabbits and a shield under the banner 'We don't want to fight' with below the caption ''Tis conscience do make cowards of us all'), yellowing snapshots of the men in Princetown, frail, ragged-looking men but not unsmiling, and cards drawn by one of the inmates who was an artist. It was not, says Hayler, a bad life; many of the men were very inventive and even constructive, offering to build a church in the village which they duly did, so that to this day Princetown possesses the only church built by prisoners in Britain.

Hayler himself was not a man to make trouble, but even he could not stay entirely outside the hostilities, both petty and more serious, that at times overran the camp. With Hayler had come men commonly referred to as 'strange religious' and they, keeping their heads down and their beliefs to themselves, posed few problems; but others, among the 'anarchists' and 'politicals', did. They argued and fought with the warders, they went on go-slows, they circulated peace material and they complained, often provoked by increasingly vituperative attacks in the newspapers.

Early in the existence of the camp, the *Daily Express* had sent down reporters who came back from Princetown with derisive stories about the good living enjoyed by 'Princetown's Pampered Pets', the 'Coddled Conscience Men' and the 'COs' Cosy Club'. In the House of Commons, a Major Roland Hunt asked whether these men might not be offered to the Germans, in return for wounded British prisoners of war, while Sir Clement Kinlock-Cooke, MP for Devonport, pursued the 'work-shy' inmates with a kind of Messianic hatred, that grew increasingly shrill over the months. 'They work in overcoats,' he rose one day to say, 'so as not to get cold, they wear woollen gloves to prevent their hands getting red . . .' He urged that their freedom and rations be curtailed, which in any case they soon were, when Lord Davenport, Food Counsellor, decided after the shipping losses to cut back on rations for prisoners, although not for civilians. By the summer of 1917 they were down to 22 ounces of bread a day; by the beginning of November to 11 ounces. Joseph King, the Liberal backbencher and member of the UDC, told the Commons that he had cases before him of 30 men, driven insane by the treatment, 'mere clerks and men of low physique' collapsed under the pressure of hard manual labour on insufficient food. He suspected, he said, that nationally that figure could be multiplied 'four to five times'.

As the bitterness at Dartmoor intensified, with local civilians jostling and even physically assaulting the conscientious objectors, Bertrand Russell led a campaign to expose the ridiculous penal nature of the work that clerks, doctors, painters and school teachers were being forced to carry out, and proposed that some serious thought now go to transforming it into what it should have been in the first place — work of national importance. Though his speeches received some support, the Bishop of Exeter, Lord William Cecil, returning from a visit to the Princetown camp and describing a state of 'seething intellectual anarchy', in a letter which received wide publicity in the newspapers, met with rather more. He had found the inmates, wrote the Bishop, pursuing seditious correspondence in 'sackloads' of letters, 'no doubt conveying instructions for those plans of bloodshed . . . which may at some future time bring ruin to England'. Why not send the conchies somewhere where they could be put in touch with enemy bombers? 'The dropping of a bomb . . . would perhaps bring about a sudden conversion: or at any rate the whirr of the midnight raid might help them to a truer view of the political situation.' In July 1917, two army officers joined Brace's committee, and yet more punitive rules were fashioned to curtail the conscientious objectors' freedom. It was not until November, and even then only after ugly confrontations at various work centres, as well as the death of a man in Dartmoor, that permission was finally won, thanks to agitation on behalf of the NCF and sympathetic MPs, for those who had not broken any rules for 18 months to seek employment under private employers.

It was not long after the first conscientious objectors started arriving in Princetown that the Revolution finally broke in Russia. News of the Tsar's abdication and the formation of the Soviet of Workers' Deputies was greeted by the socialist pacifists with great excitement; villagers recalled for years afterwards a sense of shock at realizing that in their small village hall a meeting was being held at which the prisoners from Dartmoor read out passages from Keir Hardie and sang the 'Red Flag'.

In London there was no less rejoicing. The political pacifists and the NCF seized on the idea of Anglo-Russian cooperation and read in the Russian Provisional Government's first declarations about amnesty for political and religious offenders, freedom of speech and universal suffrage, a message about civil liberties that they had long been hoping for at home. While in Russia the thousand or so religious conscientious objectors, imprisoned on the outbreak of war, were being freed, a British Charter of Freedom was drafted, with goals similar to those being propounded in Russia, calling for the release of all pacifists in British jails and camps. A vast rally was sponsored by George Lansbury's *Herald* — 'A new star of hope has risen over Europe' — to greet the Revolution, organized by a group calling itself the Anglo-Russian Democratic Alliance. It took place in the Royal Albert Hall, and while Clara Butt, the most popular singer of her day, stood on the platform and sang 'Give to us peace in our time' to 12,000 people inside the auditorium, a further 20,000 had to be turned away, and stood thronging the streets along the park.

The Russian Revolution transformed British left-wing politics. At their annual conference in April, the ILP turned the occasion into a celebration of the Revolution, while in June a newly-created United Socialist Party — the ILP and the British Socialist Party — held a convention in Leeds Coliseum to which 1,150 delegates came, among them Ramsay MacDonald, Philip Snowden, Bertrand Russell and Sylvia Pankhurst, to pledge themselves to demands very like the Revolution's own, including the setting up of a number of 'Workers' and Soldiers'

Councils'. The conference ended, to rousing cheers, with repeated choruses of the 'Red Flag' and 'England Arise'.

During the early summer the ILP's biggest peace campaign yet was launched, with calls for peace negotiations on terms voiced by the new administration in Russia: 'No indemnities and no annexations.' Snowden became chairman of the ILP peace campaign; despite unrelenting hostility in the House of Commons, he had never abandoned his hopes of bringing the country round to the notion of negotiated peace. While the Battle of the Somme went on, and while Asquith was in the throes of being replaced by the more war-minded Lloyd George, there had been little progress; but now that the Russians were professing to continue the war against Germany only on idealistic grounds, hopes for peace were in the air.

The anti-war lobby looked rather larger than it actually was. Despite the Leeds convention the Russian peace programme drew little support in the House of Commons. In May, only 32 MPs voted in its favour. That same month, the Petrograd Soviet announced that it intended to invite socialists of all nations to meet in Stockholm. While the Sailors' and Firemen's Union refused to carry men prepared to talk to the Germans across the sea — a delegation from the Labour Party Executive having decided to go — Arthur Henderson, the Labour leader, Minister without Portfolio in the War Cabinet, was sent to Moscow by Lloyd George. He came back saying that he was certain that the international congress would take place, whether or not the British were there. At a special Labour Party conference, delegates voted overwhelmingly for participation at the conference, but the Cabinet preferred to avoid it. Henderson resigned his Cabinet post, and the Government announced that no passports would be issued for Stockholm. After the Revolution and the Leeds conference, the Labour Party was in disarray; it remained in the coalition, but Henderson now turned to concentrate on post-war party reconstruction.

By now America had joined the war. Diplomatic relations were severed early in February, when Germany, having declared that it intended to wage unrestricted submarine warfare against neutral shipping around the British and French coasts, had torpedoed three American food relief ships bound for Belgium.

On April 6, further goaded by attempts to induce Mexico to enter the war on the side of the Central Powers, America declared war on Germany. American pacifists sprang into action. Petitions against the coming hostilities poured into Congress. President Wilson received several thousand telegrams pointing out that he had been elected precisely to keep America out of the war.

Right up until the day America declared war, the peace cause remained extremely popular. American pacifists had not only acquired a certain stature, smiled on by Wilson, but they had strong roots going well back into the 19th century, in the movement to abolish slavery, in women's suffrage and in the labour movement, so that by the time war broke out the 'peace movement' was gaining considerable strength. By 1916 the Women's Peace Party had a membership of 40,000, while other bodies — the Union Against Militarism, the People's Council of America — had solid support up and down the country. The Anti-Enlistment League, founded in 1915 by a high school teacher called Jessie Wallace Hughan, and two Bryn Mawr friends, Tracy Mygatt and Frances Witherspoon, who worked together for peace for 66 years and died in 1974 within three weeks of each other, had mustered 3,500 supporters behind the baldest of all anti-war declarations, with its pledge: 'I, being over 18 years of age, hereby pledge myself against enlistment as a volunteer for any military or naval service . . .' It was not unusual to see bands of well-to-do young ladies, belonging to this peace society or that, parading the streets with palm tree leaves with the words 'Keep Cool' written across them, and wearing middy blouses with peace slogans across the back. The appeal, often, was to the dainty and the cloying. Even the Emergency Peace Federation, hastily rechristened from the 'Neutral Conference Committee' after war was declared, appealed for money and help by placing an advertisement in the *New York Times* aimed at 'Wives, Mothers, Sweethearts'. It may all have been sentimental, but people rallied.

The change came with a rapidity that surprised everyone. The 'peace' so applauded by the American public had not been deeply questioning about international issues. While the Anti-Enlistment League had been speaking to volunteers, it was admirable; when men it addressed became conscripts, it ceased to be.

The opponents of war were not going to have an easy time. Thousands who had willingly given hours of their time to crusading for peace now threw themselves, with frantic endeavour, into recruiting for war. The passion that had gone to peace swung round full circle: intolerance, patriotism and, quickly, vehement attacks on all those who continued to speak of peace swept the nation. The first to fall were the peace societies, which shrank from former prominence to modest offices and tentative voices raised against persecution. These were soon followed by socialists and radicals, all identified in the public eye with seditious feelings about peace and human rights. Socialist newspapers, which tended to argue against conscription, had their second class mailing rights rescinded and many rapidly went bankrupt; socialist meetings were broken up by 'patriots' and anyone present was forced to kiss the American flag. Pro-peace movies, like the *Battle Cry for Peace* were banned, while *The Beast of Berlin* and *Face to Face with Kaiserism* drew large audiences. In a speech to the Harvard Club, Theodore Roosevelt spoke of all those still clamouring for peace as a 'whole raft of sexless creatures'.

In June, the attacks acquired a focus. An Espionage Bill, containing a clause that anyone who 'shall wilfully cause or attempt to cause insubordination, disloyalty, mutiny or refusal of duty in the military or naval forces of the United States . . . shall be punished by a fine of not more than $10,000 or imprisonment for not more than 20 years or both', became law on the 15th. Snoopers, informers, arch patriots set out in its wake to seek the mutinous and the shirkers: the American Defense Society, the Liberty League, the Knights of Liberty, the Anti-Yellow Dog League and many more. The toughest was the American Protective League, sponsored by the Department of Justice, which during 1917 more than doubled its membership. With the help of these organizations pacifists and socialist reformers were quickly identified, branded pro-German and on several occasions beaten, tarred and feathered 'in the name of the outraged women and children of Belgium'. Editors talked of the need for firing squads and the usefulness of telegraph poles. College teachers and professors suspected of pacifist leanings were dismissed from their jobs. Attacks on all things German rose to an absurd and hysterical pitch: sauerkraut was renamed 'liberty cabbage'. 'The pacifist,' wrote the lawyer Clarence Darrow, 'speaks with a German accent.'

As complaints against individuals of doubted loyalty multiplied, an amendment to the Espionage Bill was carried in Congress by 293 votes to 1, further curtailing freedom of speech, so that anyone who, in wartime, 'shall wilfully utter, print, write or publish any disloyal, profane, scurrilous or abusive language about the form of government of the United States' was committing a criminal offence. It made the Defence of the Realm Act look tame. The Attorney General could indeed feel smug when, early in 1918, he was able to announce that 'it was safe to say that never in its history has this country been so thoroughly policed'. The place to which so many thousands had fled from Europe in the 19th century to avoid persecution and conscription was now committed to the very conditions of life they believed they had left behind them for ever.

For the first few weeks of the American war, enrolment was voluntary. By June, when it was clear that there were not going to be enough recruits, national registration was brought in: a Selective Service Act instructed all men aged between 21 and 30 to register for military service and shortly after that began calling them up. The *New York Times* welcomed the move as a means of 'disciplining a certain insolent foreign element in this nation'. The only exemptions were granted to those who could prove bona fide membership of one of a small number of recognized peace sects, like the Quakers, and some 56,830 men were duly recognized by local draft boards.

For the others, there was no alternative to the army. Newton Baker, the Secretary of War, had a reputation as a 'peace man'. To Wilson's tacit sympathy for conscientious objectors, he added his own personal guarantee that the appalling brutalities that had been witnessed in Britain would never be repeated on American soil. He was wrong; they were repeated, sometimes with a vindictiveness and hysteria that made the British harshness seem almost acceptable.

Ernest Meyer was the son of a German newspaper man, who had come to settle in America where he found friends and employment with the German labour and radical publications. Ernest was at the University of Wisconsin when America entered the war; he was the first student to be expelled from a

68

campus for declaring that he would not fight.

Ordered to join a troop train bound for Camp Taylor in Kentucky, where he refused to put on a uniform, he was paraded before the new draftees while a sergeant explained that here was a traitor, a yellow dog. 'What shall we do with him?' he shouted out. 'Lynch the bastard,' the new draftees shouted back. Meyer was saved by a captain. He wouldn't accept any alternative service, even if they chose to offer it to him, he told the army, not out of religious conviction, but because he did not believe in war and could not 'bring [him]self to commit murder in its name'.

Ernest Meyer did not suffer especial brutality. He worked 14 hours a day in the kitchen of an army barracks, shunned by the men 'like you would a snake' and finding friends only among the whiskery and black-clothed Mennonite conscientious objectors whom he found 'kindly, courageous but dull'. But in September he was sent, together with a dozen of the Mennonites, to Fort Leavenworth in Kansas. His memoirs, *Hey! Yellowbacks!*, published in 1930, record what could happen to a conscientious objector in America. Wrote Meyer:

> It was not until later, that I learned of the 'hole' . . . In October . . . a number of Molokans [Russian pacifist sect] were brought to the fort . . . they refused to work under military orders and were at once put in solitary confinement in the 'hole'. They were manacled nine hours a day, in standing posture, to the bars of this dungeon, and at the end of nine hours each day their bonds were unlocked and they fell exhausted to the cement floor. They slept on a plank on the floor, which was crawling with vermin. The Molokans were kept in the 'hole' continuously . . .
>
> News of the 'hole' got out. On December 6, the War Department abolished manacling, and at Christmas the men were all taken out of solitary and placed in a special stockade. The order, however, came too late to save the lives of the Hofer brothers. The three Hofer brothers and Jacob Wipf, members of the Huttrians, an anti-war sect, were first sent to Alcatraz Island, a prison in San Francisco Bay. There they were put in a dungeon below the surface of the water. It was pitch black. Water dripped from the walls. Clad only in their underwear and tortured by a strait jacket and ball and chain, these four Christians were kept in the dungeon five days, spending thirty-six of the hours manacled to the bars. After five days they were transferred to Leavenworth and again placed in

solitary. Two of them contracted pneumonia and were transferred to the prison hospital, where they died.

As a final touch of cruelty, the body of one of the Hofers was shipped back to his family, dressed in the military uniform he would not wear while alive.

Meyer's experience and the brutality he witnessed were not exceptional. Absolutist COs received prison sentences of between 20 and 25 years. One hundred and forty-two men got life imprisonment and 17 were sentenced to death, though this was later commuted. All over America, but particularly in Fort Leavenworth, Camp Funston, Fort Jay and Alcatraz, starvation and physical abuse were used to break conscientious objectors. Often, the treatment worked. Thousands of men did change their minds, so that by the time the war was over only about 4,000 were actually found to have persisted with any form of conscientious objection. The capitulation was brought about, a number of people who later came to write up the history of the American War protesters believed, both because the men had lacked the parliamentary support that British conscientious objectors had had, and because the American labour movement was not as strong. The United States, less inclined to tolerate dissenters, produced no organization similar to the British No-Conscription Fellowship. It did however produce great eloquence. Roger Baldwin, director of the American Civil Liberties Union (ACLU), declared in his statement to his Tribunal: 'Though at the moment I am in a tiny minority, I feel myself just one protest in a great revolt surging up from among the people — the struggle of the masses against the rule of the world by the few — profoundly intensified by the war. It is a struggle against the political state itself, against exploitation, militarism, imperialism, authority in all forms.'

It was not until the spring of 1918 that President Wilson, pressed for guidelines, agreed to extend exemption for 'other than religious reasons', and set up alternative service. But even the end of the war did not bring an automatic reprieve for the hundreds of men still locked up, both conscientious objectors and all those who had fallen foul of the Espionage Law and its amendment. Repentance, a confession of guilt, were needed, and even when made were often not considered an adequate substitute for lengthy imprisonment.

Eugene Debs, the socialist who had run for President in 1900, and who opposed the war because he maintained that it resulted only from capitalist greed and rivalry, had been arrested and given a ten-year prison sentence under the Espionage Act. 'Your Honour,' he said, from the dock, in a speech of considerable dignity, 'years ago I recognized my kinship with all living things, and I made up my mind that I was not one bit better than the meanest of earth. I said then, and I say now, that while there is a lower class, I am in it, while there is a criminal element, I am of it, and while there is a soul in prison, I am not free.' Told he might hope for release if he repented, he declared, 'Repent? Repent? Repent for standing like a man?' Debs was not freed until just before Christmas 1921 and even then the prevailing mood was expressed in the *Washington Post*, which continued to refer to pacifists as 'cringing, skulking cowards'. It was not until December two years later that President Coolidge finally released the last 31 American political opponents of the war.

There remained in England one group of men who refused to come to terms with the war. They would neither obey military instructions, nor join any alternative form of service under the Home Office Scheme, nor accept civilian work of 'national importance'. What perhaps is most remarkable is that there were quite so many of them, and that their resolve appeared to grow stronger with time and hardship. Late in 1917 it was clear that a stalemate had been reached. Nine hundred and eighty-five men were systematically rejecting all alternatives, preferring to endure repeated courts martial and prison sentences, starting again each time with the severe regime of the first mattressless, solitary days; and a further 313 had been rejected as 'not genuine' by the Central Tribunal. These 1,298 men were now doing the rounds of Winchester, Wandsworth, Wormwood Scrubs and Lewes prisons.

One of them, a man whose protest and absolute refusal to cooperate in any way at all with the war seemed to give sustenance to many of the others, was Clifford Allen, the frail and clerical-looking young founder of the NCF. Allen worried constantly about whether he, and the NCF, were actually doing enough to put pressure on the authorities. Sitting sewing mailbags for hour after hour in Wormwood Scrubs, he went over the arguments again and again. 'I've become quieter,' he wrote, in a letter smuggled out to friends, 'and, I think, stronger. My determination is, I think, now inflexible.' It was how to convey this inflexibility, how to carry others with him and have influence on the authorities, that tormented him.

On May 12, 1917, Allen was released from Maidstone Jail. He had one day of liberty and spent it walking on Leith Hill. He was then rearrested, and when he refused to obey a military order was sent to an army camp on Salisbury Plain. Writing of the jailed conscientious objectors, however, he sounded satisfied: 'I don't think there is one weak man . . . Their spirit is indomitable.'

Allen had never wavered in his arguments against the war. He was, he said repeatedly, a socialist; he believed in cooperation and not competition to the death between men and nations, and he believed in the sanctity of human life. From his third court martial, on May 25 he emerged with a sentence of two years' hard labour. By now he had decided that he personally at least was not doing enough and that his duty was to refuse any order to work; he knew, of course, that the entire period of his sentence would consequently be spent in solitary confinement, in a bare cell, with no books, no visits and long spells on bread and water. To Lloyd George, outspoken and persistent critic of the conscientious objector stand, he wrote from the cells, in Parkhurst Camp on Salisbury Plain, explaining his intentions: 'It is not the fear of physical death in the trenches that has led to our remaining in prison, but rather a fear of spiritual death which we believe must follow our assent to any conscription scheme, military or civil.'

The National Committee, busy arranging for greater understanding of the conscientious objectors' position and more realistic alternatives for them to turn to, was not altogether behind him, and the tactic of prison striking remained a matter of uneasy debate for many months. In the *Tribunal*, Dr. Salter wrote a passionate attack on work strikes, arguing that they would achieve nothing for the cause. 'To win through,' he wrote, 'we must succeed in influencing the heart and mind and conscience of the nation and the authorities. We have to *convince* them; we cannot threaten or compel them.'

Allen was a brave man, but he was not physically very strong. In the *Manchester Guardian*, Bernard Shaw protested that what Allen proposed to do was virtually a 'sentence of death by exhaustion, starvation and close confinement'. Allen was not to be dissuaded. He was soon doing alternate three-day stretches in the punishment block and complaining of incessant headaches. By mid-June, the prison doctor was telling him that he had tuberculosis of the spine, certainly made worse by long hours sitting on a backless stool. 'I discount a good deal of what he says,' wrote Allen to Catherine Marshall. Over the next six months, most of them spent in the prison hospital, he continued to say how very important it was that the conscientious objectors continue their stand 'as a demonstration of our capacity to endure persecution'.

Elsewhere in the country, however, other conscientious objectors were deteriorating just as rapidly in health and sanity. When Allen proposed to move to a hunger strike, Catherine Marshall begged him not to, saying that anyone who followed his example might have to endure force feeding over a very long time.

Meanwhile, in the wider public, people were coming to accept that this small body of war resisters was unshakable in its commitment, and that it was increasingly pointless to continue to treat them with such brutality. The *Manchester Guardian* had long been a supporter of their cause; even *The Times* now began to soften its attitude. Once a man had repeatedly shown his readiness to suffer for his beliefs, the newspaper asked, 'is it either justifiable or politic to go on with the punishment?' By now, these absolutists were serving their third or even their fourth sentences, and a substantial lobby took shape, pressing for clemency in 'genuine cases'. Even the prison governors were asking to be relieved of their military detainees, whose intransigence they found increasingly hard and inhumane to deal with. However, Brigadier-General Childs continued to rule that there should be no relaxation from the rigours of the third division, although these were designed, like those of the military detention barracks, to cope with 'brute elements' and not sickly intellectuals. What was more, men were now dying, and deaths and breakdowns on any scale would probably provoke an unpleasant public scandal.

When Margaret Hobhouse, a sister of Beatrice Webb, took the case of her son Stephen, ill in Wormwood Scrubs, to his god-father, Lord Milner, the lobby spread to Members of Parliament and the Lords, particularly after she published (with the anonymous help of Bertrand Russell) a book, *I Appeal Unto Caesar*, with well-documented cases and numbers. During 1917, more than a thousand trade union branches, trades councils and local Labour parties passed resolutions calling for the release of the imprisoned men.

Mrs. Hobhouse was an articulate and formidable woman and her campaign could not easily be ignored; but then Childs was not a man easily swayed by public opinion. Eventually agreement was reached that those absolutists who were healthy would stay where they were, but be given better treatment, in the form of more exercise, and a monthly visit in a room rather than a cage, while those seriously ill would be released.

The order for the release of the sick came too late to save the lives of a number of men, like Arthur Butler or Arthur Haton, both dead of pneumonia, or the sanity of others, like Alexander Campbell, 19-years-old, and who having served two 'cat-and-mouse' sentences already, cut his throat with a razor after breaking down and agreeing to become a soldier after all. But 333 absolutists were in due course released, among them Stephen Hobhouse, only days before he would have died. Clifford Allen, whose weight had fallen to below eight stone (112 lbs), was also released; his naturally pale skin was completely white and his ears protruded from emaciated and shrunken cheeks. He was 28. With a face now deeply lined and his neck scraggy, he looked, thought his friends, like a man in his late fifties.

He was for a long time too ill to manage the NCF, but he returned to discuss its continuing role, a matter of some anxiety now that so many of its members were in prison, and that repeated tussles with the law had reduced the *Tribunal*'s print run from 100,000 to 2,000 copies. The paper, muted but not cowed, continued to press for the release of conscientious objectors and fought with its customary vigour Lloyd George's final Conscription Act, which tried to apply conscription to Ireland, and raised the maximum age to 51. Allen was out in time to replace Bertrand Russell who, during the closing months of the year, had moved strongly away from his earlier staunch attitude about the need for absolute non-cooperation with the authorities. 'I feel,' he wrote rather sadly, 'we are in some way developing the cruelty of fanaticism, which is the very spirit that supports the war.' Russell's whole approach to pacifism and war was changing; force, he had come to think, could not be condemned in all circumstances. 'If the "sacredness of human life" means that force must *never* be used to upset bad systems of government, to put an end to wars and despotisms, and to bring liberty to the oppressed, then I cannot honestly subscribe to it.' It was an argument that was to worry pacifists increasingly in the coming years.

During the first months that followed conscription Bertrand Russell had accepted that he was very likely to go to prison; by 1918, when virtually the entire leadership of the NCF was in jail, and most of the work was being done by an impressive team of militant pacifist women drawn from the suffragette movement, he no longer wished to. This did not stop him, early in January 1918, from writing a piece for the *Tribunal*, in which he argued that prolonging the war would reduce Europe to starvation and make it probable that once the revolution came it would be so violent as to bring about the end of all that was best in Western civilization. As E. M. Forster had warned, civilization in Europe would be 'pipped'.

At Bow Street magistrates court, Sir John Dickinson, objecting less to Russell's point about civilization than to his attacks in the same article on the Americans whose 'garrison' he foresaw occupying England and France with some brutality, sentenced him to six months in prison. He did not offer the alternative of a fine. Jean Beauchamp, publisher of the *Tribunal*, was fined £60 and costs. Lytton and James Strachey, who had come with other friends to hear the verdict, came away with their 'teeth chattering with fury'.

Russell had been sentenced to the second division, an improvement on the conditions that most of the absolutists were enduring, but still far from agreeable. He managed to have himself moved to the first division so that in May, when he finally went to serve his sentence, he could enjoy a larger cell (at a charge of 2s 6d a week), cleaned daily by another prisoner (at 6d a day). *The Times*, his own furniture, meals and flowers, as well as unlimited numbers of books, were sent in to him. Later, he noted that during five months of confinement he had read more than 200 books and written two of his own, *Introduction to Mathematical Philosophy* and *The Analysis of Mind*.

On October 23, 1918, the Germans accepted President Wilson's Fourteen Points. After that the end of the war came very quickly. On October 30, the Ottoman government signed an armistice with the British; on November 3 the Austro-Hungarian High Command did the same with the Italians. Kaiser William II fled to Holland and abdicated. At 5 am on November 11, starving, miserable and in growing anarchy, the Germans, having agreed to withdraw behind the Rhine, intern a great deal of their arms and railway equipment, annul the treaty of Brest-Litovsk which had ended the war between Germany and Russia, and move all German troops in Eastern Europe behind the German frontiers of 1914, signed the Armistice in the Forest of Compiègne.

Peace came into force at 11 o'clock that morning. In England, work stopped. Crowds surged through the streets. Hooters, sirens, church bells rang out. Sitting on their backless stools, stitching their mailbags, the imprisoned conscientious objectors listened to the commotion; in Wormwood Scrubs, the COs sang the 'Te Deum'. In Trafalgar Square at the foot of Nelson's column, a vast bonfire of celebration was lit. The British had been fighting for four years and three months, three quarters of a million men were dead, but the war was at last over. 'I hope,' said Lloyd George, reading the Armistice terms that afternoon in the House of Commons, 'we may say that thus, this fateful morning, came an end to all wars.'

In the election campaign that followed, candidates everywhere seemed to be pressing forward on a 'no-conscription' ticket and even Lloyd George declared: 'I wish to make it clear beyond all doubt that I stand for the abolition of conscript armies in all countries.' In the 1918 election, women, for the first time, exercised their vote, but conscientious objectors had been disenfranchised for five years. The election was a triumph for Lloyd George, who had led the country to victory and now headed a coalition government, which won a large majority in the public mood of extreme nationalism. Asquith lost his seat as

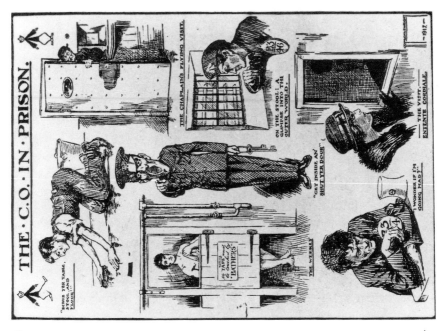

▲World War One conscientious objector in a force feeding suit.

Cartoons by G. P. Micklewright, an imprisoned conscientious objector (1917). ▲

Believed to be 15 of the men sentenced to death in France.

Members of the No-Conscription Fellowship surrendering to the police at the Mansion House, July 17, 1916. Clifford Allen is next to the post on the left; next to him is Fenner Brockway.

Women's Peace Congress at The Hague, 1915.

Banquet at the House of Commons for the 17 MPs imprisoned for political or religious reasons. Stephen Hobhouse is standing 3rd from the left; Bertrand Russell is sitting next to Mrs. Pethick-Lawrence and E. D. Morel in the middle of the centre row.

Clifford Allen at the time of the foundation of the NCF ...

... and 2 years later at the age of 29, having lost nearly 3 stone in weight.

The Honourable
Bertrand Russell
in 1910.

did all those pacifist members who had opposed the war. Ramsay MacDonald, Philip Snowden and Arthur Henderson were all out of Parliament.

Yet Lloyd George did not move to repeal the Conscription Act. Despite a popular 'No-Conscription Sunday', with rallies all over the country, and fierce opposition from the Labour Party, it was only in Germany, thanks to the Treaty of Versailles, that conscription was banned. On the official termination of war, August 31, conscription in Britain was simply left to fade away.

The Armistice did not, however, bring release to the conscientious objectors. Even if the spirit of retribution was considerably more subdued in Britain than in America, there was still much public resistance to seeing the men out of prison before the soldiers were all back from the front. During the first three months of 1919, 130 conscientious objectors, on prolonged hunger strike, had to be temporarily released under the 'cat-and-mouse' ruling, after forcible feeding, often carried out very viciously and using the same pipe on every man, had left many bleeding and wounded from the treatment.

In Wandsworth prison, 20 socialist conscientious objectors staged a rebellion, a work strike that ended with the men breaking everything they could get their hands on, before being caught and locked up in damp, filthy, long-disused basement cells; in Leicester, Leeds, Pentonville, Liverpool, Newcastle and Preston Jails similar strikes broke out, the gesture of men by now driven half-mad by their conditions.

Questions were asked in the House of Commons, and the new Secretary of State for War, Winston Churchill, who became responsible for the conscientious objectors in January 1919, kept up the battle to get them out, despite continuing reluctance within the Cabinet. In the *Manchester Guardian*, a letter was published asking the Prime Minister when the 1,497 men still in jail were likely to be freed. Signed by 'Literary and University' men, by members of the clergy, by politicians, lawyers and prominent doctors, among them Sidney Webb, Hilaire Belloc, J. Maynard Keynes and Arnold Bennett, it praised the 'preferring of principle to life' and announced: 'It is a glorious choice, and if the truth be told, fools though they may be, such men are the salt of the earth, and perhaps there is not

77

one of their persecutors, from the Prime Minister downwards, who can compare with them in high regard for things of the spirit and for loyalty to what they believe to be truth.'

At the end of May, all those who had served 20 months were released, and by the beginning of August 1919 the last conscientious objector had left prison. Harold Bing, disenfranchised, discharged from the army with ignominy, came back home to Croydon to begin applying for training as a teacher, only to find himself repeatedly turned down as a former conscientious objector. Mark Hayler went off to Paris to work with the Friends' War Victims Relief Committee. George Frederick Dutch, who had TB, was in a sanitorium started by Dr. Salter on the Sevenoaks Downs. Howard Marten, condemned to death at Henriville, returned to his bank, where he had lost most of his seniority. None of them found it easy. As a teacher called Stephen Winsten explained, the experience of being a conscientious objector in endless solitary confinement had been 'ruinous to the will . . . you have a kind of past which is outside you'.

Towards the end of July, the leaders of the NCF met to talk about shaping the future, for new generations of men and women dedicated to preventing war. Allen felt gloomy, though the meeting itself was concluded on an optimistic note. Many of the men, it was admitted, had been altered by the war, but on the whole the change had been for the better, for many 'had adopted a much more activist policy and philosophy'. The NCF was split, between those who, like Dr. Salter and W. J. Chamberlain, wished for an organization which would stand for absolute pacifism and internationalism, and the others, very much more numerous, who wanted the NCF to continue as a union of all who opposed conscription.

The split became formal at the end of November, when several hundred conscientious objectors gathered once again in Devonshire House in Bishopsgate where they had waved their handkerchiefs in silence, so as not to antagonize the sailors outside, three and a half years before. 'We are proud,' Allen told the assembled men, many of them still showing physical signs of their prolonged incarceration, 'to have broken the power of the military authority . . . We have defeated it; we will defeat it again if conscription should be continued.' At the end of the second day, the audience rose to reaffirm their dedication 'to the building of a world rooted in freedom and enriched by labour that is shared by all'. Speaking of those who had died in battle, Allen added: 'We have still the opportunities of life before us. Our lives are now forfeit.' At a great reunion held afterwards in the Central Hall, Westminster, 1,500 people sat down to eat, and heard Philip Snowden and Ramsay MacDonald talk of the hardships of the past four years. Even Bertrand Russell, whose feelings about his experiences as a pacifist were by now almost entirely negative, and to whom the end of the war had brought only the conviction that there was very little hope indeed for a better world, expressed satisfaction in the stand the men had taken. 'The NCF,' he declared, 'has been completely victorious in its stand for freedom not to kill or to take part in killing . . . You have won a victory for the sense of human worth, for the realization of the value of each individual soul.'

Good speeches and noble words; but had, as Allen maintained, the conscientious objectors really 'broken the power of the military authority'? What had they in fact achieved by their stand?

Some 16,000 British men had brought a profession of conscience to a Tribunal. Of these, 6,312 had been arrested, and 5,970 court-martialled (521 of them three times, 50 five times and three six times), and 819 men had spent over two years in prison, much of that time on bread and water and in solitary confinement. Sixty-nine — some said 73 — were dead; 39 had gone mad.

Despite this remarkable profession of a belief, the NCF had actually failed in each of its declared goals: it had been unable to prevent the passing of the Conscription Act, or, after a few months, its extension to married men. Absolute exemption was never won for the 1,330 or so men who refused to accept any alternative service, and many of its members in the end did some kind of Home Office proposed work. Their stand, their bravery, did not, in fact, either cause a repentant government to yield, or a sympathetic public to press it to do so.

But something, clearly, had been won. The conscientious objectors who emerged, one by one, from their solitary cells, did so with a feeling that they had seriously challenged the state's supremacy over the individual. Never again, many of these 16,000 men would say, was it going to be possible for man's moral stand to be ignored, nor for a democracy like Britain to take such a harsh line towards its dissenters. The war protesters had not yielded; that was the point, and the British public, having witnessed their endurance, were now prepared to understand and even respect their position. 'War,' commented Bertrand Russell, 'develops in almost all a certain hysteria of destruction — self-destruction, among the most generous, but still destruction. We have to stand out against this hysteria, and realize, and make others realize, that Life, not Death (however heroic), is the source of all good.'

This, perhaps more than any other argument, was to worry pacifists during the decades of war to come, for the First World War was not, as quickly became clear, the war that ended all wars, but only the beginning of a century of almost continuous and growing warfare. The image portrayed by the memoirists of World War I — Graves, Blunden and Sassoon — of a war lasting forever was sadly correct. How, indeed, convince people that not fighting was as robust and attractive an ideal as warfare? How, faced with this challenge, would war protesters fare? 'If there is another war,' wrote Childs in his autobiography, estimating that he personally had probably dealt with some 5,000 conscientious objectors, 'I think the problem of the conscientious objector will certainly arise stronger than ever. How it will be dealt with, time alone will prove.'

4

The 1920s: the hopeful years

For many of the British conscientious objectors, free at last after such a long period of an entirely self-sustaining solitary profession of belief, the peace in Europe was magnificent. They might not have secured too obvious a victory over their opponents, but they were alive, they were out of prison and, even if not all employers wanted them back, there were enough of them to be confident that they had done something very honourable. It was a moment for rejoicing.

Mark Hayler, in Paris with the Friends' War Victims Relief Committee, wrote to his mother on the night the Germans signed the Peace Treaty in the Hall of Mirrors at the Palace of Versailles. 'I went out in the evening and heard the guns banging away and saw the wonderful sights that one saw in the streets everywhere. Everybody seemed to be in the streets, singing and shouting in an indescribable manner . . . surging masses of men, women and children, simply jammed up the roadways. Drums and bugles could be heard everywhere . . . The throats of the cannons were stuffed with flags and torches and away up the streets they went followed by singing crowds wild with excitement.' It was enough to be free and alive; it was too soon to look ahead.

Not all who had fought so hard for peace felt the same way, especially those who had watched from the sidelines and felt frustrated by how little they had been able to do. Among the women's peace organizations the break between war and peace passed almost unnoticed, for no sooner were hostilities over than their attention was turned to ensuring that the conditions now being laid down by the allies would guarantee a lasting peace. While Mark Hayler celebrated in the streets of Versailles, the women peacemakers from America, Britain and the occupied countries of Europe were gathering again, as they had in The Hague in 1915, to devise strategies to make themselves heard by the negotiators.

They would have liked to meet in Versailles, alongside the official Peace Conference, but since delegates from the Central Powers were not allowed to come there, they met instead in Zurich. There were 16 delegations. Catherine Marshall, exhausted by years with the NCF but resolute, came from London; Jane Addams, a little stouter but just as bossy, from New York. It was an emotional reunion. The American and British women were appalled by the appearance of some of the Europeans, women so emaciated and pallid after months of near starvation that they were barely recognisable. At the sumptuous banquets held in their honour, neither the Hungarian nor the Austrian delegates dared to eat the rich food, for fear they would be unable to digest it. One afternoon, as a break from the meeting rooms, the women took a picnic up into the mountains.

The ladies in Zurich did not think much of the peace terms being discussed in Paris; Wilson's Fourteen Points were increasingly losing ground, and the reparations to be exacted from Germany sounded to them impossibly large. Forming themselves into a permanent new body, the Women's International League of Peace and Freedom, with Jane Addams as President and headquarters in an elegant 18th century town house in Geneva, the former home of the inventor of Esperanto, Zahrendorf, they now declared that all the Treaty had accomplished was to lay the ground for future wars: 'By the financial and economic proposals a hundred million people of this generation in the heart of Europe are condemned to poverty, disease and despair, which must result in the spread of hatred and anarchy within each nation.'

The Women's League was never, as such, purely pacifist. The ideal of non-violent resistance won a majority vote, but it was generally considered to be an expression for individuals, and not binding on national sections, a few of whom would continue throughout the twenties to declare that they felt that some use of force, in the cause of social justice, could not be altogether opposed. From their new headquarters in Geneva, however, under the firm hand of their first general secretary, Emily Greene Balch, an upright woman in rimless round spectacles who had lost her professorship at Wellesley College partly because of her unacceptable pacifist views during the war, the

Women's League held to an unequivocal anti-war ticket, keeping a close eye on the new League of Nations, now preparing for its first assembly in September 1920. They were full of ideals, certainly, but still, as in 1915, often either ignored or held in ridicule: on their way to a summer school in Chicago, early in the twenties, women delegates from the Women's League on a 'Pax Special' train coach were stormed by a posse from the Daughters of the American Revolution, while in Detroit a spokesman from the City Council announced that the train should be derailed and the women 'tarred and feathered'.

Where the peace women were, however, perfectly in tune with the prevailing mood was in their insistence on an international dimension to all their work. Pacifists, on both sides of the Atlantic, had entered the war clear-sighted but somewhat insular: pacifism was a faith to be exercised at home. They emerged from it confused, disjointed, splintered in many directions but with a vision that, whatever path they might individually take, it must involve other nations. The twenties, for the pacifists, were a time of meetings, of gatherings, of anti-war organizations and rallies and summer schools, and above all of talk; almost all of it was international.

But first, for the British, there were local matters to attend to at home. One unexpected by-product of the conscientious objectors' stand during the war was that many highly articulate and literate men, who normally would never have seen inside a prison, had spent long periods there, able to experience for themselves the lot of an ordinary British convict. They came out of jail outraged. 'Members of the NCF are not necessarily agreed about prisons in themselves,' commented the *Tribunal* in November 1918; 'most of us would like to see them abolished, while a few perhaps would retain them. But on one point we are unanimous: the prison system of today must go. It is brutalizing . . . Every CO should make it his business to have our prison system altered — the silence rule, the useless, soul-destroying monotony of the never-ending heap of mail bags, the degrading clothes of the convict must give way to a better regime . . .' Many of the imprisoned conscientious objectors did now answer that appeal. In January 1919 the Labour Research department set up a Prison System Enquiry under a committee consisting of Sydney and Beatrice Webb, Margery Fry, Fenner

Brockway and Stephen Hobhouse. They received no official support and were allowed no direct access to prisons, but then they hardly needed it. Their report did lead to reforms, the most important, unquestionably, being the ending of the hated silence rule, the single stricture that had most tormented the conscientious objectors. (Bernard Shaw, invited to write a preface to the report, sent a particularly embarrassing addition; while endorsing the committee's proposals, he suggested that the way to deal with incurable criminals was to put them in gas chambers. The committee was appalled. When Shaw refused to amend his preface, it appeared, but separately from the report.)

It was in this mood of do-gooding responsibility, when men relieved to have survived could deliberate over their future contributions to society, that the 1917 Club, founded during the war in honour of the Russian Revolution, now flourished at No. 4 Gerrard Street in Soho. The place was neither very comfortable, nor very glamorous: the dining room in the basement was distinctly dingy, and the narrow staircase leading up to the sitting rooms, which members complained were always draughty and untidy, smelled strongly of cat. But the membership was distinguished, if unorthodox, and almost all of it was pacifist. Ramsay MacDonald had agreed to be its first President, while Sir Charles Trevelyan, E. D. Morel, H. G. Wells, Leonard Woolf, Arthur Ponsonby were all regular diners. Elsa Lanchester, a rising star, did the cabarets.

The 1917 Club quickly became a popular target for satirists; Douglas Goldring, writing about it later, described the clientele as consisting of 'Hindus, Parsees, Puritans, free lovers, Quakers, teetotallers, heavy drinkers, Morris dancers and Folk song experts (with a tol-de-diddle-ol and hey-ho for Bradley and Bedales), members of the London School of Economics, Trade Unions officials, journalists, poets, actors and actresses, Communists, theosophists . . .' and 'sexologers', giving talks on masturbation. Some, he commented, 'would not even hurt the feelings of a vegetable by cooking it, and lived on unfired food'. Even Dorothy L. Sayers arranged for her hero, Lord Peter Wimsey, to visit what she thinly disguised as the 'Soviet Club', where, reflecting that the dinner was likely to be 'worse than execrable', he observes a fellow diner, a 'thin eager young woman in a Russian blouse, Venetian beads, a Hungarian shawl and a

Spanish comb, looking like a personification of the United Front or the "Internationale".' In the early twenties, pacifists were rapidly establishing a reputation as cranks, with bizarre and thin-blooded tastes, prone to conversation that veered somewhere between the absurdly high-minded and the dangerously revolutionary.

Many were, as critics were quick to point out, vegetarian, teetotal, feminist, unconventional and interested in crafts and the simple life, a packet of beliefs delighted reporters insisted on bringing up whenever the issue of pacifism was mentioned. Pacifists were not, of course, all vegetarians, but many vegetarians were indeed pacifist, as they now chose to repeat at each of their annual conferences. 'Vegetarianism is a new philosophy,' they announced after one summer gathering in Czechoslovakia, 'from the moral as well as the social standpoint. As military service makes a vegetarian way of living impossible, we should fight against it and refuse it personally.' This reputation, slightly mocking, sometimes affectionate, and containing some truth, of pacifists as nut-eaters and soft liberals, has dogged the movement ever since.

And there was indeed much to feed on, in the early twenties, for those eager to ridicule the pacifists. Perhaps the most peculiar of all social pacifist experiments of the post-war years was the new peaceable boy scout movement, set up by a former favourite of Baden-Powell, the founder of the Boy Scouts, who had gone through the Great War as a stretcher-bearer and emerged dreaming of a social order in which there would be no more war.

John Hargrave was 14 when, in 1908, he joined the Boy Scouts and became fascinated with the writings of Ernest Seton Thompson, a 19th century American popularizer of the Red Indians. The son of an impoverished roaming landscape artist, he was a dogged, talented, imaginative figure with highly individual and unshakably held ideals and a great deal of curly hair, worn long.

Working as a cartoonist on the London *Evening News* by the time he was 17, he began to write under the name of White Fox on woodcraft and the delights and skills of the self-sufficient outdoor life for *The Trail*, the Scout magazine. It was enormously popular. White Fox's manliness drew many admirers.

After the war Baden-Powell asked Hargrave to become his Commissioner for Woodcraft and Camping. He accepted the job, but he was a man of quick temper and autocratic views, much strengthened in his pacifism by the war, and he soon took against the militaristic patter of the elderly soldiers who saw the young scouts as a branch of the cadets. In *The Great War Brings It Home*, published in 1919, he condemned what he referred to as the 'Organized Death — Civilized Mechanical Death' of the Great War, and said that it had merely left everyone dissatisfied. 'Our trading system, our religion, our social life as a whole,' he wrote sternly, had now become 'wrong'. The Scouts did not care for this kind of talk. When Hargrave announced that what he had in mind was a new sort of movement altogether, based on handcrafts, world peace and the open air life in which he would save civilization from 'inevitable decay . . . chuck enfeebling surroundings and rely upon nature by giving our children a clean, hard, outdoor camp life' he was hastily expelled.

Taking with him a handful of other dissatisfied anti-war Scout masters, he now launched the Kibbo Kift — the words were taken from an Anglo-Saxon phrase meaning 'proof of great strength' — dividing his Kinsmen into Clans and Tribes, and bestowing on every new recruit an American Indian name. 'Be picturesque,' he told camp chiefs. 'When in camp I wear a green-fringed hunting shirt (with hood), green shorts, no hat, no stockings, sandals and a staff . . . Don't add to the general drabness and rottenness by looking black and dressing black and thinking black.'

Soon the woods where the Kinsmen gathered were filled with totem poles and brightly decorated one-man tents. Their occupants, looking like extras in a medieval pageant and speaking a private language that owed much to Anglo-Saxon and American Indian, and sounded to outsiders like a poetic, incantatory flow of mumbo-jumbo, embarked on regenerating themselves through wholesome outdoor pursuits. Rousseau and Thoreau were revered. Archery was encouraged. Until Mussolini pinched the gesture, as Hargrave later complained, the Kinsmen greeted one another with the Saxon sign of the open hand: 'How! I come with no weapons in my hand.' For special occasions, like the great annual 'Althing', the Tallykeepers,

86

Campwardens and Ritemasters, the elite of the Kibbo Kift, wore brilliantly embroidered coats and robes, of an unusually high decorative standard, for Hargrave was determined to use his talents as a designer to the full, while ordinary Kinsmen wore silk shorts and jerkins with purple cloaks. The rest of the time they hiked to places of special psychic energy where they camped and sang songs and spoke of the spirituality of the outdoor life and the beauty of peace.

Thousands joined. Not only young boys but girls, a startling departure in the all-male Scout preserve of the twenties, and even entire families. Hargrave's vision soon attracted visitors to his Red Indian camps, including the pacifist suffragette, Mrs. Pethick-Lawrence, and the Bengali poet, Tagore. H. G. Wells and Professor Julian Huxley both agreed to serve on the Advisory Committee. 'The kin stands for peace,' Hargrave told them. 'War is totally unnecessary.'

Hargrave was clearly a very odd man. He was good-looking, physically commanding and exceedingly vain, so that he refused to be photographed wearing his spectacles. He smoked heavily, while preaching a pure, out-of-doors existence. Those who feared or disliked him found him arrogant and opinionated. But he exercised a powerful attraction over his followers, and many ordinary well-educated men and women were ready to put on the most absurd costumes, speak the most ridiculous words and take to the woods. Something of his appeal, his vigour, his confidence comes through in the words he wrote in the late twenties:

> What'll we do?
> What won't we do!

> One time we'll build a new town: and if we don't like it pull it down, and build another.
> You'd rather go fishing up the river? All right, then, what's to stop you? . . . not me.

It was heady stuff, and it was fun, and after four years of bleakness it seemed full of possibilities.

The trouble, perhaps, was that, for White Fox, none of this was quite enough. The woods and the songs were fine, but how to influence the rest of mankind? In 1923 Hargrave was introduced to a Major C. H. Douglas, an engineer and economist

and the author of books which blamed all modern ills on shortage of purchasing power. Douglas believed that there was a
fundamental flaw in the world economic system, so that there
never could be enough money in circulation to be able to buy
up all the goods that were for sale. Here, then, was an explanation for the world's poverty and bellicosity. Social Credit, as
Douglas's creed was called, would, by paying an unearned
birthright income to every individual, produce a 'Leisure
State' in which no one would have to work simply in order to
live. For Hargrave, Social Credit was the Kibbo Kift's missing
link. It would solve not just current hardship, but dispel the
threat of all future wars since, as he now wrote, they sprang
'from a faulty financial system and that system can be
rectified'.

Not all his followers embraced the new calling quite so
ecstatically and in the mid-twenties a socialist group (which
became the Woodcraft Folk and survives to this day) split off
as Hargrave led his more dedicated Kinsmen down the New
Way of the Kindred towards the Great Work of National Sal-
vation. The Kindred were to be the driving force bringing
Social Credit to the people. But how? Clearly a dramatic step
was needed. Hargrave got his troops out of their jerkins and
cloaks and into a new para-military tailored tunic and shorts
and a beret. The Kindred no longer hiked; they marched.
Instructors were borrowed from the Brigade of Guards to
teach them how to drill. Amazingly, many continued to obey
Hargrave.

Social Credit's young troopers did not survive, though for a
while, calling themselves the Green Shirt movement, and frequently scuffling with Mosley's Blackshirts and Socialist and
Communist groups, they attracted a popular following among
working class unemployed of the big cities. But when Social
Credit foundered as a genuine economic movement in the
State of Alberta in Canada — which had briefly elected a
Social Credit government — the Green Shirts went down with
it, especially after the Public Order Act of 1937 banned the
wearing of all political uniforms. By the time war broke out
again Hargrave's pacifism was a thing of the past. 'Join up,' he
said firmly to whatever former silk-clad Anglo-Saxon speaking
Kinsman came to consult him. 'And get as high up as you

possibly can.' The years of self-sufficiency, discipline and drill-
ing served the boys of the Kibbo Kift well: casting aside all talk
of peace, many had distinguished war careers.

The serious business of pacifism, however, was really taking
place outside Britain, or at least on a firmly international stage.
The heart of the immediate post-war revulsion against war was
moral, with Christians calling for the return to the pacifist ideals
of the early Church, diverted from its true course by Constantine, and secular humanists looking back to 18th century
enlightenment and the rule of reason. Pacifists, whether Christian or not, rejected war because of the horror of the recent
massacre of the innocent, of the way that soldiers had been
transformed into machines of death, of the glamorization of war
and the fear that any other such conflict would be the end of
democracy. They deplored the futility of four years of
slaughter, and they condemned what they saw as the deceit-
fulness of the whole enterprise, whatever its origins or its outcome. In the early 1920s it was still perfectly possible to believe
that an international solution to the problem of war could be
found through joining the League of Nations. The principle, for
liberals and radicals, believers and atheists, was clear: war was
wrong and there should be no more of it. And, though it soon
became apparent that there was in fact little agreement about
how to tackle the problems left by the Treaty of Versailles, there
was a pause while people enjoyed the relief, a vast celebration of
the forces of peace over those of war.

In October 1919, 50 men and women from ten countries met
at Bilthoven, a sandy pine-wooded stretch of coastline near
Utrecht in Holland. They had been invited by Henry Hodgkin,
founder with Richard Roberts in Cambridge in 1915 of the
Fellowship of Reconciliation, and Cornelis Boeke, a Dutch
violinist who had left Britain during the war after meeting much
hostility as a foreigner.

In Bilthoven, Boeke, with his English wife, had set up what
he called 'Brotherhood House', a brightly, almost garishly,
painted building that was now the conference centre. When the
weather was fine, the delegates sat under the pine trees in a
marquee and ate at long trestle tables; they slept in dormitories
built with huge verandahs so that on warm evenings they pulled

their beds outside under the stars. More than anything they shared a common delight at having found each other; during the lonely years of their private stand against war, how could they have known that there were so many others like them, in other countries?

The meeting nonetheless was a somewhat sober affair. The delegates were Christians and felt personally guilty about the war. Presaging exactly the words that were to come from a similar gathering of German Christians in the early 1950s, they declared: 'We all stand condemned before God. None can cast a stone at his brother.'

Out of this gathering came an international Fellowship of Reconciliation, and the birth of a new style of international work: travelling secretaries were appointed who would move about Europe on goodwill tours, talking about Christianity and peace. These were not always very successful, secretaries returning from their often impossibly ambitious trips with reports that no one was interested in what they had to say. But their unmistakable commitment did inspire others, and occasionally led to concrete schemes, so that at Verdun, for instance, where some of the bitterest fighting of the war had occurred, a Swiss called Pierre Ceresole and an international team of workers started rebuilding the area. Messengers of peace moved in this way through Latvia, through Estonia, across the Balkans. Soon, the International Fellowship was finding expression in the gathering youth movements that spread through Europe in the twenties, at festivals, and summer schools and youth camps.

For non-Christian pacifists, holding their pacifism as an expression of international socialist solidarity, the No More War Movement (NMWM) was the equivalent umbrella. Set up in 1921 as a direct successor to the No-Conscription Fellowship, it drew its leaders from the old rank and file of conscientious objectors and believed in firm anti-capitalism as well as anti-militarism. On February 15, over the signatures of Fenner Brockway, George Lansbury and nine other prominent pacifists, a letter appeared in the *Daily Herald* calling for supporters for an 'all war is wrong pledge' and condemning the arming of any state in any way at any time as 'treason to the spiritual unity and intelligence of mankind'. When 18 committed pacifists met in the PEN Club on February 24 to launch their new grouping they took an individual vow never to 'take part in war, offensive or defensive, international or civil, whether by bearing arms, making or handling munitions, voluntarily subscribing to war loans, or using my labour for the purpose of setting others free for war service' — all views held by the conscientious objectors in Wormwood Scrubs and Wandsworth.

It sounded admirable, but these were feelings that could hardly be sustained in isolation. Like the Fellowship of Reconciliation, the NMWM needed allies abroad. There was another meeting at Bilthoven: this time not Christians but socialists, not men of the Church but radicals and former absolutist prisoners of conscience as well as the women who had supported them. Their movement, they decided, would be called Paco, Peace in Esperanto. 'War,' they announced, 'is a crime against humanity. We therefore are determined not to support any kind of war and to strive for the removal of all causes of war.' Wilfred Wenlock, Methodist preacher and imprisoned World War One conscientious objector, represented the NMWM.

Another former prisoner, who had met Fenner Brockway and Clifford Allen in Wormwood Scrubs, was a builder called Herbert Runham Brown, a thin, tall, neatly bearded man, very like Lenin in appearance. He was the eldest of seven sons of a 'fancy draper', grandson of a lay minister at Mortlake. He had emerged only late in the spring of 1919 from two and a half years in jail, and in 1921 was asked by Fenner Brockway whether he would consider running Paco, or War Resisters' International (WRI) as it was now named. His semi-detached house in Abbey Road in Enfield with its wide bay windows and pebbledash front became the centre of an extremely active organization. The sitting room, says his daughter Joyce, was made into the study, where files were kept and visitors taken. 'We fitted in where we could.' The house would never again be empty of visiting pacifists; no meal was ever taken alone. Soon, people started flocking in great numbers to north London. Some spoke little English; many were vegetarians; all shared a passionate hostility to war.

To celebrate the opening of one conference, a marquee was put up in the small back garden, covering the entire space. To it, by train, came the pacifists, reaching the house by marching

in ranks along the quiet suburban street. They were in high
spirits. Neighbours had long found the Runham Browns
strange; they found the visitors even stranger. A few who had
missed the early train were eventually shepherded to the house
by the station porter; these last few spoke no English, but by
now Enfield knew all about pacifists and where they were heading. After a great tea, a charabanc arrived to take the delegates
on to their next meeting. Joyce remembers Pierre Ramus, the
Austrian writer, with his long hair and heavy beard, leaning
from the open top deck and calling out 'goodbye, goodbye', with
a strong foreign accent, his arms outstretched as in a papal
benediction, while the neighbours peered disapprovingly from
behind their white net curtains.

Harold Bing, meanwhile, the young conscientious objector
from Croydon, had been recruited as a roving ambassador, a
socialist as opposed to a Christian travelling secretary of peace,
for the new international WRI.

Bing had not had an easy time after his release. Two and a
half years of stitching mailbags in poor light had badly damaged
his sight and, not fit enough to look for a regular job immediately, he had spent some time convalescing at Stanford Le
Hope, a pacifist colony in Essex, where he worked on the land,
regaining his strength.

Recovering, Bing began to apply for jobs. Government appointments, whether those in charge of the interviewing boards
were honest enough to say so openly or not, were barred to
former pacifists; so, too, were most teaching jobs, as was perfectly clear from the advertisements appearing each week in *The
Times Educational Supplement*, with the words 'no conscientious
objectors'. Harold Bing was hard-working, forthright and
somewhat austere: the WRI was the perfect place for him. He
had learned German and French while in prison, and in the
evenings, at home in Croydon, he would practise Esperanto,
begun with the other imprisoned conscientious objectors and
regarded by them as the ideal international language in which
to profess pacifism throughout the world. He became fluent in
all of these languages but his accent was terrible. Dorothy, too
tired after long days teaching to tackle a new language, would
accompany him instead to meetings and lectures. Her own
crusade was more personal. Her mother, never physically

strong, had been much weakened in spirit by five years of social isolation from family and neighbours. After the fighting was over, Dorothy went to see her aunts. She started with the one who had lost a son at the front. Would she make a gesture and heal the breach? After all, had not both young men, Harold and her own son, only done exactly what each had believed to be their duty? Her aunt turned her away.

The other sister, whose three sons had all gone to war, but returned alive, felt as strongly. There was to be no reconciliation. Dorothy's mother died in 1927, never having again seen the sisters from whom she was once inseparable.

Early in the 1920s, Harold Bing started travelling. He was still young, barely 24, but there was something resolute about him which offset his boyish appearance. Like the messengers of peace, he went everywhere, even to corners of Europe where his cause might have seemed absurd. From Austria and Germany, Czechoslovakia and France, Latvia and the Balkans, he returned with stories of extreme persecution of the men who had refused to fight during the war.

After 1915 little was known of what was happening in Europe, but now, as the stories came out, people were appalled to learn of persecution frequently worse than that in Britain and America, of hangings and shootings and long prison sentences under terrible conditions. The WRI's newspaper, the *Bulletin*, told of Poles shot by firing squad and of French socialist anarchists who, having continued to preach non-violence after the outbreak of war, were still serving out their sentences in the penal settlement of Cayenne.

From Hungary came the story of a small group of some 400 'liberal thinkers' who, calling themselves the Union of Galileans and strongly opposed to militarism, had banded together in 1911. On the outbreak of war the movement had dispersed, some going to join the army, others being sent to jail for conscientious objection. But, in 1917, something of the war's enduring barbarity had begun to obsess the Galileans and a number had been instrumental in organizing a strike at the munitions works in Csepel. Soldiers called in to crush the strikes refused to fire on them; the military police were sent for. Seventeen Galileans were arrested and one was sentenced to death. Their war was still not over. After the Communist revolution of

November 1918, those in prison were released, but only briefly. With the forming of the Red Army, in the spring of 1919, conscription was again imposed, the Galileans were again called up, and all now went to prison. In the White Terror that followed, they were hanged.

The picture Bing painted, when he returned to London from his travels, was of a Europe currently full of contradictions, with liberalization coming rapidly in some countries and not at all in others. Across Scandinavia, religious objectors to the continuing conscription into the post-war armies were being allowed to take alternative service, while those who objected on political grounds were not, and so were sent to prison; in Russia, on the other hand, there was no escape from jail, however widespread the Tolstoyan movement, and however initially lenient the Soviet government. Stories of the young resisters, called from all over Russia to serve, and often quite isolated in their protest, appeared in the *Bulletin*, issue after issue. 'Victor P. Bergmen; 24 years old, Peasant. Free Christian (Tolstoyan) . . . refused military service . . . sentenced by the People's Court to two years' solitary confinement . . . Ilija M. Prasoloff; 23 years old, Peasant. A Baptist . . . sentenced by the Military Tribunal at Bek-Buda to two years' solitary confinement.' One wonders at the courage of these lonely men.

From some journeys, Harold Bing returned full of hope. Progress was being made across the Continent, if only in pockets. The pockets could spread, and eventually even meet, particularly as there was such evident desire for peace among the young. In April, not long after his foreign trips began, Bing attended the peace week celebrations in Dortmund, organized by the Tolstoyans and the youth movement. If his words now sound ironic, they well convey the enthusiasm of the moment. 'It was,' he wrote about the programme of goodwill and rejoicing, 'the finest thing of its kind I have ever known. The future of Germany, one feels, is not only safe but big with possibilities in the hands of such a generation of young people as demonstrated their spirit and ideals.' War could never happen again, precisely because it had been so ghastly. Every year, from 1922 on, the NMWM was the moving force in a world-wide campaign of demonstrations held on the first Sunday of every August, to mark the anniversary of the outbreak of war in 1914: they took place simultaneously, in France, Germany, Poland, Austria, across most of the other European countries, in America, the British colonies and India. Not thousands, but perhaps hundreds of thousands, of people were involved. As a spectacle these gatherings were magnificent, brighter, more original possibly than the great anti-nuclear marches that so closely resembled them 60 years later, and as displays of feeling just as vehement. In Berlin in 1922, the People's Theatre Movement took over Max Reinhardt's theatre, carpeted and curtained the open stage in red, and invited distinguished speakers from all over Europe to stand one by one at a bare lectern, bathed in a single powerful spotlight. The rest of the auditorium, packed far beyond its normal capacity, was kept in complete darkness. After the speakers came tableaux and pageants, with a speaking chorus of several hundred men, women and children re-enacting scenes to represent the dreams of pre-war Europe, the horrors of war, the overthrow of capitalism and the hopes for a new, united, socialist, prospering world. Fenner Brockway, acting as publicity secretary, ran a press service in English, French, German and Spanish. As seemed to have become customary at these displays of pacifist faith, it was left to Bernard Shaw to cast a note of slightly sour doubt over the proceedings. Declining to speak at the meeting, he said: 'I grieve to say that I don't believe in these demonstrations. People who get emotionally excited about peace are precisely the people who get emotionally excited about war . . . Lloyd George will do all that is necessary to make the nation send Christmas cards to all the other nations until he wants to send them to the trenches again . . . I write so well that it is a pleasure to read what I have to say on any subject for the few people who read anything at all: but the world goes on just as it did before . . .'

1926 was the *annus mirabilis* for the pacifists. The celebration of peace had reached its height, and there was no reason yet to fear the future. On all sides, complacency filled the movement. Early the previous year Arthur Ponsonby, Under-Secretary for Foreign Affairs in the 1924 Labour government, published a statement about absolute pacifism called *Now Is The Time*. He followed it up with a Peace Letter, addressed to Stanley Baldwin. 'Sir, we, the undersigned, convinced that all disputes

95

between nations are capable of settlement either by diplomatic negotiations or some form of international arbitration, hereby solemnly declare that we shall refuse to support or render war service to any government which resorts to arms.' Not very different from any other call for peace, perhaps, except that his words seemed to strike some particular note in those who read the letter when it was published. Ponsonby himself was not an especially peaceable man, and had even been known to resort to his fists after undue provocation, and his objection was strictly practical, not moral or political. Possibly that was why it was so attractive to so many people. War, he said, had to be done away with because it quite simply failed to achieve 'a single desirable object, whatever the gigantic cost may be'.

This kind of reasoning fitted well with the aims of the NMWM. With their backing, Ponsonby's letter soon attracted thousands of signatures and more kept coming. The idea of the peace letter was rapidly taken up across Europe and America: in Holland, France, Ireland and Germany (where 86,842 signatures were gathered in one district of Saxony alone) similar letters found their way to ministerial desks.

By 1926 conferences everywhere, whether of cooperative movements, of women, of trade unionists or socialists, were now passing unequivocal anti-war statements as part of their manifestos, calling for an immediate amnesty for all objectors and deserters (of which there were said to be 120,000 in France alone), for an end to all colonial wars and the final abolition of conscription. It was the year that the WRI launched a worldwide manifesto against conscription, which eminent people from 15 countries signed, while newspapers gave it wide publicity, everywhere at least where there was a free press. In the autumn, at the British Labour Party Conference at Margate, Fenner Brockway, chairman of the WRI, moved the ILP resolution committing the whole Labour Party to the principle of war resistance. It was carried, without one dissenting voice. Never again, perhaps, was there so much agreement between pacifists and the outside world, or between themselves.

Muriel Lester had attended the launching of the Fellowship of Reconciliation in Cambridge in 1915 and been to both its inaugural international meetings in Bilthoven in 1919, as well as that of the War Resisters' International two years later. She was one of six children of a prosperous Essex shipwright and businessman, a tall, stately, cheerful and occasionally scatty woman with wispy fair hair wound in catherine wheels over her ears, and rather long teeth. Muriel Lester is an extraordinary figure in the history of European pacifism. Leaving aside the obvious prophets of the movement, like Gandhi and Tolstoy, she has been one of the major influences for pacifist belief on ordinary people. Never that well-known among the British public, she had a remarkable following in America and the Far East, where she was treated like a film star, and where her meetings, a compelling combination of fundamentalism and unswerving pacifism, drew thousands of admirers. She died in 1967, having made of her chosen bit of London, the borough of what was then Poplar and Bow and is now Tower Hamlets, a pacifist corner; today people there still talk of Gandhi, and how she made them see that war is wrong and futile.

Muriel Lester was born in Leytonstone in 1883, into a household of considerable comfort and a great deal of fun. Her father married three times, and she had four sisters. With aunts and cousins, they were an enormous family: Muriel was later able to count 103 close relations. At home, they were told that 'the British Empire was a glorious thing and the Boer War a righteous struggle'; and given little badges with tiny photographs of the generals to wear.

In 1904, when Muriel was 21, she was taken by her father to a factory girls' tea in Bow, given for the employees of the Bryant and May match works and presided over by the minister of the local Congregational Church. She read the Minority Report of the Royal Commission on the Poor Law, drawn up by George Lansbury and Beatrice and Sidney Webb, and attended Fabian meetings with her only brother Kingsley, named after the author of *The Water Babies*. When the match girls of 'Red Poplar' (as the area, known for its socialist rumblings, was called) went on strike Muriel took up their case.

In 1912 she rented rooms at No. 60 Bruce Road, the middle house in a row of Victorian red brick workmen's cottages, not far from the canal, the soap factory and the gas works, and opened a club for them. The following year she and her younger sister Doris, as fair-haired and stately as she was, but, as one

97

man remembers, 'floppy' where Muriel was angular, moved to live in Bow. They took rooms next to the Club, at No. 58. Walking the shabby streets, with smoke from the local factories making an almost continual haze, the two tall, rather stiff, middle class English ladies must indeed have seemed strange.

Soon after the war broke out Kingsley, to whom both girls were devoted, died, leaving them his portion of the Lester estate. Encouraged by their father, they bought a deconsecrated Baptist Chapel, Zion Chapel, and turned it into a hall for the inhabitants of Bow and Poplar. They called it Kingsley Hall and it included a soup kitchen. Pacifism was implicit, even if not much talked about for, at the height of the First War, not all the East Enders looked kindly on the conchies and Muriel was occasionally jeered as she walked home from her visits to Wandsworth and Wormwood Scrubs, or to the Tribunals of friends and acquaintances who had chosen to become conscientious objectors. One day, vitriol was thrown at her face, but it missed. War, she would declare, undaunted at the gates of the docks, was an unscientific way of settling anything.

Kingsley Hall, first in the old Baptist chapel, later rising impressively as a fine new red brick building towering over the streets of squashed two-storey houses, quickly became popular with local people. Believing that many of the social ills stemmed from the high alcoholism of the area, but not wishing to tackle it in the guise of an interfering middle class do-gooder, Muriel started out by referring to her new club as a 'pub', a teetotal pub admittedly, providing only cups of tea and cake, but a pub in spirit, with Saturday night parties and dancing. On Sundays, as a Methodist preacher, Muriel took services, and christened and married her flock.

Her style, in speech as in writing, was chatty, colloquial and persuasive. 'If you are lucky enough to live in a room with a view,' she would say, 'thanksgiving comes easily.' Like her letters to friends, which tended to begin 'Good friend, dear pal, enormously important adviser' and were full of exclamation marks and underlinings and 'How Jolly!' with 'PS's scrawled along the margins, it was all warm, homespun and a little dotty but those who came in touch with her took to it, because she so evidently believed it all herself and had such a clear vision of what was right and wrong.

Muriel and Doris went on living in Bruce Road. They found favour by shedding as much of the visible personal wealth with which they had arrived as they could, keeping only two dresses to wear, though Muriel, as she rather endearingly noted in a volume of her memoirs, *It Occurred To Me*, did not find voluntary poverty altogether easy. 'Obviously,' she wrote, 'gloves were not needed in summer time. Yet to me it is unthinkable to go down Regent Street without them. Could it be done? It took weeks to make up my mind to take this horrible step. Filled with a sense of crisis and feeling undressed, I strode down the street. No one seems to have noticed.'

By 1921 she had also become a regular speaker on Sundays in Hyde Park, and increasingly she was becoming involved with George Lansbury's schemes to fight the 'non-violent battle of Poplar', by bringing decent housing to the derelict and impoverished streets. Much of her work, however, took place within Kingsley Hall itself, where she presided over a collection of local girls and visiting volunteer friends, with a schoolmistressy punctiliousness that not everyone found easy, and a touch of sentimentality that made the more acerbic squirm. Those who grumbled about 'working in the slums' were sharply reprimanded and soon left. The others rose at 7, spent half an hour cleaning — there was always lots of hot water, which some considered wasteful but Muriel decreed essential — and polishing the immense wooden parquet floor and the many brass handles and rails, before embarking on long hours of taking classes, cooking, providing tea and entertaining children.

Soon, distinguished visitors, family friends and new Fabian acquaintances came to spend evenings at Kingsley Hall. The Lesters, captivated by Sybil Thorndike in *Saint Joan*, took parties from Bow to see her playing in the West End; the actress came back to Bow for tea. Corder Catchpool, prominent Quaker World War One pacifist, was to be found polishing the grates; John Galsworthy came on several afternoons; the Marquess of Tavistock took a Bible class.

Doris, less sophisticated and worldly than her elder sister though far more practical, had long wished to do something more specific for the children of Bow. In 1923, with money donated by their father, she set up a Children's House, the first nursery school in the East End of London. H. G. Wells came to open it. There was in fact something excellently complementary about the two sisters, who were very fond of each other but also quickly impatient when too long in each other's company. Muriel, energetic, impetuous, demanding, made acquaintances effortlessly and had no trouble in attracting rich and powerful patrons for Kingsley Hall. But it was Doris, gentler and less assertive, who cultivated these new supporters and turned them into lasting friends.

When, some time towards the end of the twenties, families from Bow and Poplar began moving to a new London County Council housing estate some eight miles away at Beacontree, drawn by the post-war promises of 'houses fit for heroes' and work in Ford's new Dagenham factories, they asked the Lester sisters whether they would not create a new and second Kingsley Hall on the Beacontree estate.

Doris was enthusiastic, Muriel rather less so, having by now begun to dream of more wide-ranging international missions. The two sisters came over to see what was involved. Doris proved persuasive, and with a characteristic burst of energy and commitment Muriel had soon arranged to buy a suitable site, intersecting two of the estate's busier roads, bought a caravan in which to sleep, pitched a tent in which to work, and arrived at Beacontree to supervise the building of a second Kingsley Hall.

The winter of 1929 was cold. The sisters, to those who had never encountered them, like the skilled car workers down from the Midlands or the families evacuated from other parts of East London, appeared peculiar and rather like gypsies. Sydney Russell, a trainee Methodist minister from Loughton, was asked whether he wanted to apply for the position of warden in the new yellow brick building, a somewhat more modest version of its original, where all had been expensive teak and good brass, but including the same large wood-panelled hall for meetings and the same spirit of pacifist, teetotal conviviality. Beacontree estate at the end of the twenties may have looked full of promise but many of its new residents were unemployed and consequently extremely poor. The houses had been built with no water heating system, and the pump and copper in the kitchen trickled the smallest flow of warm water to the upstairs bedrooms. It was not unusual to see houses sealed up, ready for fumigation, a disgrace which few inhabitants stayed on in Dagenham to brazen out. Sydney Russell, now in his eighties, still warden of Kingsley Hall, remembers the poverty well; he describes a life in which everyone who could afford one had a bicycle, but no one had a car, and in which on fine Sundays people walked across the fields, over agricultural land, past the uninhabited remains of four former manor houses, to Barking, four miles away.

Their new project launched, including a children's nursery school, designed by the fashionable architect Cowles Voyses to look like a gleaming white and painted doll's house, the Lesters returned to Bruce Street. Doris went back to running her first nursery school and Muriel turned to a growing commitment to the Friendship of Reconciliation, for whom she was turning into a roving ambassadress. She was an eloquent and endearing speaker, says Sydney Russell, but not always entirely accurate with her facts. At Dagenham, he preferred to ration her sessions from the pulpit; it was not that she didn't enthuse her listeners but he sensed that his parishioners, not educated in the Lester ways, might find her diet of spirituality and fervour, accompanied by the high-minded international peace hymns that she preferred, a little rich. 'At Beacontree we were,' he says, 'more functional.'

Some time in the early twenties Muriel had heard about Gandhi's teachings on non-violence in India. She started reading whatever of his writings she could find and soon introduced into the daily life of Kingsley Hall something of his austerity and self-denial. Gandhi's words — 'If you possess superfluities, while your brother lacks necessities, then you are a thief' — were much in tune with a small organization she had helped found called the Brethren of the Round Table, a Robin Hood gathering which talked of putting all they had on the table and withdrawing only what they needed, the rest going to the poor. When her father died, leaving his estate to be divided among his five surviving children, Muriel put her portion into a trust.

In 1926, through the son-in-law of Rabindranath Tagore, whom she had probably met when he came to London, she was invited to visit Gandhi at Satarmati. She was in India in time for his 56th birthday. Muriel found herself, as she wrote later, at the spinning wheel, producing 'something more like string than yarn' and feeling 'thoroughly silly' as she stood in the river with the other women washing clothes, 'balancing my hideous, stiff and super-British sun helmet on my head while sweat poured off my inverted face'.

It was soon clear, however, that she and Gandhi would get on well. She was greatly taken with the simplicity of his life, and his crusade against drink and drugs; they talked about the way he had refashioned the old Hindu and Buddhist idea of *ahimsa* — not doing injury to any living creature — and made of *satya*, the search for truth, a new philosophy of social action. By the time Muriel met him, Gandhi's non-violent gospel, drawn from the readings of Emerson, Thoreau, Tolstoy and the Sermon on the Mount, but expressed in Indian terms and Indian language as *satyagraha*, the seeking of truth non-violently, was already laid down. *Satyagraha*, as Gandhi saw it, was both a philosophy and a technique for solving conflicts: non-violence of spirit and, when persuasion and reasoning failed, the practice of civil disobedience, which might involve a strike, a walk-out or a boycott. Such was the power of *satyagraha*, Gandhi told her, that enough spiritual force could be released to transform the entire world.

Gandhi, in turn, seems to have liked Muriel Lester for her outspokenness, and the way in which she was not easily intimidated. She asked him to come to London and he agreed, stipulating only that she should 'rouse public opinion, stir the churches, get hold of Members of Parliament, convince Cabinet Ministers that what you have seen here as regards your government's drink and opium policy is thwarting our passion for the prohibition of these evils'.

By the end of the 1920s, Gandhi was President of the Indian National Congress and politically the most influential figure in India; the British invited him to London to discuss Indian affairs. When the first session of the Round Table Conference met in November 1930, however, Gandhi was in prison, and Congress refused to participate. Independence for India was now to become the declared goal of Congress, in support of which Gandhi had launched his Salt March in the spring of 1930. Early in 1931 the Viceroy, Lord Irwin, met Gandhi for long private talks and a pact was made, one of the agreements being that Gandhi would attend the second session of the Round Table Conference.

On August 29 Gandhi boarded the *SS Rajputana* sailing from Bombay. There had been talk about whether his costume of dhoti and sandals, his strict vegetarian diet and the rigid routine of his life should be modified to accommodate British habits and British weather, but Gandhi had been adamant. 'If I am to win their hearts as I want to,' he told an Indian correspondent, 'I can do so only by being 100 per cent truthful. Truth is like the sun. It can melt the icy mountain of suspicion and distrust.' The *SS Rajputana* docked in Marseilles; from there he took the train to Boulogne and crossed by ferry to Folkestone.

The party — Gandhi had brought with him his son Devidas and two secretaries — reached Victoria Station on a wintry wet day. Waiting to greet them was a large welcoming committee of pacifists and members of the Independent Labour Party. He was driven straight to Friends House, in the Euston Road, where the vast Quaker meeting hall was so full that hundreds of people had to stand in the rain outside. Fenner Brockway's seven-year-old daughter was at the door, wearing a homespun cap. Wilfred Wellock declared that 'India had forged a new weapon of freedom, developed and proved a new technique of revolt which ere long will supersede in every part of the world the old technique of violence'.

There had been considerable pressure on Gandhi to stay in central London, in comfortable and fashionable rooms. But remembering his promise to Muriel Lester in 1926, and preferring to be among the poor of the East End, he insisted on driving out to Bow. Newsreel film of the time shows the streets round Kingsley Hall jammed with silent staring crowds; you needed a ticket to get near the front. Not everyone was pleased to see him: a group of people from the British Anti-Imperialist League were holding up banners denouncing him as 'the cunning agent of the Indian princes, landlords and capitalists'. 'Five cells suitably bare for Mr Gandhi's party' had been set aside on the top floor, and shortly after his arrival Gandhi gave a radio broadcast live to America calling for help for India in her 'mighty struggle'. Fleet Street, which insisted on referring to his dhoti as a loincloth, admitted that his visit was going to be 'the best news value in the world, always excepting of course the Prince of Wales'.

Gandhi spent three months at Kingsley Hall. Holding to his resolution not to vary his routine, he rose at 3.30, prayed, ate fruit, nuts and goat's milk provided by a nearby Essex farmer — the newspapers liked to say that a goat was actually living on his terrace, which was not, in fact, true — then took his morning walk. Nearly always, Muriel went with him. She regarded the 'sewer walk', as she called it, as Bow's closest approach to rural English beauty. Distinguished visitors, eager for private audiences, had no choice but to drive out the six miles from central London in what must have seemed to them the middle of the night and, in their top hats or bowlers, accompany Gandhi along streets and paths of a kind that few had probably ever seen before.

It was well into autumn by the time Gandhi settled in Bow. The five cells given over to his party are preserved today much as they were then. Gandhi's cell, seven feet by twelve, with a small terrace, looking out over the low streets all around, is hung with wisps of orange, green and yellow gauze, and posters saying 'No to Hiroshima'. Visitors come, from America, Japan, all over Europe, to pay their respects, standing, bunched up on the terrace, peering in at the cell, or out, over the rooftops or to the garden where Gandhi planted a tree. In the autumn of 1931 the room was whitewashed and, apart from a mat and bed roll, bare with a concrete floor.

It would have been absolutely dark when Gandhi rose, and still dark when he set out, in dhoti and white wool Kashmiri shawl, along the edge of the canal, past three mills, past a distillery, a granary, a row of 18th century cottages and some oast houses, skirting bridges over which went the scarlet electric trains to Barking. It is not very different today. A four-lane highway separates Kingsley Hall from the 'sewer walk' but, beyond it, the fine early 19th century warehouse across the first bridge is still standing and nothing has been built on the open land that borders the canal. Walking along the narrow path, now thickly overgrown with bramble, it is possible to imagine the little group, Gandhi in white in front, Muriel behind him sensibly dressed against the cold, perhaps a politician and his secretary behind, rather awkwardly scrambling along the uneven unfamiliar path, moving, sometimes in single file, along the water's edge, looking down at the loaded barges, and hearing, through the dark, the voices of the men as they lowered bales and kegs on their pulleys from the high warehouse doors into the holds of the waiting barges.

After about 15 minutes they would have come to some steps leading up to the top of a dam, the Northern Outfall Sewer, a raised walkway at rooftop height, a wide straight grassy track with open countryside beyond and workmen's cottages backing up to the dam. The houses have changed since the thirties; they have been modernized and painted in brighter colours; but their gardens still run back towards the walkway; Gandhi and his party, now able to walk abreast and talk, would have proceeded at a brisk pace eastwards, while from the cottages children clambered up the banks to join them and people waved on their way to work.

In the evenings, when he returned from the Round Table Conference sessions, Gandhi often joined in the life of Kingsley Hall. One Saturday night, invited to do so by a local matron, Gandhi danced. Soon Kingsley Hall became a centre for many (at that time) novel ideas: a health food stall was put up in the main hall and an osteopath and nature cure practitioner came to give talks. A lot of local people became vegetarians while Gandhi was in London. Bow had turned its distinguished visitor into its particular hero.

Not long after his arrival, Gandhi asked to be taken to the new Kingsley Hall, in Dagenham. Hearing of his planned visit, local grandees had insisted on being present so that when the official car drew up the Lord Lieutenant and mayor were at the door, ready to receive him. Only Gandhi's two detectives alighted. A few minutes later, an open Austin 7 rounded the corner with Gandhi perched modestly in the back.

It turned out to be his weekly day of silence, a practice he never broke during his months in England. Seated, smiling, on the platform he indicated that he wanted a piece of paper. On it he wrote: 'Monday is my silent day. Thank you very much.' The children, gathered for the occasion and pointing out to each other that he wore nothing on his legs, called him the 'dumb man'.

Gandhi stayed most of the day. Before driving away again in

the baby Austin 7, he wrote in the visitors' book: 'Love surrounded me here.' Later, as he was leaving London to go back
to India, he gave Sydney Russell his spinning wheel, a bicycle
that had been presented to him and a bust of him done by Clare
Sheridan, cousin to Winston Churchill. The spinning wheel
and the bust are in a glass case in the entrance with other
trophies and mementoes of that day; Sydney Russell rode the
bicycle around Beacontree estate until it fell apart.

The Round Table Conference did not go well. The British
Government was inevitably more concerned with British inter-
ests in India than with Indian freedom, while Congress would
not negotiate with the government other than on a basis of
agreed equality; princes, spokesmen for the Hindus and
Moslems, found they were unable to agree with one another.
The last session, on December 1, ended in complete failure.
Gandhi went back to the flat he had been given as an office in
Knightsbridge House and sat by the fire, spinning in silence.
Four days later, having done an astonishing amount and seen a
remarkable number of people in 12 weeks — nine trips out of
London and tea with the King — he left for home. Before set-
ting sail from Naples he had a brief tour, a sort of regal pro-
cession, through Europe that took in Switzerland so that he
could see Pierre Ceresole, and ended in Rome where he met Dr.
Montessori, Tolstoy's daughter and Mussolini. He told an
English reporter: 'My last words to England must be: Farewell
and beware! I came a seeker after peace. I return fearful of war.'
Within a couple of weeks he was back in prison.

5

The 1930s: the shadow of war

The 1930s started well for the pacifists. To the mass movements of the twenties, when vast gatherings of workers, youth associations, women, vegetarians, and groups of every conceivable persuasion met to reaffirm, again and again, their opposition to war, was now added a new voice from the Churches and from writers. It shifted the emphasis a little, from reunions and conferences to the published word; it also, at least at first, gave the movement a clearer sense of direction. 'Moral sanctions' became the catch phrase of the day, a slogan to celebrate what was now seen to be a real force in the world, enshrined by a League of Nations which, though technically empowered to call on military support, in practice was extremely unlikely to do so.

Gandhi, too, had left a mark on more than just one small corner of East End London. Before the second Round Table Conference took place few pacifists would have said that any part of what they believed came from his teachings. Twelve weeks of incessant coverage by film newsreels, and many hundreds of column inches in the newspapers, had changed all that. Now there was virtually no one in the country who did not know something about the slight figure in white, smiling, nodding, climbing in and out of cars and explaining how, in situations of aggression, it was perfectly possible to avoid conflict in a non-violent way and, what was more, to make people pay attention when one did so. Here was a pacifist with a method and he was proving that it could work. If some had doubts about the efficacy of non-violence in situations like the war now raging in Manchuria, where the Japanese had occupied a large chunk of the north, then they kept them mostly to themselves.

Dr. Maude Royden was the daughter of a rich Liverpool shipowner. An Oxford graduate and a former suffragette, she had, during her twenties, fallen under the spell of a decidedly eccentric Anglican preacher called Hudson Shaw; in 1921 she acquired a pulpit in South London, in Eccleston Square. Here, on Sundays, she preached a non-denominational kind of socialist Christianity. (Her private life, tactfully very rarely commented on by her circle, was as unorthodox as her choice of career: Maude Royden lived *à trois* with the Shaws, Mrs. Shaw being something of an invalid. When she finally died, though that was not until 1944, Maude Royden and Hudson Shaw married, but only for a couple of weeks for then he, too, died.)

In her church in Eccleston Square, among the theosophists and eugenicists who peopled that no-man's-land of fashionable London, Maude Royden felt drawn to the pacifism preached by the Fellowship of Reconciliation, and in particular to the social and political overtones of its message.

Not long after the Japanese invaded Manchuria, she faced her congregation sternly one day with the words. 'I would like now to enrol people who would be ready if war should break out to put their bodies unarmed between the contending forces.' History does not record how her listeners responded. What is certainly true is that little action of any kind was taken until, early in 1932, as the World Disarmament Conference was meeting in Geneva, but failing to produce any solution to the conflict in Manchuria, she went into retreat with a pacifist friend called Herbert Gray. Out of their weekend's meditations came a decision to launch a public appeal for unarmed volunteers, willing to travel to Shanghai where they were to form themselves into a human barrier and stand between the Chinese and the Japanese. This time, 800 people replied. By the time they were sifted and organized, however, it was too late; hostilities had died down.

Maude Royden was only one of many won over by a desire to give some practical expression to the notion of non-violent, unarmed resistance. The Rev. Donald Soper, the son of devout Wesleyan parents and himself a fervent believer in the power of Christian truth, was drawn in, declaring that he saw in pacifism 'a spiritual force strong enough to repel any invader' and that, if it was harnessed, it could solve any of the world's ills. At the same time, a Dutch former pastor turned anarchist called Bart de Ligt was working out how such a force could realistically be used, preaching a plan to mobilize the anti-war forces behind a general strike in case of war, and hoping that it would transform itself into a non-violent social revolution. De Ligt's programme, outlined in an address to the War Resisters' International, and taking well over an hour to deliver, included long lists of things to refuse, as well as constructive methods. All forms of military service, of any kind, whether combatant or non-combatant, should, he said, be refused, as should the making of military toys, and the teaching or preaching of anything remotely favourable to war. Philosophers were just some of many — teachers, parents, psychologists, doctors — adjured to fight the moral and mental war. Meetings and appeals were to be launched, at which the uninitiated were to be trained, instructed, converted. It was a vast plan of action, detailed, all-embracing and utterly impractical. But de Ligt won enormous numbers of supporters and his Anti-War Plan was widely quoted and circulated, as were the works of a similar peace strategist, the Quaker preacher Richard Gregg, whose book *The Power of Non-Violence* advocated the use of Gandhi's *ahisma* as an alternative to armed violence in both domestic and international relations.

Not a great deal of purely unambiguous anti-war material had appeared in the years that followed the First War, though of course poetry of sorrow and regret had been published; it was as if the disgust and tragedy were so enormous that it took time to work through the minds of writers and poets who were at the front and who survived. In the late twenties, however, there was a sudden flood of autobiographical accounts of the war by men who had fought in it and seen its horrors. Robert Graves's *Goodbye to All That* and Eric Maria Remarque's *All Quiet on the Western Front* both came out in 1929, the year that Sherriff's play, *Journey's End*, began its long run. Siegfried Sassoon's *Memoirs of an Infantry Officer* followed in 1930. These, and others like them, together with the poetry of Wilfred Owen, Sassoon and Blunden, had an enormous impact on those too young to have taken part in the war themselves, and by 1933 Vera Brittain's *Testament of Youth*, her memories of nursing in the First War, was in its fifth impression.

> Do you remember the rats? (wrote Siegfried Sassoon)
> and the stench
> Of corpses rotting in front of the front-line trench —
> And dawn coming, dirty white, and chill with a hopeless rain?
> Do you ever stop and ask, 'is it all going to happen again?'

Edmund Blunden, who had served in the Royal Sussex Regiment but during the war did not write about his military experiences, preferring in his poetry to dwell on country themes instead, waited until 1928, and then brought out *Undertones of War* in which he spoke of the waste and futility of war, in a quiet, understated way. It was a book, said one critic, 'written by a ghost for other ghosts'. Like the others, he now felt a duty to explain his disenchantment in an impassioned appeal to the world to prevent another similar disaster from occurring. In *A Booklist on the War 1914–1918*, published the following year, Blunden named some 60 books, many of them historical and military memoirs of the war, which could, he said, serve to check a very dangerous evil, the prevailing tendency to transform the horror and wickedness of war into a 'glib axiom, a generalization which may not work at the hearts of the new generation'.

To these former soldiers, ruminating over the appallingness of war for almost a decade, was now added a completely new voice, coming from a different group of writers, some of whom at least were too young to have seen much of the war but were reading the experiences of others or who began remembering facts and events they had not found important at the time. These anti-war essays, novels and plays, for the most part looking forwards and no longer back, anticipating future trouble and urging vigilance, enjoyed a burst of enormous public popularity.

The best known of them all, certainly at the time, was by a previously somewhat flamboyant and frivolous socialite called Beverley Nichols who had spent the twenties writing gossipy books about people and gardens. Early in the thirties Nichols decided to stop 'drinking cocktails and talking nonsense while the clouds were gathering over Europe'. His new-found pacifism, he explained, came from an acute sensitivity to suffering and from 'images . . . so appalling that they cannot be exorcised by any effort of the common mind'. In 1932 Nichols wrote to H. G. Wells, with whom he had been arguing about the principle of conscientious objection: 'I believe that the discussion of war should *begin* with the personal agony of the soldier and should *end* with the political and economic functions which result in that agony. I should like to see a model of a hideously wounded soldier on the respectable tables of disarmament conferences.' Wells accused him of merely making an 'incantation to the unknown, unimplemented God of peace'.

Later, Nichols expanded his letter into the first chapter of a quite new and, to a public ready for it, instantly arresting pacifist diatribe, *Cry Havoc!* But, first, he wrote a pacifist play. *Avalanche* was set in the drawing room of the Chalet Cadenza, a summer house in the Swiss mountains belonging to a pacifist dramatist. The house party, an American, a British titled businessman, his crotchety and outspoken wife, their desirable daughter, another young woman and a butler, are cut off by a blizzard. All communication with the outside world breaks down. The host suddenly appears, back from a bold last sortie to the village, with the news that America has declared war on Britain, and that he, personally, does not intend to fight. There is consternation; the house party falls apart; there are rows, sulks, a broken engagement. They all drink *crème de menthe*. 'You're asking me to bury my face in mud and dirt,' protests the pacifist host, now reviled by all, to the outraged businessman, 'to fill *my* lungs with acid, in order that *you* may sell a few more pairs of stockings.' And then, taunted for cowardice, exposing greed and snobbery in the others, he reveals that it was all just a hoax: there is no war. *Avalanche* enjoyed a great *succès d'estime*, but rather surprisingly no commercial theatre would touch it. (In Vienna, it ran to packed houses for almost a year.)

Nichols now became involved with the Union of Democratic Control, still active in the twenties and thirties, keeping a watchful eye on international treaties. He was planning a book to expose the 'racket' of war, having calculated that £9,590,000,000 had been needlessly spent on the first one. He set off on a long tour around Europe — to Geneva, to see why the League of Nations was 'such a bore', to Barrow-in-Furness to visit Vickers, the armaments factory, to France, where, according to a recent report, various armaments firms were fomenting war scares, to wherever he sensed people were making money from selling and promoting weapons. He called it his 'pilgrimage' to those who 'trade in death'.

Cry Havoc! came out in 1933. It was chatty, written rather in the tone of a letter to an interested but not particularly well-informed cousin, proving that the growth of militarism was insane and that the forces for keeping the peace were doomed.

'Never, in any circumstances, to fight for King and Country' was scrawled across the front cover, in bold type. The very word *war*, declared Nichols, became obsolete the day in 1914 that the first shot was fired; after that the term 'mass murder of civilians' would have been more appropriate. *Cry Havoc!* with its passionate attack on the armament manufacturers, the 'angels of death', was to be the decade's most successful pacifist book.

A few weeks after publication Nichols was the toast of the lecture circuit. Wherever he spoke, he was cheered. (A film was made of one of the speeches he gave. Nichols met Noël Coward going into the newsreel theatre where it was being shown, and was told that the latter had come to hiss it.) From California came a telegram from a peace enthusiast: 'Arriving England Wednesday next with largest book in world measuring sixteen feet across when fully opened stop propose obtain signatures in favour of peace from every prominent man and woman in Europe beginning with King of England stop kindly arrange for open truck to transport book with full publicity from Savoy to Buckingham Palace.'

A. A. Milne, the most acclaimed children's writer of his time, who had served as a Signals officer between 1915 and 1919, now joined in the literary celebration of peace. 'I think war wrong,' he wrote in *An Enquiry into the War Convention*, 'as I think slavery and the burning of heretics wrong, and the corruption of the innocent . . . I think war silly. I think that war is the ultimate expression of man's wickedness and man's silliness . . . If the virile patriot still feels that a violent hatred of war can only come from the cowardly and the effeminate . . . let him think of war in terms of Profiteers, *Embusqués*, Nepotism, Job-wrangling, War Diaries, Propaganda, Rumours, Spy-mania, Honours Lists, Staff Appointments, Patriotic Songs, "Combing out", White Feathers, Business-as-usual, and Keeping the Home Fires Burning; Hatred and Malice and Uncharitableness; and then lies and lies and still more lies . . .' There was something very similar in all these books, some common note in their tone and approach. They were usually discursive, rather rambling, written a bit as if the author were talking to someone in a pub, with pauses for soliloquies, or imagined snatches of dialogue between statesmen and Christians, or invented dinner parties at which MacDonald, Hitler and Mussolini gathered to discuss the futility of war. But there was no mistaking their passion. Storm Jameson, the novelist, spoke for many when she declared at the end of an autobiographical essay called *No Time Like the Present*: 'If this country, I say, is got into another Great War I shall take every means in my power to keep my son out of it. I shall tell him that it is nastier and more shameful to volunteer for gas-bombing than to run from it or to volunteer in the other desperate army of the protestants. I shall tell him also that war is not worth the cost, nor is victory worth the cost.' Storm Jameson's only brother, a much-decorated soldier, had died in France. She was not a great joiner of movements, nor an attender at the pacifist gatherings. Early in the 1980s, looking back on those years, she said that the thirties pacifists, with their peculiar tastes in vegetarian food and what seemed to her excessive goodness, were not her kind of people. 'They were, well, rather dull, many of them, you know, not very interesting as people.' But, in her own shy, somewhat disbelieving way, she felt as did other writers, that she must speak.

Hardly surprising, then, that those in the political arena who now publicly advocated disarmament also enjoyed considerable popular support. Talking of the horrors of war had become the mood of the day; those who had ideas about the future were much needed. One of the most outspoken champions of disarmament was Arthur Ponsonby, the author of the famous Peace Letter of 1925, as well as of a very successful book about the use of lies in wartime, the propaganda effects of telling people that babies were being bayoneted and soldiers crucified, called *Falsehood in Wartime*.

Ever since the end of the twenties Ponsonby had been moving towards a purer pacifist position. Had China in fact been unarmed, he declared when Japan invaded Manchuria, then the Japanese would never have attempted to attack her, since in so doing they would have been branded 'self-confessed aggressors before all the world'. Disarmament, argued Ponsonby, is the 'only absolute security'. Ponsonby's position was not universally popular, but he soon found support of a most prestigious kind, in the form of Professor Albert Einstein, whose overturning of the Newtonian view of the universe had won him international renown. Einstein is one of a great number of 20th century

113

intellectuals who made a widely-talked-about appearance in the theatre of pacifism, which at the time did much to impress the world and enthuse followers, even if, like Bertrand Russell, H. G. Wells or Bernard Shaw, his commitment vacillated and was sometimes contradictory.

In 1931, Einstein was 52. Before the First War he had taken no part in the many European pacifist gatherings, being drawn into discussions about the morality or immorality of war only when he experienced for himself the disruptions it could bring to science. 'My pacifism is an instinctive feeling,' he later explained. 'A feeling that possesses me because the murder of man is disgusting.' In an introduction to a handbook on pacifism, called *Die Friedensbewegung* he maintained that any human being who considered the spiritual values supreme had no alternative but to be a pacifist. By 1920 he was an absolute pacifist himself.

If the next 15 years saw a gradual eroding of that belief, as he came to see that dictators were not persuaded by pacifists, by the early thirties he was still nonetheless calling for proper education to remove the misunderstandings which made war not only possible but popular. 'Is there any way of delivering mankind from the menace of war?' he asked Freud, in a celebrated letter, later published. His own view was bleak. Man, he felt, 'has within him a lust for hatred and destruction'. (Freud's reply was long and in patches inconsistent. Referring to himself and Einstein firmly as 'pacifists', and agreeing with him that an international peace-keeping court was necessary, he said that he felt nevertheless that it needed 'investment with adequate executive force'.)

It was in New York, on December 14, 1930, at the Ritz Carlton Hotel, at one of those great gatherings of people often used by pacifists for their pronouncements (in this case the New History Society of New York), that Einstein delivered what was to become an enormously-quoted appeal to pacifists the world over. True pacifists, he announced, should stop talking and replace their words with deeds. 'Even if only two per cent of those assigned to perform military service should announce their refusal to fight,' he declared, 'governments would be powerless, they would not dare send such a large number to jail.'

The speech prompted a canny manufacturer to come up with badges with the words 'Two per cent'. Soon, they were everywhere. In England, they caused considerable muddle, being assumed to be yet another tactic in the drive to reduce the proof in alcoholic drinks. Bertrand Russell, in a letter to Herbert Runham Brown, commented that two per cent would never be enough: the next war was likely to be greatly more brutal than the first and the two per cent would be quickly shot.

On Saturday, May 2, 1932, three months after the opening of the World Disarmament Conference, in the Salle de la Réformation in Geneva, the largest international conference ever held, Einstein arrived in the Swiss town on a visit. At a press conference held soon after, he declared that the conference itself was the 'greatest tragedy of modern times, despite the cap and bells and buffoonery'. He called the delegates 'unintelligent and insincere' and nothing but 'puppets moved by strings in the hands of politicians at home — politicians and ammunition manufacturers'.

Einstein was far from alone in his reaction. The World Disarmament Conference, which for so many people, pacifists and non-pacifists alike, was the answer to their fears over Manchuria, their regrets about the harsh terms of the Treaty of Versailles, which had exacted from the Germans what seemed to them unnecessarily punitive losses of land, industry and colonies, and their anxieties about the all-too-obvious build-up of armaments all over the world, was proving a hopeless failure.

What made it all so particularly depressing was that people had really believed it might work. The Kellogg-Briand Pact, signed in Paris by 15 countries in August 1928, renounced war as an instrument of policy and pledged that all disputes and conflicts 'of whatever nature or whatever origin' would be settled by peaceful means. After the Kellogg-Briand Pact had come the Five Power Treaty to halt capital ship building and limit the size of aircraft carriers and submarines. The pacifists could be forgiven for a touch of optimism, especially after Arthur Henderson, the senior British delegate and now named chairman of the conference, told a meeting in London: 'at a disarmament conference as elsewhere the government will do what the people want. If the people want disarmament, they can have it.'

Many people, to judge from the signatures gathered in a

series of immense international efforts — eight million by the women's organizations alone, and three million of those from the League for Peace and Freedom, who organized a Peace Caravan to travel 9,000 miles crisscrossing America from Hollywood to Washington — did indeed want it. But they were not about to get it. By early 1932 the world was not in a mood for disarmament. In the countries most involved, the economic situation was worsening all the time. In Britain, the Labour Party, faced by the repercussions of the world economic crisis, had been forced to resign in August and a National Government under Ramsay MacDonald, including Conservatives and Liberals, had taken over. In the Far East, war was raging; the League of Nations' request to Japan to withdraw from Manchuria — she now controlled the whole northern province — had ended in nothing except an agreement that Lord Lytton would travel the area with a commission of inquiry. In America, unemployment towered above all other issues.

In July 1932, after much talking, much disagreeing, the conference adjourned. In January 1933 it opened again, inside the 1850s greenish-yellow building, four storeys high, filled with the mists and fumes of tobacco, from innumerable pipes, cheroots and cigars; but by then Hitler was in power. The talk was all of military systems, of how 'security' could be agreed through power politics. The World Disarmament Conference was, after all, doomed.

Just the same, despite Hitler and Mussolini, 1933 was a good year for the peacemakers, perhaps the last good year, particularly in the opening months. Like 1926, it was a year in which widely-publicized meetings and gatherings, not only in England but across Europe and America, seemed to be voting for peace, and measures to keep peace, rather than talking of war. It was also possibly the last year in which pacifists of the old school, idealistic, full of memories, could continue to blind themselves to the inevitability of the events that were about to shape the world. But it became, as the months wore on, a year of muddle. Emotional pacifism was still the mood of the day, but somewhere along its edges it was going a little sour.

It opened, for the pacifists, gloriously. On February 9, the University Union at Oxford met to debate 'that this house will in no circumstances fight for King and Country'. Beverley

116

Nichols was to have proposed the motion, but he was in Geneva, doing research for *Cry Havoc!*, and his place had been taken by Cyril Joad, disciple of H. G. Wells and Bernard Shaw. Joad was a slight, mischievous figure with a small beard. By 1932, after many years as an ILP socialist, he was describing himself as an 'uncompromising pacifist' and had drawn up what he called a 'Charter for Rationalists' advocating the abolition of censorship, repeal of the divorce laws, education for birth control and, above all, 'complete disarmament' on the part of Britain, and war resistance in the eventuality of war. Having toyed with Mosley's New Party, he was now the founder of something called the Federation of Progressive Societies and Individuals, intended to put into practice Wells's vision of a gathering of inspired thinkers solving the ills of the world through reason.

Joad was an inspired speaker. In the debate 275 undergraduates voted never to fight for their King or country; only 153 opposed the motion. The newspapers gave a lot of coverage to the event, much of it incredulous. 'Seldom have we seen anything more diverting than the rage and astonishment caused by the Oxford Union resolution,' commented the *New Statesman and Nation*. 'The pages of the *Telegraph* and *Morning Post* are wet with the tears of sexagenarian Oxonians lamenting over the decadence of their Alma Mater.' A week after the debate, 30 enraged undergraduates raided the minute book and tore out the page referring to the pacifist triumph. Before it was rewritten, agreement had been won to hold a second debate a couple of weeks later.

This time, Randolph Churchill led off, against the pacifist case. The number of undergraduates present had more than doubled. The barracking, the noise, were extraordinary. Once again, the pacifist victory was total: 750 to 138 votes, a majority of 612 young men declaring that they would never fight. In the *Manchester Guardian*, a leader writer had spoken of 'youth's deep disgust with the way in which past wars "for King and Country" have been made and in which, they suspect, future wars may be made; disgust at the national hypocrisy which can fling over the timidities and follies of politicians, over base greeds and commercial jealousies and jobbery, the cloak of an emotional symbol they do not deserve.' In the serious papers, the motion received much support; in the others, there was angry talk of the 'yellow bellies' of Oxford. Winston Churchill remarked that he 'felt the lips of young Frenchmen, Italians and Germans curl'.

The world's students, however, were behind their Oxford colleagues. The Manchester University Union carried the Oxford resolution by 371 votes to 196; the London School of Economics passed it unanimously, while in Wales, Aberystwyth University College voted in its favour by 186 to 99. The pacifists, everywhere, were jubilant. The *War Resister*, the paper of the WRI, which was in the process of doubling its supporters, hailed it as a gesture 'for intellectual and personal liberty and a revolt against the whole inhuman paraphernalia of *machtpolitik*'.

In Canada and New Zealand, students voted with the Oxford 'yellow bellies'. In America, a nationwide poll was rapidly carried out and, of 21,725 students, 8,415 took an uncompromisingly pacifist stand, while a further 7,221 said that they would bear arms only were their country actually under threat of invasion. Their fervour turned to public anti-war declarations as young men renounced war at the annual Armistice Day eve services, held by the War Resisters' League and organized by Tracy Mygatt and Frances Witherspoon of the World War One Anti-Enlistment League. In the mid-thirties, dozens of No More War Parades, with up to 20,000 marchers, were laid on by the radical and pacifist groups, while a procession of Vassar women in gowns and caps took to the streets of Poughkeepsie, New York, chanting, 'No more battleships. We want schools.' 'This is the time for us to work fast,' warned Jessie Wallace Hughan. 'Not when war comes.'

1933 was undeniably a year for political developments which seemed to many to spell unmistakable support for pacifists. In 1931 the Conservatives had won Fulham East with 23,000 against the Liberal-Labour vote of under 11,000. In 1933 at a by-election a young Labour candidate called J. C. Wilmot, preaching a mixture of disarmament, cooperation with the League of Nations, and criticism of current economic policies and in particular abysmal housing in Fulham, came top of the poll with 18,000 votes. According to Winston Churchill, it had all been due to the 'wave of pacifist emotion', though there was much talk that the issue had in fact — and unfairly — been decided by accusations against the Tory that he was nothing but a 'warmonger'. Whatever the truth — seven other by-elections, held at around the same time, but fought without the slightest pacifist overtones, showed much the same swing away from the government — victory at Fulham East was widely heralded as proof of a strong pacifist mood.

More interesting, perhaps, because it provided a far clearer and considerably more subtle picture of the actual feelings of the time, was the National Peace Council's Congress, held a little earlier that summer in Oxford. The Peace Council was one of the most powerful forums for pacifist debate in the thirties. The 1933 meeting drew an exceptionally large audience of well over 500. Cyril Joad was there, and Sir Norman Angell (knighted in 1931), as well as Clifford Allen, now Lord Allen of Hurtwood. Afterwards, a public demonstration gathered outside the town hall and flowed out on to the surrounding streets. The tone of the day, however, was somewhat different from much that had gone before, more analytical and contemplative, as if the emotional response to pacifism was now giving way to more stringent examination. Absolutists seemed to be abandoning the purity of their earlier stands. Was the world such a very different place, or were they now all just rather older?

Allen had spent the twenties and early thirties in semi-retirement, tinkering with socialist issues and the ILP, opposing the death penalty, throwing himself behind the 'new school' movement of Bedales, the Russells, A. S. Neill and Dartington Hall. At the Oxford Congress he seemed to be reaching back to an earlier view — that pacifism is in the end without power, suitable only for the wilderness, for 'educators' or 'religious propagandists'. To have any real value, Allen now argued, pacifism had to be constructive; war resistance was no longer enough. What pacifists ought to do was to unite and to press the British Government to take a bold step at all international meetings, and propose that all countries disarm completely within ten years. At the same time there should be formed an internationally-controlled force just strong enough to 'provide the security essential for international peace'. 'That,' said Allen, by now a somewhat stooped and frail figure, having never fully recovered the vigour of his pre-war days and, though only 43, soon to die, 'is what I mean by pacifism. Not a tightrope dance of logic about whether force should ever be used, or when; not a negative advocacy for resisting war; but something quite different, namely testing out the possibility of using reason and initiating bold proposals, hitherto considered impracticable, not because they were undesirable but because no one would propose them.' The choice, added Allen, 'is between an armed anarchy and an armed society. Both are evil. But I suggest that the armed society is less evil; that a good society, though armed, is on the way to becoming an unarmed one . . .'

A far cry from the absolutist pacifist position of 1916 and 1917, perhaps, but by 1933 the world was very different. Reason, not pure belief, was going to have to cope with international problems, which by now seemed to have lost some of their earlier simplicity, just as reason was going to promote 'collective security'. Among the pacifists there were few who were not internationalist, seeing only in joint action any true hope of keeping the peace. (Even so, there was some disagreement, even among otherwise united pacifists: given that an international police force — seen strictly as police and not as army — might be considered necessary, would it be like a domestic force, and established after general disarmament, or would it be something a little more military, and provide security before disarmament? Pacifists who advocated the need for such a body, but insisted that they would never serve in it themselves, tended to be accused of having double standards.)

The issue of sanctions was also a test. That economic pressure was an effective weapon in the world had been proved by the First War. But how humane a weapon was it? Pacifist visitors to Germany soon after the Allied blockade was lifted came back wondering whether starving children was really non-violence. Just how popular these two measures were in the minds of the general public was put to the test when a coalition of 38 separate peace organizations, under the auspices of the League of Nations, agreed to hold a peace ballot. Citizens were asked to vote on six questions concerning the League, rearmament and war. The crucial questions were 5a and 5b, which tested the readiness for 'peace at any price' by asking: 'Do you consider that, if a nation insists on attacking another, the other nations should combine to compel it to stop by a) economic and non-military measures? b) if necessary, military measures?' When the votes were counted, almost six in every ten people said they were prepared to back collective security with military force; nine out of ten with sanctions short of war. What had been demonstrated was a willingness to resist aggression with militancy; but also continuing support for the idea of collective security.

The question now, perhaps, in the confused mid-thirties, was who was in fact a pacifist at all? Some argued that the word should only be used to define conscientious objection in time of war; others that its meaning was far broader and could really be used to embrace 'friend of peace and enemy of war'. Letters on the subject poured into *The Times*. *Headway*, the journal of the League of Nations Unions, came out with the definition of a pacifist as someone 'desirous of peace at practically any price; one who is probably a conscientious objector; and who disapproved of military service' — which did not make the situation very much clearer. It was left to Frank Hardie, the young man who so brilliantly organized the Oxford Union debate, to sum up the confusions and dilemmas of the time in the *New Statesman*. 'In the sense of preferring peace to war,' he wrote, 'we are all pacifists now. But that kind of pacifism is not enough. There would be less confusion if the word "pacifist" were always taken to mean one who, on account of certain principles, philosophical or religious, will, in no circumstances whatever, take part in war.' Few, by 1933, could feel quite so clear; and, in the years that followed, even that clarity was to be shattered.

In almost all ways, of course, it had always been easier for the purely religious pacifists. Their doubts, in a final way, could be met by a return to pure faith. And, as the thirties grew even more confusing and belligerent, it was about to become the only easy form of pacifism. In general, committed Christians had spent the twenties and early thirties supporting the view that man could grow in grace and that the Churches, acting within society, could provoke a real moral awakening. If the Churches, argued Richard Roberts of the Fellowship of Reconciliation in 1929, refused to endorse warfare, then governments would in the end be obliged to think up other ways than armies to deal with international conflicts. More theologically minded believers followed the fashionable teachings of Karl Barth, the Swiss pastor, and Reinhold Niebuhr, who said that to demand progress in a secular world was to show too little humility in the face of God's mystery. The more liberal churchgoers took the view that, on the contrary, the setting up of an international police force was a perfectly acceptable first move, and well in keeping with the practical necessities of the times. A council of Christian Pacifist groups in England — Methodists, Congregationalists, Quakers, Baptists and Anglicans — started meeting to promote a more united Christian opposition to war. What was to give them a distinctive voice was the emergence of the most important pacifist figure of the thirties, a pug-nosed, pale-skinned, plump and somewhat foppishly dressed Anglican clergyman called Dick Sheppard. It was Sheppard's particular brilliance that he was able to attract not simply Christians but the widest range of pacifists, even the purely political ones. He exasperated a lot of people; but most loved him. 'When he comes into the room,' Max Beerbohm once said to Rose Macaulay, 'everyone feels happier and comes more alive.'

Sheppard had not always been a pacifist. He was born in 1880, the son of a canon at Windsor. As a boy he was a good mimic, with a soft rubbery face, and he could make people laugh. At 19 he volunteered for the Boer War, but was hurt in an accident in the hansom cab that was taking him to Waterloo station to join his regiment, and was left with a permanent limp. He went to Cambridge instead, where he boxed and played cricket and spent his holidays working in a settlement in Bethnal Green, moving to live full-time in the East End and manage a local boys' club when he graduated. In 1909, after long hesitation, he was ordained and went to be deputy priest-in-ordinary to King Edward VII.

On the outbreak of war Sheppard was sent to the Western Front as a chaplain, but only briefly, for he was soon offered the post of vicar at St. Martin-in-the-Fields, a very worldly church, though better known for its glorious past, having seen Charles II baptised at its font. Sheppard liked large congregations; he also believed in social work. He kept the crypt of the church open all night for the destitute and those sheltering from air raids, and he so raised the style and pomp of the daily services that one sidesman was soon remarking disapprovingly that he had not seen such absurd ceremonial since visiting a Shinto temple in Japan. By the end of the war, Sheppard was attracting 1,200 people to his Sunday services. Soon afterwards, to the disgust of many of the clergy, and on John Reith's suggestion, his services began to be broadcast. As the first radio parson, chatty, avuncular, his name was soon widely known.

Sometime late in 1929 or early in 1930 Dick Sheppard became a pacifist. 'I do not think a Christian can take part in any work of killing,' he wrote to a friend, a supporter of the No More War Movement, 'or do anything that he cannot believe Christ would have done.' He spent increasing amounts of time with Maude Royden — he was with her and Herbert Gray during the weekend retreat in Kent at which the idea of the Peace Army was discussed — and went to The Hague to hear Einstein talk against war and conscription. Always a restless, energetic man, despite frequent attacks of bad and debilitating asthma, he complained to friends that he was beginning to feel lonely in the Church of England.

On October 16, 1934, on what looked almost like a whim, and possibly inspired by a stirring sermon preached by Dr. Harry Emerson Fosdich on Armistice Sunday the previous year in New York — 'I renounce war for its consequences, for the lies it lives on and propagates, for the undying hatred it arouses, for the dictatorships it puts in the place of democracy, for the starvation that stalks after it' — Sheppard wrote a letter to *The Times*. It spoke of the growing violence, the urgency of the international situation and increasing fascism. The average man, said Sheppard, was clearly now beginning to look round him for some other solution to modern society and some other escape from a war which would not only be a 'denial of Christianity, but a crime against humanity, which is no longer to be permitted by civilized people'. Nothing very new; it had all been said many times before. But then, towards the end, he added that any men who felt as he did and wanted to do something about it should send him a postcard with the words: 'We renounce war and never again, directly or indirectly, will we support or sanction another.'

Sheppard had given as his address the Walton-on-Thames house of Brigadier-General Frank Crozier, a somewhat eccentric former soldier who had turned against the 'dirtiness' of war, and was one of the keenest supporters of Dr. Royden's Peace Army. For a few days nothing happened. Sheppard was puzzled and disappointed. Then the telephone rang. It was the village postmaster to ask what he should do with several sackfuls of postcards, building up unmanageably around his office. Within the first few weeks 30,000 cards had arrived; soon, they numbered over 100,000. 'The trouble,' wrote Sheppard in the *Sunday Express*, 'is [that] I am now what is called a peace crank'.

The question was what was to be done with all these cards and all this goodwill. Sheppard did not really want to start a new organization, and in any case was still far from clear himself about what correct pacifist thinking and behaviour should be in the world of the early thirties. 'Abyssinia and Italy simply beats me,' he wrote to a friend. 'I don't know what we pacifists ought to be at.' A meeting seemed called for, and on July 14, 1935, on a particularly hot summer's day, thousands of people converged on the Albert Hall. Apart from Sheppard himself, Crozier, Edmund Blunden and Maude Royden all spoke; Siegfried Sassoon read some of his war poetry. It was, declared Sheppard, 'the finest pacifist meeting I was ever at'. What became known among his friends as Sheppard's 'beastly blooming organization' was born.

It started life, as the Sheppard Peace Movement, in rented rooms in Grand Buildings overlooking Trafalgar Square, with 200 new pledges each day to be turned into members and a distinguished cast of sponsors: Storm Jameson, Arthur Ponsonby, George Lansbury, Ellen Wilkinson and Siegfried Sassoon. More meetings followed, with Dick Sheppard insisting on parading the streets in sandwich boards to announce them, and more members. Sheppard's personal stamp on the organization, despite the arrival of yet more distinguished sponsors in the form of Bertrand Russell, Aldous Huxley, and Vera Brittain (making it possibly the most prestigious of all British pressure groups), was enormous and, though the name was soon changed to the Peace Pledge Union (PPU), it was unanimously agreed that, for the time being at least, 'the direction should rest largely in one man's hands'. That man could only be Sheppard.

He was a strange and sometimes slightly contradictory figure. People today remember him as a not particularly inspired or brilliant speaker, tending sometimes to the sugary and the sentimental, but all agree that he possessed such warmth, sense of humour and integrity that he rarely failed to charm and dazzle. If his rather autocratic manner, his plummy, mild voice, and his hand-made Lobb shoes disturbed the more austere and self-denying pacifists, they had the desirable effect of making him attractive to circles normally extremely suspicious of the scruffy Left. He might have been their doctor, their family solicitor. Sheppard was not an intellectual; but he was intuitive and highly pragmatic and and he had great faith in the middle, rational position.

The first members of the Peace Pledge Union had all been men. In 1936 women were invited to join, by sending similar postcards; some did, but not in quite the same number. Yet the movement continued to grow; peace shops opened, and some 800 separate groups around the country held pacifist meetings.

But what was the PPU actually going to do? Sheppard had not given much thought to anything beyond the formal signing of his pledge. In meetings with his more active sponsors there soon emerged clear agreement that some sort of 'non-violent resistance' should be the binding theme among members; somewhere among the talk, though not very precisely spelt out, was the idea, rather as with Einstein's two per cent, that if enough men refused to fight then there could clearly be no war. The natural prophet to shape this feeling was Richard Gregg, a Quaker lawyer and preacher who had just spent four years living in India with Gandhi. 'Greggism', as it quickly became known, held that a trained corps of resisters would be able to stop soldiers from fighting and to win support and approval from the public. A manual, *Training for Peace*, was now produced and sold to PPU members. It recommended meditation, group singing and folk dancing, and, along with rather precise directions for the peace cadres, suggested that 'spinning or knitting clothes . . . would provide significant work for the inarticulate, for mothers who cannot easily go to meetings or old people who cannot go out'. 'Greggism' was not altogether popular. One pacifist called it 'Yogie-bogie exercises' and even Sheppard did not greatly care for it. The trouble, as with the other much debated pamphlet by Ronald Duncan, which advocated setting up small cells of pacifists, trained like a religious order to convert the public at large, particularly in the slums, was that no one could quite see how it could be made to deal with international aggression, of the belligerent variety now being seen in

Italy and Germany. It had been seen to work in India against the troops of the British Empire, but could such 'reasonable' behaviour be expected of Hitler? And was non-violence possibly not just another form of coercion, just as violence was?

If the PPU was not going to provide a force of non-violent resisters, what, then, was it to do? Clearly the only alternative was to become a movement of the masses, so large and so persuasive that its voice had to be attended to. Sheppard's touch of the mystic, couched sometimes in public school language — he announced at a peace gathering in Manchester that he had just had a dream: 'In it George Lansbury and I were playing tennis against Hitler and Mussolini. George had a game leg and I was asthmatic but we won six love' — did not always help. There was often muddle over direction. Not every sponsors' meeting was harmonious. 'What we want,' an exasperated Sheppard was heard to say at the end of one, 'is a bloody massacre.'

Just the same, the PPU continued to grow. Not only Christians, but socialist pacifists and humanitarians, bewildered and appalled by the steady rise of Hitler and the failure of the League of Nations over Mussolini's invasion of Abyssinia, saw in the simplicity of the pledge a last reassuring beacon. The organization received further support when, in 1935, a Quaker teacher and member of the No More War Movement called Humphrey Moore, believing that the pacifist message was not reaching out to enough people, raised £56 and printed 1,500 copies of a first issue of a paper he named *Peace News*. Moore ran the paper from his house in Wood Green, North London; because he was also working for the National Peace Council he was able to recruit well-known pacifist writers like Storm Jameson and Vera Brittain. As the copies of *Peace News* came from the printer, young men and women from his congregation sold them on street corners.

After the first six issues, the PPU suggested they might merge forces, and by the late thirties there were known to be about a thousand PPU members around the country selling the paper. Circulation rose to 24,000. *Peace News* was filled with stories about conscription in other countries; with details and reports of meetings; with advertisements for 'pacifist' lodgings; and with passionate leaders about peace. It was lively and widely read, but it never had much money: the same photographs — a policeman grappling with a protester, a group of marching soldiers, the identical portraits of Ponsonby and Gandhi — appeared again and again.

Sheppard referred to his pacifist followers as 'rebels against the world as it is'. Certainly they were a curious and often ill-assorted lot; perhaps the strength and distinction of the PPU lay precisely in the very diversity of the men and women who had signed its pledge. At the summer school gatherings so beloved of pacifists between the wars the somewhat older, non-conformist, non-smoking, teetotal vegetarians were to be found deep in talk with young men and women who, if asked, would have described themselves as humanitarians and said that they believed in individual freedom and the right to pleasure. While the first sat late into the night debating the more esoteric issues of life, the second larked in the dormitories and introduced a fashion for taking their baths in public. At Swanwick, setting for the first PPU camp, the vegetarian table and the meat-eating table formed themselves into teams and challenged each other to a game of cricket. They played lawn tennis, in the very long shorts of the day, and danced to the piano at night. They were earnest, and not at all elegant, but it was fun. Away from the camps, they banded themselves into groups and sat down in the paths of Black Shirt marchers, lustily singing a rather feeble verse:

> Loving Sheppard of thy sheep
> Keep us all in Peace Pledge keep

while the more political were now beginning to stand as candidates at local elections.

Sheppard was tireless. As friends noted, and complained, he rarely worked less than a twenty-hour day, struggling to keep control of an organization that was bursting; he kept coming up with new ideas, like writing to Hitler, suggesting that he go to Germany to preach (Hitler did not reply). As symbol and star of the PPU, he was greatly in demand, on platforms, at rallies, at interminable meetings, receiving endless visitors. So widespread in fact was the cult that grew up around him that, when at one point he developed acute appendicitis, it became a serious item on the news. And he was often ill.

The asthma that had bedevilled him since childhood was

127

growing worse. On October 31, 1937, Sheppard was found dead, sitting at his desk. He was 57. For many of his supporters, their last memory of him had been at the most recent PPU summer school, when he had been particularly boisterous and cheerful. He had not even lived to see himself confirmed as Rector of the University of Glasgow, a position he had won, against enormous odds, on a straight pacifist ticket.

Sheppard had asked to be buried in the Cathedral Cloisters in Canterbury. Before his coffin was carried there he lay briefly, in state, in his church at St. Martin-in-the-Fields, surrounded by the staff and senior members of the PPU, while over 100,000 people filed past. 'He worked himself to death,' Ramsay MacDonald remarked. 'He was unique I think. It is nice to have known him.'

MacDonald was right. There was something unique about Sheppard, and the PPU found it very hard to do without him. After his death his place at the head of the organization was eventually filled by Canon Stuart Morris, a Cambridge graduate with a long, thin face, chaplain to the Royal Flying Corps in World War One, who owed much of his pacifism to his appointment as secretary to Bishop E. W. Barnes, one of the rare truly pacifist senior clergymen of the time. Morris was a considerable figure and an able organizer, oratorial and exhortatory in manner, but he lacked Sheppard's powerful attraction. He was not cosy. The inherent divisions in the PPU now grew sharper, with the younger, humanitarian pacifists maintaining that theirs should be a political movement and a pressure group, while the more religious-minded held that the PPU should really see itself as a group of believers, rather in the mould of the Fellowship of Reconciliation. In March 1938 the PPU sponsors produced a political manifesto, while *Peace News* carried articles advocating practical pacifism, both along the lines that Morris believed were closest to Sheppard's thinking, though many members grumbled. A truce was declared, influenced largely by a shared fear of what lay ahead. Spurred on by the sponsors, who were now to be elected rather than just nominated, the PPU raised the money to buy a house off the Euston Road, at No. 6 Endsleigh Gardens, and there, to Dick Sheppard House, they moved in March 1939. They are still there, shrunk from the entire house to a few small rooms scattered between basement and attic, the others long since let off to conservationist and other pacifist bodies.

By now, in any case, the great pacifist dreams of the entire 1920s and a good part of the 1930s were fading fast. With the final subjugation of Abyssinia by the Italians and their subsequent departure from the League of Nations, the remilitarization of the Rhineland and in July 1936 the outbreak of civil war in Spain, the hope that non-military sanctions might prove effective was collapsing. The League of Nations continued to argue for collective security, but it had become clear to most people that what they were talking about was virtually indistinguishable from conventional defence. Hardly surprising, then, that the spirit of the great pacifist illusion began to drain away, though the direction this took and its speed varied considerably from one end of the movement to the other.

It was easier for the PPU members who continued to move down the path of an ultimately religious or even mystical pacifism. Indeed, the religious pacifists, ousted from their prominence by the universal enthusiasm for peace that had overtaken socialists and intellectuals and humanitarians, began to regain their ascendancy. The tendency to dwell heavily and a little nostalgically on 'man's yearning for peace', and on the importance of being a 'witness' when all else failed, was beginning to seem increasingly attractive to pacifists who had become depressed at the utter inability of statesmen and world leaders to reach a common ground. Retreat, of an individual and mental kind, was appealing. A number of pacifists began to withdraw into mystical and religious contemplation, while the world foundered about them. The best known guru of contemplative pacifism was Aldous Huxley.

When, in the mid-thirties, the BBC had arranged for a series of lectures on the 'Causes of War' Aldous Huxley agreed to give one on the psychological phenomenon of war. 'Wars,' he declared, 'are not fought by climates or political or economic systems, they are fought by human beings . . .' What was needed, therefore, was long-term research into the human mind, into why the 'barbarian and the sadist are strong within us'.

It was through Gerald Heard, writer and simplifier of scientific advances, that Aldous Huxley drew close to the PPU, finding particular agreement with Sheppard's insistence that the future for pacifists lay in their organization and their willingness to prove themselves united and courageous. 'The only hope,' he wrote to a friend soon after the great Albert Hall rallies of the summer of 1935, 'lies in the pacifists being better disciplined than the militants and prepared to put up with as great hardships and dangers with a courage equal to theirs. Not easy. But I suppose nothing of any value is easy.' Like Heard, Huxley agreed to become one of the PPU's sponsors; he seemed, at least at first, to have hopes that pacifism could avert another war, even if he continued to view it as a creed. 'If enough people address themselves to living up to this belief . . . then there will be peace,' he wrote, 'for peace . . . is a by-product of a certain way of life.'

Whenever Huxley was in London, he gave up a great deal of time to the pacifist cause, writing pamphlets and speaking for the PPU and producing a brief, concise *Encyclopaedia of Pacifism* for Chatto and Windus. In one of the most read of his pamphlets, 'What are you going to do about it? The case for constructive peace', he argued that 'man is unique in organizing the mass murder of his own species. War is not a law of nature . . . Constructive peace must be first of all a personal ethic.' C. Day Lewis, replying in the *Left Review* in a piece entitled 'We're not going to do nothing' and attacking this drift towards private and internal protest, criticized Huxley's position as a 'great, big, beautiful idealist bubble — lovely to look at, no doubt; charming to live in, perhaps; but with little reference to the real facts and inadequate protection against a four-engined bomber.' To claim, as Huxley seemed to, that violence is morally wrong because any end achieved by violence will itself be morally unsatisfactory was, argued Day Lewis, fallacious and self-contradictory. Huxley's was nothing but a 'doctrine of despair'. What was in fact needed was a coordinated and effective peace front, an international alliance of people united against fascism and not a retreat into the saving of individual souls and 'spiritual exercises'.

Day Lewis had a point; Huxley was indeed retreating. United pacifist fronts were beginning to seem to him increasingly feeble. By early 1937 both he and Heard were becoming discouraged about the peace movement; despite the enormous size of the protest against war, there now seemed little chance of anyone making the kind of impact that would actually push the government into action. All that was left, perhaps, were personal ethics. In April Huxley left for a lecture tour of America; and there he stayed for the next 25 years. Though he remained a sponsor for the PPU for the rest of his life, he gradually shifted backwards into a pacifist cul de sac. *Ends and Means: an enquiry into the nature of ideals and the methods employed for their realization* became something of a bible for a number of British pacifists, but its message was not likely to appeal to all those who still hoped that international common sense was going to avert a war. Seek ultimate reality by freeing yourself from everyday behaviour and thought, he seemed to be saying; there is little else that you can do. In both Britain and America, a number of the more deeply religious pacifists were now moving rapidly to the point where they were seeing themselves as a 'redemptive minority', witnesses to a code of ethics that might one day allow society to advance spiritually. Pacifism, for them, was fast becoming a pure act of faith; if they seemed to be opting out, they were doing so, they argued, because it was all they could do for society.

It had never been easy for the socialist pacifists. For a large number of them, the Spanish Civil War meant the end of their commitment: it was simply no longer possible afterwards to be both pacifist and socialist. If pacifist, how could you argue that it was all right to kill a fascist, but not a communist? If socialist, how could you stand by and see fellow-workers massacred? In some ways, the clarity must have come as a relief; there had been a terrible buffeting of loyalties.

The early thirties had seen a tacit understanding that the left-of-centre in Britain needed to stand together, to revitalize the thinking behind a new British economy and to uphold democracy in the face of the growing strength of fascism and communism. The pacifist veterans of World War One, like Clifford Allen and Herbert Runham Brown, stood firmly behind the League of Nations, even if they had to live with its many contradictions, recognizing that to be effective the League needed force, but seeing in that force a policeman's truncheon and not a soldier's gun.

The attitude of the Conservatives, with their enormous majority in Parliament, was described by Alfred Salter as 'more insolent, arrogant, imperialistic and jingo than any I have known before'. This undoubtedly helped Labour to swing towards pacifism. At the Labour Party conference in Hastings in 1933 a resolution was passed unanimously against participation in any war in any circumstances. 'Labour,' announced Salter triumphantly, 'will have nothing to do with any more mass murder.' His enthusiasm was slightly premature: there was little true intention within the Labour Party to implement their declaration that they would rather strike than see a war, and the second resolution, proposed by Arthur Henderson in favour of collective security, received the same unanimous applause.

It was Italy's invasion of Abyssinia in October 1935 that really dealt the socialist pacifists their first major blow. If nothing was done about Mussolini, the pacifists realized, then the League might well be destroyed. If, however, economic sanctions were imposed, then war might follow. Many now drifted into the Peace Pledge Union and sought reassurance in a movement that seemed united at least in its fervour, while those inside Parliament, like George Lansbury or Albert Salter, redoubled their attempts to make others understand that the way to avoid aggression was to remove its causes, by pooling the earth's resources. 'Appeasement' was not yet a dirty word. It went hand in hand with 'collective security'. Illegitimate demands were to be met by collective security; legitimate ones should be handled with appeasement. Clifford Allen, most outspoken supporter of the view that the rise of Hitler and the Nazis was due more than anything else to the failure to meet German grievances after the Treaty of Versailles, kept pressing that Germany should be brought back into the League of Nations, to play her part in collective security. In Parliament, on a series of private members' motions, Lansbury and Salter, who formed a Parliamentary Pacifist Group, called for a world conference to give all countries access to raw materials. The pressure of population and the need for more food and prosperity were such, they argued, that they were driving Japan, Italy and Germany to war.

But then came the Spanish Civil War. Was it actually possible to support one war and yet condemn all warfare? A few confused pacifists, like Kingsley Martin, editor of the *New*

Statesman, and Victor Gollancz, whose Left Book Club had been enormously important in drawing attention to the issues of peace and war, tried the impossible, arguing that it was in fact perfectly all right to support the war in Spain and yet be a pacifist in Britain. Others did not find it that easy.

Fenner Brockway, most staunch of the absolutists of the First War, had spent the late twenties and early thirties in a growing mood of uncertainty. Now he went to Spain, and returned saying that he feared for the 'incompleteness of pacifist philosophy'. Among the peasants of Catalonia he had found equality and armed men, prepared to die in order to defend their freedom and their equality. Was their violence and that used by the Fascists the same? Fenner Brockway concluded that society which resulted from anarchist violence would be fairer and freer than the one resulting from a Fascist victory, and thus 'I came to see that it is not the amount of violence used which determines good or evil results, but the ideas, the sense of human values, and above all the social forces behind its use'. Socialism, in the end, was what counted, and a 'full, free and fraternal life' was possible only when material poverty was banished, exploitation brought to an end, and with it all class and national divisions.

The No More War Movement, on which Fenner Brockway had put so strong a stamp, though he was no longer its chairman, wound itself up, after a small section of the membership had tried to get civil wars exempted from its pledge. The remaining members, refusing to condone any war, carried out with modern weapons, went over to the ranks of the PPU, which simply absorbed the war resisters.

And what of the intellectuals, for whom the word 'peace' in the thirties had held such magic? Nancy Cunard, Ivor Montagu, Stephen Spender and Louis Aragon organized a poll, later published as *Authors Take Sides on the Spanish Civil War*. One hundred and forty-eight authors received letters. 'It is clear to many of us throughout the whole world that now, as certainly never before, we are determined, or compelled, to take sides', read the text. 'The equivocal attitude, the Ivory Tower, the paradoxical, the ironic detachment, will no longer do . . . This is the question we are asking you: are you for, or against, Franco and Fascism? For it is impossible any longer to take no side.'

Those who received the letters nearly all agreed. One

133

hundred and twenty-eight writers declared themselves for the Republic. Leonard Woolf, Rebecca West, V. S. Pritchett, Fenner Brockway, C. E. M. Joad, all the most unambiguous pacifists of the time, voted against Franco. Rose Macaulay and Storm Jameson announced they felt the same, but would go no further than a formal declaration of hatred of fascism.

Five voted for Franco; among them Evelyn Waugh and Edmund Blunden. Sixteen professed themselves neutral: some, like Norman Douglas, because they did not want to take sides; others in idiosyncratic ways of their own. 'I am not an "anti" of any sort,' said H. G. Wells, 'unless it is anti-gangster or anti-nationalist.' 'Questionnaires are an escape mechanism for young fools,' objected Ezra Pound, 'who are too cowardly to think . . . You are all had. Spain is an emotional luxury to a gang of sap-headed dilettantes.'

It was left to Vera Brittain to make the one uncompromisingly pacifist statement. 'I hold war to be a crime against humanity,' she replied, 'whoever fights it and against whomever it is fought . . . I detest fascism and all that it stands for, but I do not believe that we shall destroy it by fighting.'

The British Left had given up their pacifism; but they had done so slowly. Right up until 1936, through the great defeats of the League of Nations, through the remilitarization of Germany and rise of Hitler, they had gone on hoping that pacifism was still realistic, that order was somehow possible in a world where the one policeman, the League of Nations, had no truncheon. Reluctantly, they now realized that the moment was past. The fascist advance had to be stopped, even if there was still profound disagreement about how.

'Although the world is arming at an ever increasing rate and civilization is apparently rushing to destruction, I refuse to despair . . . Pacifism is not on trial . . . Hard and difficult though our path may be, we pacifists must preserve our faith that love alone will save the world . . .' The writer of these optimistic though not exactly practical words was George Lansbury, a whiskery and benign lifelong pacifist and socialist, Guardian of the Poor for Bow and Bromley, whose squared-off moustaches and small, shining eyes peer in a kindly way out of a hundred photographs of the twenties and thirties, leading deputations

134

and marches, planting commemorative trees, embarking on journeys and missions. No account of the closing days of the pacifists' thirties would be complete without him. As the world crept towards war, Lansbury threw himself into one of the last great schemes for avoiding it; it was unsophisticated, even a little dotty, and it could never have worked. But there was something hopeful about it, and Lansbury's particular voice, questioning, naïve, as if incredulous of man's stupidity and greed, is sometimes a little like that of Bob Geldof in the 1980s, marvelling that the world can be so venal while half the African continent starves to death.

In 1938 George Lansbury was 79. The son of a contractor, employing gangs of workers on railway construction, he had spent his entire life in the Labour movement, having come into politics with Keir Hardie's Independent Labour Party in 1906. Like Hardie, Lansbury was an excellent speaker but a rather flat, inelegant writer. He was small, modest and approachable, a teetotaller much embarrassed by drunkenness, but addicted to tea (and cold mustard, which he ate in small pots in the House of Commons dining room), who wore a reefer jacket and baggy trousers for all occasions right up until the day he became a Cabinet Minister, though even after that he still refused to wear gloves, sock suspenders, spats or tie pins. He never learned to shave, preferring to walk to the barber's every morning to have his mutton-chop whiskers trimmed, in summer occasionally still wearing his bedroom slippers. His wife Bessie, also small, had a round face and hair piled up in a neat cottage bun on top of her head; she looked rather like him. A charming photograph taken of them in 1925 as they were leaving their house in the East End of London shows George Lansbury in top hat, clasping, under one arm, an umbrella, and under the other Bessie's hand; both are smiling, in a slightly self-mocking way. Bessie looks wary. The Lansburys had twelve children and lived at No. 39 Bow Road, not far from Muriel Lester and Kingsley Hall, a cheerful, not always very affluent life, with much singing in the evening, for Lansbury was a fine baritone; he kept his desk in the main room facing the window, overlooking the street so that he could watch the trams and steam wagons go by.

By the thirties Lansbury was famous as champion of the

women's suffrage movement, for which he had been to prison in 1913, then as first Commissioner of Works in the Cabinet under Ramsay MacDonald, when, nicknamed 'His Majesty's First Commissioner of Good Works', he had reformed the London parks by pulling down the railings and opening the Serpentine to mixed bathing (*The Times* complained that he had turned Hyde Park into Coney Island); and later as editor of the *Daily Herald* where he had spent the First War as an unshakable anti-war crusader. By his late seventies he had lost none of his vigour. He inspired both great affection and irritation. Friends would say of him that he was the sort of man who seemed to look rather hopeless and ineffectual, but then turn out to be extremely wily.

Lansbury's last days in government came about purely on account of his pacifism. In 1931, he had become leader of the Labour Party, where he found it hard to square his own personal and increasingly pure brand of pacifism with the party's allegiance to the League of Nations' collective security. By the time the Labour Party met in October 1935 for its annual conference in Hastings, Italian troops were invading Abyssinia, and Hugh Dalton moved to call on the government to use 'all necessary measures' through the League to stop the Italians. There was much debate, swinging towards the pacifist side, then back away from it again.

In the afternoon, Lansbury rose to speak. Almost as if sensing what drama was to come, the entire conference, except for two small groups of trade unionists, got to their feet and sang: 'For he's a jolly good fellow.' Lansbury's speech was uncompromising. 'I have no right to preach pacifism to starving people in this country and preach something else in relation to people elsewhere . . . I have never under any circumstances said that I believed you could obtain socialism by force . . . I am ready to stand as the early Christians did, and say "This is our faith, this is where we stand, and, if necessary, this is where we will die."'

Marvellous and stirring words; but the mood of Conference was not with him. Ernest Bevin rose quickly and spoke, with a sharpness later much criticized as 'virulent' by the delegates, of the distastefulness of taking 'your conscience round from body to body asking to be told what to do with it'. Next day a resolution to call on the government to use 'all necessary measures' through the League to stop the Italians was carried by 2,168,000 to 102,000. George Lansbury resigned as leader of the party.

He lived another four years. He was frail and he had lost his much-loved Bessie two years earlier, but he was not broken. He intended to concentrate what energy he had left on the one cause in which he believed without reserve: trying to stop a war. At the next general election he was returned for Bow with an increased majority, became Mayor of Poplar yet again and started helping refugees from Germany.

Later he was to journey to America with Dr. Salter, a gauche and intolerant figure but just as passionate about peace, on a tour for the American Emergency Peace campaign, and greatly enjoying the stunts put on for his benefit in the 56 towns in which he lectured (flocks of carrier pigeons bearing messages of peace). While he was away the FOR voted to set up 'Embassies of Reconciliation'. Their idea was to send men and women anywhere around the world where trouble seemed to be brewing in order to do what they could to prevent it. Lansbury returned to find himself made an 'Ambassador'; he was to be their only real one.

He was a natural choice, since he had been doing this sort of thing all his life. As early as 1920 he had called on Lenin in Moscow and reported him to be as 'gentle, reasonable and understanding as Lloyd George or Winston Churchill'. Lansbury was always a very charitable judge of character.

In August 1936 Lansbury set off for Paris to see Léon Blum. He hoped the French leader would help him see the other leaders and he wanted to talk about the Belgian Prime Minister Van Zeeland's report on the economic and financial causes of war, as well as his idea for setting up a £1,000 million international development fund to be levied as a proportion of existing military expenditure. Blum, he imagined, would help him sound 'the clarion call for a peace conference'.

In September, Lansbury was in Brussels; then in Denmark, Norway and Sweden. World leaders were affable, but none would take the first step. It was like 1915, when the peace women travelled Europe. So, in April 1937, he set off for Berlin. He had been told that an interview with Hitler could be arranged, and had sent on a list of topics he wanted to discuss, to avoid any 'ranting' stemming from unpreparedness. On his return to England, he told reporters that he could not tell them what he and Hitler had spoken about, because the Führer had sworn him to secrecy. What he could say, however, was that Hitler was a man who fully understood the futility of war, and longed for peace.

Privately, to friends, he added that his impression of the German chancellor was of a 'dreamer and a fanatic . . . I think history will record Herr Hitler as one of the great men of our time . . . free of personal ambition, not at all ashamed of his humble start in life, simple in his mode of living . . . I thought he looked rather a solitary man.' To Clifford Allen, he wrote: 'He will *not* go to war, unless pushed into it by others.'

There was still Mussolini to see. In July Lansbury was in Rome. Once again, he was captivated. Mussolini assured him that he was making a start towards averting war by entering into trade agreements with neighbouring countries and that he would be delighted to play a part in any conference. Lansbury came home describing the Fascist leader as a mixture between Stanley Baldwin, Lloyd George and Winston Churchill (were *all* visionaries and despots like Lloyd George and Churchill?), a man whose face brightened up at any talk of children and the 'masses'. 'It is hard, indeed impossible,' he declared, 'for me to understand how anybody can believe that violence and war is necessary and right when he thinks of children.' It was Candide, in the land of the monsters.

Lansbury, who insisted on travelling modestly, was often tired. Everywhere, he was offered wine and coffee; he longed for tea. To divert himself on these interminable train journeys, he played chess. Still, he had not finished. There was as yet no conference arranged. In December he was off again, to Prague, Warsaw and Vienna.

And then he could do no more. The Foreign Office had not been helpful; and Baldwin was silent. To Lansbury's repeated requests for an interview there was always an excuse. He came back to Bow and started travelling around England, speaking on behalf of the Peace Pledge Union, and writing a book about his missions. He called it *My Quest for Peace*. It ends on a wistful note. 'Surely,' he wrote, 'it is not too much to hope that very soon a better spirit of mutual forbearance and toleration will appear and enable us to live free from such terror.'

Lansbury lived to see the war begin. He died on May 7, 1940. For a week, he lay in state at 39 Bow Road, where the people of the East End, formed and nurtured on Gandhi, the Lester sisters and their implacably pacifist MP, came to pay him their respects. There was often a queue all down the road. Later, when the RAF took to dropping leaflets over Germany, they called it 'Lansbury's war'.

As the world moved into the last 18 months of an aggressive peace, Hitler annexing Austria and soon after Czechoslovakia, followed by the Munich settlement, the pacifists kept on urging negotiations, despite increasing unpopularity. *The Week*, Claud Cockburn's radical news-sheet, was reflecting the communist attitude, attacking the 'pacifists and the do-nothings of the Labour Party'. From Bow, Muriel Lester sent a telegram to Lord Halifax, the Foreign Secretary, asking whether the government could not be courageous enough to acknowledge publicly the mistakes of the Treaty of Versailles. The pacifists may have lived in Utopia, but they were resourceful and persistent. They were fast losing their allies, however, for not even the League of Nations now universally believed in trying to placate the contestants. As Max Plowman, soon to become influential within the ranks of the PPU, remarked, 'The nations of Europe are like a collection of drunken men in the bar-parlour just before closing time'. While the arguments now turned to preparing for war, only a few pacifists were prepared to praise Chamberlain for preserving the peace at Munich, hoping the settlement reached there might be permanent because any alternative seemed too terrible to contemplate.

The others, seeing in Hitler and Mussolini a challenge they had never faced before, a form of evil and malignancy they did not think existed, crumbled. In Britain, as in America, where liberal supporters of the anti-war movement were abandoning their former position and going over to support Roosevelt's views of preparedness, pacifists now accepted that military force was all that was left. Rabbi Judah Magnes, an American World War One pacifist, declared that war with Germany was immoral, but 'we do not know what else to do'.

139

A filmed newsreel remains of the Peace Pilgrimage, one of the last great peace rallies in a decade of almost incessant peace gatherings, peace meetings and peace debates, that took place in February 1939. The film is silent. There is something very moving about the people who file past the camera on their way to Trafalgar Square. They are carrying banners with the names of their towns and universities; the students are wearing gowns and mortar boards, the men dark suits, the women neat white blouses and the tightly curled hair of the moment. It is a sober, joyless occasion. Their expressions are apathetic. They are marching, not because they believe that they can no longer do anything, but because, like other pacifists before them and others after, it is all that is left for them to do.

The early summer saw the last Fellowship of Reconciliation conference before the war, held in Fanø, in Denmark. The early days in Bilthoven had set a pattern: there was something about the northern shorelines and orderly villages that was especially attractive to the pacifists. Muriel Lester joined the delegates after a round of frenetic visits as travelling secretary to Vienna, India, Palestine, France and Germany, where she had made friends with the man who looked after the bears in the Berlin zoo, who turned out to be a pacifist. At Fanø, in between sessions, the peace people, British, Germans, Scandinavians and many Americans wandered along the white sand among nesting colonies of birds; in the afternoons, they spread rugs in the woods near the hotel and slept, and when they woke, they talked about whether it would still be possible to set up an office somewhere in Asia for the duration of a European war that no one any longer believed was not about to come.

In the East End of London, at much the same moment, Sydney Russell was witnessing what was to remain one of his last images of peace. One afternoon, a troop of Hitler youths came to Kingsley Hall, by bicycle. He remembers standing at the door, later that evening, watching them leave: the leader whistled, the boys in their leather shorts, and neat fair hair, stood to attention by the bicycles, formed up in orderly rows. The man whistled again, the boys mounted and waited, right feet on the ground, heads turned to face him. The man whistled a third time and slowly, in perfect, rehearsed unity, the Hitler youths cycled away.

140

The mood, today, is against the 'appeasers' of the thirties. Figures like Lansbury seem misguided, even a little ridiculous. By the 1950s it had become familiar to question whether the strength of the British pacifists of the pre-war years had not enabled Hitler to start his great build up of armaments, as it became known that he was encouraged by the Oxford debate. Except for a small wing of the pacifists, however, none of them really had anything to do with appeasement policy. On the contrary, peace movements as a whole stood for resistance to Hitler, to Mussolini and to Japan; pacifists were passionate anti-fascists and many tried to push the government into resisting Italian aggression in Abyssinia. What was more, after 1935, they were really not very strong. When pacifism was at its height, in the late 1920s and early 1930s, there was little immediate danger of war. As the decade wore on, opposition to rearmament weakened. By Munich, the Labour Party was supporting the 'organization of manpower', even if it remained opposed to conscription.

Because the supporters of the peace movement hated war, they hated fascism, seeing in it the danger of war; because they rejected power politics and the uncontrolled build up of armaments, they advocated collective resistance to aggression and the indivisibility of peace. And when it all failed, they turned quickly to their own personal dilemmas: what should pacifists do in wartime?

6

1939: redefining a faith

William Heard comes from an old naval family. Ancestors, for several generations back, have been officers in the British navy. One, a surgeon, served with Nelson on board the *Victory*. Some time early in 1939, as a schoolboy of just 17, Heard went to the naval barracks at Mill Hill, not far from his home, and asked the officer at the desk whether he might join up. Wait until you reach 18, he was told. Come back then.

When war broke out, Heard was working as a trainee on the switchboard for a firm making electrical instruments. He volunteered for the auxiliary fire service, but was soon dissuaded by his employers, for the electrical instruments had been replaced by essential war equipment and his job was now a reserved occupation. Heard worked shifts; from six o'clock to two one week, two to ten the next.

Among the electrical parts, working not far from him, was a young woman with whom Heard soon became friendly. She was, she told him, a Jehovah's Witness; she talked to him about the Bible. It wasn't anything he knew much about. After work, when they were both on the same shift, they went to Bible meetings together. Heard was an orphan. He and his sister lived with the grandmother who had brought them up; widow of an inventor of seaplanes, she kept a sweet shop and made her own ice creams, sold door to door by a black man wearing a white hat and a white coat. 'She had,' says Heard about his grandmother, 'ambitions for me.' They didn't, apparently, include religious conversion. The day soon came when Heard returned home from the evening shift to find the door locked against him. He had no possessions; his grandmother had not chosen to throw a suitcase of clothes out with him. He never saw her again.

It was not surprising, then, that Heard now drew nearer to his new friends. He began to feel the appeal of a faith that dealt in absolutes and spoke of the Kingdom of God as a real place, with its own paramount laws, based on love and not the confusing messiness he saw all around him. He found it clear, sane and comforting. He liked the Bible study classes, and the sense of excitement that came to him when a person on whose door he knocked during his evening rounds expressed some interest in what he was telling them. He began to feel that he was wasting his time as a clerk in an electrical firm, given over to the laws of a government he no longer felt bound to. One night, when his shift came to an end, he took his tin hat and put it on the table alongside a note telling his employer that he had gone. The firm could have prosecuted him, but he heard no more.

The Jehovah's Witnesses now took him more closely as their own. In March he was baptized, by total immersion, in Bayswater, at the headquarters of the movement. It was a symbol of all he had decided to do, the carrying out of God's will on earth. The elders assigned him to Reading, to live in a caravan and preach their work. But by now the authorities were after him, for, deprived of his reserved occupation, he was just another young man bound for the army like any other.

'I went before my Tribunal,' he remembers, 'and they turned down my request for total exemption. The Appeal court offered me non-combatant work, but I turned that down. Then I waited.' Today, Heard is a recently retired civil servant, living in a semi-detached pebble-dash terrace house in Seaford, on the South Coast. He is a slight, rather serious man, with neat glasses and neat clothes. His manner suggests carefulness, due regard for things; as servants of God, he says, Jehovah's Witnesses look after themselves. He is friendly, but distant. The street on which his house stands is blowy, perched above the water, buffeted by the sea winds so that the plants in the kitchen garden behind are bowed, though orderly. In front, a healthy green hedge protects the small patch of grass and the sitting room window from passing eyes; some six feet tall, it looks forbidding, giving the small house an enclosed, secretive look. It is the only front hedge in the road.

The next summons took the form of an order to report for a medical examination. Heard did nothing. The third directive could not be so easily ignored. It was an order to appear before Acton Police Court. There, the magistrate overruled his explanations, and directed that he be taken under guard to the nearby drill hall for medical examination. Marched there, he was marched back, having declined to remove his clothes. The authorities were polite, disbelieving, a little bored. The mother of his first Jehovah's Witness friend stood his £10 overnight bail. Next morning, the same magistrate sentenced him to six months in prison. It was borstal, Heard being barely 18.

World War Two is not remembered for its cruelty to conscientious objectors, whatever the origins of their pacifism. On the contrary, it is remembered for tolerance, something it had learned from the previous war. But cruelty did occur, even if it was random and unfortunate. There may have been something about Heard, about his slight build, his seriousness, that was provocative, even threatening.

He was one of 30 in his borstal dormitory. One man stood guard. There were no lavatories, only big buckets in the middle of the room. The other boys were a mixed group, young offenders and a few deserters. Heard was the only conscientious objector and the only Jehovah's Witness, though, already wary of people's feelings about his chosen religion, he took care to keep that fact to himself. Night after night, buckets of urine were poured over his head. It was ragging of a vicious kind. Boiling cocoa, when there was some to spare, went down his neck. The warder had not taken to him either. Heard took size five in boots; he was issued with a six and an eight. He asked for and was refused a Bible.

'By day,' says Heard, 'I worked in the tailor's shop. I used to wonder, before the war, who darned in prison. I discovered; it was me. On Saturday mornings I scrubbed the long dark corridors. When they let me have a Bible, I kept it tucked in my shirt, for if I forgot and put it down the boys took it for cigarette papers. Then a Christadelphian conscientious objector came in. He was a panel beater. He didn't have such a bad time. He was my one and only friend.' Heard became an observer of the tyrannies and petty brutality; he watched them, from somewhere in his mind, intent on the Kingdom of God, where he could not be reached by man. He was unhappy, and he did not feel himself to be like the other boys he now called 'ruffians' all about him. He felt different. It did not occur to him to give up his stand. After all, he says, 'I had decided'.

After two front teeth had been knocked out in a fight, Heard was told that his appeal had come up. It was a wasted occasion.

The next prison was Wormwood Scrubs. It was better there; in the mailbag shop he stencilled 'GPO', on the inside and outside of the bags, at a table with three other conchies. One had a long beard; Heard thought him a fool.

The third prison was Oxford. Heard was taken there from Wokingham Police Court, handcuffed to a bigamist. He was told to work in the kitchens. Together with Alfie, the Cat Burglar of Bath, he washed up for 133 men. There was no other pacifist. An old lag by now, he was kept away from other prisoners. He walked the cinders path on his own, round and round, day after day. He was 20. When his sentence ended, a prison committee gave him a shilling with which to return to civilian life. He was not told that he was to stay free, but the authorities had evidently had enough of him. Heard was never arrested again. He spent the remaining years of war on the move, finding what work he could, watching the way that when people felt frightened they took refuge in hating Jehovah's Witnesses. Then he married a girl he had known since he was 11. After the war, he joined the tax office and rose to be inspector before he retired, 36 years later. In Seaford, he has seen the Jehovah's Witness congregation grow from two old ladies to 80 vigorous members. He feels heartened.

Heard remembers his three sentences in prison very clearly, but without bitterness. What he minded most, what sticks in his mind most painfully, was the feeling that he never quite knew what time it was, so that one summer night he got up thinking that it was morning, when it was not yet properly dark. Otherwise, he says, it was really quite simple for him. He could not fight and he could not serve. Jehovah's Witnesses may not put themselves into positions in which they might shed blood; he could not carry a gun, for unwittingly it might be used. 'Neutral' is the word he prefers, neutral in the world's affairs. When one contemplates God's Kingdom as an attainable state, man's wars seem ephemeral things.

The arrival of the Second World War found the British pacifists quiet, even resigned. There was little of the passionate intensity and rancour of 1916, not least perhaps because so many continued to insist, long after the signs of war were plain, that there would be no fighting, that there *could* be no fighting, as long as the British and the French and the Americans did what they should have been doing all along, and redeem the mistakes of the Treaty of Versailles. 'An intelligent population, like the Germans,' remarked Philip Snowden not long before his death in 1937, 'could never have rallied to the call of a leader like Hitler if they had not felt he expressed the national indignation.' The British pacifists, right up until September 1939, went on repeating his words. They spent the closing years of peace in a frenzy of attempted and postponed negotiations, continuing to believe in the unbelievable, that war could be prevented by appeasing the dictators. Even as Hitler was marching into Austria in March 1938 Salter was still insisting: 'You will either have truck with them round the council table or you will have truck with them on the battle field. I believe it is better to have a conference with them now rather than see 20 millions of men slaughtered and all the great towns of Europe laid in ruins.' Only once war had actually been declared did they transfer their allegiance elsewhere, with deep regret and some weariness, and that was to a new movement, for negotiated peace.

Well before any fighting broke out, however, it was obvious to everyone that, for the pacifists at least and particularly the pacifists of war age, this war was going to be a very different affair. The conscientious objectors of the Great War had been pioneers; those of the Second War were about, in Fenner Brockway's words, to 'tread the path they prepared'. Somewhere between 1916 and 1919 a principle had been established: that the final judgement about taking part in a war is made, not by the state, but by the individual. Now that principle was about to be tested, and found to stand up. There was going to be no need for a body as crusading and courageous as the No-Conscription Fellowship, while the one that took its place, the Central Board for Conscientious Objectors (CBCO), was more a welfare organization than an upholder of conscience.

If the official attitude was soon to be much altered, with reason replacing intolerance and incomprehension, the conscientious objectors themselves were also very different men. Pacifists, by definition, are lonely people, especially in wartime. As a statement of faith, opposition to war appears to be

146

reached most often along a private, individual road. In the First War, there was at least camaraderie among the imprisoned men, a feeling of belonging which intensified as the persecution grew stronger; it gave them determination, the sense of being right. As Clifford Allen, serving his second sentence in solitary confinement, in Maidstone Prison, had written to a friend: 'True, my vitality seems to get lower and lower, but I am overflowed with a strength and happiness . . .' There was no such certainty in the Second War. Opposition became a matter of pure faith, a hard kernel of conviction, if not religiously, then at least morally, held, and almost always in solitude. What was most surprising, perhaps, was not that so many entered the war pacifist, but that so many remained pacifist for five years of fighting: for World War Two saw the number of British and American conscientious objectors not diminished, but quadrupled. In Britain alone, just over 60,000 men and women refused to fight.

In the 20 years of peace, furthermore, the pioneer pacifists had largely faded away. The distinctive and learned voices of peace of the Great War were about to be replaced by a less vociferous and generally more ordinary body, whose strength lay in numbers rather than individual heroism. Many of those already in middle age when they made their stand in 1916 — like most of the peace ladies — were dead. Philip Snowden had died, as had Clifford Allen; Lansbury had a few months left to live, Salter a couple of years. Others had gone abroad: Bertrand Russell, Aldous Huxley and Gerald Heard were all in America, as was Rosika Schwimmer, the 'very, very radical feminist', who had made audiences laugh with her jibes against men and who was now fighting a solitary battle for citizenship in New York, blacklisted as a spy, and continuing to refuse to sign the necessary clause about bearing arms. As for the true absolutists, the men like Howard Marten, Mark Hayler, Frederick Dutch or Harold Bing, who had preferred repeated sentences of solitary confinement and even the possibility of death to conscription, well, it was no longer a war for them. In any case, the acrimony had gone. 'It was a bit sniffy perhaps,' remembers Dorothy Bing, soon to be evacuated with her school to the country. 'But we could say openly that we were pacifists.'

On April 1, 1936, the Prime Minister, Stanley Baldwin, was asked in the House of Commons to give a guarantee that conscription would never be introduced while peace lasted. 'Yes, sir,' he replied. 'So far as the present government are concerned.' Slightly less than two years later, when Chamberlain was Prime Minister, the same question was put; the same answer came back. The pledge was reaffirmed during the Munich crisis.

But, as the European chaos worsened, the government grew rather more circumspect in its answers. Conscription, a highly emotive topic for over 20 years, was beginning to creep back on to the front of the stage. In March 1939 Hitler completed his occupation of Czechoslovakia. On April 26, in a mood of some apology, reassuring the House that such a move would be useful in that it would alert the world to the firmness of British intentions, the government announced that they intended to bring in a scheme for six months' compulsory military training for men aged between 20 and 21.

The Labour Party put up a mild fight. Their tone was one of regret, not anger. The way was now clear. In the House of Commons, the principle of conscription was accepted by 376 votes to 145; it was soon followed by the Military Training Bill (1939) under which all 20 and 21-year-old male British subjects were to register, with the exception of men already in the armed services, lunatics and the blind. If the peace movement, elsewhere in the country, seemed to be vigorous and healthy, it was evident that in the Commons it was ailing: when the Bill had its second reading in May it occupied 14 hours of parliamentary time, but considerably less than an hour of that was allocated to the pacifist group, while the MP for Tottenham, a pacifist called Fred Messler, rose 30 times trying and failing to catch the Speaker's eye. Within eight days of the Royal Assent, 240,757 men had been registered. The machinery was all in place, though there was as yet no war.

The remaining months of peace were spent by the political pacifists in battle; they had just one campaign left in them, and they fought it hard. These powers were all very well, they argued, but they might still not be needed. In June, Ernest Bevin told the Labour Party conference that the policy they were pursuing — defence alliances with European powers and rearmament at home — was not encouraging for peace. There was still time, he argued, to pool the resources of the world and tell 'our friends in the middle of Europe, Italy and Japan . . . that we are offering them a place in the sun'. Ten weeks later, Germany and Russia had signed their pact, Germany had invaded Poland and Britain had declared war.

For the few men who had entered Parliament as pacifists and stayed profoundly pacifist, there was really very little left to do. It remained to Alfred Salter, as broken, said his friends, by the declaration of war as Keir Hardie had been in 1914, to sound the valediction. It was an appeal or, if not exactly an appeal, a record, a testimonial that, as Europe returned to war, one parliamentary voice could be found raised in protest. Salter was in his late sixties and not well. He scrutinized the coming programme of the House of Commons and chose a day when he was sure of being called. He stood up very stiff and straight and spoke somewhat softly. There was complete silence and, despite the unpopularity of his words, some sympathy. He was, he said, still a socialist, but it was as a Christian that he seemed to speak. It was his 'Christ in khaki!' speech all over again, a little muted perhaps, but fundamentally unchanged in 25 years. The teaching of Jesus Christ was that 'any creed, however brutal and bestial, could only be overcome and finally eradicated by spiritual weapons, and never by destroying men, women and children indiscriminately . . . Britain and all Europe are rushing down the steep slopes to collective suicide and damnation. Will not somebody, for the sake of Christ, demand sanity and peace?'

There was no one so minded available. By mid-September 1939, 340 Members of Parliament had voted for a National Service (Armed Forces) Bill (there were only 9 votes against) and 230,009 men had registered. However, 5,073 or 2.2 per cent had claimed conscientious objection — the highest percentage ever, before or since. In no less a place than Parliament and by Chamberlain himself, their rights and, more than that, their moral status had been made clear. At the second reading of the bill, six months before the outbreak of war, the Prime Minister had declared that the abuse of conscientious objectors was 'an exasperating waste of time and effort'. 'I want to make it clear here,' he said, 'that in the view of the government, where scruples are conscientiously held we desire that they should be respected and that there should be no persecution of those who hold them.'

In the first few months of the war the young pacifists of fighting age rallied in such numbers that the Tribunals could not handle them. Registering not with the Military Training Boards but with a special new body known as the Register of Conscientious Objectors, there came a moment when they had to wait up to six or even seven months before they received a date for their hearing. All that first winter, the percentage of conscientious objectors to soldiers stood at and around two per cent. To the authorities who had with such pride announced the new spirit of leniency towards men with conscientious scruples, it must at times have seemed an alarming trend, as if the pacifists might swamp the system. But then the numbers fell. By March they stood at 1.6 per cent and then they went on falling, to little over 0.5 per cent.

As in the First War, the 51,419 men who had registered an opposition to war by the middle of 1940 were a mixed bunch, described by Derek Stanley Savage, himself a conscientious objector, as an 'amorphous mass of ordinary well-meaning but fluffy peace lovers'. They were, in this war as in the previous one, teachers and clerks, musicians and shopkeepers, journalists, bank employees and farm labourers.

They were not, however, as politically inspired as they had once been. Rather, British World War Two pacifists were more concerned with morality and the spirit than with questions of socialism or anarchy. True, from the very first, Tribunals were invariably better disposed towards the religious objectors than the political ones, but it is interesting to find that of 3,353 cases dealt with by the south-western local Tribunal in Bristol, over two years, 75 men said that their objection was political, 54 gave a 'humanitarian' or 'moral' reason, for their stand, while the remaining 3,000 or so wrote down 'religion' on their papers. The Methodists headed the list, with 662; the Quakers accounted for 302. Of the 17 organizations that made up the Central Board for Conscientious Objectors, 12 were religious. Religion came in many forms; one Tribunal, in its post-war report, listed members of 51 different religious bodies.

Most of the young men who now refused to serve had not

been born in World War One. They were schoolboys when Japan invaded Manchuria. And, if many had in fact joined the PPU or the League of Nations Association during the heady pacifist thirties, they tended to say now, when questioned about their stand, that it was really their fathers and the Great War that had most strongly influenced them. They might never have described themselves as pacifist, and without a war might well have lived their lives without it. All that was needed was the most subtle of spurs, the reading of some verses by Edmund Blunden, perhaps, or hearing a priest talk about politics and Christianity, to keep the instinct alive. It was as if a little band of men, many unsuspecting but all in their very different ways touched by the 1914–18 war, were primed to turn pacifist. It was all so volatile, so much a matter of chance. The declaration of war was enough to make the resolve harden. And, as with the First War, once the decision was made, very few turned back.

Because, in memory of the unpreparedness and consequent chaos of January 1916, a great deal of planning and thought had gone into this new machinery of conscription, the system for dealing with all this conflicting and often inchoate conscience was considerably better laid down. Men objecting to the war were to be given three choices. They could apply for unconditional exemption on grounds of strict conscience; they could ask for alternative work, within the army but of a non-combatant kind. Or they could request civilian work. The Tribunals to hear them were set up by the Ministry of Labour, with a chairman and four others, one to be agreed on after consultation with a trade union. The chairman was to be a county court judge, a man deemed by the government to possess, by definition, the necessary 'impartiality' though not the 'great and deep understanding of human nature' called for by the Labour MP, C. C. Poole. Those who served under him were academics, solicitors and barristers, chartered accountants and doctors, men, nearly always, and usually in their mid-sixties. George Lansbury was scornful. What was really needed, he said, were not old men like himself 'but persons much younger and persons with an appreciation of what conscience means'. What, however, was a man's conscience? What did the word really mean? That had been, and was to remain, the real question.

The British Tribunals of World War Two have left a picture

151

of fairness. Those appointed to serve, recalling the much-publicized injustices, the horrors of the infamous 'cat and mouse', took satisfaction in the openness of their minds, the tolerance they observed when faced with young men who spoke of the glory of heaven, or the wrongness of this particular war, while admitting that there might indeed exist 'just wars' in which they would be willing to fight. They were eager to understand, bending over backwards to accommodate. Just the same, the Tribunals varied greatly in their different interpretations of conscience.

North Wales rapidly became known for its leniency, handing out 74 per cent of conditional exemptions and rejecting altogether only 6 per cent of the cases laid before them. South-West Scotland was particularly severe, turning down 41 per cent of the men summoned before it. Every applicant, at every Tribunal, was invited to submit a written statement and bring witnesses to help him defend it. In practice their objections to the war ranged from one-line statements, to 30-page essays, which filled their judges with despair. Artists brought their drawings and cartoons; writers their books. It was the duty of the Tribunal not to argue the merits of their case but to ask themselves whether they were really satisfied that the case itself was genuine. One man held to the Kingdom of God, another to an international fraternity of socialists and workers: it was not up to the solicitors and doctors to impose their own preferences, simply to decide whether the young man standing before them actually meant, in full sincerity, what he was saying. The judges could be forgiven some confusion.

The young men themselves, however, could also be forgiven some alarm. If the tone of the Tribunals differed markedly from that of World War One, the actual event did not. The solemnity was all there, particularly as they were usually held in court rooms. 'Would you help a wounded man?' a chairman might ask. To the would-be-conscientious objector's 'yes' would come back. 'Then you have no objection to serving in a non-combatant corps;' to his 'no', the chairman might reply: 'Then you are inhuman. You can't be a genuine Christian [or Quaker, or Christadelphian, or whatever the applicant was claiming]. We won't exempt you.'

At times, the young teacher or bank clerk must have

wondered whether he were not back in the court rooms of the First War, especially when confronted by officials who seemed to take delight in sophistry and ruse. Gone, admittedly, was the old chestnut: 'If your mother was attacked by a German, what would you do?' But in its place was something far subtler, more insidious: 'Don't you think your present work is helping the war effort?' or 'Your church has approved the war; what right have *you*, at *your* age, to question its wisdom?' or 'If you object to taking life, why aren't you a vegetarian?' It was all a bit schoolmasterly, somewhat stern and often very confusing. And not all judges were friendly. 'We will call you the "new contemptibles",' Sheriff Brown, chairman of one of the notoriously harsh Scottish Tribunals, told one unhappy applicant. 'You are a lot of cranks,' said Judge Richardson of Newcastle, to two Jehovah's Witnesses.

This scorn, reminiscent of the bad-tempered dismissals of the Tribunals of the First War, was largely confined to political objectors. Judge Richardson was unusual in dismissing the religious-minded so scathingly; most judges supported them. It was the men with political consciences who had, if not a rough, certainly a chancy time. The spirit of tolerance towards all forms of conscience was certainly implicit in the wording of the Act, but once again it suffered from not being properly spelt out. Up and down the country, young men appearing to oppose, not all wars, but specifically this capitalist war, were regarded with some suspicion, many tribunal members expressing considerable irritation that they should be allowed to 'pick and choose their enemy'.

At the first sitting of the Appellate Tribunal on December 6, 1939, the validity of a man's political conscience arose in the shape of George T. Plume, member of the ILP, originally granted exemption by the London local Tribunal on condition that he remain in his present employment, but now summoned back by an appeal brought by the Ministry of Labour. The Ministry wanted guidance about how they should be dealing with applications of this kind. Was all political objection acceptable providing it was held with sufficient fervour? Or only some kinds? Fenner Brockway agreed to represent Plume.

Denis Hayes, in his book on the conscientious objectors of the Second World War, *Challenge of Conscience*, reprints the hearing at some length. The historian, H. A. L. Fisher, was chairman of the Appellate Tribunal. He summed up what he thought *he* saw in the Act: 'The intention of the state was not to protect every form of conscientious objection; it was not intended to protect the fascist who has an objection to fighting for the government; it was not intended to protect the Welsh or Scottish Nationalists, who may have a conscientious objection to fighting for Britain . . . and it was not intended to protect a socialist who may have a conscientious objection to fighting for a capitalist state.'

Fenner Brockway then rose to give his own interpretation. 'I suppose,' he said, attempting to define something that exercised tribunals for the entire duration of the war, the exact nature of a 'conscience', 'it is a combination of intellectual and moral conviction which is held so deeply that the individual holding it will not recognize any authority which attempts to impose on him a different course from the course which expresses those convictions . . .'

Fisher and his colleagues were not persuaded. The Tribunal upheld the Ministry of Labour's appeal and Plume's name was taken off the Register of Conscientious Objectors. On paper, matters might now have become grim for future political objectors. In fact, little changed. Some local Tribunals continued to reject most political claims, while others continued to respect them, and the Appellate Tribunal resisted laying down any unbendable rule. 'Intensity of conviction', whatever its roots, went on guiding many doctors, lawyers and accountants in their search for true consciences.

It was one of the anomalies of a system characterized by its anomalies that artists and authors fared particularly well, perhaps because the art and writing that came out of the Great War had left such an indelible mark, even on the Tribunal members now in charge of men's consciences. There was considerable tolerance for a view much despised when the young men of Bloomsbury had espoused it 25 years earlier, that creativity was something easily destroyed, possibly for a very long time, by war. Benjamin Britten and the pianist Clifford Curzon both won total exemption, their Tribunals finding that artists devoting their full time to their art were doing so to national advantage. Raymond Farrell, a young dancer, won his plea to be allowed to continue dancing after George Bernard Shaw, ever a quixotic figure in matters of war and conscience, sent a postcard to be read before his Tribunal: 'Skilled dancers are very scarce and their recreative value for tired soldiers enormous.'

These reluctant conscripts were not, of course, on their own. The tribulations of the pioneering conscientious objectors had done more than simply ease the passing of more understanding laws: they had encouraged the growth of anti-conscription bodies which, like the government itself, had learned from the experience of the First War and were now well prepared to take on their side of the struggle. Long before September 1939 there were already some dozen organizations founded on the principle that military conscription is wrong, in that it infringes civil liberty.

During the 'phoney war' Fenner Brockway, still opposed to conscription, though after the Spanish Civil War no longer the absolute pacifist he once was, became chairman of the Central Board for Conscientious Objectors, a federation of 15 different societies. It was all very harmonious. What the young objectors needed, as the veterans well knew, was information: they wanted to be told how to prepare their cases. Soon, 100 different groups, mainly composed of World War One conscientious objectors, were busy around the country. They sent reporters to every Tribunal, so that records could be efficiently kept, and so that any suggestion of bias or excessive bellicosity on the part of individual chairmen could be noted and challenged. As in the First War, members of the Board vanished from their posts from time to time to serve short spells in prison; like Clifford Allen or Fenner Brockway, the men who ran it were more extreme in their pacifism than many of the people they were helping. They never went for long, and in any case there were many others to take their place.

The CBCO attracted, as its predecessor had, mild-mannered and legalistic men who saw in conscription a straight abuse of human rights. One of these was Denis Hayes, a law student from Newcastle who, in 1941, became publications officer for the Board. The CBCO had opened offices in rooms lent by the Peace Pledge Union in the new Dick Sheppard House off the Euston Road. The Quakers donated furniture. Here, three secretaries, a man who kept records, and Denis Hayes worked, as monitors and welfare officers. There was little of the militancy of the First War.

What they were witnessing was a system that now worked. Between the autumn of 1939 and the summer of 1940 over 50,000 men were processed by Tribunals all around the country; while the vast majority of men of military age were setting off to join their regiments or leaving for training, a parallel, though of course much smaller group, was packing for its own pacifist war. They were not allowed to stay at home. In the next few years, teachers and bank clerks, lay preachers and shop assistants were to become road-builders, foresters and miners.

At the start of the war a number of men had been sent to the Royal Army Medical Corps (RAMC), but that quickly became what the papers referred to as a 'lily-livered conchy corps', and then only medical specialists were taken on. In the late spring of 1940 a Non-Combatant Corps (NCC) was finally set up, with 14 companies, and 6,766 men were sent to build and maintain roads, hospitals and barracks. Their officers came from the Auxiliary Military Pioneer Corps, and were for the most part veterans or reservists. There were, of course, truculent and ill-tempered exchanges, particularly with civilian women who, like the Conservative press, led a mild sort of witchhunt against those they considered to be, by definition, cowardly. But, on the whole, the Non-Combatants thrived.

Of the others offered and prepared to accept alternative work, but of a civilian kind, a huge new unskilled but by and large willing force swept out from the cities into the British countryside, assigned to farms where they were to dig ditches, cut down thickets and bring in the harvests. Many had never seen a pitchfork in their lives. But since pacifist teachers were not to teach, and shop assistants had to be carrying out the 'equivalent to war' it was to farms that they went. If the Second War is remembered by the pacifists for anything, it is not for organized brutality or hostility on the part of civilians as much as for the extraordinary randomness of what became of them. Edward Blishen has recorded the sheer incongruousness of the farming conscientious objector's life in *A Cackhanded War*. Blishen was offered exemption on condition that he worked on the land. He was young and fit and perfectly willing. He was told to report for 'ditching, hedging and land clearance' at a farm near the North Sea. Among his fellow pacifists were a member of the Particular People, a very small man with a leathery white face and a vast pair of gumboots; a good-natured Quaker, and a bank clerk who called himself a Muscular Christian and wore his City suit to the fields, where he changed behind a haystack. The fields of his first farm were filled with an assortment of colourful and vague young men, in trilbies, college scarves and plus-fours. There was much lusting after the land girls, almost persistent hunger at the hands of timorous and ungenerous landladies, incessant cold and enduring inefficiency and 'cack-handedness'. It was, records Blishen, a world that was both a bit batty, with several of the pacifists believing in Armageddons and millennia dominated by the devil, and intensely boring.

Blishen makes light of the discomforts. He recalls the cold and the tedium with humour. But not every conscientious objector found this profound sense of isolation and mild pervasive chill of disapproval tolerable, especially when they were billeted on their own, with uncongenial and frankly critical employers. Early in the history of the farming war resisters, a Methodist minister called Henry Carter, a man who had long been preaching temperance and pacifism from his pulpit, began receiving pathetic letters from conscientious objectors working on the land saying that they felt ill-used, lonely and confused. He had the idea of setting up a sort of welfare service for the small pockets of pacifists grouped in farms and forests around Britain. He called his scheme the Christian Pacifist Land Units, and his Methodist supporters were soon joined by people from other churches; then he started recruiting men to act as informal mentors to his units.

One of the people he approached was Sydney Russell, warden of the second Lester sisters' settlement in Dagenham. Russell well remembers his first visit to a group of men working on a chicken farm in Hook in Hampshire. The chicken huts stood barely five feet from the ground, so that even men of average height had to stoop as they worked. After ten hours groping and mucking out in half-light, this depressed gaggle of teachers and accountants would set off on foot for a long tramp to their rooms in a leaky abandoned cottage in the middle of the New Forest. The local villagers would have nothing to do with

157

them, making it unmistakably clear that they were welcome neither in the pub nor in the church. It was not so much inhuman as deeply, humiliatingly, demoralizing. Russell did not feel unreservedly approving of the men he came to comfort, even if his own feelings were totally pacifist; he considered some to be arrogant and others lazy or prickly. But he tried to patch up quarrels that spread rapidly among men who felt themselves punitively and wrongly employed. Things improved, he says, when he was able to persuade the lady of the local manor house to lend him her large and cheerful hall for the men to use as a club twice a week and put a ping-pong table in it.

It was not only the question of poor morale, a sense of being punished for your views by being made to do insanely dull and inappropriate work. Not many conscientious objectors, wherever they were working, found it easy to escape a constant reappraisal of what they had decided to do. The believers in Armageddon, of course, were not so plagued by inner debates. But the others, particularly those who could attribute their pacifism to nothing very much clearer than a Methodist Sunday School teacher or the reading of Siegfried Sassoon's poetry, found the decision not to fight, when so many others were, and were being killed, a tormenting dilemma, particularly as the news from the war grew worse. The fall of Paris found the Tribunals growing tougher in the kind of exemptions they were prepared to grant; it also found the pacifists more troubled.

Ted Milligan was at Reading University when the war broke out. His parents had moved from the Presbyterian Church to the Society of Friends before he was born; he grew up a Quaker. His father was an engineer, a World War One conscientious objector. Neither of his parents was very communicative.

When Milligan was 14 he heard Norman Angell speak on the subject of collective security. It provided the subtle spur, the next layer in what was fast becoming pacifist certainty. Selling *Peace News* on the streets of Reading, he watched the faces of the people who brushed past him: some were disapproving, others looked away embarrassed. No one was openly hostile.

Milligan was a solitary young man. He did not care for the interminable conversations about war and peace inside the PPU meeting rooms and he cared still less for the fashionable Richard Gregg and all his talk about how non-violent power was not really violent at all. He approached his Tribunal with clarity, if also with some loneliness. He was offered, and turned down, conditional exemption, suggested by men he found kind and sympathetic and perplexed that he appeared so un-cooperative. They wanted him to go on doing what he was already doing, working for the Society of Friends, and seemed astonished when he said he would appeal. He felt 'unkind and bloody-minded'. The Appellate Tribunal repeated the same offer; this time he accepted. His protest had been made.

Milligan did not find his war easy; the memory of what he did seems to have affected all the rest of his life. It was hard to remain a pacifist when his best friend was killed fighting, hard to really believe another Quaker pacifist called E. R. Morris, when he said: 'I took my conscience out in 1939 and gave it a thorough spring-clean and don't intend to give it another until the war is over.' Milligan found that his conscience needed constant attention.

He stayed with the Friends' Service Relief until 1946, run-ning hostels for the elderly and those whose homes were de-stroyed in the bombing. Then he went back to Reading to finish a degree in Philosophy and English Literature before training to become a librarian. Later, he wondered whether, confronted with the same dilemma, he would have done exactly the same. 'I was producing a witness,' he says. 'I'm never certain that one changes anything except oneself. But I felt then and feel now that any change in oneself must have, somewhere, some ultimate effect on other people.'

Along the margins of all this work now being carried out across Britain by the conscientious objectors came a number of interesting experiments, especially medical and social ones, that were to endure long after the war ended. It was as if, some-where in the corridors now given over to the pacifists, there was the room, the time and above all the will to explore conditions of ordinary life, often in fact having very little indeed to do with war, in a way that had not been possible before. The sort of men who chose to become conscientious objectors were, by and large, people disposed to be socially useful, people with odd and individual views and ideas of their own. In peacetime they were citizens with more than an average feeling of responsibility. In war, anxious often to prove themselves, they became willing volunteers in a great number of somewhat bizarre schemes. Two of the more unusual had to do with infection.

In 1940, having been turned down by the army as belonging to a reserved occupation, a biologist called Kenneth Mellanby, working as a research fellow on insects, dreamed up the idea of using conscientious objectors as guinea pigs in a study of scabies, which appeared to the authorities to be alarmingly on the increase, particularly among soldiers. The question that no one could answer was how exactly it was being transmitted. Bedding and underclothes were the currently popular explanations.

Henry Carter helped Mellanby find recruits through his Pacifist Service Units. In December 1940 the research biologist moved into a large Victorian villa with a small garden at No. 18 Oakholme Road, Sheffield. The evening he arrived the city was blitzed, casting some doubt over his experiment, since scabies was commonly believed to be highly infectious and he began to wonder how effectively he could segregate his guinea pigs during air raids.

The first to arrive were a former mathematics teacher and an artist. They were joined by an electrician, a milkman, a shop assistant, a ladies' hairdresser, a clerk and a baker. The cooking, washing and housekeeping was shared out equally among them; during the day the men minded a small number of chickens and worked on an allotment. The artist produced a coat of arms, with a small bug and the motto *Itch diens*. There was much good humour.

To test the infectiousness of scabies, the blankets and underclothes from soldiers with the disease had been delivered to Oakholme Road. The pacifists were asked to sleep naked between the blankets and wear the infected vests. The days passed. The baker baked; the hairdresser grew cabbages; the chickens produced eggs. No one contracted scabies. Were scabies, Mellanby asked himself, perhaps something to do with IQ? Was it a venereal disease? Was it connected with dirt? The experiments went on. At last a volunteer came out with scabies; then another. Soon the men were in such an agony of itching that they were to be found prowling around the house at night, naked.

When Mellanby was satisfied that scabies was incubated in

160

the warmth, that it took a surprisingly long time to develop, and that benzyl benzoate was a satisfactory treatment, he switched his volunteers over to different experiments. They ate pound after pound of wholemeal bread, in a research project on calcium deficiency and diet, and then went for days without water, to see how long shipwrecked sailors might reasonably be expected to survive without liquid. It was a surprisingly good-tempered household; the pacifists complained hardly at all.

In London, a somewhat similar experiment, though on a larger scale, had taken shape. When the bombs had first fallen on the city, vagrants along the Embankment, like all other Londoners, had looked for shelter. The problem was that they were covered in lice. The shelter marshals did their best to set up some form of isolation system, but in the dark and the panic it was not always easy. The lice spread.

Soon the vagrants came up with their own solution. When the bombing continued, they took to congregating in one particular shelter in Hungerford Lane, underneath Charing Cross Station, known as Arch 173. It quickly grew filthy. Passers-by would peer into the gloomy depths, where the vagrants had lit fires and crouched around the flames, only their backs and legs visible, their heads and shoulders hidden in the smoke that hung over the cave. Arch 173 reminded people that Dickens had spent part of his boyhood here, in Hungerford Lane, in a blacking factory.

The idea then came to Westminster Council to set up an experiment that would be both socially useful, providing help for the vagrants, as well as medically important, as an enquiry into lice. They approached the Anglican Pacifist Fellowship, a body of Christian conscientious objectors, and Arch 173 reopened as the Hungerford Club, with bunks, baths and a cooking area, on February 26, 1941.

Arch 173 was a highly popular shelter. Police searched the Embankment for suitable candidates, who had to be over 30 and destitute. They came willingly. Regulars were issued with blue tickets, entitling them to permanent accommodation. Then the lice-collecting began. The pacifists, working closely with the Medical Research Council, embarked on a Herculean task of ridding their nightly guests of lice, which had to be caught, stored in containers and sent off to various laboratories.

One visitor was rumoured to possess a record herd of some 15,000 insects.

Within a short time, the lice had been eradicated. The pacifists were delighted, the Medical Research Council rather less so. Calls came in for more lice. The conscientious objectors gamely took to breeding them themselves, wearing small collecting boxes strapped to their upper arms, bare to the skin on one side, while the top was covered over with fine gauze to stop the lice escaping. Arch 173 saw 4,500 people pass through its dormitories by the time the war ended. It remained a cheerful but determinedly ragged place, the vagrants continuing to light their fires and hang their washing from nails in the brickwork.

These experiments suggest a widespread sense of good humour towards and on the part of the war resisters. This gives a somewhat false impression. There were absolutists in the Second War, men who would have no truck at all with the military system, as there had been in the First, and not all of them won unconditional exemption at the Tribunals. These were men whose conscientious scruples were not thought convincing, or who had the bad luck to appear before more sceptical or choleric Tribunals.

For those men, offered alternative service and refusing it, trouble began early. The first court martial took place on March 12, 1940. Kenneth Makin was a 22-year-old Christadelphian, and his request for total exemption had been refused by Newcastle-upon-Tyne Tribunal. He was told to report for duty at Dalkeith, and sent a subsistence allowance and a travel warrant to get there. He returned them with a covering note: 'I do not need the one and I have not earned the other.' On the night of February 20, just as he was going to bed, a policeman arrived and took him off to a military guard room. His court martial, held a few days later, decreed that he should serve 60 days' detention and he was driven away to prison in Glasgow, where he was forcibly stripped of his civilian clothes and locked up in his cell with a uniform. He did nothing. Three times, soldiers came into his cell and forcibly dressed him. Each time, he took the uniform off again. It was very cold. He was kept in solitary confinement, on bread and water. After nine days, he was taken back to Dalkeith where he was put in hospital with suspected pneumonia.

Forcible dressing in military uniforms and medical examinations became the spark for repeated courts martial and sentences. In the First War, medical examinations had been of little significance, carried out only after induction into the army, and even then only cursorily. In the Second War the army wanted only fit men. Examinations were to take place before induction. Prosecutions against those who refused them began in May 1940. The sentences started out as fines; rapidly they led to 'indefinite detentions', the men held simply until they accepted an examination, but after repeated failures this was changed to a maximum two-year prison sentence or a £100 fine. By the end of July, 68 conscientious objectors had been prosecuted. The notorious 'cat and mouse' was back, men being given sentences too short to permit them to apply for a Tribunal hearing, 84 or even 90 days, when 91 would have been enough. The passing of a new bill in March 1941, making civil defence compulsory, and in particular fire watching — which many conscientious objectors had been doing perfectly willingly on their own initiative, but refused to do under compulsion — produced a fresh number of prosecutions and prison sentences. The prisons to which they were sent were rated, much as in the First War, according to their 'pleasantness'. Lewes came top, then Dorchester, then Maidstone, said to have a particularly sympathetic Governor. Birmingham was regarded as the worst. In Wakefield, there was a moment of resistance, a mild sort of strike, when a dozen prisoners refused to accept army blankets or parade in gas masks, but that was small stuff compared to the confrontations of the First War, and soon quelled by punishment on bread and water.

Inevitably, it was not long before stories of brutality were heard. As more arrests were made, as the war grew more intense, as the blitz caused more civilian casualties, so resentment grew. During air raids, conscientious objectors in prison were left locked up in their cells. Later, many recorded the particular terror, when they felt themselves to be like helpless rats locked up in small cages from which there was no escaping a bomb. In June 1941, two men died when their cells received direct hits in Walton Jail, Liverpool.

Two places, Dingle Vale and Ilfracombe, where conscientious objectors in any number were held in detention, have left stories of intentional, systematic cruelty. The accounts of the men who suffered it are revealing, because they show how normally sane men, in this case soldiers and prison officers, can be reduced to incoherent fury and an irrational, overwhelming desire to hurt, when confronted by pacifist stubbornness. It was as if there was something about these opponents of war, for the most part quiet, well-mannered but absolutely intransigent men, that was provocative beyond all enduring. The more bellicose among their jailers could, quite simply, not bear it. They resorted to an inarticulate attempt to destroy them, physically as well as mentally, until forcibly restrained, and eventually prosecuted, by the authorities.

Arthur McMillan was a chartered accountant in his early twenties, living in Forest Gate in East London, when war was declared. He and his wife to be, Muriel, were both Methodists, recent converts, regular attenders at a church where pacifism was much debated and generally much applauded. More than other religions, pre-war Methodism was extremely outspoken on the subject of war and peace: among the many pacifists I have talked to, a remarkably large number said they owed their belief to Methodist teachers.

The last months before the war were spent in endless talk about Christianity and warfare and what the local young men should do if conscription were introduced. Arthur McMillan, like the others, joined the PPU and the Fellowship of Reconciliation, and during the long summer evenings of 1939 other young Methodists came from surrounding parishes to this edge of the city to talk. They vowed to stand firm in their pacifism, to act as witnesses in the event of a war they deplored; Muriel McMillan remembers that people spoke of grains in a desert, and how they felt at the same time very strong and very helpless. When the call-up papers came, all the young men applied for exemption. Only Arthur was unlucky enough to have his request turned down.

Arthur McMillan died some years ago. His widow lives in a house outside Saltdean, on the South Coast, with her brother, another pacifist who survived the war years in alternative civilian work. They have an impeccably neat garden, with highly-coloured herbaceous borders curving round rockeries up and down the sloping terraces, for their house is on a steep hill overlooking the sea. There is a loggia, which catches the sun. Muriel has kept her husband's letters from Dingle Vale, Ilfracombe and Hull. She received them, week after week, while working in the Hungerford Club among the lice in London. They show how very anxious a young pacifist could be, how very perplexed but also how very tenacious, and it is possible to see, in McMillan's measured, concerned tone, something of what it was that drove the guards to impotent and insane fury.

McMillan had been offered alternative service, in the Army Medical Corps. He refused it. Orders came for him to report to Dingle Vale, in Liverpool. There he stayed until his court martial. When he refused to put on a military uniform, he was jostled and pushed about, but he was not hurt. From a neighbouring cell, late at night, he heard sounds of a man being beaten up. It was not until he reached Ilfracombe, late in the winter of 1941, that his bad time really began.

Ilfracombe
21/2/41

It has been a most awful day for me — I promised to let you know when I felt depressed and I will keep my promise. I really have felt absolutely rotten today . . . The officers and NCOs are all very friendly and decent but the trouble is that all the other fellows here are going to do the work . . . it would be so easy to do the work, doing it in harmony with others instead of standing alone and wrecking what is a grand relationship . . . You must not gather from the foregoing that my resolution has weakened. Far from it, but it is very hard.

27th Feb 1941

Yesterday there was a parade for dental inspection and as usual I refused to parade (I have never paraded yet of my own free will — they have always had to push me and of course I do not resist) . . .

Then we had to left turn and march. They left turned and marched. I maintained my status quo and for my trouble got a push, and then, in my weakness, I, too, marched. I have never felt more ashamed of myself in my life — a c.o. in military

165

uniform marching with a hideous mask on his face — a would-be follower of Christ, one who claimed to be born again, being trained to help murder his fellow men . . .

When the roll-call was finished, it was left turn, so I just stood there. Quick march. They all marched and I stood still. The sgt. maj. came up and said 'Go on, march' and pushed me. I went as far as his push took me. Again a push and again a halt. Again and again. It must have been a funny sight to see him push me up Ilfracombe High Street . . . One feels so obstinate to keep refusing, but what else can be done? We dismissed on returning, but I did not salute.

On March 13, 1941 Arthur McMillan was again court-martialled, for refusing to obey military orders. He was one of ten conscientious objectors to appear, and the only one to have finally accepted a military uniform. They were sent off to Hull prison to serve their sentences. It was here that ill treatment started, of a regular, relentless kind, though McMillan himself escaped the worst of it. They arrived to hear that a conscientious objector had just broken his neck, having been ordered to do something by a sergeant while standing at the top of some stairs who had then lost his temper and flung him down to the bottom. The man was dead. It was not an auspicious arrival.

Three of us arrived at Hull in the charge of an armed sgt. and three other escorts and we marched to the prison, a huge building with great big strong gates which denied all possibility of escape. Those doors give a sort of feeling of being utterly cut off from the world and indeed it is so. We passed in and were met by a sgt. who instantly ordered us to face a wall . . . The language of the warders is the filthiest it is possible to imagine . . . They call you all the dirtiest names imaginable and everything is said at the top of the voice in a hoarse yell or a hysterical scream. To a Christian it is simply revolting and extremely shocking . . .

However, the other two fellows with me were not in uniform (they had not been forcibly dressed) and they had also refused to carry their kit-bags . . . They were then lifted up bodily and literally thrown at this great gate, with such force that it shook. I thought they would be knocked insensible, but they were not and they were then punched and ill-treated by the sergeants who were yelling and screaming at them in a really terrifying manner . . . in an hysterical manner with falsetto voices, and it seemed just like men in an asylum. . .

... still in civvies they refused to put on Army uniform. They were each seized by several sergeants and thrown on the stone floor and their civilian clothes were literally torn off them ... They were then brutally assaulted. They were grabbed by the throats and held till they got red in the face and I got really alarmed ... Then they were held up against the wall by one sergeant while others took turns at punching them in the stomach and below the belt ... My two friends were naked when we went up to the cells and for a long time in that first evening I could hear the hysterical screams and yells at them and the noise of slaps and punches on bare flesh ...

There are more letters, in the same tone, almost dispassionate. Brutality gave way eventually to petty tyranny; the men were half-starved and not allowed to use a lavatory. Arthur McMillan did one further prison sentence, three months in the civil jail in Shrewsbury, before an Appeal Tribunal directed him to land work, which he accepted, in one of Henry Carter's units near Epsom. In time, a number of soldiers responsible for acts of cruelty towards conscientious objectors were court-martialled but few received more than reprimands, not least because the pacifist witnesses proved too forgiving, vacillating, while giving evidence, between a desire to tell the truth and a desire to be charitable.

By the end of 1946, the Central Board had recorded 1,050 conscientious objectors who had been court-martialled. One, a Gilbert Lane from Wallington in Surrey, was court-martialled six times; 106 men were tried three times, 210 twice. Many, like William Heard, the Jehovah's Witness from Mill Hill, unexpectedly found themselves released into civilian life for no very good reason, except perhaps that Sir James Grigg, Secretary for War, was one of the least conventional of Cabinet Ministers, and it would have been in his style to order their release.

In the world outside, well away from the military and the courts martial, the British pacifists led a muddled, uncertain existence. It was all a question of luck. People could comprehend the stand that was being made, but they could, as Dorothy Bing noted, be 'sniffy'. If the real vitriol levelled against those men and women who had failed to support the First War was missing, there was still a certain amount of abuse. In the *Daily Mail*, Charles Graves described the young men appearing before their

Tribunals as 'youths . . . actuated by motives which turn out to be pure selfishness and personal cowardice, and which they try to disguise by bogus theology and claptrap phrases . . . but most of them are scared stiff'.

Though there were few persistent polemicists against the war resisters, a certain taunt, that they were at heart pro-Nazi, was repeated in some literary circles. In a celebrated piece in the *Partisan Review* George Orwell called them the 'fascist gang'. If they imagine, he wrote, 'that one can somehow "overcome" the German army by lying on one's back, let them go on imagining it, but also let them wonder occasionally whether this is not an illusion due to security, too much money and a simple ignorance of the way in which things actually happen . . .'

The PPU, that once stalwart pacifist voice, was not weathering the war well. After the first declaration of hostilities there had been a sudden sharp rise in membership, so that early in 1940 the sponsors were able to report a record figure of 136,000 (even so, barely half their original target), but with the blitz and the fall of France supporters dropped sharply away. Before he died, Dick Sheppard had warned that, if war should come, then half the men and women who had signed his pledge would disappear. He was right. It was not easy keeping members, and practically impossible recruiting new ones, against a background of stories about concentration camps and the Gestapo, and ever-growing casualties.

Then the sponsors themselves began fading away as well, the writers and philosophers and politicians who had made of the PPU the most intellectually prestigious lobby in the country. Storm Jameson wrote to announce her resignation and switched her energies to helping refugees; after her came Ellen Wilkinson, Rose Macaulay and Bertrand Russell. Russell's defection was scarcely a surprise. As early as 1937, he had been writing to Gilbert Murray from America: 'Spain has turned many away from pacifism. I myself have found it very hard . . . You feel "they ought to be stopped". I feel that, if we set to work and stop them, we shall, in the process, become exactly like them and the world will have gained nothing. Also, if we beat them, we shall produce in time someone as much worse than Hitler as he is worse than the Kaiser. In all this I see no hope for mankind.'

More surprising perhaps, and possibly more wounding to pacifist morale, after C. E. M. Joad and Dr. Maude Royden also defected, was A. A. Milne's betrayal: the apostle of the anti-war movement of the early thirties, the best-selling author of passionate books about peace at any price, who not so long before had insisted, 'In the next war I shall be a conscientious objector . . . No law of God or Man can ever persuade me that it will be my duty . . . to kill any of those boys', now rushed into print with a pamphlet, *War with Honour*. It was a reversal of all he had said before. Just as passionately, Milne now argued that 'one man's fanaticism has cancelled rational argument'. Hitler, he said, was something different and thus this war, too, was different. 'It is a war for the destruction of all Christian and civilized values. Not a war between nations, but a war between Good and Evil.' Hitler 'is the self-elected, self-confessed anti-Christ', announced the man who had probably won more converts to the pacifist position than any other writer of the decade; 'Evil is his God.'

Much of the spunk now seemed to leave the PPU, which looked for a time as if it might even be closed down by the authorities. Questions were asked in the House of Commons about its 'pernicious propaganda'. The PPU was not, however, seeking controversy. When, in early 1940, it printed a poster reminiscent of Tolstoy, with the words, 'War will cease when men refuse to fight. What are YOU going to do about it?' and was prosecuted, the poster was rapidly withdrawn and the six PPU officials who had been summoned and bound over for 12 months swore to take more care in the future. (In some people's minds the PPU had acquired a taint that it never quite lost. In *The Meaning of Treason* Rebecca West was later to refer to it as 'that ambiguous organization which in the name of peace was performing many actions certain to benefit Hitler'.)

Peace News itself, squeezed by paper rationing down to four tightly-packed pages, reported in each issue whatever news it could discover about pacifists in other countries. On two separate occasions, early in the war, it took passages lifted from the Indian weekly, *Harijan*, edited and largely written by Gandhi, urging the Jews to take the course of non-violence. Jews, he wrote, should start to practise, 'not the passive resistance of the weak' but the 'active non-violent resistance of the strong'. 'If the Jews can summon to their aid the soul power that comes only from non-violence, Herr Hitler will bow before the courage which he has never yet experienced in any large measure in his dealings with men.'

From all round the country now came dozens of stories about individual acts against the civilian pacifists — in 1940, in Blackpool, an Anti-Conscientious Objector League was formed — particularly on the part of councils, many of which were busy voting to dismiss or not to employ war resisters. Of 63 County Councils, 19 sacked their conscientious objectors. Councillors professed themselves disgusted and unwilling to succour the conchies, particularly when local dignitaries threatened to stop paying their rates unless they dismissed them, or when council buildings where conscientious objectors were employed, as in Manchester, were stoned.

Debates in council chambers everywhere were interminable and acrimonious. Was it, members asked each other, practical to rid themselves of all pacifists? Was it legal? Was it *right*? Some spoke of 'leprous sores' or 'yellow streaks'. Arthur Smith, Muriel McMillan's brother, the gardener in Saltdean, was a school dental officer with the London County Council when war broke out. Pacifist like his sister, he registered as a conscientious objector. A paragraph about him appeared in the local paper. Soon, his case filled the entire letters column. Correspondents were universally hostile. How could a man work for the state, and accept public money, but then refuse to take his responsibilities seriously and fight for his country? Going home in the evenings, he found the neighbours distinctly cool. The LCC decided to place him on unpaid leave for the duration of the war. Smith began applying for jobs. He was short-listed for a job in Brighton, then called back and offered the job. 'I said to them: you should know that I am a conscientious objector. They asked me to leave the room. When I came back in, the chairman said: "Get your fare from the office and look sharp about it!"' From then on, he always put 'conscientious objector' on his application forms; he was never again short-listed.

Particularly victimized were teachers, since the local education committees tended to take their cue from the Council decision. It was not unusual, whatever the protest from central government, which spoke angrily about 'heresy hunts', to hear

170

that teachers had been asked to sign a declaration saying that they were not conscientious objectors, members of the PPU or against the war. It was as if pacifism was a contagious disease, especially harmful to children. In time, the hostility mellowed, though it was always to reflect the fortunes of war, intensifying during losses and great battles, diminishing at times of victory. By the end of 1941 many councils had swung round, not least because so many pacifists had proved themselves so courageous in the blitz, and there was in any case by now a growing shortage of labour.

Against all this sniping, both muted and simmering, has to be set the admittedly small, but extremely articulate and committed, group of men and women who held firm to their pacifist convictions and spent the war campaigning, in a long uneasy truce with the authorities, broken from time to time by confrontations. The war brought out the skills and talents of renowned pacifist speakers, many of whom congregated around Muriel Lester and Kingsley Hall, and whose oratory is still well remembered in the 1980s by people who gathered in hundreds round the soap boxes in Victoria and Hyde Park.

The Methodist preacher Donald Soper was particularly powerful; his voice was firm and carrying, and with his somewhat phlegmatic expression and rather long face he would stare out from behind his glasses, pacing up and down before enormous congregations, gathered at Tower Hill, scene of the dock strikes of the 19th century, preaching a pacifist Gospel, in which he interpreted Jesus's teachings as categorically forbidding the taking of life or the use of violence. War, for Soper, was quite simply contrary to the will of God. Most of the best-remembered peace speakers of the war were ministers, and many of them, like Soper, Methodist. But there was also the Rev. Paul Gliddon, of the Anglican Pacifist Fellowship, who held a communion service much liked by the pacifists in the crypt of St. Paul's Cathedral on Thursday mornings, and Patrick Figgis, of the Congregational Church, who thundered out his message of Christian pacifism to an increasingly uneasy congregation of stockbrokers in Sanderstead in Surrey. These meetings, recalls Soper, for whom listeners turned out in thousands rather than hundreds, were on the whole good-tempered, though they attracted a small group of hecklers, who jeered and

171

yelled; he was apparently very good at handling them. Soper speaks now of the euphoria of the marches, the meetings, the rallies, but has some note of regret: 'We were,' he says, 'more concerned with the pilgrimage than surveying the towers of the New Jerusalem.'

The peace speakers tended to be men. But the Second War produced its own crop of peace women, and if they had little of the panache and exoticism of a Rosika Schwimmer or a Jane Addams they were tireless and convinced in their crusade. From the very first issue of *Peace News* in 1936 there was a definite feminist corner: 'Women must be earnest about peace! Eliminate warlike toys.' By the middle of December 1939 Vera Brittain, Sybil Thorndike and Ruth Fry had taken the Central Hall in Westminster — 'women say: stop the war!' — and founded a Women's Peace Campaign. When the call-up extended to women, the PPU opened its own women's section. And it was Vera Brittain, later to become chairman of the PPU, who helped to form a Campaign for the Abolition of Night Bombing, which, though it singularly failed to influence the outcome at Hamburg or Dresden, did touch people's consciences and later made a considerable mark when it turned to highlighting the appalling starvation in occupied Europe. America did not produce her fiery peace ladies of 1915, but it did produce Pearl Buck, the writer, who, from West Virginia, declared: 'The power of women is a subtle thing. It is the influence which every woman has upon some particular man. Let that woman convince that man that war is foolish because it gains nothing and that he is a ridiculous figure when dressed up in a uniform, and the first step to world peace will have been taken.'

Public feeling was not always easy to gauge, especially about those not in government service. Individual pacifists tended to keep their heads down, trying not to provoke antipathy. No one has left a more vivid impression of the randomness, the perplexities of the war for those who opposed it, than Frances Partridge, whose published diary of the time, *A Pacifist's War*, spans the years 1940 to 1945.

Frances Partridge grew up very much within the fringes but not precisely in the centre of Bloomsbury. Though a visitor to

George Lansbury planting an inaugural tree at Kingsley Hall; behind him to the right are standing the two Lester sisters.

A Kibbo Kift rally.

Gandhi leaving Friends House in September 1931; on the left are Krishna
Meran and Lawrence Houseman.

Muriel Lester and Bayard Rustin on a pre-war Fellowship of Reconciliation
tour of the United States.

Dick Sheppard.

A World War Two woman
prisoner in Holloway Prison.

Alternative service on the land in World War Two.

Pastor Martin Niemöller.

Garsington Manor, she was too young to share in the endless deliberations on war of the Stracheys and the Bells. Rather, as an 18-year-old girl, with a 'belligerent Irish mother', she remembers the excitement. In her eighties, a lined, charming, highly rational woman, she says: 'Now war is seen as insane, people who aren't as old as me don't realise the glory with which men went off.'

It was not in fact until the thirties, when married to Ralph Partridge, a much-decorated soldier but full of horror about the war that he had fought, and when she travelled around Europe and heard people talking about Nazi Germany, that something of what war meant really came to her. She never went to the PPU or any other pacifist meetings; Bloomsbury didn't.

Between 1940 and 1945, Frances and Ralph Partridge and their small son Burgo lived at Ham Spray, Lytton Strachey's house on the Hampshire Downs. Ralph Partridge applied for, and was granted, exemption, having spent agonizing days preparing an eloquent testimony. 'The ethical basis for my profound conviction that war is wrong in itself and all its consequences,' he told his judges in March 1943, 'is that I believe human behaviour should be governed by reason which is all that distinguishes us from brutes . . . that the organized violence of war is infinitely worse than individual acts of violence because for political reasons it is exonerated by the state and even glorified . . . I respect the authority of the state wherever my conscience is not at stake, but I claim the right to refuse to take lessons in murder, which is what military service is about.' For five years, Frances was an observer of a war she deplored, following its victories and defeats from afar. But she was also a wary and acute commentator on people's attitudes to it, and to those of her friends who had taken the pacifist path. She writes of the people, like Gerald Brenan, who stopped being friends once Ralph Partridge had formally become a conscientious objector, and about the mild, unpredictable disapproval that came from the village. The Partridges were devoted readers of the *New Statesman* and she was much irritated by the way the paper seemed to her to switch its attitudes all the time. In August 1940, she noted that there was a 'Spanish war addiction', the view that the Spanish Civil War was the only one worth fighting; a 'line that war isn't so bad' in that it was good for

173

democracy and unemployment and that in any case not all that many people had died; a 'quiet natural-history attitude of Vita Sackville-West ("Our village in an air-raid")' which she found silly. 'Last, but one I find more and more painful, is the semi-erotic excitement about the brave young airmen in danger.'

It is an onlooker's war, private, always sane, sometimes humorous, with its visiting refugees and occasional trips to London. When finding herself next to a woman on the train she would talk about the pacifist position and try to explain how sons sent to kill for their country would not necessarily die but they would probably kill some other mother's son. 'Wrote letters,' she records, on April 12, 1941, as Cyrenaica was being retaken and the Balkan Campaign beginning and Germany prepared to invade Russia, 'sitting on the verandah most of the morning — the sky perfectly blue: peace visible, tangible and audible; the cows lying down in the field; Burgo and R's voices by the bonfire under the glossy leaves of the Portugal laurel, the bees buzzing in the grape hyacinths; far off the hum of a tractor. No aeroplanes. Positive happiness invaded me, and though I know that it is achieved at the cost of ostracism, I cling to it and do not want to lose it.'

7

Back to the Tribunals

The German military breakthrough in Europe in the early summer of 1940 was a moment of decision for many British pacifists. The movement split. Those who had never been absolutely clear, those who had been swayed by Spain, or momentarily seduced by the rhetoric of A. A. Milne, now resigned themselves to the war. The others seemed to react by turning sharply inwards, away from everyday facts, away from broadly-based socialist pacifism and towards a far narrower Christianity and sectarianism. It was hard, now, to think of pacifism as a practical measure. The only honest alternative seemed to lie in Canon Morris's 'redemptive minority', the notion that pacifists should become witnesses, upholders of a morality that would in time enable society as a whole to advance spiritually. It was not, these pacifists appeared to be reassuring each other, selfish to turn away; it was all for the greater good of mankind. Aldous Huxley and Gerald Heard had been saying as much from California. It was time for those who stayed in Britain to re-examine and re-affirm the depth of their own consciences. In surprisingly large numbers, they now turned to the idea of setting up pacifist communities.

There was nothing altogether new in Britain in the idea of a retreat into spiritual witness at a time of war, in order to live a life dedicated to getting ready for peace, so that when it came a new social order might be born with it. It had strong roots in the late 19th century cult of the garden and the land as a regenerative power for a sick society. At Letchworth, in 1903, enthusiasts for the simple life, Tolstoyans, trade unionists, socialists, followers of Ruskin, had all welcomed a Garden City that was to be a 'Utopia of clean, pure air, flowers and perpetual sunshine', in which the inhabitants were to wear knickerbockers and sandals, eat vegetables and read the works of H. G. Wells, Tolstoy and William Morris.

D. H. Lawrence had also been drawn by this talk of countryside. In 1910, while a teacher in Croydon, Lawrence had lectured on social problems, with a view, as he wrote, 'to advancing a more perfect social state and to fitting ourselves to be perfect citizens — communists — what not'. At Garsington Manor, just before the First World War, he and Lady Ottoline Morrell would discuss their revolt against 'the rule and measure mathematical folk'. In January 1915 Lawrence was describing his dream to gather together 'about twenty souls and sail away from the world at war and squalor and found a little colony where there shall be no money but a sort of communism as far as necessaries of life go, and some real decency'. His listeners included Aldous Huxley, Bertrand Russell and John Middleton Murry. Lady Ottoline was to be President, and Garsington Manor the retreat 'where we will come and knit ourselves together', washing off the 'oldness and grubbiness and despair' of England.

The others did not appear to take it all very seriously. It was fun, over dinner, to talk as if a new world could really be founded. Russell was soon a central part of the No-Conscription Fellowship and on his way to jail; the others went back to their books. But Lawrence, observing that 'we are hardly more than ghosts in the haze, we who stand apart from the flux of death', started a magazine he called *Signature* to recruit disciples; and, when that foundered, he began to talk about going to live in America, possibly in Florida, with a group of people who shared his views and would help him establish a new life, in a community he called Rananim, from the first line of a Hebrew dirge. In preparation, he moved to a cottage in Cornwall and invited friends to group around him and explore the possibilities of communal life. The Middleton Murrys came down, but did not care for the countryside, finding it bleak and stony. Eventually Lawrence left England; there had been several rather merry dinners at the Café Royal, musing over the Andes and Mexico, but in the end he and his wife Frieda, made wretched by local suspicion and general anti-German feeling, left, with Dorothy Brett, his only recruit, for America, to a 9,000-foot-high ranch in the Sangre de Cristo Mountains north of Taos.

His preoccupation with a new society had, though he was not to know to what extent, left a mark; something of his spirit lingered with John Middleton Murry. In 1933, three years after

Lawrence's death, Murry bought a house near Colchester called The Oaks, at Langham, and named it the Adelphi Centre. It was to be a place where socialists 'could keep fit for the battle of life against death by constantly renewing their morale'. The Adelphi Centre, wrote Murry, a Marxist and strong supporter of the League of Nations, was to encourage monasticism, and train socialists, real socialists, not 'socialist politicians'. In 1934, Murry resigned from the ILP which was ideologically anti-war but not in the spiritual way he wanted, and organized the first of what were to be three very successful summer schools. Blake's proverb, 'Religion is politics and politics is Brotherhood', became the Adelphi's motto.

Not very long after its foundation Max Plowman took over the editing of the Adelphi's paper. Plowman was a disciple of Blake and a good friend to the supporters of the Garden City dream. He was also a convinced pacifist, having been fired by the First War to write a 'paean in praise of creative peace', though he disliked the word 'pacifist', saying that to him it sounded unpleasant, too Protestant, too odd. Plowman referred to war as 'race suicide' and was intent on marrying pacifism to the idea of communities, which he saw as places governed by 'elders' who decided their policies. When, in the summer of 1936, Murry seemed to be turning away from pacifism over Spain it was Plowman who drew him back, during a week spent together on the Norfolk Broads, largely by pressing on him his own book *The Faith Called Pacifism* which had just been published, and by introducing him to Dick Sheppard.

Murry now underwent a complete change. He joined the PPU, left the Adelphi Centre, somewhat to the consternation of his followers and produced a book of his own, called *The Necessity of Pacifism*, in which he declared that true socialism is by necessity pacifist, and the true socialist, having failed to find answers in economics, must find them in 'human' solutions, while becoming a member of 'a movement which has something quite simple to say: "Refuse all complicity in war and take the consequences."'

By the time war broke out Murry had reached the conclusion that the only true role for a pacifist socialist was that of witness 'against the total dehumanization of humanity'. The Adelphi was turned over, largely on the insistence of Max Plowman, to a home for refugee Basque children from the Civil War, and Murry, having accepted the editorship of *Peace News*, began encouraging people around him to start up pacifist land communities. He had read about the kibbutz experiments in Palestine. The communities he envisaged were to be witnesses of goodness in the coming age of darkness, models for a new social order and bastions against the collapse of the old one. 'Henceforth,' he announced, 'the true concern of pacifists is to help build a religious political movement which could endure the incalculable moral and material stresses of total war . . . I see in the pacifist movement the raw material of a new Christian Church . . . the leaven that will leaven the lump of the new civilization which must come, for assuredly we are in the death throes of this one.'

Murry was not dreaming on his own. Communities were now opening every week, in Essex and Norfolk, Gloucestershire, the Rhondda Valley and even London, where a small group of pacifists living in Kentish Town survived the war by reconditioning and remaking old clothes and selling them. There was no exact model for these new Utopians to turn to, though many now began to examine the Brüderhof, the fundamentalist Anabaptist Christians who had arrived from Liechtenstein as a group of strolling players early in 1936 and had set up their commune at Oaksley in the Cotswolds.

The Brüderhof had been founded in Germany in 1920 as a community based on obedience and brotherly love by a German academic and organizer in the Student Christian movement called Eberhard Arnold. The universe, believed Arnold, involved a death struggle between good and evil; God was at the head of the forces of good, which would ultimately triumph. Man could help, if he renounced his own ego, allowed himself to be filled with the Holy Spirit, and listened to God's calls for him to bear witness to the spirit of peace and love in all simple daily activities.

The Brüderhof were not in tune with Hitler's Germany. By the early thirties they had merged with the Huttrian Church in Alberta, and, having adopted its customs, were now dressed the Huttrite way, the men in heavy beards and the women in long skirts, bodices and head scarves. Under threat from the Nazis, they moved, first to Liechtenstein, and then on to England.

Organized, hierarchical and extremely disciplined, the Cots-
wold Brüderhof thrived; their farms prospered; they took in
refugee children and, as conscription came, conscientious objectors who were looking for alternative work on the land. The
rules were strictly enforced; all wealth and property were
shared, and no brother could take part in politics, whether of a
national or local kind. (Only once in their history, it is
thought, have they wavered. A community in America not
long ago, much caught up with the civil rights movement, con-
templated voting in the Johnson–Goldwater presidential elections. In the end they refrained. 'We decided,' the community
announced, 'that politics was just not our way.')

The communities that were coming together around
England had other, somewhat less esoteric, roots. Kingsley
Hall had been the natural choice for a conference that took
place one day in 1937 when some 150 people from various
churches and societies agreed to meet to discuss how best to
express Christian pacifism and Christian political thought in
action. By next morning, 25 were found to be still there, sleeping in odd corners of the warren-like settlement, in Gandhi's
former cell up on the roof, or in one of the many spartan,
highly-polished little rooms above the hall, smelling of
beeswax and soap. Further long discussions resulted in the
birth of a Community Service Committee whose plan, the
records show, was to promote small rural communes professing personal allegiance to Christ.

In keeping with the spirit of these communes — some
formed expressly by pacifists, for pacifists, at the outbreak of
war, others Christian in spirit and taking conscientious objectors as agricultural workers — a small literature was now
building up. Early in 1942 delegates from some of the hundred
or so groups met in Epsom and agreed to produce a regular
bulletin, to act as a clearing house for sale, loan or barter.
Queen bees, cockerels, pullets and cuttings began to circulate
around the countryside, sometimes followed by poultry
breeders, beekeepers and market gardeners, willing to share
their particular talents. A clear picture of these ventures comes
through the now very rare copies of the bulletin, with its
earnest, somewhat pious notes; there is a lot of talk about the
good Franciscan life, and the necessity for pooling incomes. It

is all rather high-minded and Protestant and peculiarly English: hard work, denial of the flesh but almost sentimentality of the soul.

At Nova Scotia Farm, near Ipswich, the pacifist communards rose at seven, ate porridge, observed a few minutes of silence, took it in turns to read from a passage in the New Testament, then went out to tend 41 acres of wheat and vegetables, and to milk the goats. After lunch, they listened to Debussy's *La Mer*. On Saturday evenings, known as 'social nights', a schoolmaster played the piano, while an accountant proved unexpectedly good at impromptu plays. At Norley Wood, near Lymington, the 21 residents rose from their bunks at 6.30 and after a certain amount of horseplay (holly in the bed) cycled ten miles to ditch and plant for a Christian Pacifist Forestry and Land Unit. During their picnic lunches (210 slices of bread for sandwiches) they read Shelley and the *Spectator*; over dinner they talked of Marx and Maupassant. There was cocoa at nine. It was sober and uncomplaining, and how, on occasion, they must have longed for something else, a little glamour, perhaps even a little sin. In the bulletins, correspondents remembered D. H. Lawrence with warmth, and quoted to each other a letter he had written to Lady Ottoline in 1915: '. . . Let us be good all together, instead of just in the privacy of our chambers . . . Let us laugh at each other, and dislike each other, but the good remains and we know it . . .' Out in the countryside, on 12s 6d a week pocket money, rising in the dark to milk strange beasts, completely cut off from the outside world since very few had either the money or the desire for a radio, the pacifist hairdressers, accountants and shopkeepers were doing their very best.

For the authorities, the pacifist communities were clearly an unexpected bonus, and whatever their eccentricities they intended to maintain a decent relationship with them. What they were doing, after all, was providing an outlet for some hundreds of conscientious objectors released from the Services on condition that they find work, but very often, having no country skills of any kind, being totally unable to do so. But there could also be a more suspect side to them. A number of war resisters opposed to conscription itself carried their antagonism to the war to the stage of refusing all dealings with the military authorities, including even registration. Many of these men, faced with imminent arrest and having nowhere to go, turned to the pacifist communes, using these isolated farmhouses and sympathetic households as temporary refuges, until the police caught up with them, when they moved on. Since there were enough places to go to, and their addresses were well-known in the community world, it was just a question of keeping moving, from one to another, and sometimes back again. One of these men was Tom Carlisle, a 20-year-old anarchist from the East End of London.

Carlisle is now in his sixties, a short, stocky man with a neat moustache who talks rapidly and willingly; he is finishing a degree at the Bradford School of Peace Studies after many years in the trade union movement. Nine years ago he had a nervous breakdown; he had read somewhere that it helps to associate with what he calls 'moral superiors'. The only ones he could think of were the Quakers, who have welcomed him to their meetings. Tom and his wife Maisie live in Keynsham, near Bath, on a red brick compact housing estate. His war was a community war.

Tom Carlisle grew up in Poplar, Red Poplar, Lansbury's Poplar, where the talk was all against war. His mother was a suffragette and one of his aunts used to tell stories about the way she knocked off policemen's hats during suffrage rallies. When he was 15, in 1935, Tom joined the ILP youth group; he had friends who went to fight with the International Brigade in Spain.

Tom remembers Gandhi coming to Kingsley Hall; he followed the crowds along the roads and watched from between people's legs when the small man in white climbed out of his car, surrounded by towering officials in suits and huge policemen. The Carlisles admired the way Muriel Lester chose to 'live just down the road, only a little better than us'. They went to the Hall in the evenings and heard Sybil Thorndike recite. Maisie, Tom's future wife, was one of the children sent off to the Essex countryside to get out of the East End fumes. In her family, Lansbury was God; her mother felt about him 'as she did food'.

Nowadays Tom says that though he was not a religious boy, and by 1939 going through a decidedly anti-religious phase, there was nonetheless something of the spiritual and the philosophical in his violent opposition to war. Basically, though, he was against the idea that anyone should have the authority to demand his conscription. He is a little embarrassed now by what he regards as possibly ill-considered youthful anarchy, though he insists that his belief — that peace is not a condition which is achievable without radical changes in society — is as valid for him today as it was then.

When his orders to register arrived in 1940, he replied to say that he would not be doing so. His family were not altogether pleased; to be against the war was right and proper, but prison was strictly for criminals. While waiting for the inevitable summons, Tom worked in Poplar library and spent his evenings with the conscientious objectors at Kingsley Hall. He and Maisie happened to be selected as the two youth delegates to pay their respects to Lansbury, as he lay in his coffin in Bow Road. They thought he looked different, sad.

In February 1941, the police close behind him, he took off. Through Muriel Lester, who kept a list of them, he knew of a community near Gloucester, started by the Quakers; they were short of labourers, having just taken on some additional land and were pleased to take him in. They gave him 12s 6d a week and his keep, and he dug, milked, planted and drained ditches with a journalist from the *Daily Herald*, a teacher from a progressive school in Uttoxeter, a few local conscientious objectors and a member of the Horniman family. The more philosophically-minded quickly moved on. Tom stayed a year and was eventually joined by Maisie.

The Whiteway Colony, as it was called, was older than many of the others. It had been started in 1899 by a woman called Nellie Shaw, who had anarchist leanings and burnt the deeds to the land; its heyday was the 1914–18 War. The Second World War pacifists held weekly meetings to allocate the work, rising in turn to cook breakfast. Once a week they devoted an evening to discussing their pacifism. The local people called them Dutch Quakers because, says Tom, they looked shaggy and unkempt, with ragged beards and probably very ragged shorts, when they took their vegetables into market.

When the police finally tracked down his address and he knew that a new summons was on its way, Tom moved off. Next came a spell as a gardener in a TB sanitorium, the other side of

Gloucester, then work for a local bus company. Maisie stayed on in the commune. A detective was on his trail, so he kept going, this time to Stoke, to agricultural work, living in a hostel for conscientious objectors, then to a community in Essex, to another in Wiltshire and finally to one at Weston-super-Mare. The life appealed to him: tough, solitary, rather dour but not unfriendly. On one land community scheme the men lived in a cricket pavilion. It was terribly cold. There was no insulation to the plywood walls, and a single stove, burning scraps of wood from a nearby timber yard, gave out a feeble heat from the middle of a long hall. Furnishing was sparse: a trestle table, a bench, two chairs and a sofa without springs. In the mornings, the men used a stone to break the ice on the washing butt. There was no radio, but on Saturday nights they listened to a collection of old and soon extremely scratchy classical records on a creaky gramophone. The pavilion possessed a number of bicycles, on which the young men in their whites had once ridden home, after summer evenings at the nets; the pacifists used them, on Saturday afternoons, to go visiting, to see how other conscientious objectors, in other pacifist communes, were faring. But no one bothered about the war news. 'We weren't really interested,' says Tom. By 1942, he was heartily sick of moving. He packed his few possessions and returned to Gloucester and to Maisie and there the police got him.

Tom, as the judge at the Gloucester Assizes soon observed, was an outlaw. 'In the old days, we would have sentenced you to death. This is serious. If we get more like you, we'll have anarchy.' The following morning he decreed nine months' hard labour. Maisie was pregnant. Tom began to think that his protest had probably gone far enough and he appealed. Transferred first to Bristol and then on to Wormwood Scrubs, he found himself with over a hundred other sentenced conscientious objectors, among them the composer Michael Tippett; he was there the evening that Benjamin Britten came in to give a concert, after which he and Tippett exchanged scores, Tippett's being his own work, written surreptitiously, so that, when Britten left, he was able to carry the new work out with him, in absolute defiance of the prison rules.

At his new trial, Patrick Figgis, now in charge at Kingsley Hall, came to give him a good character. It was rare to hear of a

pacifist released in this sort of way. Tom volunteered for the
mines, at this point of the war acutely in need of men, too many
having gone off to fight and too few having been willing to
return, and to North Somerset minefield he went, knowing that
Maisie was living in an income-pooling commune in Bristol;
and there he stayed, working in the pits, on and off for much of
the next 20 years.

The four Carlisle children, born towards the end of the war
and after it, are not pacifists. One is a teacher in a private boarding school, another works for television. Maisie and Tom still
go to PPU meetings, but in a desultory way, saying that they
have become nothing more than reunions for old people, who
talk about the good old days of peace. They prefer CND, which
they consider has more meaning and more vigour. But their
views, their absolute pacifism, have not changed. 'In our world,'
says Tom, 'if you were a socialist, well then, you were anti-war.
It was our part of the world. I've always felt you've got to stick to
your original principles. You haven't got anything else.'

The pacifist communities had entered the war, if nothing else,
optimistic. Theirs was going to be a witness to the pacifist faith,
as well as to the viability of harmonious egalitarian life. When
the hostilities ended, members told each other, working models
for a healthy new society would all be there, waiting for those
returning from the fighting to copy. They knew that it would
not be easy, but perhaps that was part of its charm. As Gerald
Heard, writing from California, warned Max Plowman, 'a
single member lacking in full consciousness is enough to wreck
any community'. Early copies of the bulletin were full of
caution. What were needed, one editorial observed, were 'men
and women to whom food, dress and sex are secondary inci-
dents in life, not primary preoccupations; people who can get
up early; people who are efficient in making lives with hand and
brain, because community in its initial stages is rather like life
on an uninhabited island.' Young children, 'pure consumers',
were not to be welcomed, as being too expensive. It was a little
like John Hargrave's Kibbo Kift, good, pure, and idealistic,
and the weaker spirits might have done better to attend.

The notion of this pure hard work was attractive from the
start to a great many university graduates who had come down

from their colleges at the time of the General Strike and wide unemployment, who had spent the thirties talking socialism and the League of Nations and who now, as the bombs fell, vented their rage against the betrayal of their ideals in hard, pacifist commitments. Ronald Duncan, friend of the Bells and the Stracheys, was one of these; having pounded the country for the PPU in the closing months of peace, he set up a farm community for fellow intellectual pacifists on the Devon–Cornwall border. Eric Gill, the sculptor and engraver, who saw in pacifism a retreat from the mass-produced civilization he deplored and often wore the habit of a Dominican Tertiary, was another who chose to live out the hostilities in small communities up until his death in 1940. On the island of Iona, off the western coast of Scotland, a Scottish minister called George MacLeod was busy establishing a community of disciplined Christians round the rebuilding of its medieval abbey. In all these places, really hard work and deeply-held dreams carried the pacifists rapidly and by and large smoothly well into the second year of the war.

The trouble was, as Gerald Heard had remarked, community life was not at all easy. The men now trying to live off vegetables, to rise at dawn and to make a living from often very meagre land, were for the most part city dwellers, with soft hands, bad backs and a taste for meat. They knew about tax exemptions, French grammar and company law, not about lathes and manure. What is more, at heart many never really wanted to know; they longed for the day when they could get back to their files and their classrooms. Their failures on the land depressed them, as did the incessant hard manual work which made their muscles ache; they grew bored. All of Ronald Duncan's ten pacifist companions were intellectuals; not one had worked on the land before. The animals died; the crops failed. 'At least,' Ronald Duncan wrote later, a little wryly, 'we were not dropping bombs on each other.'

All round the countryside, well before the war was over, intellectual farm hands were trying to drift away, back to the comforting and familiar cities, away from their ploughs and seed beds, or, if they had resigned themselves to sitting the war out, were resorting ever more frequently to petty arguments. Tom Carlisle, sampler of so many different households, is reluctant to say that the pacifist communes did not thrive, but even he will admit that as the men revealed themselves singularly unsuited to work that they had previously imagined so simple, and to a way of life that was both very isolated and very disciplined, so the spirit drained away from the movement. Only those held by religious faith seemed strong enough to overcome the cramped housing, the loneliness and the disagreements. The others, the socialists and the anarchists, the humanitarians and the rationalists, grew fractious, their minds full of Welsh and Scottish independence, Thoreau or Marx and not potato blight, especially when the crops came up, yet again, diseased, and funds fell intolerably low.

No one has chronicled better the collapse of the community ideal than John Middleton Murry, the man who had begun the war with such hopes for a united pacifist witness. Together with Max Plowman, aware of the dangers of relying too heavily on unskilled men, he had been a supporter of the Community Land Training Association, which in March 1941 began to train younger men as farmers and craftsmen of agricultural tools. A farm in Lincolnshire was acquired. But then, in May, Plowman died. Murry turned to Frank Lea, assistant editor of the *Adelphi*, biographer of Shelley, and later of Plowman and Murry himself. Lea, whom Murry's brother Richard, a weekend visitor to the farm, remembered in the 1980s as the man who tended the goats, rejected Plowman's notion that communities should be medieval monasteries, governed by elders, and returned to Lawrence's vision of them as providers of 'a new level of technical achievement and social awareness'.

The day came when Murry heard from the Air Ministry that his land at Langham was to be requisitioned. Still believing in the perfect community, he decided to buy 183 acres of land at Thelnetham on the Suffolk–Norfolk border and, during the winter of 1941, he settled in with some ten pacifist followers, though the numbers soon rose. He was 52. The farm had cost £3,325 and all the profits were to be shared. Three cows, five heifers, 20 ewes, and four horses were bought and installed.

Murry believed that his cooperative dream had to fulfil two very specific goals: it had to work as a farm, and make money to support its workers, and it had to become a true philosophical community of men who lived well with each other. At the opening meeting, he spoke of the importance of promoting a 'continual increase in personal responsibility'.

It was quickly obvious, however, that Thelnetham was about to fail at both. Two of the first lambs died and the mares remained firmly barren; the land, which at first sight had looked so full of promise, turned out to be hopelessly poor so that even the mangel-wurzels grew no larger than small oranges.

Far worse than the vegetables, in Murry's eyes, were the people. From the start the pacifists seemed more eager to explore their own consciences for the true meaning of community than to set to at hard farm work, and while the crops failed and the herd diminished they mused and bickered. One of the more committed and serious of the men soon left, describing the others as 'irresponsible and adolescent'. Murry, commuting for half of each week to his job as editor of *Peace News*, returned to find friction and disaster. The farm fell into debt. 'A chapter of cranks . . . social misfits . . . sexually unfulfilled and frustrated' was how Murry was soon referring to his companions, with whom he too bickered, about hierarchy and ownership. Soon his disillusionment was total. Though Thelnetham limped on right through and on after the end of the war, Murry's faith in it as a scheme was dead. Only two kinds of people, he declared, were actually at all suitable for community life: a man and a woman in the process of achieving physical love, or those capable of healthy spiritual love. The young who came to his community farm had been neither. Later, and not without malice, friends were to wonder whether Thelnetham had not perhaps provided Murry's friend George Orwell with his model for *Animal Farm*.

Murry's experience was extreme. Elsewhere there were some very real successes, where members not only worked hard and made their farms profitable, but remained good-tempered. Spicelands, an enormous and very remote mansion with views over Dartmoor and Exmoor, former home to the Society of St. Francis, was made into a training centre-cum-community for conscientious objectors: many were Quakers; the turnover was rapid, men departing to work in hostels, hospitals, or other labouring communities once they were trained. Though eight miles from the nearest village, and short of funds, the inmates kept in good spirits, building up, by the end of the war, a library

187

with over 3,000 books. In 1970, at their annual reunion, they were able to muster 70 of their former communards, people actually pleased to see each other again.

And the Brüderhof remained what it had been at the outbreak of war, a model of a community that could work. At the height of the Battle of the Atlantic, when submarine attacks were at their peak, 350 Brüder, having been told by the Home Office that, because of their German origins, they would have to be interned, emigrated to Paraguay. They left behind them three men to wind up what had been an exceptionally successful farm of 70 shorthorn cattle, 120 sheep, 1,000 chickens and 30 beehives. But round these three men quickly gathered 19 others, British conscientious objectors, and in the spring of 1942 they moved to a new farm near Ludlow, with superb views over the Welsh hills. Though the land was poor, and few of the men had any farming experience, the community prospered. By the end of 1942 it numbered 33 people and the following year it doubled, when some of the Brüder were able to return from Paraguay. These men at least had been able, in Lawrence's words, 'to laugh at each other, and dislike each other', yet hold to the original purpose of the venture.

No account of the British pacifists of the Second War is complete without the women who, early in 1942, began receiving their call-up papers and demanding that their consciences against war also be listened to. It was something quite new and quite unforeseen, and there was no machinery to deal with it. Men had laid claim to a conscience in the First War, so were assumed to possess one in the Second; women, never called up by the army, had no immediately recognizable consciences.

Under a new bill passed in March 1941, all men liable for call-up and all conditionally registered conscientious objectors were informed that they were expected to do civil defence. Civil defence, said the authorities, was civilian work, not military work; there were to be no exemptions. Thousands of conscientious objectors disagreed; hundreds went off to prison. And there were still not enough men. On December 2, the Prime Minister, Winston Churchill, announced his intention of calling on single women, between the ages of 20 and 30. The Tribunals began. The War Office had not felt that there was any point in setting up non-combatant sections in any of the women's services, and those registering as pacifists were directed to civilian work — when they would take it. Not all would.

For refusing 'direction' to work, 257 women were prosecuted and 214 sent to prison; more than 200 others soon joined them for refusing to fire-watch. As with a number of the men, some of these sentences were all the more absurd in that the women had been perfectly happy to fire-watch without compulsion, and had indeed been doing so, but, when conscripted, said they would do so no longer. It was the conscription, not the fire, that counted.

The first woman to go to jail was Constance Bolam, a 21-year-old housemaid from Newcastle-upon-Tyne. In January 1942, Miss Bolam told her Newcastle Tribunal that she disagreed with war in every form or shape and had no intention whatsoever of taking up any work she was conscripted to do. She spent a month in Durham Jail, in the laundry.

The Tribunals did not much care for the women applicants and some steps were taken to avoid hearing their cases at all; when interviewing officers discovered that a woman intended to object to the war, they were instructed to offer her work in agriculture, market gardens or hospitals. Only if she turned all these down, and could not be cajoled into any kind of compromise, was she to be sent before a Tribunal. There was considerable nervousness that women faced by the court room might prove very emotional, quickly upset by hostile questioning and prone to introduce time-consuming irrelevancies. Women members were hastily drafted on to the boards, presumably to act as a softening influence.

Judges, their tolerance tried by the 45,000 or so cases that had already passed before them, seemed to have reached a pitch of extreme censoriousness at this new stubbornness. Their manner was often curt. Hazel Kerr was told that, if she cared to carry the argument she was presenting to its logical conclusion, then she would be forced to eat no food at all and thus starve to death. 'And that,' declared the chairman, 'might be the most useful thing that you could do.'

Most of the women, in fact, were extremely resolute and well prepared for their Tribunals and the consequences. They had been watching the prosecutions of the men pacifists for months and knew precisely what to expect. They neither quaked nor cried. If anything, they were rather less easily intimidated than the men, arriving for their hearings with a very clear idea about why they were there and what they would or would not accept.

Nora Page was 27 when she was called up, early in the women's draft, for war work; on being informed it meant working as an assistant in a greengrocer's shop, thereby allowing the girl he employed the freedom to move into war work, she refused. The authorities did nothing. But when some months later she refused when she was asked to register for fire-watching — though she was at the time a volunteer fire-watcher in Wood Green — they prosecuted.

She was very calm about it all. Nora Page is a small woman in her early seventies, with bifocal glasses, pale skin, white hair and a soft voice, round and gently obliging. She lives today as she lived then, in North London, in one of the areas that produced a high number of pacifists in both wars; Tottenham, Edmonton, Walthamstow, Wood Green and Enfield (home of two of the men sentenced to death at the Western Front in 1916), all had well-attended branches of the PPU throughout the war. Her street, of semi-detached two-storey houses, is impeccably neat with small front gardens; she has beds of multicoloured tea roses. In her sitting room she keeps files of contacts from the war days; she ticks them off; few are alive.

Nora's father had been an engineer, mending aeroplanes in the First War; he lost two brothers in France. In the twenties she remembers a teacher at her school breaking down on Armistice Day and crying, for the fiancé she had lost in the war; other girls cried too, recalling lost fathers. Nora felt guilty that she had not lost her own.

By the mid-thirties, when Dick Sheppard came to speak in Wood Green, Nora was working for a firm making musical instruments. She had become friendly with other young women in Europe and Germany, because the firm had many international contracts and through them she knew a lot about German rearmament and the coming war. In 1938 she signed Sheppard's pledge and went out selling *Peace News* on North

London's street corners. By then, several members of her family felt as she did, and both a brother and a sister were destined for jail sentences as pacifists.

The local PPU branches had been excellently prepared for war; enthused by Denis Hayes and the Central Board for Conscientious Objectors in Dick Sheppard House, they were soon issuing leaflets of advice to local war resisters and sending members to stand outside Tribunal hearings, ready with information about how to plead and what exemptions were available. Nora often sat in at the trials as an observer; she remains scornful: 'They were absurd. How could any three men sitting on a board judge if a man had a conscience or if he was pulling your leg?' When her own Tribunal hearing came, she was a familiar figure around the court, friendly policemen having often let her take fish and chips to the men queuing interminably for their hearings to come up. 'We've been waiting for you,' the chairman at Tottenham Court Road told her, but not in an unfriendly way. 'We can't do nothing about you, or we'll get no more fire-watchers. What's the minimum sentence?' The clerk told him it was 14 days.

Nora spent them in Holloway, the main prison for women conscientious objectors. She arrived in a Black Maria, directly after her hearing, having been so certain of the outcome that she had her ration book packed with her. The wardress who let her in was suspicious at such preparedness. She was inspected by the doctor, told to have a bath, then issued with a linen dress, dirty white cotton vest and pants, black stockings but no suspenders, second-hand stout shoes and a dark blue shawl-like cape. She felt like a very tatty nurse. The conscientious objector inmates were considered a nuisance, not a threat; the Governor was impatient, the wardresses indifferent and the other prisoners, mainly in Holloway for theft or soliciting, disbelieving. Long afterwards women prisoners recalled that they knew when it was Friday because they woke to a dank smell of bad fish.

Holloway had no proper black-out for its roof. When air-raids came the vast Victorian star-shaped building, reminiscent of some chilly Gothic castle, was instantly immersed in complete blackness and wardresses patrolled the corridors with dimmed torches. Nora remembers watching the fire bombs

191

from her cell window. Air raids were moments of nightmare in prison life. When the lights went off, the women prisoners would begin to scream, working themselves up to pitches of frenzy and hysteria as the bombing intensified, banging on their cell doors with a shrill, keening noise of caged creatures. When it grew too bad, the Governor would order the cell doors to be opened. On her release, Nora was once again directed to war work in a shop. She visited the Labour Exchange in Wood Green to explain that she would still release no one else for war service by taking their place. The authorities were sick of these troublesome women; the man behind the desk, shuffling the many papers in front of him, said: 'I can't actually withdraw this. What I think I'll do is lose it.' She heard no more and went back to voluntary fire-watching in Wood Green.

She would do as much today. In 1939, she believed that war was wrong; Methodism had taught her that Christ forgives his enemies, and her musical instrument firm had shown her that her foreign friends, in any case, were hardly enemies. She feels exactly the same. To her husband's embarrassment, she talks to people at bus stops, much as Frances Partridge did to the women between Hampshire and London that she met on the trains. 'You can make them think,' she says. 'At the end of the day, people remember conversations.'

In Holloway, Nora had joined a select company of women pacifists. Sybil Morrison was there at one point, charged with a breach of the peace, having spoken out against the war in Hyde Park, and Kathleen Lonsdale, the distinguished researcher into X-ray crystallography and first woman Fellow of the Royal Society, mother of three young children, had spent her 40th birthday in a cell not far away. In October 1943, some nine months after her release, a Quaker woman working in the fruit and vegetable business in Covent Garden, followed her there, for a 60-day sentence, consisting of two separate 30-day charges for refusing to fire-watch. Joan Layton knew only that she owed her prosecution to someone from her building in Russell Chambers who had alerted the authorities to her views; she never discovered who it was.

Joan Layton's pacifism was a more troubled affair. Looking back at it now, from the position of a convinced Quaker and absolutely opposed to war, she can remember at the age of nine reading a story about Quakers in a child's encyclopaedia and asking her mother what Quakers were. 'People who don't believe in war,' she was told. 'I thought to myself: just like me.' She hoped that no one would notice that she did not cheer the soldiers when they came home after the Armistice.

But it was not really until war broke out, when she left the Church of England parish that had meant so much to her, after being asked in church to pray for British soldiers but not for German ones, that she began moving in the direction of the Society of Friends. By this point war was in full swing and she was employing conscientious objectors for her firm in Covent Garden while serving herself on various government committees dealing with the rationing of apples, tomatoes and oranges. She had read Beverley Nichols's *Cry Havoc!* and was already thinking of herself as a pacifist; her friends were all conscientious objectors, the other men in her new Quaker circle having already gone off to the war. Unlike Nora Page, she found Holloway hateful; she felt constantly degraded and dirty, and remembers the distinctive dress, and in particular the cape, with loathing. But it never occurred to her not to go to prison. Pacifism, for her, was never anything but an absolute, once held, never shed; it has shaped her entire life since 1942. She finds it hard always to understand friends who changed their minds.

By early 1945 it was becoming possible to make a fairly precise tally of what had happened to British conscientious objectors in five years of war. It was clear that their numbers had risen dramatically since the First War, but it was clear too that there was something very altered about their experience, both in their own attitudes towards war and in the way that they were treated by society.

The First War had seen 16,000 men register as conscientious objectors: about 0.125 per cent of the six million men who fought in Flanders, Gallipoli, Palestine and on all the other fronts. Four times that number, 62,301 people, 1.2 per cent of the five million called up, of whom 1,704 were women, appeared before Tribunals in the Second War, according to meticulous records kept by Denis Hayes and the CBCO. Two thousand nine hundred and thirty-seven were awarded total exemption, and spent the war in their own homes, getting on with their own lives. The rest were scattered almost evenly between civilian work, non-combatant work and a constant state of confrontation with the authorities; 6,500 of these last, 500 of them women, at one time or another between 1940 and 1945, served time inside prison.

The drama of the First War had lain not so much in society's disgust at its conchies, as in the many abuses that had come from the way in which the 'conscience clause' had been administered. There was, after all, not much brutality in World War Two towards the pacifists as a whole, and not much intransigence; it was a feature of the Second War that after a series of Appellate Tribunals exemptions were regularly given to men objecting to no more than some wars at some times. An individual had truly won his right to his own conscience, whatever its origin.

The war itself had, of course, been a very different affair. The effect had been to make most of the men who asked for, and won, exemptions, in 1939, 1940 and 1941, quieter, more eager to prove their courage in other ways. The struggle had thus been one of establishing a right to an individual conscience so unalienable that it would never again be questioned. The conscientious objectors were not the pariahs they had been in 1916; they were everywhere, a part of the fabric of Britain at war, and furthermore, after the bombing began, they were part of it, not able, as they had been in 1916, to consider themselves distant spectators, observers of two distant armies, killing each other on some faraway battlefield.

'I think far-seeing men of philosophic judgement . . . would say that the life of the community had been enriched,' Fenner Brockway told the second annual conference of the Fellowship of Conscientious Objectors towards the end of the war. 'The conscientious objector has stood for eternally desirable values, when they were threatened with suppression, and the world is a less evil place because they have done so.' A declaration of conscience should not however be regarded as sufficient in itself, Fenner Brockway added; it was only a beginning. 'The conscientious objector has no right to reject war in the present unless he spends his life in helping to make a future without war.' This impulse was very marked for many of the objectors of the Second War; it was behind the work of the Friends'

Ambulance Unit, behind the Hungerford Delousing Club, behind the pacifist communes: that war had to be sat out, endured, but that when peace at last came, because of their labour, the world was going to be a better place.

In 1945 it was also becoming clear that Britain's pacifist response to war had not been equalled in other countries. There had, of course, been war resisters everywhere, but nowhere else had they been so numerous and so organized. In France, Italy, Belgium, Holland and across Scandinavia, pacifists had lain low but, when identified, there had been little tolerance for them.

In Germany, the peace movement had been suppressed well before the war and many of its leaders had fled the country by the late thirties. Now news reached the offices of the PPU giving some better idea of the fate of conscientious objectors who had not got away. Survivors of the concentration camps told how Jehovah's Witnesses and Bible students objecting to militarism had been among the camps' first inmates; in Buchenwald they had been formed into a punishment corps and few lived to see the war end. Of 83 known Bible students sent to Belsen, 18 were found alive by the Allies.

Max Josef Metzger, a Roman Catholic priest, founder of a movement for renewal within the Church and closely involved with the international peace meetings and congresses of the 1930s, had been beheaded in Brandenburg Prison in Berlin, accused of high treason. A memorandum on post-war Germany, with passages about securing peace, in his hand, had been given to the Gestapo. Another prominent pacifist, Dr. Hermann Stohr, former secretary of the German FOR, was also dead, executed in June 1940. Of the flourishing pre-war peace world, with its warm contacts with Britain and America, there was very little left.

America, to a surprising extent, had mirrored the fortunes of Britain. There had been more conscientious objectors than in the First War, and more of them were concerned with private witness than public protest. Everywhere, they had been better treated, with none of the public hatred of 1917, though as at Dingle Vale and Ilfracombe there had been pockets of cruelty. The Selective Training and Service Act of September 16, 1940, which called for the draft of all able-bodied men between 19 and 44, contained a clause for exemption for anyone who 'by reason of religious training and belief' objected to warfare. Local draft boards had to decide whether they were sincere and then direct them into civilian work or non-combatant service. There were no women conscripts. This time, however, the Protestant Churches were drawn into the argument, and in October 1940, largely prompted by the Quakers, Mennonites and Brethren, a National Service Board for Religious Objectors came into existence. Only non-religious absolutists ran into any serious trouble, and some were lucky enough to appear before reasonably humane boards.

Jim Bristol is in his seventies, a quiet, solid-looking man with a square face. In 1941, when America entered the war, he was 29, pastor of the Grace Lutheran Church in Camden, New Jersey, not long married and father to a 20-month-old baby called Lea. Bristol was a pacifist, a man who had spent his years in Lutheran Seminary 'reading stuff no one put my way' and convinced that either Christianity was right, or war was right, but certainly not both. He had spent the thirties, as a supply pastor, trying out his liberal views about civil rights and integration on a small, poor congregation who were, he says, very tolerant of their role as guinea pigs for his progressive views.

When called to register, on October 16, 1940, Bristol did so, preaching the Sunday before from his pulpit that he would make his registration an act of dedication to work more positively for God and peace. Later, he regretted his decision. When, in April 1941, he received the next stage in papers towards call-up, he sent back an eight-page statement explaining why he would not be joining the army. It was almost five months before a marshal came for him.

Bristol's Church Council voted to accept the resignation that he offered them; his congregation turned it down. He served 18 months in a federal penitentiary, not unhappily; what he remembers now is that the fortunes of the conscientious objectors fluctuated with the fortunes of the war itself. The experience changed his life, however. When he was released, he returned to his congregation, but was appalled to find that, when voting ten dollar gifts for local men in the army, they also voted to send nothing to the town's two conscientious objectors.

Soon, he left the Lutheran Church and went to work for the Fellowship of Reconciliation, moving in the fifties to the Quakers and the American Friends' Service Committee (AFSC). Faced today with the same choices that faced him in 1940, he would do precisely the same thing. 'There are some things,' he says echoing Tom Carlisle's words, 'well, things one had to say, that's what I feel, and let things fall where they may.'

There have never been as exact figures for the United States as those collected by Denis Hayes in Britain, but some 72,000 men are believed to have registered a conscience against the war. About 6,000 of them, much the same number as in Britain but only a fraction of the proportion of fighting men, went to prison. A number of the others were employed clearing trails, making roads, building dams and fighting forest fires, under the aegis of the Civilian Public Service and much along the lines set up by the Civilian Conservation Corps under the New Deal during the Depression. As in Britain, physicists cleared swamps, and eminent economists dug ditches.

Not long into the war, largely to cope with the dissidents, the 'social actionists', conscientious objectors who were confusing everyone with their talk about socialism and human rights, the government opened some camps of its own. They had a mildly punitive air about them. To these came Jehovah's Witnesses, Black Muslims and black Jews whose consciences forbade them to struggle in what they believed was not a holy war. Mulford Sibley and Philip Jacob, later writing a history of the American conscientious objectors, called them 'the ultimate penal colonies'. In time, these camps became places of considerable friction; men preferred to return to prison rather than stay in them, while those who did staged sit-ins and walk-outs though their preferred tactic of protest became complete non-cooperation in all work, along Gandhian lines. Confrontations between the authorities and the inmates of these camps went on long after the fighting had actually ended.

In prison, there was also a programme of resistance. During World War Two, one man in every six in a federal prison was a conscientious objector. They were, for the most part, either Jehovah's Witnesses, or men ineligible for the camps on a number of different scores, or Americans opposed to conscription itself, who, rather like Thoreau 100 years before,

197

chose prison over denying the freedom of their own consciences. 'Prison,' wrote one pacifist, 'seems to be the mother of civil rights.'

The first pacifist prison rebellion took place in Danbury Correctional Institution, where, on April 23, 1941, 16 prisoners refused to work or to obey the prison routine. Though they were quickly released from the solitary confinement in which they had been placed — one of the protesters was a baseball player much needed by the prison team — odd isolated acts of disobedience went on occurring. In the middle of 1943, more systematic striking began. It started over segregation, and then spread, with frequent hunger strikes, to other causes and other jails. 'We . . . are compelled,' the pacifists of Lewisburg announced, 'to a non-violent revolutionary movement.' One prison superintendent remarked that he longed for a return to 'the good old days of simple murderers and bank robbers for prisoners'. Prison life was to provide an important grounding for pacifists in the civil rights struggle to come; it made them radical, and it made them interested in the practical application of Gandhi's non-violent resistance in a way they had not been in the thirties.

Early on the morning of August 6, 1945, in bright, clear weather, an American B-29 bomber, *Enola Gay*, flying at 9,300 metres, dropped a uranium bomb over the city of Hiroshima, a port on Japan's eastern coast. The bomb was called *Little Boy*. 'This is the greatest thing in history,' President Harry Truman told the crew on the ship on which he was travelling. Three days later, on August 9, a second bomb, *Fat Man*, fell through a gap in the clouds on to one of Japan's southernmost cities, Nagasaki. By the end of the year, some 210,000 Japanese were known to be dead from the two bombs.

Though the precise nature of what the Americans had done was not apparent to the world for many months, the Second War was effectively at last over. According to an estimate put out by the United States War Department, 80,000,000 people, throughout the world, had been injured or killed. *Little Boy* and *Fat Man* closed the era of conventional defence and opened the nuclear age. For the soldiers, it was going to mean a very different kind of war. For the pacifists, it was really a kind of beginning: what would become of conscience, when no army at war would ever really again need fighting men in such numbers that conscription of the unwilling would be necessary or worthwhile? And could protest against war survive, in the countries which had so successfully enshrined it as an unalienable right, when the means to wage it had been so profoundly altered?

PART TWO

8

Getting used to the bomb

It took a surprisingly long time for the world to react to the new weapons of mass destruction. As the war in the Pacific came to its sudden stop, and the Allied soldiers started to come home, thoughts in Britain turned more readily and optimistically to the new Labour Government and social promises heralded by the Welfare State, and to contemplating the almost unimaginable task of reconstruction, while in America there was simply relief that it was all over. Hiroshima and Nagasaki were a very long way away.

In December 1954, the British public was asked what changes it imagined might be brought about by the splitting of the atom. There were many replies, most of them positive. Only a very few people, a bare four per cent, wondered whether there might not be some change in military techniques of a kind that would affect international relations. Even among the pacifists, those who had endured the war as conscientious objectors, or spent it dreaming of the social improvements peace would surely bring, there was reassuring talk about how peace with a bomb was really a great better than no peace at all. More sensible, certainly, to look ahead: for an uneasy shadow of doubt, that the vast pacifist fervour of the thirties might in fact have actually contributed to the war, continued to prod at people's minds.

What protest against the bomb there was came from a few isolated voices, mainly among scientists and clergymen, particularly once John Hersey had published his book on Hiroshima in 1946 and people could no longer avoid knowing just what an atom bomb could do. In the United States, the radical pacifists and the atomic scientists together were the first to mobilize their forces for a world without nuclear war. By the middle of that year, a Federation of American Scientists, with over 2,000 members, was already arguing that the 'arms race must be stopped'. Meanwhile, in Britain, an 'atom train' toured the countryside during the winter months of 1947, stopping for a few days in one large town after another, while atomic scientists tried to tell the audiences who gathered of the power and destructive potential of the bomb. Kathleen Lonsdale, the physicist, who had spent a month in Holloway Prison for her refusal to fire-fight under conscription, was on board. It was not enough, she said later, to give people the facts: what was needed was to convey some sense of good or evil in what had been done. Dr. Lonsdale was a Christian, a devout Quaker, as well as a scientist. 'The people want guidance,' she wrote in a pamphlet called *Effective Christianity*, 'and that science is not competent to give. . . The feeling of horror, I think, was not so much at the deaths of many thousands of Japanese as at the fact that we had invented a new crime against humanity itself. And that feeling remains, I believe, as a very deep-seated neurosis; a sense of guilt, of unrest . . . When will the Church be ready to speak with a prophetic voice to declare these things? And if she cannot, who will?' No one, it seemed; and certainly no one in 1948. Even those who attended to Dr. Lonsdale seemed to prefer to discuss the manner in which the decision to drop the bombs had been made, rather than the properties of the bombs themselves. When Attlee announced that year that Britain was to make its own A-bomb, there was almost no protest at all.

In any case, the early post-war years were not good times for pacifists anywhere. The fighting was over; pacifism had become a little boring. The signing of the peace had not been followed, as it has been in 1919, by a sudden rush to renew old international peace links: there were no emotional gatherings in Bilthoven, no nostalgic and exhortatory dances among the pine groves or meetings of women's peace movements beneath the potted palms of European congresses. It was all more a question of tentative and somewhat exhausted regrouping, in the church halls and North London sitting rooms which had seen so much vigorous protest while there was something clear to protest against.

The Peace Pledge Union was sickly, if not actually moribund. An incendiary bomb had hit Dick Sheppard House, but it was the general air of failure rather than war damage that hung over the place. Sybil Morrison, statuesque, passionately feminist, somewhat bossy, was full-time national organizer; the staff of five met at 11 and 4, over cups of tea, to talk. The members who had not dropped away, disappointed that their voice had not been enough to prevent war, had left later, having convinced themselves that this had been after all a just war. The few who remained were middle-aged, middle-class, prosperous and largely without politics. They were cosy and devoted. Every week, Stuart Morris spoke from a soap-box at Hyde Park Corner; Sybil Morrison took Lincoln's Inn. She used to say how she loved hecklers; at least they brought the crowds in. She herself was deft with those who came to jeer, could turn their sneers amusingly; the crowds loved her. And if the meetings were sometimes a little bleak, the poster marches somewhat lonely, the office at least was cheerful: Donald Soper, Kathleen Lonsdale, Benjamin Britten, Vera Brittain all coming by from time to time, for news of what was happening elsewhere, for tea, for the copies of *Peace News*.

It was no better in the other pre-war pacifist strongholds. The War Resisters' International, at its reassembled gatherings across Europe, was finding that conscription remained in force in most parts of the world, and that battles they had fought and believed won in the heady pacifist days of the twenties and thirties now needed fighting all over again. Those who met and talked were remarkable people; but events were against them. The newly-independent countries like India and Pakistan were busy building up military forces and the Cold War was fostering militarism.

The Fellowship of Reconciliation, determined to keep alive some of the social experiments pioneered by its pacifist members during the war, sometimes seemed to be concentrating more on welfare than on peace. The pacifist fervour was not so much diminished as ousted by more important matters. The stauncher pacifists could be forgiven for fearing that they were heading rapidly down into a very blind tunnel.

And yet there was a rumbling among the pacifists, a new voice, soon to be louder than any previously heard. There was something about these new weapons that could not just be ignored, some qualitative leap of a very different order from anything that had gone before. It was not about war, exactly; it was about survival, and it demanded a new form of protest. It was as if, seemingly with one bomb, the notion of 'witness', of a single man's refusal to be conscripted, had become, if not unimportant, at least to many a little irrelevant, almost foolish. But what was to replace it?

In August 1949, the Soviet Union exploded its first atomic bomb; there was surprise; no one had imagined their military testing to be so far advanced. Soon a small group of people began to meet at Dick Sheppard House in London; they had been helping with the famine in Greece caused by the war and as they talked they returned to the subject of Gandhi and non-violent resistance and how the new civil rights movement in America seemed to be using sit-ins so effectively in their protest. These were not the familiar, older PPU members; they were, for one thing, very young, barely in their twenties and most of them still at school during the war. They were full of ideals, and increasingly disappointed that the new society promised by the Labour Party seemed to be so slow in coming. Michael Randle was a 17-year-old reporter working on *Peace News*; Pat Arrowsmith, a Cambridge history graduate and social worker, granddaughter of missionaries stoned to death in China, whom *The Times* was later to describe as a 'brisk young woman'. Then there was Hugh Brock, a rather older man, who had spent four months in prison as a conscientious objector, and was much revered by the young supporters. And if their main concern was now the atomic and hydrogen bombs, which governments appeared to be making and testing with complete impunity, at heart most of them were also pacifist.

During 1950 and 1951 a Non-Violence Commission took shape: it was ambitious and it must have appeared, to the outside world, deeply impractical. The Korean War was at its height and what these young people were suggesting was that Britain should stop producing nuclear weapons, that it should get out of NATO and that it should expel the American forces based in the country. Michael Randle remembers how, meeting in Hugh Brock's house in Stoke Newington, there would be long discussions about whether obstructive non-violence was justified in a democracy where other debate was possible, and how the arguments went backwards and forwards over whether or not the decision to make the bombs had been a truly democratic one in the first place, and whether, even if it had been democratic, any government was justified in threatening the annihilation of thousands of people?

The talking might well have simply gone on, and the Non-Violence Commission have remained small, articulate and impotent, had not events shifted them along. On January 31, 1950, President Truman announced that he had directed the Atomic Energy Commission to continue with its work on all forms of atomic energy weapons — including a hydrogen or 'super-bomb'. Now the talk became more purposeful. The moment had come, agreed the new nuclear pacifists, to challenge these weapons of mass destruction used against civilians, and put Gandhian tactics to the test. 'Operation Gandhi' was launched and, because those who believed in it were not always supported by the main body of the PPU, they decided to go their own way, out on their own.

The first 'action' as it would later be known, in the jargon of the sixties, was a mild, courteous affair. There is something touching about its tentativeness and its meek regard for manners. Not long before midday on January 11, 1952, 11 people met by the bookstall in Charing Cross Station. Some had come to the meeting by bus, others had walked or taken a train. The twelfth, a woman, was late, and they decided to go on without her. The little gathering, looking rather like a respectable outing of young schoolteachers, walked to the War Office in Whitehall and, as Big Ben struck 12.00, sat down on the steps.

The police, politely informed in advance, politely led them away. Three times they came back, and sat down again. A crowd, friendly, curious, gathered. A photograph which appeared next morning in the *Daily Mail* shows the demonstrators smiling, embarrassed, somewhat awkward. The women are wearing headscarves, tied in small knots under the chin; the men have good navy blue overcoats worn rather long in the fashion of the time. They are, above all things, respectable. At last, a lorry was fetched and the 11 protesters, smiling sheepishly, were driven off. As it disappeared, a breathless young woman hurried up. She asked a constable where the War Office was and, on being shown, sat down defiantly on the steps. The police led her off to join her companions in Canon Row police station. Next morning, they were fined 30s. each. The methods of the group, in the couple of paragraphs devoted to the event in the papers, were described as 'family', which was somehow intended to denote their Gandhian non-violent stand.

Back in Stoke Newington, there was considerable satisfaction at what had been achieved: the event had been peaceful, the onlookers friendly, the police tolerant. What was needed now, everyone agreed, were more sensational targets. A man called Jack Salkind, who as a hobby collected bus timetables, reported that there was something very odd about a bus route that went from Reading and ended in a place with no proper name, just the AWRE. Hugh Brock offered to take the bus and find out where it went. He came back saying that the stop was for the Atomic Weapons Research Establishment just near the village of Aldermaston. 'Operation Gandhi' talked about staging a demonstration round its perimeter fence, but concluded that their very few numbers would make little splash. Instead, they settled on handing out leaflets to the workers, as they came off their midday shift. The group, having by now swelled to 20, hired a bus as far as Aldermaston and walked the last three miles to the Atomic Research Station gates.

It was all still a very long way from anything to do with real influence, particularly as other fears seemed more pressing — nuclear testing, irradiation, continuing conscription in the world. The protests went on — at Mildenhall American Air Base, where two girls lay down in the sun in front of the main gate and American soldiers with walkie-talkies circled round them in jeeps; at the Microbiological Research Centre at Porton on Salisbury Plain — fuelled mainly by the odd items that kept appearing in the news, showing the relentless build-up of the bombs, but they were never very big.

The actual transformation into a real movement of many people, was, however, to come from another direction, or rather from several different directions at once. Within the Labour Party, the debate was intensifying, while around the country small groups of people began forming themselves into committees to protest against the continuing weapons tests. When Christmas Island was named as the place where Britain was going to explode its bomb, 'Operation Gandhi' wrote to the *Manchester Guardian* saying that they were raising money to send a Quaker called Harold Steele and a number of other supporters into the Pacific. The letter was signed by some of the more famous names in pacifist circles: Laurence Houseman, Ruth Fry, Bertrand Russell. Three days before the test, a small procession of women wearing black sashes marched from Hyde Park to Trafalgar Square, in pouring rain.

On both sides of the Atlantic, it was all waiting to take off; only the sparks were needed. They came in 1957. That year, the first Sputnik was launched, a new Soviet challenge to American military superiority, while the continuing testing of weapons was beginning to make growing numbers of people anxious. (Though when Albert Schweitzer appealed over the radio to 50 countries to stop the testing of all nuclear weapons, the *New York Daily News* advised its readers: 'Laugh off this Schweitzer manifesto' since it contravenes 'the assurances of most nuclear scientists that fall out from test explosions . . . is not dangerous at all.')

On November 15, a first advertisement for the newly formed National Committee for a Sane Nuclear Policy — SANE — appeared in the *New York Times*. 'We are facing,' read the headlines, 'a Danger Unlike Any That Has Ever Existed.' By the following summer SANE had 130 chapters, representing 25,000 people; its members were pacifists, advocates of civil rights and proponents of world government.

In June 1957 an ad hoc committee under the name of the Committee for Non-Violent Action (CNVA) had been formed to bring *satyagraha* into play against the tests. CNVA was skilled at civil disobedience, its members quick to dream up imaginative gestures that attracted publicity and kept prodding at the fears of ordinary people. Its most successful, perhaps, was the voyage of a ketch called the *Golden Rule*, the sea mission that was the model for so many of the later anti-nuclear naval exploits.

Captain Albert Bigelow was a lieutenant-commander in the US Navy who had served on three combat vessels in World War Two. When the atom bomb fell on Hiroshima, he was appalled. By 1952 he had moved so far from his earlier military way of life that he resigned his commission in the naval reserve one month before he became eligible for a pension. Captain Bigelow became a pacifist, joined the Society of Friends, and when two of the Hiroshima 'maidens' arrived in the United States for surgery they came to live with his family.

Later, Bigelow described his moment of conversion to a more radical pacifism. 'What can a man do? . . . Spontaneously,

209

intuitively the idea was born. The idea was an act . . . an act that could not be bypassed, could not be brushed aside, could not be ignored.' Like the draft raiders later, Bigelow had become an 'actor', a witness.

In 1958, he set sail, with three other Quakers, on the *Golden Rule*, bound for the American bomb testing site in the Pacific. In Honolulu, he was served with an injunction restraining him from entering the testing area. He ignored it and continued on. The boat was stopped and the men on board arrested. They were serving prison sentences when the bomb was exploded.

Another boat, the *Phoenix*, had meanwhile arrived in Honolulu. It was captained by an anthropologist called Earle Reynolds, a former resident of Hiroshima, sailing round the world with his wife and children. Reynolds was not by inclination an 'actor'; he was reluctant to embark on any form of civil disobedience. But some time around now the need to 'act' clearly came to him too. On July 1 he was able to radio to a coastguard patrol in the area that he had entered the nuclear test zone and intended to remain there. The *Phoenix* was located and seized; Reynolds went to prison. He came out a hero and went off to give 58 talks around the country.

In Britain, the transformation of doubts into protest came about more abruptly. Duncan Sandys, in his annual Defence White Paper of 1957, had promised an end to National Service, a reduction in defence estimates and greater reliance on nuclear weapons for Britain's defence; the White Paper called for an independent British nuclear deterrent.

On November 2, an article appeared in the *New Statesman*. It was by J. B. Priestley, the novelist and journalist. Its tone was urgent, emotional. It seemed to him, he wrote, that the world was about to turn into a 'radio-active cemetery', while trigger-happy, power-mad politicians and scientists debated in the 'stifling secrecy of an expensive lunatic asylum' and spectators sat by like rabbits waiting for the massacre. No one had quite said these things before, or at least not so publicly, with such passion, at such a perfect moment. 'The catastrophic antics of our time have behind them men hag-ridden by fear, which explains the neurotic irrationality of it all, the crazy disproportion between means and ends. If we openly challenge this fear, then we might break the wicked spell that all but a few uncertified lunatics desperately wish to see broken, we could begin to restore the world to sanity and lift this nation from its recent ignominy to its former grandeur. Alone, we defied Hitler; and alone we can defy this nuclear madness into which the spirit of Hitler seems to have passed, to poison the world.'

It was heady stuff and there was more to come. It was none of it strictly, purely, pacifist: Priestley was suggesting neither parting with the Americans nor abandoning the defence of the country; it was a question of peace as a force for sanity and above all morality. Three weeks later, the *New Statesman* published a letter. It came from Bertrand Russell and was addressed to President Eisenhower and Nikita Khrushchev in the Soviet Union. 'Never before,' announced Russell, 'has such a sense of futility blighted the visions of youth . . . Individual death we must all face, but collective death has never, hitherto, been a grim possibility . . . One thing only is required to dispel the darkness and enable the world to live again in a noonday brightness of hope. The one thing necessary is that East and West should recognise their respective rights, admit that each must learn to live with the other and substitute argument for force in the attempt to spread their respective ideologies.' Britain might appear a militarily weak power, but morally the country's voice was still strong.

Events now moved quickly forward. On January 16, 1958, there was a meeting near St. Paul's Cathedral at the house of Canon Collins, veteran campaigner for the relief of starving Europe and founder, with the publisher Victor Gollancz, of a group called Christian Action. Those who came were a different lot from 'Operation Gandhi', who were now calling themselves the Direct Action Committee (DAC); they were older, established, politically cautious, respecters of position and law and order. They came from the arts, but not many from politics or the sciences. J. B. Priestley and his archaeologist wife Jacquetta Hawkes were there, and Kingsley Martin and Rose Macaulay, Michael Foot, Bertrand Russell, Doris Lessing and Denis Healey. The names of 13 of these first 19 supporters, as someone soon remarked, could be found in *Who's Who*. Something, they agreed, had to be done to halt the drift into a nuclear world out of all control. A further meeting was suggested, a public meeting, to be held at the Central Hall, Westminster, on February 17.

And, when that day came, it was successful beyond all imagining. Five thousand people pressed their way into the hall; hundreds more flowed into the smaller side halls. There was a single message, and the speakers carried it from audience to audience, like runners in a relay race: Britain must renounce the bomb. Canon Collins put it across in the name of Christianity; J. B. Priestley in that of common humanity; Bertrand Russell for the sake of survival; Michael Foot, the future Labour leader, for sanity; A. J. P. Taylor, the historian, for morality. 'Is there anyone here who would do this to another human being?' Silence. 'Then why are we making the damned thing?' Thunderous applause. The biologist and poet Alex Comfort, who was later to say that this was the most significant movement since the Chartists, sounded a rousing battle cry. 'The people,' he called out, to an audience very ready to rise up and respond, 'must take over — *you* must take over. The leaders of all parties are waiting, as they always wait on any issue of principle, to follow public opinion. We can coerce them . . . Let them make this country stand on the side of human decency and human sanity — alone if necessary.'

After it was all over, after £1,750 had been raised, some 1000 people, light-hearted with a feeling that they might really be about to influence events, walked round the corner to Downing Street and shouted 'Ban the Bomb' in a good-tempered way until a few arrests were made and Doris Lessing complained that she had been jostled by the police who, observers commented later, were to be seen inciting their dogs to 'snarl'. The Campaign for Nuclear Disarmament (CND) had been born. Its appeal was wonderfully simple: it was a force for life, rather than death, and you didn't have to belong to any faith or political group to feel part of the huge moral indignation.

Though the various local groups which had been working against the nuclear tests now readily merged into the new Campaign for Nuclear Disarmament, not everyone was yet in harness. The new body was somewhat wary of provocative gestures and confrontations with the police, seeing itself basically as a prestigious and opinion-forming pressure group,

212

rather like the anti-hanging lobby, aiming to work on the Labour Party and to change policy. The Direct Action Committee, on the other hand, had no intention of abandoning its street politics. What was more, it had a new scheme well underway, one which promised to be more spectacular than any that had gone before. The decision had been made to march from Trafalgar Square to Aldermaston over the Easter weekend; with only 13s 8d in the kitty, Pat Arrowsmith had been working out the incredible logistics of shepherding an as yet unknown quantity of people over the intervening 60 miles. An ex-army colonel called Michael Howard had offered to handle the marshalling of walkers through London. The Labour Party, the trade unions, the New Left socialists and the Communist Party had all expressed interest. Then one day a commercial artist from Twickenham called Gerald Holtom wandered into the offices of *Peace News* with a curious drawing: combining the semaphore letters of N and D, he had superimposed a white circle on a purple square with a droopy purple cross inside. The organizers wondered what to make of it, but eventually agreed that, stuck onto lollipop signs along the route, it would indeed make a striking image, particularly if it was just on its own, with no words, no explanation. What would become one of the most memorable of all modern symbols had just been found.

On Good Friday, April 4, 1958, 5,000 people gathered in Trafalgar Square and 600 of them set out to walk towards the Atomic Weapons Research Establishment at Aldermaston, singing, to the tune of 'Home on the Range':

> Oh give me a land that is peaceful and grand,
> With concern for the whole human race,
> So we can be proud that the dread mushroom cloud
> In our future will not have a place.

It was raining hard. Next day, the BBC announced that it was the wettest Easter since 1900. The young men in jeans, the girls in pony tails, kept on marching. They spent the night in Hounslow. It began to snow. A friendly farmer handed out hard boiled eggs to the marchers as they straggled by.

Fenner Brockway was there, with his wife, celebrating their 20th wedding anniversary; and Donald Soper, who declared: 'The marcher is a marked man. He has nailed his colours to a

213

mast . . .' and Peggy Duff, first General Secretary of CND, who
was to write later, in her political autobiography, *Left, Left, Left*,
'Peace and the right to liberty and the pursuit of happiness . . .
are indivisible.' Bayard Rustin, soon to be widely known for his
work with the civil rights movement, had come from the Non-
Violent Action Against Nuclear Weapons in America, and
from West Germany there was the pacifist pastor Dr. Martin
Niemöller. For the last mile, they walked in silence, and at the
end of it all there was a vigil, organized by a serious 20-year-old
girl with fair hair cut severely straight called April Carter, who
had been working for the Foreign Office. Later, she
remembered the first Aldermaston march as a somewhat sober
affair, very unlike the more festive ones to come. 'It was terribly
un-English,' wrote Alan Brien next day in the *Daily Mail*. 'But it
was proof that 1984 is still a long way off.' The marchers, he
went on to say, were the 'sort of people who would normally
spend Easter weekend listening to a Beethoven concert on the
Home Service, pouring dry sherry from a decanter for the
neighbours, painting Picasso designs on hardboiled eggs . . .
The quiet suburbanites were on the march.' *Peace News* was
jubilant. 'It's only the beginning! . . . Britain will not be the
same again . . .' They were, in a small way, right. The movement had indeed reached the people.

The first Aldermaston march did not, as many hoped, bring
about a smooth merger of the two main anti-nuclear factions.
The differences, in style, in image, in intent, were just too
different. CND went right on producing its leaflets and agitat-
ing through the columns of establishment newspapers, lobbying
those in power, while the Direct Action Committee, reaffirming
its commitment to non-violent protest, returned to its plans for
civil disobedience. Between them hung a distinct cloud: a little
patronizing on one side, a little contemptuous on the other. And
there was more than just style to keep them apart: those drawn
into CND were impelled by a feeling that the survival of the
human race was at stake and that to be deflected from this single
idea was absurd, while the Direct Action Committee, more
dedicated in its approach, was also more ambitious: it was not
just nuclear pacifism that inspired them but pacifism generally,
the transformation of an entire society through peaceful means.

'People like me used to think: what we're talking about is nuclear destruction,' says Michael Randle. 'That was our way in — then pacifism followed.' Young, penniless and almost monastic in their sense of purpose, they set off on fresh forays into the countryside in search of worthy targets. Pat Arrowsmith, by now national organizer while April Carter was general secretary, remembers how they hitchhiked around the country lanes, or when they could borrowed scooters and drove about, peering behind huge perimeter fences in search of secret missile bases.

In East Anglia they came across a new base under construction at Swatham. The strategy for their particular kind of non-violent action was by now well laid down: a period of talk with local union leaders and workers, explaining what the site was really about, and trying to convince them to black it; then on to more direct tactics.

The first weekend in December was frosty; a thin film of ice had formed on the mud. Fifty demonstrators marched out cheerfully from Swatham; when they reached the base, watched curiously by the workmen, they pulled back a loosely fitted fence, entered the site and sat down in the mud. Pulled away by policemen who had been waiting for them, they got back in again. 'It was,' says Pat Arrowsmith, 'the coldest night in my life.' At one point fire hoses were turned on to the protesters who were now soaked as well as cold. The police were far from friendly; there were scuffles, a certain amount of roughness.

Two weeks later, the demonstrators came back. This time the police were better prepared; there were no scuffles, the first having led to some unflattering publicity. But, as the protesters scrambled onto the base, the police simply yanked them off, and drove them away in vans. On December 20, over 30 people were sent to jail. Bound over to keep the peace, they had refused to do so. April Carter went to Holloway, the prison for so many women pacifists; she found the stripping, the uniform, the lack of privacy, hateful. Like the others, she was destined to see a great deal more of prison life, for the leaders were to return to jail again and again, like the resisters in both wars, and nuclear protesters ever since, with very little fuss.

The Direct Action Committee was now working extremely

215

hard, on a divided front. From the first days of 'Operation Gandhi' much of their interest had always been international, looking to America for tactics and allies and to wherever nuclear testing was being carried out for their targets. Events in Britain were only intermittently at the forefront. Hugh Brock knew Julius Nyerere and Kenneth Kaunda, later Presidents of Tanzania and Zambia, and had long supported the anti-colonial movement in the columns of *Peace News*. It was, says Michael Randle, a time of 'sparking': civil rights and anti-nuclear groups in America; the nuclear movement in Britain; each pushed the other a little further on.

In Britain, the movement against the bombs was making progress. As CND took shape, a number of bishops and suffragans in England and Wales emerged to declare a unilateral position. By early 1959 CND had tens of thousands of active supporters and by the end of the year branches in some 500 places. Trade Unions, under the determined lead of Frank Cousins and the Transport and General Workers, were also moving towards unilateralism, and at the TUC conference in 1959 a TGWU unilateralist resolution received 2,755,000 votes. It was defeated, but a motion protesting against the installation of nuclear bases was carried.

The movement was soon to take other, more militant, more exciting forms; it was to become more visible, seemingly more powerful; yet this was perhaps its best moment. There was hope, and everything appeared to point towards success. The pacifists, who had failed to bring about peace in the First War, and failed to prevent a second, were optimistic as they had never been before. Left-wing intellectuals and scientists filled the pages of *Peace News*, *Tribune* and the *New Statesman* with a message, like the one delivered in Central Hall, Westminster, that took different forms but was in essence always the same: nuclear war was horrifying and insane. It had to be stopped.

One day, the journalist James Cameron sat in on a talk given by a 'head lady' of the Women's Voluntary Service on civil defence. She was briefing her troops about the effects of radiation. It was powerful stuff, all on its own, but Cameron chose to intercut her talk with extracts from Hersey's *Hiroshima*. 'One good thing about it you ought to know, it isn't infectious. Nor contagious. You can't *catch* radiation sickness, except if the

216

fall-out drops on you; what I mean is you can't get it from a friend . . . (and they were all in the same nightmarish state; their faces were wholly burned, their eye sockets were hollow, the fluid from their melted eyes had run down their cheeks . . . their mouths were mere swollen, pus-covered wounds . . .) Also of course you must remember there are quite different *sizes* of bombs. They wouldn't use a big bomb on a small area, would they? . . .' Cameron's piece appeared in *Lilliput* magazine under the title 'One in five must know' and was distributed as a pamphlet. Thousands read it.

The message, now, was everywhere. In the *New Statesman*, Jacquetta Hawkes, returning to a feminist theme that carried those who could remember back to Pearl Buck and Rosika Schwimmer, appealed to the women of England:

> Now we women must rouse ourselves to resistance,
> For this is our business . . .

And for those who did not read, who did not care for poetry, there was pop music with its lyrics of despair:

> The first day there'll be lightning,

sang Tommy Steele in 'Domesday Rock',

> The second day there'll be hail,
> The third daybreak there'll be a big earthquake,
> So brother, forward my mail . . .

It was hard not to be involved. 'It was,' remembers one regular marcher, 'a very frightening time, especially for young people.'

The second Aldermaston march was a glorious affair. It was, as April Carter says, considerably more jolly than the first. The weather was again appalling, with rain that never seemed to stop, but it hardly mattered. The organizing of the march itself had been relinquished by the Direct Action Committee into the more numerous hands of CND, who decided to reverse the order, starting from Falcon Field at Aldermaston on Good Friday and bringing the message to the government in London, rather than taking it to the workers at the base who were in any case all too familiar with what was being said.

The organizers expected 700 people. Four thousand three

hundred gathered on the Green, then set out in the rain, with Jacquetta Hawkes and Canon Collins in the lead. The arrangements were efficient: lorries went on ahead with the baggage, groups marched in disciplined ranks under their distinguished banners and international delegations had turned up in great number. Onlookers, who admired a steel band, remarked that the marchers seemed older and that there were fewer beards and sandals.

Fifteen thousand reached Trafalgar Square on Easter Monday: they found the streets lined with onlookers, the square itself filled with another 5,000 to welcome them. Families had brought their babies; girls jived in brightly coloured stockings and bands played every kind of music. Several marchers were brandishing placards with Einstein's remark: 'If I had known, I would have been a locksmith.' In just two years, the Aldermaston march had become an institution. People today remember it not as a solitary event, but as a way of life. Tony Smythe, later to hold a series of distinguished positions in the world of human rights, and then not long out of prison as a rare fifties' conscientious objector to National Service, recalls it simply as one outing in what had become an engrossing continuous preoccupation: 'It provided,' he says, 'almost everything: friends, social life, politics, a moral cause. All our friends were on it. We automatically took our kids along. We believed we were doing something.'

On the Tuesday, when the cleaners were busy clearing the leaflets and the lollypop sticks from Trafalgar Square, James Cameron wrote a long piece in the *Daily Mail*; his tone of respect was one now shared by increasing numbers of people. 'The resurrection,' he wrote, 'is visible in the backyards . . . The sparrow chooses a piece of old string for his gesture of resurrection. The Aldermaston marcher selects a funny hat . . . How is it that this Aldermaston march, which brought 20,000 people into Trafalgar Square yesterday, trailing a two-mile plodding queue from Berkshire to London, did not — as some feared, or hoped — become a bore, an annual Easter exercise for the crackpot fringe?

'How did it, on the contrary, become far bigger than last year, more purposeful and more moving? . . .

'This is not a demonstration; it is a movement; like it or not it is here; any government, however secure and smiling, will ignore them at its peril.'

When polls began to be carried out on who precisely these protesters were, a number of interesting facts emerged. Twenty reporters were despatched by *Perspective* to interview a random sample of marchers. They came back saying that teachers formed the largest group, followed by librarians, clerks, civil servants, journalists and social workers. Forty-one per cent were under 21; 60 per cent considered themselves active politically and only 4 per cent believed they belonged to the working classes. Most interesting, perhaps, was the reason people gave for being there in the first place: 90 per cent of all those interviewed spoke of their support being essentially a moral one. What they seemed to be expressing was a feeling of revulsion: it was the sheer scale of the destructive power of these weapons that made them different, and the indiscriminate way in which they killed. It was not simply more; it was new and it was different. And, because most British people still saw themselves as a moral force, if no longer a physical one, they seemed to feel that it was up to them to give a moral lead.

So the teachers turned out, and the civil servants, and many former conscientious objectors, elderly veterans from Wandsworth Jail and Prince Work Centre of World War One, and middle-aged fathers from Dingle Vale and the pacifist communes and mothers from Holloway Prison of World War Two; and a great wave of young radicals, readers of E. P. Thompson the socialist historian and the *New Left Review*, appalled by the apparent lack of morals in all parties and by the specific horrors of an H-bomb.

Almost the only people who were not there, in fact, were the diehard thirties pacifists, the purist PPU members, who chose to see in the new nuclear pacifism a blinkered, over-simplistic reaction to the growing militarism of the world. Sybil Morrison, increasingly beleaguered as the issue of nuclear weapons began splitting the PPU in two, declared that simply getting rid of the bombs was like 'scraping spots off measles'. The breach proved bitter. Hugh Brock, editor of *Peace News*, as well as founding father of 'Operation Gandhi', had become a total convert to the battle against the bomb. The day came when he judged a divorce of the two factions unavoidable. *Peace News* left the PPU

219

and became an independent paper. Other supporters crept away, not because their commitment to pacifism was any the less, but because they felt that there was so little time left in which to save the world from extinction, and that they could no longer do nothing about it. Antagonism became sharper when Sybil Morrison decided to tour the country, campaigning against CND. 'Weapons are not the cause of war,' she would tell gatherings that seemed to diminish in size and approval from city to city. 'It is because of war that weapons are made.' Soon both she and Stuart Morris, whose lives had been moulded in the crusade against war, resigned. In the wider movement they were not much missed. The young supporters professed themselves tired of such self-righteous stubbornness. 'We found', says one, 'their puritanical views deeply irritating.'

Bertrand Russell had been one of the first people to remark that, with the arrival of the hydrogen bomb, a war between nuclear powers 'was no longer Clausewitz's continuation of politics by other means, but a recipe for mutual destruction'. How to save the world from nuclear annihilation was to remain a central preoccupation for the rest of his life, and Russell was to lead a third and new crusade in the British anti-nuclear debate. Two days before Christmas 1954, he gave a talk on the BBC under the heading of 'Man's Peril'. It was a kind of signal of a new and absolute commitment, a return to the cause of peace with all the passion he had brought to the No-Conscription Fellowship in 1916. 'I appeal as a human being to human beings.' Russell was 82, his slightly quavery upper class voice very precise and arresting. 'Remember your humanity and forget the past. If you can do so, the way lies open to a new paradise; if you cannot, nothing lies before you but universal death.' Encouraged by the response to his talk, he began exchanging letters with Frédéric Joliot-Curie, the French physicist who, 16 years before, had shown that a nuclear chain was possible, and with Einstein, the man whose name was most inextricably linked with the bomb, and who now so publicly regretted the way in which it had been used. There was something particularly persuasive about these two now ageing men, Einstein continuing to argue that a travesty had occurred at Hiroshima and whose scientific brilliance added great influence to the debate, and

Russell, a veteran of so much peace work. In February 1955 Einstein received a letter from Russell. 'I think,' he wrote, 'that eminent men of science ought to do something dramatic to bring home to the public and governments the disasters that may occur.' What he was proposing was a statement, signed by men of 'opposing political creeds', outlining the perils of the bombs and of bacteriological warfare, and which would emphasize 'the general proposition that war and science can no longer co-exist'. Einstein replied warmly and in April he wrote again, suggesting a further resolution to bind governments to find peaceful means of settling their disputes. Though Einstein did not live to see it, a manifesto was duly written, signed by 11 prominent men of science, nine of them Nobel Prize winners, and conveyed to the world at a meeting in Caxton Hall, attended by over 100 journalists in the summer of 1955. 'We have to learn to think in a new way,' read the text. 'The question we have to ask ourselves is: what steps can be taken to prevent a military contest of which the issue will be disastrous to all parties? . . . Shall we put an end to the human race; or shall mankind renounce war?'

Cyrus Eaton, a benefactor of Bertrand Russell's from an earlier visit to the States, had a house at Pugwash on the St. Lawrence River in Nova Scotia. After the manifesto was launched, Russell asked him to lend it for a conference of scientists, and in July 1957, 22 physicists, chemists and biologists met for five days of talks. It was the first time that scientists of this eminence from East and West had met so openly. Pugwash became a regular event. At first, particularly within North America, the meeting was viewed warily as an enterprise with dubiously communist leanings. Later, as its statements were so plainly without bias, and Joseph Rotblat, its Secretary General, was such an undisputed figure of probity, respect for the gathering increased. Russell himself, as Pugwash became more obviously established, grew somewhat less interested. 'He felt,' Rotblat later explained, 'he had too little time left: he must try everything.'

Russell himself was not, however, directly responsible for what came next. The new move came from an outsider, and was made easier by the unpalatable but growing realization that the huge fire kindled by the movement against nuclear weapons was not spreading in quite the way it was meant to. The third Aldermaston march of 1960, though a success in terms of numbers — 10,000 the first day, 15,000 the second, 40,000 in Trafalgar Square on Easter Monday, and even William Hickey, the gossip columnist, there to spot celebrities — was not greeted with quite the admiration it had been in earlier years. To judge by his column, Hickey's man was bored. *The Observer*, *News Chronicle*, *Sketch* and *Mirror* praised the orderliness and tenacity of the marchers but cast doubts on the sensibleness of their views. In the *Express*, René MacColl went a great deal further. 'Who are these people?' he demanded, somewhat truculently, as if they were unwanted gatecrashers at a party, 'What do they really think they're doing? Have they used their heads? Far too many of them, I thought, are exhibitionists, show-offs.' The great Easter parade had been fine while small and colourful; Establishment Britain was not really ready for more.

What was worse, the political support that had seemed to be flowing their way was now setting sharply back on a different tack. When, in 1959, the Labour Party had again failed to win the General Election, the issue of nuclear weapons had become central to debate on both the left and the right of the party; and a number of key organizations had come down firmly on the side of unilateralist policy. At the 1960 Labour Party Conference, the unilateralists scored an unexpected victory, but Gaitskell, in a long and most passionately argued speech, had promised to reverse that decision; 'What sort of people do you think we are? . . . Do you think we can become overnight the pacifists, unilateralists and Fellow Travellers that other people are? . . . There are some of us . . . who will fight and fight and fight again to save the party we love.' After the conference, the parliamentary Labour Party rejected both the unilateralist pledge and any move to unseat Gaitskell as party leader.

In any case, the government had cancelled the Blue Streak Missile project; the Labour Party now turned to a British defence policy based on commitment to a nuclear NATO. It was a setback not easy to recover from; many had felt that CND's ultimate victory lay in Labour hands. 'It was,' as Ian Mikardo observed, 'the only arena in which the campaign could ride.' The Labour Party was not about to become, as had for a moment seemed possible, the party of unilateral peace.

The outsider who now emerged to blow new life into the vast but slightly flabby movement was a 24-year-old American,

Ralph Schoenman, in London doing post-graduate research in politics at the London School of Economics. Schoenman was short, thick-set, with a neat strap of brown beard, and full of charm. He came from Brooklyn, New York. He was abrasive, dogmatic, unscrupulous and without timidity, and quite unlike anything the British campaigners were used to. Though not many liked him, most were excited by his vigour, his irreverence when faced with petty difficulties.

Russell had been thinking that CND, of which he was a founding sponsor, was proving over-cautious in its approach. When Schoenman went down to see him in his house in Wales, Russell was delighted. What the young man was soon proposing — a committee of 100 prominent people to promote civil disobedience against the 'ever growing menace of nuclear war' — seemed to him most attractive, particularly now that he had begun to feel, as his biographer Ronald Clark later wrote, that CND and Canon Collins were 'little more than a whisper in the parish magazine'. Russell was not altogether in favour of civil disobedience. He regarded it as a highly dangerous doctrine, liable to lead to anarchy, but there were clearly times when it was justified. This was one of them; CND had tried, with more accommodating tactics, and it was failing. The moment had come to move on.

The actual launch of the Committee of 100 came about in a spirit of some acrimony. Canon Collins had asked that any new move be postponed until after the Scarborough Labour Party Conference. Nonetheless letters had been sent out secretly by Schoenman to leading figures, to see whether they might take part in the sort of committee that he was intending to set up; one destined for John Connell, the well-known anti-nuclear supporter, went by mistake to John Connell the Tory journalist, who promptly sent it on to the *Evening Standard*. Canon Collins was dismayed; he declared that he could not and would not endorse civil disobedience of the kind being proposed. Russell resigned from CND.

The Committee of 100 was formally born on October 22, 1960; its hundred dignitaries were writers and journalists, actors and doctors and scientists, many of them young, and all attracted by Schoenman's vision that the British government could not but be swayed by '10,000 or 100,000 people' committing acts of civil disobedience. More coverage was needed and more coverage was going to be cajoled out of the world's press. Russell's presence was a never-fading asset: it was not just that he was so famous, or such a fine speaker, but the fact that he brought conviction and that his speeches, eloquent, rousing, were widely reported. And he could handle hecklers magnificently, deriding their sneers with courtesy and total authority. As his lieutenant, Schoenman was everywhere: bumptious, energetic, bringing in new blood, going to meetings of the New Left in the Partisan coffee house and returning with fresh injections of support and people.

Though the Direct Action Committee pursued its own path and activities for another ten months, the two groups were natural allies, even if the first nuclear pacifists were somewhat purer, the second more diverse. After one last major protest, when 35 members of the DAC trekked 465 miles in seven weeks to Holy Loch, to demonstrate against the stationing there of a Polaris submarine, the supporters joined ranks, Michael Randle becoming general secretary in a 'mini-coup'. Randle saw the Committee of 100 as the direct successor to the DAC, even if he was not quite as optimistic as Schoenman; he thought a true change of heart more likely to take 'millions', rather than thousands. Theatrical, imaginative, highly-publicized exploits, involving as many people as could be persuaded to attend, were now embarked on: demonstrations outside the Ministry of Defence in Whitehall, sitdowns in Parliament Square, rallies. Arrests followed quickly, on a scale not seen before. As the international situation appeared to be deteriorating and rumours spread that nuclear testing was to be resumed by both the Russians and the Americans, the Committee announced that a major rally was being planned for Sunday, September 17, 1961, in Trafalgar Square.

This time the authorities acted first. They did not want a demonstration and they did not want trouble. Thirty-six of the better-known members of the Committee were summonsed to appear before a magistrate and invited to bind themselves over under an act of 1361 to keep the peace for a year. Thirty-two refused. Two of these were Bertrand Russell and his wife Edith, who received a month's prison sentence each for inciting the public to civil disobedience, reduced to one week in deference to his great age. Russell was delighted; he had repeatedly told the conscientious objectors of World War One that prison sentences were excellent publicity; he instructed his lawyer to make no move to have the sentence quashed altogether. Photographs of him, frail, very thin, with wispy white hair and beaked nose, appeared in newspapers all over the world, above the words of his short statement, delivered from the dock: 'No one can desire the slaughter of our families, friends, our compatriots and a majority of the human race, in a contest in which there will be only vanquished and no victors.' It was wonderfully emotional stuff.

Russell was borne away to prison, where he was to serve his week's sentence in the hospital, in a Black Maria, commenting with satisfaction on his means of transport and pointing out that in World War One he had gone to Brixton Prison by taxi. He spent the time reading detective stories and a life of Madame de Staël and composing a melodramatic and slightly self-indulgent pamphlet; 'along with valued colleagues,' he announced, 'I am to be silenced for a time — perhaps for ever, for who can tell how soon the great massacre will take place?'

Russell was in prison when the Trafalgar Square rally took place. It was a strange occasion. Copies of the Public Order Act had been posted up at every police station and thousands of extra policemen had been brought into the city. At 5 o'clock in the afternoon, immediately after a big Battle of Britain parade, thousands of protesters sat down and began to sing. It was raining. At one point, observers estimated there were nearly 12,000 people crammed into the square; photographs show hundreds of well-known faces — John Osborne, Vanessa Redgrave, Lindsay Anderson. The occasion might have stayed peaceful had the police not so rapidly turned hostile and had protesters not begun dodging them, disrupting those sitting as they zigzagged through their rows. Fire hoses were produced; protesters were dragged kicking to police vans. Between 6 o'clock and 1 am next morning 1,314 people were arrested; 658 were released on bail; the others spent the night in jail. It was dawn before Trafalgar Square emptied.

Something, now, was changing. There was no longer much warmth towards the anti-nuclear movement, even if wide publicity was given in the newspapers to stories of police brutality. There seemed, commented the more serious newspapers, to be

225

too much noise and too little thought about it all. In *The Guardian*, Christopher Driver remarked on CND's 'extensive failure to engage the energy and the sympathy of many who share its premises about the usefulness of the British deterrent', while the *Economist* commented that the Committee were now behaving as 'if Britain were a police state'. It was left, once again, to René MacColl, in the petulant tones of a bad-tempered prefect to voice the true note of Establishment contempt. 'The fact remains,' he wrote in the *Daily Express*, 'that they are, every last one of them, willingly or unwillingly, communist stooges and agents . . . It wasn't so much their clothes (predictably outlandish for the most part) as their expressions; a sort of ox-like, staring-eyed air of eager martyrdom.'

For all the bad publicity, the Trafalgar Square rally was perhaps the highest moment of glory for the Committee of 100. Twelve thousand people had shown themselves prepared to risk, if not severe punishment, at least arrest and possible prison for a cause that seemed to them so important that it could not be ignored. The problem was: where to go next? How to increase the spectacular nature of the demonstrations? How to escalate the process of defeating the government? There was talk of selecting specific military installations and bringing all work there to a complete standstill through massed civil disobedience.

But the police equally were growing tougher, more resolute. Early in December 1961 men from the Special Branch raided the Committee's offices and the houses of six of its leading members, whom they arrested on charges of conspiracy under the Official Secrets Act. Outside, the winter's plans were in a state of collapse: transport was hard to find, and though people did turn out at selected targets the impact was not as great and arrests continued.

The trial, the Official Secrets Trial, as it was known, was held at the Old Bailey. It was a little as if the whole movement against nuclear weapons was in the dock. On trial were not simply five men and women, but the very notion that citizens could challenge the state and hope to get away with it. It lasted several weeks. The public gallery, every day, was full of supporters with CND badges: outside, pickets walked up and down, while a persistent curate held up a sign saying: 'For Christ's sake, Ban the Bomb.'

Those in the dock were very young. The eldest, the only woman, Helen Allegranza, daughter of two parents in the armed forces and herself in the ATS until drawn to CND by the disastrous Suez expedition of 1956, was only 34. The others were all under 30. There were Michael Randle; Terry Chandler, who had come to pacifism through reading Thoreau and Gandhi; Trevor Hatton, an accountant, convert to the movement after hearing Donald Soper speak in Hyde Park; Ian Dixon, who had done his military service as a conscientious objector in a hospital, after watching the film of *All Quiet on the Western Front*; and Pat Pottle, a printer, whose father had been in prison as a pacifist in the First War. They had been charged with violating the Official Secrets Act, by 'conspiring together to enter Wethersfield air base for a purpose prejudicial to the safety and interests of the state'. Documents taken from their homes — including the names of the guests at Michael Randle's sister's 21st birthday party — were quoted against them. The Attorney General, Sir Reginald Manningham Buller QC, spoke at length of their intentions to 'flout the law'. Pacifism, nuclear weapons, the tactics and rationale of civil disobedience were all put in the dock and knocked down.

Witnesses for the defence were called. Professor Linus Pauling, Nobel Prize winner, and Professor of Chemistry at the California Institute of Technology (later better known for his work on Vitamin C and colds), told the court that he was personally a supporter of civil disobedience, but was then dismissed before he could give his views on disarmament. Bertrand Russell, refusing the seat offered to him, announced that his intention in setting up the Committee of 100 had been to 'try and avoid the extermination of the people of this country and many millions elsewhere' and said that he felt at least as responsible and 'as President perhaps rather more' than the people in the dock. 'Of course, they are a nuisance to the authorities . . .' Jeremy Hutchinson QC for the defence agreed, perhaps recalling Bernard Shaw, 'and to a great many people. They are an irritant . . . and you may think that they are an irritant to the consciences of a great many people as well.'

Neither his words, nor those of the distinguished witnesses, nor of Pat Pottle, who chose to conduct his own defence, had much effect. Never in the history of the Old Bailey, declared the

Attorney General, had there been such 'effrontery'. Non-violence was quickly disposed of. The effect of holding up an aircraft, said Mr. Justice Havers, would be exactly the same whatever the method with which it was done, violent or non-violent. He announced that he would be lenient, providing the defendants agreed to give up all illegal demonstrations. All six refused. Mr. Justice Havers then said that he felt obliged to impose the sort of sentence which would deter others: 18 months for the men, 12 months for Helen Allegranza. Michael Randle had been married just one week.

The Easter march to Aldermaston in April 1963 was the sixth and last. The manufacture of weapons at the site was coming to an end. It was not a great success. Though still drawing huge crowds and popular spectacles — a saffron-robed monk from Hiroshima, a group of anarchists with a banner 'Ban the Lot', a party of folk dancers from the Punjab — the headlines were seized by a splinter group called Spies for Peace, who had managed to find details of Britain's nuclear shelters and were now busy telling the world about them, while Canon Collins was pelted with flour and eggs in Hyde Park. *The Times* commented that it had all become a 'slightly tedious annual parade in which the earnest bonhomie of a tube station in the blitz and the opportunity for remarkably uninhibited carousal have been welded to a formless sense of protest against authority'.

In any case, events themselves had taken a different direction. The Cuban missile crisis of October 1962, greeted in America with an enormous pacifist protest, had proved to many people that the anti-bomb movement was totally impotent where a major decision was concerned. Whatever their numbers, whatever the ingenuity of their tactics, the protesters quite simply had no international voice. No one was listening to them. What was more, the very fact that the superpowers had pulled back at the edge of nuclear annihilation demonstrated that peaceful resolutions were possible. Confrontation had taken place, but the worst had not automatically followed. The Partial Test Ban Treaty, forbidding all nuclear tests under water or in the atmosphere, had at last been signed, in the summer of 1963, after interminable years of apparently hopeless negotiations, removing further cause for immediate alarm. Had CND's reaction been a little alarmist? Something of the public mood of boredom at their antics was summed up when a Japanese flowering cherry tree, symbol of Nagasaki, which had been planted by a local CND branch in Ipswich, was instantly chopped down, and a clump of rhubarb planted in its place. As for the protestors themselves, they were tired, exhausted after five years of continuous planning and agitation.

Increasingly, too, there had been schisms in the movement. When in July 1963 Queen Frederika of Greece paid a visit to London, the Committee of 100, remembering Gregory Lambrakis, who had once walked with them the route to Aldermaston and who was now dead, believed murdered by the police, organized a series of demonstrations against her. The CND leadership was furious, arguing that this was in fact quite irrelevant to the nuclear issue. Yet this was precisely what was now happening: the cause was turning into other things, into the environment, into housing campaigns, into ecology and any number of different extra-parliamentary campaigns. Of all these the most directly related and the one most reminiscent of the aftermath of other pacifist drives was the movement to better prison conditions. Put together, many thousands of weeks had been served by demonstrators in prisons all around the country. Pat Arrowsmith alone had served six sentences. In February 1963 appeared a report called *Inside Story*: written by the occasional pacifist inmates of 12 of Britain's prisons, it had considerable impact, even if details like porridge coming from bags labelled 'Grade II pigmeal' and jam being given to vegetarians in lieu of meat were not altogether believed.

The movement evaporated slowly. The bumptious Ralph Schoenman, so brilliant for a brief time at enthusing others and injecting fervour where it had died away, moved on, into the fight against the war in Vietnam and into further plans with Russell, though not before he was unfortunately quoted as saying that 'every major political initiative that has borne the name of Bertrand Russell since 1960 has been my work in thought and deed'. Russell himself, having now passed the age of 90, but still pursuing peace, seemed to believe, after Cuba, that it was the United States that presented the greater threat to the world, a belief soon reinforced by events in Vietnam. He left the Committee of 100 and, in September 1963, announced that he was setting up a Bertrand Russell Peace Foundation, with communication and education as its aims, 'to oppose institutionalized violence and campaign against them, and to further the cause of peace with freedom and justice'. In 1966 Russell launched his International War Crimes Tribunal, based on a premise that the Americans were conducting the war with appalling barbarity; it was soon widely dismissed too for being one-sided. By now he had split totally with Schoenman, though characteristically his valedictory note was one of praise for the young man 'whose companionship was as welcome as a delicious fresh breeze on a muggy day'.

The others, those who had spent so very much time trying to preserve the world from nuclear destruction, moved off in directions of their own: April Carter to the London School of Economics, 'to get educated', the leaders of CND to their own interrupted lives, and a few people, among them the purer pacifists, to a rather lonely pursuit of peace, talking of forming 'crisis contingents', to intervene where peace was in jeopardy, rather in the mould of Dr. Maude Royden's Peace Army of the thirties. Helen Allegranza committed suicide, apparently much disturbed by her months in prison. 'A radical non-violent society', not nuclear pacifism, became the fashion of the time.

Afterwards, people asked themselves why had CND gone wrong. Why, when everything seemed to be pushing for victory, had the sense of urgency evaporated? Pat Arrowsmith would later say that she had never 'felt that they had been bound to win, only bound to try'. Others blamed the collapse on a failure to attract working-class support, and on the fact that in the end no one had managed to capture the Labour Party, whose leaders were never quite convinced by the tactics of civil disobedience.

The 1964 General Election was now in everyone's mind; the movement was played out, the arena taken by the war in Vietnam. But what no one would be able to take away from CND, from the Direct Action Committee, from the Committee of 100, or from those who had given five years of their lives to getting rid of the nuclear bomb, and who had gone to prison again and again in an attempt to make themselves heard, was that an entire country had been alerted to the dangers of nuclear weapons and that politicians had been persuaded to work a little harder towards producing international agreements. At its peak, the movement in Britain had been the largest single extra-parliamentary demonstration the century had seen. 'I thought,' says one of the Committee of 100's founders, 'that it might change people. And it did: enormously. It changed what they were prepared to do; it made them lose fear of standing their ground and it taught them discipline.' 'I think people want peace so much,' President Eisenhower is quoted as saying, 'that one of these days governments had better get out of their way and let them have it.' Even in their present failure, there was something very comforting in his words.

9

Japan: a new meaning for peace

In the spring of 1954 Senji Yagamuchi, a 23-year-old technical engineer from Nagasaki, crept around the back of the station yard and on to a train bound for Tokyo. He was hiding, trying to keep out of sight, because he was a *hibakusha*, a survivor of the A-bomb that had fallen on Nagasaki on August 9, 1945, just nine years before. He was a thin, wiry young man without a job, so severely disfigured by burns that no firm, despite his excellent degree, would give him work; he was also without money and could not buy a train ticket to Tokyo.

Earlier in the year, he had tried to commit suicide. There were thousands of others like him, he knew, leading stealthy and lonely lives among the shacks on the edges of Hiroshima and Nagasaki, away from the busy construction sites of the gleaming new cities that were rising rapidly from the devastation, young men and women who were ill, desperate, deformed, and still, after all those years, completely confused about what had happened to them.

Today, with the bullet train, the journey from Nagasaki to Tokyo takes rather less than ten hours. Then, by local express, it took over 26. Yagamuchi had no friends in Tokyo and only wooden open sandals on his feet, but the skin graft hospital ward full of other survivors from which he had just been discharged had filled him with determination to visit the government offices in the capital, until then strangely silent on A-bomb matters, and ask them why they could not at least pay something towards the many operations that had been made necessary by the particular ferocity and peculiar properties of thermal burn and radiation.

A friend in the station office had told him how to board the train from the yard, unobserved. He had also warned him that there would be three ticket inspections on the journey to Tokyo, so Yagamuchi kept himself awake, going to hide in the lavatory each time the inspector entered his compartment. At Tokyo station, he gestured over his shoulder as he approached the

232

barrier, as if another passenger behind were carrying his ticket. Then he disappeared quickly into the crowd.

The Diet was not in session. Nonetheless, hungry and extremely sleepy, Yagamuchi made his way there across Tokyo on foot. 'My long peace march,' he calls it. When he reached the gates he asked an official whether there was a member from the prefectures of either Hiroshima or Nagasaki in the building. The members were all away, he was told, but there was a secretary of a member for Hiroshima; Yagamuchi was shown to his office. There, he asked for writing paper and a pen, and sat down to draft a number of requests agreed on in the ward by the survivors during those long weeks between operations: a medical fund, so that all future operations would come as a matter of course and not from the charity of local citizens; a special bath house so that maimed survivors would not have to expose their wounds to ordinary people; perhaps some money towards employment or housing.

Yagamuchi now needed a ticket home; he had no friend at Tokyo station. He was directed to the Juvenile Crime Division, where a police chief redirected him back to the Welfare Department. The officials were not exactly friendly; but then Yagamuchi was hardly pleasant to look at, his face puckered up along his right cheek bone, his right ear missing, his head held at an awkward longsided angle, and whatever skin that was visible beneath his shirt collar and sleeves purple and drawn. Even so, they treated him with the scrupulous attention to regulations for which Japanese bureaucracy is famous.

At the Welfare Division, they informed him that he needed a letter from the secretary of the member for Hiroshima, proving that he had in fact been there on official business. But when he returned to the Diet the secretary admitted that since he was only a private secretary and not a parliamentary one he was in no position to issue such letters. Eventually, after lecturing Yagamuchi on the unpreparedness of his mission, the Welfare chief produced the money for a train ticket home to Nagasaki and, with some reluctance, a little more for food.

Nothing came of the journey. Yagamuchi never heard a word from Tokyo or from the Member of Parliament for Hiroshima. But he went back to Nagasaki, to the ward full of survivors, to the next in what turned out to be ten major skin grafts to straighten his neck and remove the keloids, the growths of wrinkling scar tissue that disfigured so many of the A-bomb victims, with a new resolve to win some sort of recognition for the maimed survivors of the A-bombed cities, men and women who can still recall with absolute clarity the two August mornings 42 years ago when out of a fine, mildly cloudy summer sky fell two atomic bombs.

The facts are worth recalling, briefly. Very early on August 6, 1945, a United States Army weather observation plane took off from Tinian, one of the Mariana islands. As it neared Hiroshima city, some 2,700 kilometres away, it sent a message to the B-29 *Enola Gay*, flying just behind: 'Fair weather, ready for air raid.' In the streets of Hiroshima the people were on their way to work. Earlier that morning the city had filled with volunteers, many of them high school students, drafted in from the suburbs and neighbouring towns to start tearing down buildings as part of the city's self-defence measures.

It took 43 seconds for the bomb to fall 9,600 metres and explode, flooding the whole city with a bluish-white glare. Instantly, the epicentre of the blast reached a temperature of several million degrees centigrade; a fireball formed, emitting heat rays and radiation in all directions. No atomic bomb had ever been used on human beings before.

The bomb on Nagasaki, three days later, was almost a mistake. It was intended for Kokura, in the north-east of Kyushu Island, a city with a major arsenal. The skies over Kokura were covered by heavy clouds that morning, so, after circling for ten minutes, the plane headed off for Nagasaki, its second, alternative target. There was cloud there too. But, as it approached, a gap appeared through which the pilots could see below the Mitsubishi Heavy Industries Nagasaki Arsenal. At 11.02, *Fat Man*, rounder and a little longer than Hiroshima's *Little Boy*, and bearing plutonium rather than uranium, exploded over Nagasaki city.

Though different in composition, the bombs had much in common, particularly for those below. In both Hiroshima and Nagasaki the fireball was soon followed by blast and shock waves, killing all those close to the epicentre instantly while destroying all buildings, and leaving those further away in agony from thermal burns and radiation. At 500 metres from the epicentre reinforced concrete buildings fractured, steel girders and beams dissolved and cracked; at three kilometres, electric light poles and trees charred and roof tiles splintered.

Half an hour after the bomb fell a fire storm broke out in Hiroshima; it quickly reached its maximum speed of 18 metres a second and by late morning some 13 square kilometres of the city had been reduced to ashes. In Nagasaki, where the city was more spread out, 6.7 kilometres disappeared. In both, during the morning, 'black rain', minute particles of carbon turned into water vapour, poured down on to the city for several hours; it contained large amounts of radiation.

Half of all those within 1.2 kilometres of the epicentre of *Little Boy* and *Fat Man* died quickly. By the end of 1945, some 118,000 were dead in Hiroshima, 73,000 in Nagasaki. Mostly, they died of thermal burns. Those who survived for a few days or weeks suffered from nausea, vomiting, anorexia, high fevers and diarrhoea; their hair fell out; they had gingivitis and gangrenous ulcers. Those who lived on showed signs of blood injury, especially to the bone marrow, one of the most important consequences of radiation illness.

By no means all of this, or even very much of it, was actually known to Yagamuchi, as he made his way to Tokyo in 1954. It is one of the less well documented facts about the bombing of Hiroshima and Nagasaki that enormous efforts were made in Japan to keep all details of the bombs' effects from the people, in case they led to outbreaks of hostility towards the American occupation forces. Right through the 1940s and well into the fifties it was forbidden to discuss the bombs at all.

The official policy of silence had started immediately. A cameraman, filming around the ruins of Hiroshima in September 1945, only weeks after the event, had been arrested by October and his film confiscated. By the middle of that month, a press code was issued to silence all reporting. Newspapers were not allowed to write about the cities. First the American Forces, then the Japanese Government, made absolutely certain that no detail and no pictures of the aftermath would disturb the public apathy. Even in the universities, there was little hard information.

Dr. Tatsuicho Akizuki was a 29-year-old doctor working at the Urakami Dai-ichi Hospital, 1,500 metres from the bomb's epicentre on August 9, 1945, one of the only medical figures to survive the explosion and able to help with the wounded. He is a now frail and somewhat stooped elderly man. 'In September, a month after the bomb fell, we started hearing about radiation sickness. A rumour spread that for 70 to 75 years the area around where the bomb had fallen would be uninhabitable.

'Most of those who died, died within the first 40 days. There wasn't anything that we could do for them. We couldn't even keep their wounds sterile. After that, the deaths diminished. As a doctor, how could I be sure what my patients were dying of? I seemed to be seeing a lot of tuberculosis, many stomach ulcers. But how could I blame those on the bomb? In any case, pretty quickly, I was seen as a dissident for being so active in these matters.'

Within a year of Yagamuchi's journey to Tokyo, a Japanese peace movement was born. It wasn't his inspiration alone, of course, or even mostly his. But, as so often with a popular movement, it came into existence out of an almost spontaneous national feeling among survivors all over the country that they deserved recognition and that they had been too long without it. The spark they had been waiting for came in the spring of 1954, when the wider Japanese public heard, and were revolted by, the news that the Americans had decided to conduct a new atomic test, an H-bomb this time, on Bikini Atoll, and that a Japanese tuna fishing boat called *Fukuryu-Maru 5*, ('Lucky Dragon 5'), had returned home to the port of Yaizu covered in the 'ashes of death'.

After that, things happened very fast. In Hiroshima and Tokyo, small groups, mainly of students and housewives, began to collect signatures protesting about Bikini Atoll. Out of this, in 1955, came *Gensuikyo*, the Council Against Atomic and Hydrogen Bombs, an all-party, national, anti-nuclear group. That same year, in Hiroshima, on August 6, was held the first World Conference against Atomic and Hydrogen Bombs. In Nagasaki, Yagamuchi now found the spirit to gather his friends into an Association of A-bombed Youths. 'At last, after ten despairing years, I began to find hope again,' he says. 'All of us survivors who had been so isolated began to think that there would be other voices speaking for us.'

Since those months of 1954 peace has become a word of great

potency in Japan. In May 1947, the new Western, democratic Japanese constitution, renounced 'war . . . and the threat or use of force as a means of settling international disputes'. Round this legal package has gathered committees and movements, appeals and amendments, a vast, confused, elaborate web of peace politics.

The *hibakusha*, the A-bomb survivors, occupy a special place in Japanese life today. Of the 366,523 survivors still alive and registered in the spring of 1977, there were some in their thirties, since foetuses of those two August days — a figure put by the authorities at 4,989 — are considered *hibakusha*.

The survivors are both symbols, and as such revered, and pariahs, bearing the taint of perpetual contamination, the marks of a completely new 20th century plague with its constant exhaustion, sterility and loss of hair — and, of course, leukaemia and cancer. Many of the *hibakusha* stay in close touch through Yagamuchi's now emerged Nagasaki Association of A-bombed Youths and Maidens, whose 60 surviving members gather once a month. Suicides, very frequent in the first ten years after the bomb fell, are now uncommon, particularly among those campaigning for *hibakusha* rights, though a co-founder of the movement took her own life in 1983. She had undergone, says Yagamuchi, 14 operations for keloids, and had been told that another was necessary.

It is not only the disfiguring physical marks that hold together those who shared a common moment of nightmare 42 years ago, nor their mutual terror of finding within themselves the symptoms of leukaemia and cancer. Many feel themselves to be special, to have been singled out. 'They say "Hiroshima and Nagasaki only happened because we were infamous yellow people,"' explains Yagamuchi. '"It would never have happened to the Germans. We were an experiment for the Americans." Especially in Nagasaki, that is what the *hibakusha* say: "The Americans used a different bomb on us. They needed us as guinea pigs."'

Though many of those who did survive the bombing — the 'A-bomb' is how they refer to it, pronouncing it in English 'Ebam', as if it were one distinct word — left Hiroshima soon afterwards and went to look for a new life somewhere else, those who stayed appear to have been often better treated. They suffer far less from the feeling of horror that clings to the memory of the great mushroom that rose over each city, and are better protected from the rejection and repulsion widely felt towards survivors in the other large cities of Japan. At his meeting each month Yagamuchi carefully chronicles each recent episode of discrimination he hears about: the cases of those who have been unable to find work, who have lost their jobs once news of their whereabouts on August 6 or 9, 1945, becomes known, of those who have gone to enormous lengths to keep their past a secret so that their children will be able to marry. Though no evidence of the radiation sickness has been found in 'second generation' survivors, the children of the *hibakusha*, it is generally believed that it is there, and they are widely regarded as on a par with the *eta*, the untouchables, as unsuitable brides. Even the potatoes grown in the soil around Hiroshima are suspect; they go to market under other names.

In Kyoto last year, the *hibakusha-nokai*, the Association of A-bomb Victims, who need their label to acquire their blue health books, entitling them to free medical care, renamed themselves; to outsiders, they are now the *Friends of Kyoto*. Yagamuchi knows the stigma well. After two years of intensive treatment in the late forties, he was considered well enough to go back to school to continue his training in engineering. His dream as a boy had always been to work for the Mitsubishi yards in Nagasaki, whose defences against aerial bombings he was in the middle of helping construct as a schoolboy volunteer, when the bomb fell. When he graduated, he applied to the firm for a job. Though he learned that he had passed the exam with credit, they turned him down. Until he became involved in *hibakusha* work, he made and sold rice cakes in the streets of Nagasaki.

In September 1984, I went to Japan, to visit Hiroshima and Nagasaki. Because modern pacifists live their lives filled with the images of a nuclear holocaust, I wanted to see the only two places in the world where a nuclear bomb had fallen. It became important to talk to the people who had survived it. I wanted, too, to ask: what effect did these two bombs have on the Japanese peace movement? Are Japanese pacifists different?

In the middle of Nagasaki just 100 yards from the epicentre

of the bomb, stands the peace museum, a six-storey undistinguished grey building of brick and glass. On one side is a long rectangular plot of garden, with box hedge and a stone pool full of giant goldfish and carp. Because of the scented box, and the gravel path, and a surprisingly unkempt grass lawn, it has a slightly Italian air, like the neglected formal garden of a Florentine villa.

Inside, the museum is always full. By nine in the morning orderly parties of schoolchildren assemble in the empty ground floor hall, many carrying brightly-coloured paper garlands in the shape of storks, linked one to the next, symbols in Japan of good health and good wishes. They hang them on hooks round the life-size photographs of the maimed bodies and the cabinets full of pieces of charred and twisted masonry and metal collected in the streets in the days following the bombing. They give the place an almost festive air.

Across the road, above the souvenir shop and restaurant run by the *hibakusha* to bring an income to the survivors' organization, is Yagamuchi's office. This too is filled with pictures taken in days after the bomb fell. There is still much to be done for those who remain, explains Yagamuchi, who says that a recent project has been carried out by the local social services of the city to gather the memories of those who had been blind and deaf from birth and yet survived the bomb, and whose experiences have been locked inside them for 40 years. Once they are helped to express them, he says, they experience enormous relief, because though they neither heard nor saw what befell the city, they felt the shock and the blast, and the memory has haunted them ever since.

Then there is the matter of compensation. While free medical care is available to all those who were that day within a certain radius of the bomb's epicentre, to those inside their mothers' wombs, and to those who entered the city shortly afterwards in search of relatives, there has still been no money for those who lost their homes and their livelihoods in Hiroshima and Nagasaki.

After our talk, Yagamuchi guided me, as he guides all visitors, to the peace park to look at the enormous copper god-like man whom Seibo Kitamura, himself an inhabitant of Nagasaki, designed as a memorial stone to the bomb. Yagamuchi likes to see the ways foreigners react. The almost Grecian figure, with his distinctly Aryan features and apparently blond curls falling to his massive shoulders, gazes staunchly forwards from under seemingly closed eyelids, one arm pointing outwards, the other up towards the sky, index finger extended. I said, hesitating, that the statue looked out of place. 'The inhabitants of Nagasaki hate this man,' said Yagamuchi, maintaining that he is too Western in appearance and bears too military a stance. He is, they say, a gross and menacing presence, with no delicacy or subtlety.

In Hiroshima, where I went next, peace is smarter, a more professionally organized affair. The city itself was more profoundly obliterated by the bomb than Nagasaki, for it lay contained in a valley, enclosed on three sides by hills, so that the blast and the fires were better able to build up within its walls, a fact drily recorded in the museum where there is a small note explaining that Hiroshima was selected as a target for the high density of its population and its ideal setting. Ninety-two per cent of the city was affected by the bomb; 40 per cent of it was burnt out altogether.

Today, Hiroshima is a prosperous, modern, industrial city. It is an agreeable place, having managed to retain some air of the past, with old trams that rattle through the city centre. It even boasts a pleasant tourist excursion, in the form of Miyajima Island, 15 minutes by ferry across the bay, a shrine island dedicated to the daughters of the Shinto wind god Susanoo, on which for many years neither births nor deaths were allowed to take place. Dogs are banned from the island; fallow deer graze among the visitors.

There are people in Hiroshima who want to see the city further smartened up. They feel uneasy about the image of contamination that seems to hang over the modern city blocks like an immutable, indestructible memory of fall-out. There is a new Hiroshima, they say, a port of considerable industrial vitality. What is more, only 18 per cent of Hiroshima's present inhabitants are *hibakusha*.

Zen Matsutani is a man who thinks this way. He was three when the bomb fell and he was saved by an aunt who threw herself over him as the blast brought the wooden house in which they lived down onto their heads. She died at once. He remembers the flash of light and running through the streets already on fire.

In the years that followed, the family lived in their weekend house by the sea, beyond the bomb damage, and Matsutani's father, a builder, became a millionaire rebuilding the city, and later a bankrupt, trying to govern it. Zen Matsutani is a Harvard and Heidelberg-trained lawyer who made his own fortune out of a hideous pottery doll in the shape of a baseball player before setting up an organization called the Pan Pacific Fund, which brings foreigners to Japan. Fifteen years ago, he became a Zen Buddhist. He is unusually tall, with a flat open face and teeth spaced very far apart; he wears a blue blazer with gold buttons. The present mayor of Hiroshima is a 'telegram man', he says, good only at remembering to record bomb anniversaries. With a number of friends, Matsutani has set up a new dining club and from their members he hopes will come a new mayor, with a taste for the future.

Matsutani took me to see Professor Naomi Shono, a nuclear physicist who graduated from Kinshu University in the summer of 1945 with dreams of pursuing Einstein's theory of relativity. Shono entered the burning city, three days after the bomb had fallen, in search of his parents and his uncle's family. His parents had in fact left Hiroshima just before the bomb fell and were safe; his uncle, aunt and their three children were never found. In the fifties, Professor Shono became obsessed with a 'sense of sin'. 'Since similar scientists to myself had made nuclear weapons, how could I, a physicist, go on with my work?' He said that 3,000 separate projects have now been carried out on the physical and mental effects of nuclear bombs; and that Hiroshima University has preserved 6,400 internal organs of those who died.

Zen Matsutani lives in a wooden chalet overlooking Miyajima; flags hang from the balustrades and in the garage are two large new Mazdas. The sitting-room is full of half-bottles of Beaujolais and Chianti, stacked around the walls in racks: Mrs. Matsutani manages one Italian and four French restaurants in the city, having inherited the running of a geisha house from her mother-in-law 15 years ago. Driving home from our meeting with Shono, Matsutani suddenly said that his wife was ill, that he had sent her to his brother-in-law doctor in Tokyo, and that her white blood corpuscle count was below 4,000. It should be 10,000.

'You see,' he said, with very little expression. 'I can't understand. It should be me. My wife does not come from Hiroshima.' Leukaemia in Hiroshima was running at 17 times above normal when it reached its peak in 1951. Of people who die early in the city, the inhabitants of Hiroshima say: 'He could not beat the bomb.'

A decent amount of space has been left for the peace museum, park and memorial in the centre of the city. The space is important, for Hiroshima has become the altar of the world's nuclear pilgrims, who arrive here in busloads, so that the coach park is constantly full. Hiroshima is a stop on most Japanese tours. It is also an obligatory outing for all classes at all schools. There is a feeling that visitors will willingly come as far as Hiroshima, a mere three hours from the great tourist sites of Kyoto and Nara, but that they cannot quite face the extra five by bullet train on to Nagasaki. And who can blame them? What will they find, after all, so very different?

Even attendance at the museum is somehow more muted, more reverential than in Nagasaki. The displays, in the long gallery of the ferro-concrete structure up on legs, are better lit and more formally laid out, with long textual explanations in both Japanese and English, while the whole gallery itself is dimmed. There is less chatter than in Nagasaki, and few stork garlands. Part of the display concentrates on the bomb's peculiar radioactive properties, the way it photographed both men and objects and left their imprint on the sides of walls, imprints which endured, like X-rays, after the bodies themselves were turned to ash.

The director of the museum, Yoshitaka Kawamoto, is himself a *hibakusha*, a thick-set, smartly-turned out man in a pinstripe suit. He has an interpreter, a long, thin boy with a strong American accent. Through him he explained that he believed his function to be that of witness: 'I was 13 when the bomb fell. I was standing 800 metres from the epicentre. When I look at photographs of the devastation at that point I cannot understand why I am still alive. I cannot explain why I survived. That's why I make every effort to tell children what happened.

Children aren't foolish. They will realize they have to protect themselves.'

Every year 1.4 million people come to the museum. Eighty thousand of these are foreigners, and these are increasing as businessmen add Hiroshima to their schedules. They record, in lesson books laid out for the purpose, their impressions of what they have seen. Nearly all are exclamations of horror. But in one book an American has written: 'You deserved it. What about Pearl Harbour?'

Outside the museum, at the end of the long walk that leads to the trees and the domed shell of the city hall which has been left as a reminder of the physical destruction of the city, is a small stone memorial, a curved object inside which burns a perpetual flame. It is here that visitors come to pay their respects to the dead.

On the wide platform that leads up to the stone, on the morning I was in Hiroshima, a small ceremony was being held to commemorate a nuclear test, as happens whenever a weapon is exploded.

The gathering had been fixed for midday. At 12.10 journalists and a camera crew from Hiroshima television still outnumbered the demonstrators. But then others arrived holding cushions, which they laid out in orderly rows. They were a middle-aged collection of people, housewives in neat dresses, office workers in suits, sitting cross-legged, an unsmiling, sober group; many wore straw hats to keep off the sun. A few held placards. At the back, slightly apart, sat three Buddhists. Two were elderly men, in crumpled white suits and panama hats, mildly and in unison beating two small drums. Between them sat a woman in her mid-fifties, in a dark-blue-and-white-spotted silk dress; on her head was a pale straw hat, and she held a brightly-patterned paper parasol. Looking around her at no one in particular, she kept up a steady, soft chant.

The ceremony lasted an hour. Around and among the protestors, parties of school children, in their very short blue shorts and brilliant white shirts, the girls sporting yellow, red or purple hats, formed up, advanced, bowed and filed away. A few Western tourists took pictures. Above, kites circled, then came to settle along the edge of the ferro-concrete museum building.

Up until August 6, 1945, Japan had no proper peace movement. The twenties and thirties, which saw such passionate
pacifism elsewhere in the world, saw almost none in Japan. If
the Buddhist believers found it hard to reconcile the built-in
pacifist credo of their faith with the order to fight, they usually
found it harder to disrupt the harmony for which Japanese life is
famous. When the call came in 1941, they joined the army.

The communists, who might have resisted conscription, had
been effectively crushed in the thirties when at Tokyo University alone several hundred students were arrested and tortured
for their dissident ways and as an example to others. Among the
Christians, some members of minute and often esoteric sects,
like the Mennonites and the Nonchurch, did oppose the war,
but they were quickly arrested and spent the years in prison, or
drifted away to hide in the heavily-wooded mountains of
Japan's northern islands. There was no open resistance to the
war.

Today, Japan is said to possess the largest and most effective
peace movement in the world, able without difficulty to collect
30 million signatures for any nuclear protest petition. In the 40
years of its existence in Japan, this modern concept of peace has
become politics. It has also become wise company policy, and
essential in all religious doctrine, trade union debates and state
education. There is even a cigarette called 'Peace'. In peace
affairs, however, the last 40 years have been extraordinarily
contorted and fragmented ones in Japan, with the *hibakusha* acting as major players, yet also in some ways regarded as unset-
tling in a country where the very word for peace, *'hi-wa'*, also
means 'harmony'.

After 1945, students returned from the battlefields to their
universities feeling that they had been deceived by the military;
what had been heralded as a sacred war had turned into no more
than mindless butchery. In the early fifties, as it became clear
that first the occupation authorities and then successive
Japanese governments were shifting their attention from
radical reforms towards anti-communism, and as Japanese
leaders appeared on the verge of accepting remilitarization, so
students turned towards the peace protestors in Hiroshima and
Nagasaki and rallied to the anti-nuclear cause. In 1960, for the
best part of a year, Tokyo University was constantly emptied of

students flocking to the Diet to protest against the proposed Security Treaty with America.

At the foot of Mount Fuji, where the American Marines drilled their men, small groups of housewives started complaining about this use of their land; their protest grew into peace camps. In Okinawa, outside the American base, particularly as the war in Vietnam escalated, there were repeated and bitter anti-war demonstrations.

It was not, of course, only the students who protested. *Gensuikyo*, the Japan Council against Atomic and Hydrogen Bombs, grew steadily in size and power during the fifties, establishing itself as an all-party national movement, supported *de facto* by the labour movement, and becoming largely responsible for the peace march that leaves Tokyo for Hiroshima each year. In 1963 the Socialist Party, the General Council of Trade Unions (*Sohyo*), and other groups decided to boycott the Hiroshima and Nagasaki conferences and form their own *Gensuikin* (Japan Congress Against Atomic and Hydrogen Bombs), on the grounds that *Gensuikyo* had refused to condemn Soviet nuclear tests and so become an agent of the Communist Party. All the same, the peace movement seemed healthy and widespread: peace protesters marched, carried banners, made up slogans, collected money for the *hibakusha*, staged conferences and talked. And not in vain. President Eisenhower's planned visit to Tokyo to ratify the Security Treaty was cancelled for fear of riots (it was signed instead in Washington). Towards the end of the decade, in fact, the government confirmed its non-nuclear credo. Japan, it agreed, would neither manufacture, nor use, nor bring into the country, any nuclear weapon. In 1977, *Gensuikyo* and *Gensuikin*, mollified by years of relatively harmonious co-existence, agreed to ally themselves once more, at least to the extent of working together for the peace conferences and the annual march.

It was what they were agreeing to that was sometimes in doubt. For, while 'peace' was rapidly becoming the great national slogan, it was as rapidly losing any real meaning. At best, for those who pursued it realistically, it meant stopping Japan from rearming, from acquiring her own nuclear weapons; it meant defending Article 9 of the constitution

245

forbidding the creation of any military force, against the attempts of politicians to erode or modify it. In a country previously known for its excessive militarism, this represented a cry of disillusionment over policies that had failed, a changing mood in favour of internationalism as much as anything, a seeking of links with other nations where the anti-war movement seemed a promise of modernity and democracy. The young, escaping the oppressive bonds of Japanese family society, looked abroad and saw how others of their age were going on marches and waving flags.

Perhaps not surprisingly peace in the late sixties and early seventies came to be all things to all people, so that the form it took depended on the institution adopting it. For the politician, it became a matter for negotiation, a clause on which to hang other clauses, a way of preserving the apparent status quo while bargaining quietly behind closed doors, but also a yearly matter for re-evaluation, as some factions pressed for more spending on the Self-Defence Force and others on closer ties with America. For the Labour movement, it meant an utterly reliable rallying cry; for the religious, a symbol of renewed faith in a country with little faith left. Around Japan, in the cities and in the countryside, in the name of the peace movement, many things started to happen. They continue, in ways that are not always peaceful, in fact often contradictory, today.

By tradition, a relatively small Buddhist sect, the Fujii Nittatsu, leads the peace march to Hiroshima. Unlike many other sects, it has been totally committed to pacifism. In their now distinctive yellow robes, members are encouraged to earn their own livelihoods and not depend on the temple for their keep. They are also urged to travel. One monk was at Comiso in Sicily, protesting against the arrival of Cruise missiles on Italian soil. A peace pagoda has been built by them in Britain in Milton Keynes. In Tokyo the group is called, sometimes a little disparagingly, the 'drum beaters'.

But if the Fujii Nittatsu are the most visible religious exponents of peace in Japan they are neither the best organized nor those with most power. Soon after the war ended, as if to rekindle national pride in a country where the most solid symbol of religion, the Emperor, had just been ousted from his

246

position as Shinto God, a whole collection of new religions was
born. Some were old Shinto or Buddhist sects, refashioned;
others formed around spiritual leaders, many of them women,
who called for a new belief in mental and physical well-being.

By 1951, 156 of these religions had registered themselves with
the Ministry of Education. Some have vanished: *Denshinkyo*,
which worshipped electricity as the main deity and Thomas
Edison as one of the four lesser deities has long since gone. But
others, like the Dancing Religion, founded by a farmer in
Yamagushi prefecture who wore men's clothes and was the first
woman to ride a bicycle in her district, are flourishing. What
these new religions have in common is that they demand very
little from those who join them, that they preach optimism —
the 'religion of happiness' is what many call themselves — and
that they say they intend to return to man on earth a sense of his
own importance and dignity. For this, peace is a necessity; and
virtually every new religion founded since 1945 leans heavily on
its pacifist credo. The nearer the organization to Hiroshima and
Nagasaki, the louder its affirmation of peace.

The most influential and certainly the most solidly established of these new religions revolves round the figure of a 13th
century monk called Nichiren who came to believe that he was
the only person who could save Japan from ruin, through his
own interpretation of Buddhism. Nichiren taught that all the
truth that a man needs to know is revealed in the Sutra of the
Lotus, or the Good Law, and that he must chant his homage to
the Lotus Sutra as a constant act of faith.

In the thirties, Nichiren's teachings were the inspiration of
two of the new religions, though neither came to prominence
before the mid-forties. One was Soka Gakkai, which for a long
time was the fastest-growing religion in the world, particularly
among trade unions; it has now acquired a slightly unpleasant
flavour of aggression and a reputation for militarism among its
cadres of young recruits. The other was Rissho Kosei Kai, or
the Society of the Establishment of Righteousness and Friendly
Intercourse, which preaches family life, social work and a firm
commitment to 'world peace'.

In London, a member of the Anglican Pacifist Fellowship, a
small gathering of mainly elderly Christian pacifists, had given
me an introduction to the founder of Rissho Kosei Kai, Nikkyo

Niwano, a former milkman in Tokyo, who, in 1937, followed the path of Nichiren and chanted the Lotus Sutra with 20 friends.

I had been told that the Rissho Kosei Kai headquarters were at Honancho, a suburb of Tokyo. It seemed a likely address, a suitably obscure district, far from the fashionable city centre, perfect for a small gathering of probably cloistered elderly religious pacifists. I changed underground trains three times and emerged on a wide boulevard of office blocks and local shops. Following instructions, I started walking west, looking out for a small house, perhaps a couple of rooms above a shop. It was very humid. After 20 minutes, I gave up. Nothing seemed to correspond to my directions. Hot, petulant, I went to find a telephone; an English-speaking secretary redirected me.

It was only now that I noticed that just off the main road, partly hidden by some trees, stood an immense Buddhist temple, made of pink ferro-concrete. From a platform to one side two men in black suits and a third, in the sky blue and gold-braided uniform of a doorman at a grand hotel, were waving energetically. As I drew near, I saw that behind lay a second enormous temple, a round building with Indian domes, and beyond again a third edifice, a vast square hall many storeys high, like a United Nations headquarters. All the buildings were pink, the favourite colour, I was later informed, of Mrs. Naganuma Myoko, co-founder with Nikkyo Niwano of Rissho Kosei Kai.

President Niwano is not accustomed to being kept waiting. I was hurried through the lobby of the temple, with its panels of the Four Noble Truths, up in a lift and down a main guest hall with tapestries of the 'All Sidedness of the Bidhisattra Regarder of the Cries of the World' and into the large conference room, decorated by a ceramic panel of a Zen master sitting in a tree, in which waited six aides with tape recorders and two men with cameras. The President himself, a tall, toothy, smiling man in his 77th year, was ushered in by a further cortège of aides, and wrapped into a blanket for our audience. When secretaries and the two women clearing tea left the room, they walked backwards.

Rissho Kosei Kai, the President announced at once through his interpreter, has 5.7 million members throughout Japan.

They are all pacifists. Since all are brothers and sisters, killing each other is clearly impossible.

President Niwano is used to audiences. He declared, unprompted, that true light about pacifism came to him only immediately after the war, when he learned that 450 of his followers had walked into a battle and not one had been killed, though the rest of their regiment had been slaughtered. Since that day, he said, he has studied Gandhi, and found in his teachings many similarities to Buddha's words; he was also much impressed by the sincerity of a party of anti-war American Unitarians who had visited Tokyo at the time of the Vietnam War.

The Rissho Kosei Kai claim 10,000 people at their daily morning service in the pink temple. Aides talk about good works, about group counselling and the importance of blending deep faith with daily life. Nikkyo Niwano is a vice-president of the World Conference on Religion and Peace and spends much of his time travelling, addressing peace conferences around the world. He is not a supporter of the Japanese peace movement, which he considers divisive and unproductive. I asked him what he would say to his members in the event of Japan becoming involved in another war. 'I would instruct them to refuse to fight,' he replied, smiling his warm toothy smile. Each morning, when the 5.7 million of the faithful assemble in their meeting places all round the country, there is a moment's pause, followed by 'Good morning, Mr. President', as they humbly address their unseen founder in Tokyo.

In the Labour movement, peace has quite another face. Harmony has taken a battering in recent years. In April 1984, the Communist Party newspaper *Akahata* carried an article condemning the leadership of *Gensuikyo*. It was working far too closely with *Gensuikin*, the paper warned, and *Gensuikin* was a 'divisionist organisation . . . clearly swinging to the right'. In a mood of rapidly escalating mutual hostility *Gensuikyo* was suddenly purged of its most dissident, that is to say most moderate, members.

One of these was the Venerable Gyotsu Sato, a former Air Force captain and graduate of Japan's foremost military academy who, so people say, was prevented from disembowelling himself at the gates of the Emperor's palace in 1945 by a passing Nichiren monk who persuaded him that Japan's dishonour could be better exorcised following Buddha's path than in ritual suicide. The Venerable Sato is stout, affable and wears a crew-cut and huge leather boots under his yellow robe. He has a room in a small house in a shabby suburb of Tokyo which he calls his 'peace office'. While *Akahata* continues to slight him by refusing to use his title in its editorials, he is seeking supporters for a new, politically unaligned peace organization. In the little office bare of everything except a row of school tables and some fold-up chairs, with a mop leaning against one corner, far from the glass and chrome splendour of *Gensuikyo*'s modern central headquarters, there is much talk of grass roots, a sentiment finding increasing expression among peace workers, who are beginning to declare that the monolithic structure of the 30-year-old peace movement is quite irrelevant to peace.

Among the peace campaigners there is not one who does not volunteer that the movement was born of the two bombs that fell on Japan in August 1945. Without those, they agree, there would be no Japanese peace movement. The bombs, says the Venerable Sato, are the 'inherited property of our movement. Just as the *hibakusha* are.' When not long ago national television showed a new documentary on the Nuclear Holocaust, 33,000 people tried to reach the television station by telephone. The 3,000 who were put through all said the same thing: 'We don't want to die.' If anything, the cult of the anti-bomb grows stronger. In 1975, 59 per cent of the population of Japan declared that Hiroshima and Nagasaki were matters that should never be forgotten. In 1982, that number had risen to 77 per cent.

But what, the protesters ask themselves, does the peace commitment amount to? Except among a very few Christian minorities, 'pacifism', as an idea, does not exist. The term is seen as woolly, impractical. Even those most active within the peace movement look confused, slightly affronted, if asked whether they would call themselves a 'pacifist', a person opposed to all wars, all fighting, at all times. 'Peace,' explained the Venerable Sato, 'means protesting against what happened to us in 1945. It means preventing Japan from rearming and hoping possibly to influence world leaders about nuclear weapons. What it doesn't mean is a philosophical discussion about past military behaviour or even whether or not to spend more on defence.' This is especially true among the young, born long after the bombs fell, but brought up in a country where peace education (post-Hiroshima peace education) and a visit to the Hiroshima Peace Museum (which records nothing, no act of war, other than the bomb and its aftermath) are made an important stage in growing up. No one talks about what happened before August 6, 1945. That is history.

Peace work, like being a *hibakusha*, can also have its dangerous side. On a train to Kamakura, the old capital of Japan, an hour's journey by train from Tokyo, I was approached by a girl who wished to practise her English. She told me she had just joined *Gensuikyo* as a volunteer in the international department and that she was much upset by the recent squabbles. Yasuko Kusachi is in her early twenties, a part-time teacher whose union, affiliated to *Gensuikyo*, actively encourages her to become involved. But both her elder brother and sister work for Japanese companies, industrial concerns where harmony is valued. Belonging to the peace movement is not considered harmonious; it suggests extreme feelings, perhaps even conflicting interests. Both are anxious about having a sister so publicly caught up with peace.

Inside the universities the spirit of protest has waned in the last few years. The combination of the savage battles between students and police in the late sixties, in which protest turned more rapidly into bloody confrontation than on Western campuses, combined with a canny political decision to shift the debate from peace to economic growth (so that prosperity came to equal peace) has resulted in a generation of students, uneasy at heart, yet more interested in organizing concerts than in becoming involved in mass movements. When the Prime Minister, Yasuhiro Nakasone, began talking sympathetically about the desire evinced by the Americans to see Japan rearmed and her defence budget increased, and hinted that conscription might be brought in for the Self-Defence Force, it was the Conservative Women's group in Parliament who protested. The students said nothing. This has not prevented a growing involvement with America, as the constitution made inevitable,

251

but it has meant that there is a resistance among politicians to dwell on it too openly.

Every year, in the decades that preceded the Second World War, the Prime Minister of Japan and his Cabinet paid a formal visit to the Yasukuni Jinja Shrine near the Imperial Palace in Tokyo, the memorial to all those who have died for the Emperor. With its ferocious scenes of the Russo-Japanese war, its oddly carved monuments to the spirits of departed soldiers, the military used it as a kind of symbol of nationalism. After MacArthur separated state from religion, the Yasukuni Shrine lost its government support and its status; for many years no official Japanese went near it.

Since 1980, however, government ministers have taken to paying their respects once more before the shrine, though in a private capacity. In 1984, Prime Minister Nakasone suggested that these visits should perhaps be made official once again. United in nothing else, the many splinters of the Japanese peace movement have become united in this: Rissho Kosei Kai, Buddhists, Christians, *Gensuikyo* and *Gensuikin*, students and grass roots activists, all rose up in fury at what they have declared is the symbol of an official desire to see Japan remilitarized. It is as if, suddenly and with a sense of panic, they have become fully conscious of the frailty of their peace organizations, enormous and vocal though they are.

10

The United States: civil rights and beyond

There is something about American pacifism that is different; and also too large to take in easily. As if, having cut its teeth on so many other issues it has become in the process more virile, more sophisticated than other forms of pacifism, with a grandeur that carries it well beyond single causes. It means that one can understand it only by looking at the lives of a few, often isolated men and women, at different times in pacifist history, and by hoping that something of their style and enormous diversity will come across.

Over the decades, the pacifists seem to have rolled in waves. Drawn in by their Quaker upbringing, they turned at first to civil rights; tutored on the freedom rides and the lunch counter sit-ins, they embraced the marches on Washington against the war in Vietnam, then hastened on to challenge the threat of nuclear war; children at the time Saigon fell, they now work for the Sanctuary movement, giving refuge in Arizona and Texas to those fleeing persecution in Central America. It is as if, along the way, they pause, reflect, then dive back in again. It gives pacifism an excitement that it does not quite have elsewhere. Nowhere is this more true than with the fight for civil rights; seldom has pacifism taken such a forceful direction.

Bayard Rustin was in England for the first Aldermaston march, at Easter 1958. He had been sent from America by the Fellowship of Reconciliation and the War Resisters' League of which he was Executive Secretary, to see what he could do to help. He was 47, a tall, thin man with a small moustache, a conscientious objector who had served 28 months in various federal penitentiaries for his anti-war views, and far more experienced in pacifist confrontation than any of the young 'Operation Gandhi' supporters by whose side he marched in the rain down the damp Berkshire roads. He was also black. They must have seemed very innocent to him, very carefree, with their childlike banners of exhortation, and their belief that the bomb was the one great enemy to destroy. That they liked him so much, that they followed his advice so willingly, says much for the tact with which he must have treated their opinions.

Rustin had always been a pacifist. He was born in West Chester, Pennsylvania, and grew up under the sway of a Quaker grandmother whom he remembers as a woman with very clear precepts about anger and retribution. 'In my family,' he says, 'I never saw anyone express frustration or anger. We were taught to do what they did.' Rustin is now in his mid-seventies, his hair white, his manner a little statesmanlike, dispensing world thoughts from an office in New York where he is director of the Philip Randolph Institute, a politically shrewd civil rights educational body. He is somewhat disorganized, relying frequently on the memory of a young assistant, but expansive; he talks quickly, tipping his chair back, his informality and gestures those of a much younger, athletic man. In recent years he has become a somewhat controversial figure. But it was in his hands, and those of others like him, that pacifism, in the two decades that followed the war, took one of its most distinguished turns.

In the thirties, Rustin came to New York to sing in cafés with Leadbelly and Josh White, and to listen to the Young Communist League on its strong stands on war and racism. He had heard about Gandhi in high school, where a teacher who took an optional early morning class in current events — 19 students out of a full complement of 500 rose to hear him — had been so impressed by Gandhi's work that he wrote to India for material for his students. When Muriel Lester came to America from Bow in 1937, on the third of her great speaking tours as travelling ambassador for the Fellowship of Reconciliation, it was natural that Rustin should find a way of meeting her. He was already in awe of her reputation, as host to Gandhi for the Round Table Conference, and as representative of the British Christian pacifists, who were widely admired among American pacifists of the thirties. He found her extraordinarily compelling. 'She had,' he says, 'a prophetic voice.' Rustin was drawn towards the Fellowship of Reconciliation, as many who listened to her were; he felt that she had helped him to see that he had to find some other way of dealing with conflict. Her words and

Gandhi's teachings 'caused my basic sense of non-violence to flourish: without them I might have ended up ashamed'. When Muriel Lester left New York to continue her tour, Rustin went with her. In 1945 he was to lead the Free India Committee and face repeated arrest for sitting down in front of the British Embassy in Washington.

There was a small coffee house in New York near City College where students went to talk in the late thirties. Rustin, being black, was not allowed to join them. He was not the only black student, nor the only student of any colour, to feel the injustice, and in other cafés, other meeting rooms, much discussion took place about how young blacks should go right on into the café and insist on being served. One day they did; the age of sit-ins had begun. Their small success was not all that remarkable; coffee shops rely on students and the students felt very strongly. But they were served, and they had been successful, and that, says Rustin, mattered: success made the next step possible, and the one after that, and so it continued. Rustin was neither the first to challenge the system, nor the front-runner in the sit-ins: civil rights marches and boycotts, on a small scale, were well under way, much encouraged by more prominent people like A. Philip Randolph, President of the Brotherhood of Sleeping Car Porters, one of the most powerful black groups in the country and already well aware of the value of Gandhian tactics. But Rustin, an instinctive campaigner and personally very brave, kept up the pressure on white store-owners in Harlem and was good at getting his petitions signed. In 1942 a small gathering of FOR people, with the example of Gandhi in mind, agreed to 'confront racial injustice without fear, without compromise and without hatred'. They called themselves the Congress of Racial Equality, CORE. Rustin was their first field secretary. Word spread from Chicago, where the group had originally met, to other cities; new groups, still under the aegis of the pacifist Christian FOR were set up in Detroit, Syracuse and New York. To celebrate their first national conference, held in June 1943, CORE arranged for 65 people to stage a sit-in at Stoners, an expensive all-white Chicago restaurant: when they won, and Stoners agreed to change its segregationalist policy, they must have felt their movement was going well.

By this time, however, Rustin was on his way to his first

prison sentence as a conscientious objector to the war in Europe and the Pacific. As a Quaker, he could have taken alternative service, gone off to one of the work camps set up for men like him; he refused the offer, saying that it was conscription itself that he objected to and that in any case he judged it wrong that Quakers almost alone should have such an option. The Tribunal judge, at his hearing, proved sympathetic to the aims of CORE; he gave its field secretary six months in which to put his work in order before serving his prison sentence.

In the autumn of 1943, Rustin reported to Ashland prison, in Kentucky, to serve a three-year sentence. It was a limited security jail; the men could work outside the prison walls, keep their cell doors open and take what exercise they wished. What they could not do was mix: sleeping and eating were both segregated. There were few criminal offenders at Ashland: many of the inmates were Kentucky moonshiners, men in their fifties and sixties, serving short sentences for brewing illegal whisky. A third, perhaps, were conscientious objectors, and many of those Jehovah's Witnesses. It was a good moment to try out a few of CORE's new tactics.

The conscientious objectors were, as Rustin remembers, very young; at 33, he was older than most, and nearly all of them, of course, were white, the Second War seeing relatively few black war protesters. 'We were anxious to satisfy ourselves that we weren't what people called us: cowards, traitors. We wanted to show that we didn't reject the necessity to face injustice, but that we intended to engage in conflict in another way.' Some of the white young men had never thought of this sort of thing before; they were devout, moral people, from close-knit homes, where obedience was insisted on. For them confrontation was a very alien and often frightening idea. Rustin says that he learnt a lot about courage, about men's limits and their endurance, in these months.

Having asked for, and not surprisingly been refused, an end to segregation in the prison, as well as closure of the jail's solitary confinement cells, and for more books, 150 men went on a hunger strike. Twenty-eight days later most were very weak; three seemed to be on the point of dying. Faced by the prospect of transferring so many men to a hospital to force feed them, the Governor, supported by his Washington superiors, who had other things on their minds than the requests of a few recalcitrant conchies, agreed to lift segregation. The battle had been won in part because of the moonshiners. These men were on the whole illiterate; they warmed to the conscientious objectors when they took time to write their letters home for them and to read them the funnies. A few casual classes in literacy were begun. Furthermore, many of the pacifists were vegetarians: by sitting with them the moonshiners could get more meat. So they supported their aims and fought the cause of desegregation with them. It helped that the governor was a decent man, a doctor with relatives in the Church of Brethren; he was lonely and he was interested in why people became pacifists.

Desegregation, for a few blacks, had been a small affair. Solitary confinement, in Rustin's words the 'solar plexus' of the penal system, was quite another matter. Demands for no more punishment of this kind were not tolerable. Twenty-eight of the more prominent troublemakers, Rustin among them, were now moved to Lewisburg Penitentiary in Pennsylvania; after Alcatraz, it was the prison with the tightest security in the entire country. The conscientious objectors were known as the 'poisonous protest'. Thirty-seven men — other intractables from other jails had been sent to join them — spent 18 months confined in the prison library, which had been cleared to accommodate them. Here they ate and slept and worked, isolated from all danger of contaminating the other prisoners. They had 30 minutes' exercise each day. At the end of the war, they came out of prison very determined, and with new confidence, resolved both to keep up their Gandhian tactics and to bring reform to America's jails. As in Britain, a serious move for prison reform, prodded by the conscientious objectors, took shape: rehabilitation, education, training, all became issues that were never again dropped.

There had been about 35 key leaders, a few of them black, most of them white, among the conscientious objectors. When they returned to civilian life they found the country full of black ex-soldiers who had spent their war years in Europe being treated, in the main, with toleration. These men, remembering the segregation of their own childhoods, came back 'prepared to do war'. Harnessed to the Gandhian pacifist tactics of CORE, they were to prove a formidable army.

257

Up until now CORE's activities had been local. In 1948 the Supreme Court ruled that inter-state travel would no longer be segregated. The first freedom ride to test the ruling took place the following spring. Some ten men, all of them pacifists, some black, some white, set off in twos and threes to ride the Grey-hound and Trailways buses through the upper South. Photographs show tidy, respectable men, in wide-brimmed hats and suits, carrying the square functional suitcases of the day; hair cut short and brushed well back, folded overcoats over one arm, they might have been, like the early British bomb protesters, teachers heading for a convention in a small suburban town. Rustin alone sports a raffish bow tie.

The freedom riders encountered more surprise than actual harassment. But soon some were arrested. In North Carolina, Rustin, and two whites, Igal Rodenko and Joe Felmet, served 30-day sentences in segregated chain gangs for sitting together at the front of a bus. Rustin returned to write up his experiences for the newspapers.

FOR had ridden high during the war, its membership rising to 15,000. People found its purity and its return to a sober Christian morality comforting. After the war ended, the idea of extending its activities to civil rights at first seemed exciting, but not all the Christian pacifists, brought to their faith by a steady consideration of the Bible, found these new and testing issues easy to absorb. By the end of the forties, CORE had left FOR's umbrella and set up on its own. Its origins were palpably pacifist; its new followers sometimes less so.

The real thrust of the movement took another seven years to develop. During that time Rustin went to India, at the invitation of the Indian Congress Party, to study the Gandhian movement. On December 1, 1955, in an episode familiar to an entire genera-tion of people all over the world, a seamstress in a Montgomery, Alabama, store called Rosa Parks was going home from work on a city bus when she was ordered by the driver to give up her seat to a white passenger, as directed by law. Mrs. Parks declined. The driver had her arrested. The seamstress was well liked by Montgomery's black community. She had once been secretary to Ed Nixon, a divisional head of the Brotherhood of Sleeping Car Porters; she asked him to bail her out.

Next day, Nixon phoned Ralph Abernathy, pastor of the

First Baptist Church of Montgomery, to propose a one-day boycott of the city buses. Martin Luther King, Jr., pastor of the Dexter Avenue Baptist Church, was one of about 40 local community leaders to endorse the boycott. He asked Rustin to come and help organize the 42,000 blacks now drawn in. After the boycott was won — though it took 55 weeks — Rustin went north again, saying that the event had been significant, not least because 'it reveals to a world sick with violence that non-violent resistance has relevance today in the United States against forces that are prepared to use extreme measures to crush it'.

Montgomery, for Rustin, was the start of seven years' work with Martin Luther King, who was soon to win far greater renown for his crusade for civil rights, and for his widely-quoted words on non-violence and peace. It was King who said of the bus boycott that 'Christ furnished the spirit, while Gandhi furnished the method'. Early in 1957 they formed the Southern Christian Leadership Conference (SCLC) to carry the lessons proved in Montgomery throughout the South. So as to spend more time in the movement, King resigned his pastorate, and early in 1960 moved to the headquarters of the SCLC in Atlanta, his home city. Later, speaking of his own 'intellectual pilgrimage to non-violence', he said how much he had been moved by Gandhi's Salt March and how it was in Gandhi's emphasis on love and non-violence that he had discovered a method for social reform he had long been seeking. 'It must be emphasized,' he wrote, 'that non-violent resistance is not a method for cowards . . . The phrase "passive resistance" often gives the false impression that this is a sort of "do-nothing method" in which the resister quietly and passively accepts evil. But nothing is further from the truth . . . The method is passive physically, but strongly active spiritually. It is not passive non-resistance to evil, it is active non-violent resistance to evil.' To win the friendship and understanding of opponents, to accept suffering without retaliation, to keep believing that the universe is fundamentally on the side of justice — these, said King, were 'basic facts' for the non-violent resister to remember.

His followers did not always find it easy. The confrontations were met by hostility, jeers, physical attacks and arrests. From now on, CORE in the North and SCLC in the South kept up a steady pressure with boycotts and sit-ins, while in 1960 the Student Non-violent Coordinating Committee (SNCC) was set up to act as an umbrella to the thousands of students engaged in 'sit-ins', 'jail-ins' and 'kneel-ins' to highlight segregation throughout the country. For the first time, the non-violent techniques introduced by CORE 15 years before were being used on a mass basis.

Zohara Simmons, from Atlanta, Georgia, left the black university, Spellman College, in September 1962. Atlanta was still totally segregated: white and black neither ate, nor travelled, nor went to hotels together. She joined the Rev. Abernathy's church and was often there when Martin Luther King came to speak; soon a friend of Abernathy's sister, she was invited to their houses. Faces she had only seen before on television turned into people whose dedication impressed her. In tone, much of it was religious, not only among the Baptists, but with the Quakers, of whom she had known nothing before but whose homes, in Atlanta, provided one of the very few places blacks and whites could meet.

It was inevitable that she should be drawn in. By the time Zohara Simmons was involved, sit-ins had spread to 50 cities. 'There was,' she says, 'a lot of talk about the philosophy of what we were doing. Dr. King was certainly pacifist: he wasn't just talking about strategy. I was often troubled about letting people push me around. But tactically he convinced me that we would win the hearts and minds of US citizens by being well mannered.' Training in non-violent techniques went on continuously: how to go limp when picked up, how to remain calm, how to reduce tension. 'In big meetings you'd get men who gave money but said: "I can't march. If someone hit me, I'd hit them back." We weeded them out.'

Zohara Simmons is a tall, lanky woman with big round glasses and a halo of frizzy hair; she is energetic, purposeful and serious. She works in Philadelphia for the American Friends' Service Committee, founded in 1917 to provide alternative work for conscientious objectors and radical ever since in its opposition to all war. Zohara worked for the SNCC right through the sixties, active across the South, watching the tactics of non-violence, to which she felt instinctively wedded, erode as civil rights campaigners in the front line found it ever harder to contain their anger, and as emphasis shifted away from non-violence and towards black power. The gains the early resisters had made seemed at the time small. Now, when she travels back to cities in which, 15 years ago, she could get no hotel reservations and could ride only in black taxis, she is amazed by the speed with which so much changed. What she has not done is lose her faith in non-violence; tough, clear-sighted, she is almost sentimental on this question. 'I think Dr. King and those genuine in their hearts were pacifists. Their loss to the movement is something we've never recovered from. When I look back to those many local leaders, spiritual people whose names I probably never even knew, particularly the women who housed the workers and baked their suppers, I know that love is a force for change. Then we admired them but thought it all a bit sentimental. Looking back now I know it was important. And when the struggle moved away with the young Turks, much of that was lost.'

In August 1963 Rustin led a march on Washington, inspired, at least in part, by what he had seen at Aldermaston. It was the largest demonstration in the history of America: 250,000 people, among them 150 members of Congress, with a mission to gain federal support for the drive against segregation in the deep South. Martin Luther King spoke, as did Rosa Parks and Ralph Abernathy; Bob Dylan, Joan Baez and Peter, Paul and Mary sang the songs of integration. In 1964 Congress passed a Civil Rights Act, outlawing job discrimination on the basis of race, colour, religion, sex or national origin, and banning segregation in all public places. The civil rights movement was not over yet; marches, sit-ins, arrests were to go on for the rest of the decade, but non-violence as a tactic had lost some of its charm, and attention was swinging round to Vietnam. King, a year before his death in Memphis, Tennessee, on April 3, 1968, spoke out publicly about the war in South-East Asia, but there was considerable doubt among some of his followers, like Bayard Rustin, as to how wise it was to combine both issues; the philosophical lines at least, many felt and said, should be kept clear.

The battle for civil rights had not precisely been about pacifism; but its founders had been pacifists, schooled in the pacifist traditions of America, and its tactics had come from

Gandhi and non-violence. After Indian independence, so people would argue, the civil rights victories were the most important political successes of pacifist methods.

During the summer of 1963, the War Resisters' League set up a peace action committee to consider America's support for the war in Vietnam. A first, very small, gesture of protest: the house of South Vietnam's permanent observer at the United Nations was briefly picketed. It was not until the following December, 1964, in sub-freezing weather, that 1,500 New Yorkers turned out to listen to one of the great 20th century labour leaders and peace campaigners, A. J. Muste, denounce the war. Muste was a Presbyterian from Newton in Massachusetts, one of 70 ministers who lost their pulpits because of their pacifism in the First War. He was a tall, thin, long-necked man with glasses, who would become more long-necked with age, like a frail and dignified eagle. Veteran of the labour strikes of the twenties, active in every pacifist and civil rights issue in the decades that followed, he would give the growing protest against the war in South-East Asia great distinction. Sparked off by the rally in New York, other war protesters spoke in Minneapolis, Miami, Austin, Sacramento, Philadelphia, Chicago, Washington, Cleveland and Boston. In San Francisco, Joan Baez sang.

America first bombed Vietnam early in February 1965. The pacifists greeted it with a Declaration of Conscience. By that summer, some 6,000 Americans had pledged 'conscientious refusal to cooperate with the United States Government in the prosecution of the war in Vietnam', saying that, among other things, they believed that 'all peoples of the earth, including both Americans and non-Americans, have an inalienable right to life, liberty and the peaceful pursuit of happiness in their own way'. A. J. Muste and Bayard Rustin were among the first who signed, as were a large number of clergymen, intellectuals and academics. That year, a year of marches, demonstrations and acts of civil disobedience in Washington, in which hundreds of people were arrested and splattered with red paint by angry patriots, an 82-year-old refugee from Nazi Germany burnt herself to death in protest against the war, and was soon copied by a Quaker and a young Catholic worker.

Randy Kehler was in all things unlike Bayard Rustin: he was white, from a liberal Republican family living in an affluent New York suburb. He was raised, as he puts it, to have 'a social conscience of sorts', but it was not one which was concerned with war or peace. Kehler came to pacifism through the civil rights movement.

He was 19, on his way to meet a friend with whom he was going to a concert, when his train stopped in mid-Harlem and he had to get out and walk. It was 1963, an evening in early summer; he did not feel particularly afraid. On the pavement, at one end of 123rd Street, he saw a large group of people collecting round a speaker; he wandered up, thinking it might be to do with Malcolm X and the Black Muslims, something he had earlier that day been reading about. Almost at once, he was surrounded by four blacks about his own age who, with a certain urgency, pulled him into a nearby building, saying that the meeting was dangerous, no place for a young white. The building turned out to be the offices of CORE, currently busy arranging the August march on Washington. While the crowd dispersed outside, Kehler offered to stuff envelopes.

Kehler never got to his concert. Instead, he listened to the CORE supporters talking and by the time he left much later that night he had agreed to start raising money towards the march. His parents, surprisingly sympathetic, suggested names of possible contributors among their friends.

The bus that was to take the marchers to Washington left from Harlem at midnight; Kehler found himself sitting next to the only other white man on the bus, an elderly man reading through a War Resisters' League calendar that seemed to include short biographies of famous pacifists. Stopping at a page on Max Sandima, the repeatedly jailed anti-war exile from Russia, one of the few conscientious objectors to be sentenced to death by an American tribunal in 1917, the old man passed the calendar over. Kehler looked at it and passed it back. 'I'm Sandima,' said his neighbour. 'And pacifism is not a word in my vocabulary.' Kehler remembers that what he chiefly felt was curiosity. 'This was all so new to me. The word pacifism raised so many images. I said to him: "If a man was holding a knife at your mother's throat, what would you do?" He looked at me. "I can't tell you what I'd so. I can only tell you what I've done." He must have been about 90, and here he was on his way to Washington, but he still wasn't willing to consider hypothetical situations. That impressed me.' Several years later, when Kehler was refusing to fill in the papers that would have entitled him to request alternative service to the war in Vietnam, he did so partly because, remembering Sandima, he would not consider the hypothetical.

The civil rights campaign was giving way to the protests about the war in Vietnam while Kehler went to Harvard; he disliked campus life intensely, feeling claustrophobic and spent his free time teaching inner city children in a nearby settlement house. In his senior year a petition came round: 'I publicly declare,' it said, 'that if called to serve in Vietnam I will refuse.' He signed it, one of 50 out of some 10,000 Harvard students to do so. 'It was clear to me that it was an illegal act,' Kehler says. 'I kept imagining the hand on my shoulder and the dungeon.' He had no taste for martyrdom.

At Stanford for a postgraduate fellowship to study teaching, Kehler heard about a course on non-violence at the Free University; he joined it. It was not all theory. The students were taken to a military induction centre in Oakland to prepare for a non-violent sit-in. 'I went along,' says Kehler, 'but I wasn't certain it was a good idea.' He had said that he would be there only in the role of supporter; in the event, he was impressed. He had thought it would be rowdy, disorganized, a little absurd; he liked the calm, the sense of dignity. At the last moment he sat down with the others and, when they went to jail, he went with them, to serve a ten-day sentence.

What intrigued Kehler, when he looked around at his fellow inmates, was who they were. They were not just students, members of a hippy generation for whom he felt no natural sympathy. There was a doctor, a landscape architect, a psychologist, a bookshop owner, family men in their fifties and sixties. There is something of Candide in Kehler; he is mild, shrewd, good-tempered with gentle and courteous manners. 'I kept asking them: do you really mean to say that you can have a profession, and raise a family, and *still* do this? What I couldn't get over was that these were normal men, for whom protest was a normal way of life.'

In prison, Kehler met people who worked for the War

Resisters' League, which from the very start had strongly opposed the draft. When he came out, he left his studies and stayed to work for them on the West Coast. It was, he says now, the most exciting time of his life: for three years he organized demonstrations, arranged and carried out acts of civil disobedience, taught Gandhian non-violence as a technique and worked to get military deserters to Canada and Sweden. It was not until the summer of 1969 that he was picked up, by three plainclothes FBI men, purporting to be newspaper reporters. In Wyoming, in February 1970, he received a two-year prison sentence. He had thought it might be longer, this being conservative cattle country. He did not appeal. He put down the lightness of the sentence to the fact that he was middle class and that his respectable parents testified to his good character.

Kehler served 22 months in all, in two separate prisons. The first, Safford, Arizona, was a minimum security jail; like most other conscientious objectors he made trouble and was soon moved on. The second jail was near Pasco, Washington, medium security, and he was put there for helping organize a strike. He was told that he had a negative attitude towards prison life. 'I guess,' he says, 'that I'm an inveterate organizer.' Released from the 'hole', after three weeks of dank, dark, solitary punishment, he spent the rest of his time quite peacefully, studying Spanish, playing the guitar his parents had been allowed to send him and meditating. Towards the end, when the novelty wore off, he longed to get out.

The war in Vietnam gave rise, in America, to quite new patterns of resistance and to a whole new rhetoric of protest. Starting in 1967, non-cooperation with the Selective Service Act led thousands of young men to return their draft cards to the government or to destroy them in public acts of protest and so risk felony indictments. The wider movement, which took real effect when 175 men ceremonially burnt their draft cards after a march on the UN in April, became cohesive and national in a way that the war protest had not quite been before. It led to much-publicized trials, unusual in the history of the pacifist movement, and to exploits in which draft boards were raided and their files seized and destroyed, symbolic acts that seemed to entrance the whole of the American intellectual left.

The early draft board raiders were mainly Catholic, and exempt from the draft either because of their vocation as priests or because of their age. Only later were the raiders young and secular. They were given no particular name, but their deeds produced a language: their exploits became known as 'actions', and they themselves 'actors'; raiders raided in order to 'witness', consciously using the Quaker word and the Quaker idea that a man's witness can move the conscience of an entire people. The draft board raiders wanted to be brought to trial; they wanted the chance to speak, to turn the courtrooms into places where the illegality and the immorality of the war in Vietnam would be put on show. As one defendant, speaking of his particular raid, would put it: 'I entered that building with much of the same intention with which I'd entered the Society of Jesus, in order to be of service in some way to other men . . .'

The first draft raider was a 19-year-old Minnesotan called Barry Bondhus, who broke into his nearby draft board and emptied two enormous buckets of human faeces into a cabinet containing several hundred draft records. Barry and his 11 brothers had spent the two previous weeks carefully preserving their excrement. His action became known as the Big Lake One action, after Big Lake, Minnesota, his home town. After him, came the Baltimore Four (October 1967: 600 draft records defiled with blood); the Catonsville Nine (May 1968, 378 draft files destroyed with home-made napalm); the Boston Two (June 1968: hundreds of draft records obliterated with black paint); the Pasadena Three (May 1969: 500 records burned); and many others. When three young men mutilated some of the records at the Selective Service office in Silver Spring, Maryland, with a mixture of blood and paint, they issued a statement: 'We accuse you, the American Government, of mass murder in Vietnam, of economic oppression in underdeveloped nations, as well as in our own cities, of the creation of a life-style based on the priority of property over lives . . .' It is doubtful that the trials these actions led to would have been the same anywhere else. There is something more radical, more accusatory, more grandiloquent in the purity of the stand the men took than in similar trials elsewhere. In comparison the Old Bailey Secrets Trial of the five young British anti-war protesters seems a little drab. These seminarians were bookish men, carrying out their own defence, and their learning filled the little courtrooms of the small conservative cities where they were tried with an eloquence they had rarely encountered before.

The sentences the raiders were given were usually stiff — three, five, seven years in jail — but those convicted seemed to view them with indifference. Once their imprisonment was over, many emerged for only a few hours before setting out on another 'action' as certain as the first to bring heavy penal sentences. Charles Muste completed a first sentence at the age of 20. Eighteen hours after being discharged from parole supervision he joined 14 others to raid the draft board on Chicago's South Side, where they seized some 40,000 draft records and celebrated Pentecost by burning them in a nearby side-street. 'I feel guilty about having it so good,' Muste is quoted as saying to a friend. 'It's not really so different out here from in there.'

Across the United States, people felt very different emotions towards the raiders and their trials. Some found them silly, some objectionable, some rather threatening. On the Left, there was something approaching hero worship for the small band of martyrs in whose hands the country's conscience sometimes seemed to lie. And, as most of the seminarians vanished into prison, there was concern that the splendid tactics might not be achieving their aim, that the forum for discussion had not been large enough, that, in the words of Francine du Plessix Grey, who covered many of the trials for the *New York Review of Books*, they had become 'like chamber music played to the intimate audience of the peace community'. What worried her, and others like her, was that if the actions were forced to become more violent, the movement would 'lose its moral force and its dimension of hope'.

The judges did not find these trials so easy either. The Vietnam War was posing them a terrible dilemma: they were obliged to uphold the statute 'against counselling, aiding and abetting the erosion of the draft' and still come to terms with the fact that, Dr. Benjamin Spock, America's most celebrated paediatrician, or William Sloane Coffin, the Chaplain of Yale University, who from time to time stood before them in the dock, were not the kind of person they had ever sent to jail before. The state seemed to be trying men who, once in the dock, lost no time in bringing the state itself to trial.

As the war went on, thousands of men and women signed statements of 'complicity', in much-publicized and often televised ceremonies, so that they could be seen actually 'abetting' and 'aiding' the draft resisters by accepting the draft cards offered them. The impression grew that many Americans were now willing to break the law in order to bring the war to an end: the most honourable strategy for an honourable and moral man had become that of breaking an unjust law. It reduced those in power to disgust. 'These naïve men,' Richard Nixon, then Presidential candidate, said of the Columbia University students and professors after they had risen up to protest against the war in May 1968, 'are failing their country. They are chipping away at the fragile structure of liberty which it has taken mankind thousands of years to perfect.'

By the end of the war, one million draft cards were said to have been burned, mutilated or destroyed, and 3,000 young men had been convicted, and gone to prison or to alternative service. Some 170,000 in all had taken a conscientious objector stand and won a victory of sorts: at the start of the war, religious reasons alone entitled an objector to demand conscientious objector status; in 1965 the US Supreme Court ruled that pacifist beliefs based on convictions other than orthodox religion would be considered. Non-cooperation with the draft was only, however, one corner of what became generally known as 'The Resistance'. An estimated 80,000 to 100,000 military deserters and draft evaders are believed to have left the country. And pacifist 'actions', of a more public sort, multiplied: in the autumn of 1967 a 'confrontation with the war makers' took place outside the Pentagon, with hundreds arrested, while in Oakland a Stop-the-Draft-Week, arranged by pacifists, succeeded one morning in closing down the Induction Center for three hours with a sit-in. Who attended these actions, who responded and how, can never precisely be pinpointed. As in all protest, cause and effect are hard to calculate. David Halberstam later wrote that when Pentagon officials advised President Johnson, back in 1966, that their computers forecast victory if he would authorize the bombing of Haiphong and Hanoi, the President refused, saying that they should ask their computers: 'How long it will take 500,000 angry Americans to climb that White House wall out there and lynch the President?'

Michael Randle, Michael Scott and Bertrand Russell during a CND
demonstration.

Anti-war protestors burning draft records in Milwaukee, September 1968.

The last leg of the Mississippi march to Jackson, June 1966; front row from the left are standing the Reverend and Mrs. Ralph Abernathy, and Dr. and Mrs. Martin Luther King.

A pacifist boarding the atomic Polaris submarine *Ethan Allen*, November 1960.

A sitdown at Greenham Common during the Easter demonstration, 1980.

'Mutants' on a CND demonstration, 22 October 1983.

Tax resistance, always popular after Thoreau, was another tactic that acquired a completely new dimension at the time of the Vietnam War. As a form of protest, the non-payment of taxes towards military expenditure had been going on in a small way since the Revolution. It now built up rapidly as Americans realized that 10 per cent had been added to their telephone bills to support the war. Soon the numbers refusing to pay these bills reached 200,000, with 20,000 more declining to pay income tax. Response was confused and arbitrary, it being against American law to cut off telephones for non-payment of taxes. The Internal Revenue took to seizing cars instead, and bicycles and television sets, and stereos, loading them into vans and taking them off to be auctioned, then returning what money they fetched over and above the 10 per cent of the telephone bill. It became something of a game, a constant seizing, auctioning, buying back, seizing again.

On January 20, 1973, thousands of people came to Washington to protest against the inauguration of Nixon as president, and to denounce the Christmas raids over North Vietnam and the 36,000 tons of bombs American planes had dropped. Though the war was shortly to be over, the protests went on, against the holding of political prisoners in South Vietnam, and for an unconditional amnesty for all Vietnam War resisters. Peace did not really come before April 1976 when the war in Vietnam and Cambodia finally collapsed. In New York's Central Park, some 80,000 people came to celebrate; they flew white balloons. The war was over, not, as pacifists have always dreamt it might be, because enough men had refused to fight, but at least partly because never before in America had there been such opposition to war, and never before, in any country, had so many people resorted to so many different tactics in order to bring the war to an end.

Eclipsed by the battle for civil rights, and then by the war in Vietnam, the protest against nuclear weapons merely simmered on until the late seventies, when President Reagan's belligerent pronouncements and the inescapable fact that the superpowers were rapidly building up their arsenal of nuclear weapons triggered off a fresh movement of peace protest. It has been growing, in various forms, ever since. Furthermore,

269

nuclear pacifism possesses a new moral dimension that makes it different from the vast but more diffuse pacifist fervour of the thirties. It is not just about war. Alongside the question of how to avoid the mass slaughter of mankind which advances in science have made possible, it is also attempting to grapple with the greater problem of how to secure some measure of justice in the world without betraying human values. It is common sense, the desire not to be obliterated by an arsenal of nuclear weapons out of all control, allied to a wish to live a more decent life. The note finds an increasing echo even among the more political in the anti-nuclear lobby.

By the end of the seventies, when anxieties about nuclear energy were adding to fears about nuclear weapons, the American peace movement began to acquire a new set of 'actors'. These were religious women, increasingly determined to challenge some of the major social issues of the day. Peace has been one of them. Their influence on the bishops has been enormous.

Catholic nuns — women religious as they are called — came to America originally to minister to the needs of a predominantly very poor Catholic minority in a mainly Protestant country. For over 150 years almost the whole of the social service network of the Catholic Church was run by communities of nuns, accountable to the Church hierarchy, but in practice acting with considerable independence. They built and ran schools, hospitals, orphanages and academies. They were very busy, but the contradictions in their lives — minimal wages, negligible responsibilities, the fact that, while in their work they were handling thousands of dollars, they still had to ask permission to read a newspaper — irked them. When, in the late sixties, Vatican Council II called for a renewal of religious life according to the 'charism of the Order, the intentions of the founder and the signs of the times' many nuns removed their habits, left their hospitals and their classrooms and moved into soup kitchens and neighbourhood action centres, into legal aid offices and refuges for battered women; and into the peace movement. Just over a thousand out of 1,500 nuns canvassed said they felt their work should be 'outgoing and open to the secular'.

Pam Solo is an intelligent, strong-looking woman with brown hair cut short and straight and great determination of manner;

she is in her early forties, the third Peace Fellow at the Bunting Institute in Boston, considering the work and implications of the Nuclear Freeze Movement. She works without stop, going to and giving countless seminars, preparing papers, travelling, speaking at public meetings, and has time for nothing else, spinning around the fine quads and squares of the university town in jeans, with a worn briefcase, and several piles of books under each arm. She is a nun, from the Order of the Sisters of Loreto. Pam Solo was a small child when the craze for building bomb shelters came to America. At her school there was much talk about 'duck and cover', about civil defence, about where to put your bomb shelter and how big it should be. The Solos had no shelter; they could not afford one. 'All my friends did,' she says, 'it made me wonder.' She wondered more at the age of 15 when she read Hersey's *Hiroshima*, then *The Diary of Anne Frank*, then went to see the movie of *On the Beach*. The holocaust, the nuclear bomb, and being told to curb her terrible temper and yet always stand up for and protect her brother, who had been born a dwarf: conflicting messages and she grew up confused.

In 1964, she became a nun. She was 18, aware only that she wanted to lead an interesting life and that the Sisters of Loreto seemed to her to offer it. She had not long been teaching at a girls' academy in St. Louis, Missouri, when the tranquillity of her order was disrupted by one of the sisters going off to burn Vietnam draft records. Until then, she says, the idea of civil disobedience had been 'low key and acceptable'. But now the community, by this one move, was made to define its stand. There was a great deal of personal struggle; 'the privacy of the person over the institution, the fact the individual had the responsibility to act according to her own conscience.' By 1969 the sisters were beginning to come out of their habits, and leave the large mother house for small houses and flats, deciding for themselves with whom they wanted to live and the kind of work they intended to pursue. Some left the order altogether, then returned to it, in a lay capacity, forging new and to the sisters exciting possibilities of religious commitment. Not all that many, at first, turned to the peace movement. They went on teaching, but changing the things they taught and the way in which they did so. A very few became involved in the war in South-East Asia; the others observed.

Pam Solo was one of the women religious who turned early towards peace, in an active, organizing way. At weekends, when not teaching, she would set off to campaign for the immigrant farm workers and the labour movement, and on picket lines she met people busy with training in non-violence. For a while she thought of starting an institute to study non-violence in Denver. The end to the war in Vietnam did not greatly reassure her; she sensed militarization would only increase.

The Rocky Flats nuclear plant campaign began with a decision to block the delivery system to a local plutonium plant. No one could have imagined that it would go so far. Pam Solo was one of ten people, concerned like herself, but with no great scheme or direction. 'We said: let's expose the fact that the nuclear race is not abstract but affecting our day-to-day lives.' The programme was organized meticulously, with a regard for structure that has characterized much of the modern anti-nuclear protest: the ten protesters visited government offices in search of information; they held public meetings; they arranged a symposium; they mounted a demonstration outside the plant with helium-filled balloons released with messages saying that anyone who found one should send back the tag, rather like ringed birds, tracked to winter or summer quarters. The campaign went well; it was exhilarating to be doing something and others found the enthusiasm infectious. By 1978, the issue had become of national concern; across the United States the public had come to hear of Rocky Flats. Pam Solo travelled about, telling people. What had started as a small action in Denver was now a spreading movement.

It did not become so all on its own. If the recent history of American pacifist concerns is about anything, it is above all about diversity, imaginative local schemes of protest that swell up, become national, or remain local, linked to others like themselves. As in West Germany, pacifist feeling, intense, often religious, develops many different forms, explodes in pockets and bubbles of rebellion against government policy. Pam Solo's feelings were mirrored by those of many others, whose interests had also started out local, but who, as they discovered the dimensions of what they were tackling, were turning to national, even global plans.

The Catholic Bishops' pastoral letter of May 1983, arguing

that whether you start from the premise of a Just War, or from a position of non-violence, man has no alternative but to condemn nuclear war, was one highly encouraging strand, and has been looked upon with admiration and envy by Christians in other countries. Another was the formation of a band of nuclear protesters to focus not on the vast panoply of possible nuclear disasters but on one limited idea: that the superpowers, the 'two most overarmed states', should be persuaded to halt their production of new weapons, simply to stop where they were, cease testing, production and development, as a first step towards later reduction. Much of the planning was done over the telephone, on conference lines, with some ten to 12 local enthusiasts plotting strategy. They called their idea 'Freeze': a catchy, memorable name. Like CND in the late fifties, its strength lay in its deliciously simple message: you did not have to be a Christian, or a Democrat, or white, or well-educated, or even pacifist, to belong: you just had to be sufficiently concerned about nuclear annihilation to request one single and infinitely logical step.

Freeze's founders are a curiously homogeneous group. They are of an age, in their early forties, and of a social class — middle; they are articulate, disciplined, and they work extremely hard. Randy Kehler is one of them, coming to Freeze quite naturally, from the civil rights movement and Vietnam. Carla Johnston is another, an elegant, outspoken Boston woman, who has spent 20 years in local government, promoting citizens' rights and better education and who has recently been trying for a seat in Congress on a Freeze platform. A third is Helena Knapp, English and an Oxford graduate, formed in the old school of dedicated girls' education. These campaigners have a style which distinguishes them from other crusaders for peace, a knack for organization and public speaking that makes them seem, at times, more like high-flying executives of a successful company than idealists struggling to save a recalcitrant world from a nuclear catastrophe. Pam Solo explains it. 'You look around Freeze,' she says, 'and you see people raised on civil rights, on Vietnam, on Hiroshima, on civil defence, on women's movement, on Vatican II — it's as if these strands have bred a whole new generation of peace protesters.' It was, as Randy Kehler puts it, a wave, and they rode it.

273

Freeze's campaign has been forceful, superbly efficient and increasingly political. One branch of it, Freeze Voter, was set up in 1983 in a smart large block of offices in Washington, not far from the White House. Freeze Voter is a lobbying body, and has scored some successes. If the leaders are of a kind, the supporters are not. They come from everywhere, from every age, though mainly from the middle classes, attracted by an organization that has seemed to promise so much, through the power of well-informed argument.

The beauty of Freeze, say its leaders, is that it is realizable. Its problem, perhaps, is that it has not been realized. Freeze Voter, at its peak in 1984, attracted 25,000 volunteers and donations from a further 40,000, and Freeze itself, between 1980 and 1984, was the largest peace organization the United States had ever had. Some say that a million people turned out for a Freeze rally in New York's Central Park in 1982. But it has not made the next leap. No one is quite sure why. They worry about whether to promote civil disobedience, or whether to avoid it, as counter-productive. They talk about a possibly mistaken but totally conscious decision to eschew personality cults and identifiable gurus and to rely on democratic leadership, of the inherent difficulty that all such movements face in keeping up impetus, in the face of greater public concern over the economy and employment. 'We are the victims,' says Pam Solo, 'of rapid success.' And Freeze has not attracted black support. Interestingly, American blacks have not played a leading role in the current anti-nuclear movement. The protest against the war in Vietnam grew naturally from the civil rights movement; nuclear pacifism has not followed on. Michael Simmons, Zohara's former husband, who was intensely active with her in the struggles for desegregation, is a member of what he calls a crisis intervention team in a poor part of Philadelphia, born in the seventies to try to temper the aggression of gangs of young black Philadelphians tearing each other apart in street battles. Simmons is a big, burly man with a heavy beard. He was a conscientious objector during the Vietnam War; his brother was in the Marines and died later of the defoliant Agent Orange. He was arrested and sentenced to three years for refusing induction. He served them in full; he never made parole.

Simmons has tried nuclear protest; he finds it too abstract.

Driving me to the station, in an unusually scruffy car, the seats
cluttered with leaflets, jerking in heavy traffic and heavy rain
through a bit of the city so broken down it was hard to believe
anyone lived there, he said that he could not help seeing what
people now call the peace movement as a white, middle class
concern. 'My point,' he said, 'is that, when Reagan built the
missiles, the bomb had already dropped on the inner cities.
There are in fact two peace movements in the States: the civil
rights movement and the nuclear movement. And those are
quite different things.'

Freeze is not, of course, on its own. There are doctors, lawyers,
housewives, feminists, students, accountants all over the States
who, together in small groups or as members of larger ones, are
protesting against a nuclear end. In the summer of 1985, on
Sunday, August 4, shortly before the 40th anniversary of the
dropping of the bomb on Hiroshima, several miles of decorated
and embroidered ribbon were wrapped slowly round the Pentagon. When there was found to be very much more than
enough to go round it, the US Capitol was taken in as well,
while other Washington landmarks, other symbols of political
and military power, like Arlington Cemetery, where America's
unknown soldier is buried, and the Washington Monument,
were encircled as well. It was like a vast Christmas present, to
the citizens of America.

Right up until the morning of the 4th there had been considerable worry about the weather, lest the great heat and
humidity prove too much for the crowds, many of them middle-
aged women who had come to see their sewing on display. The
day proved exceptionally pleasant, neither very hot nor very
damp; people brought picnics and sat around telling each other
the story of their lives and how they had come to design a ribbon
for the day.

The idea had come from a 61-year-old school teacher called
Justine Merritt who, so it is said, had returned from a spiritual
retreat with a vision that people should construct a great ribbon
long enough to wrap around the Pentagon, made up of sections,
each a yard long, depicting 'what I would hate to lose in a
nuclear war'. When Justine Merritt sent out her Christmas
cards she wrote about her idea along the bottom, suggesting to

275

friends that they spread the message. Using guidebooks and street maps, Mrs. Merritt had calculated that what was needed was a mile of ribbon, some 2,000 separate segments. It did not seem too much. By August 4, 15 miles of ribbon were being assembled, from boxes and cases and bags, in sections and groups and divisions, orchestrated by civic leaders. The organization was phenomenal. The ribbon had become a national symbol. At 2 o'clock, in an atmosphere both carnival and tearful, balloons were released, to indicate to those grouped along the ribbon's path that the final knot had been tied.

The ribbon was a quintessentially peaceful affair, a matrons' call for peace. Not all the peace movement's exploits have been as quiet, and the question of how effective civil disobedience can be in times of peace continues to split some of the more politically conscious members of Freeze. Is it better to carry out 'actions' and provoke? Is it better to lobby and conciliate? The fact that civil disobedience has been endorsed so thoroughly by at least some of the Catholic bishops gives the actors a strength that cannot easily be ignored. Bishop Hunthausen, signatory to the Pastoral Letter, and one of the strongest figures in the movement, a man who had consistently refused to pay his taxes towards the military machine, was himself drawn into it by one of the more remarkable of America's most recent 'actions', a movement of national protest that has been enduring on the West Coast since the late seventies.

Jim and Shelley Douglass were looking for a piece of land on which to start a centre for non-violent action when in 1977 they came across a house standing on a hill overlooking the gate where railroad shipments enter the Trident submarine base at Bangor, Pennsylvania. The spot was too remote for a centre, but it gave the Douglasses an idea. They would use it to observe 'one critical means towards nuclear holocaust', shipments of missiles that travel the United States by rail from factory to base. In July 1981, having taken some years to acquire the house, they moved in, founded a community called Agape ('the love of God operating in the human heart'), and began their vigil. It has grown steadily, to become a national preoccupation, the tracking of the great white train, and a symbol, for the destructiveness of American nuclear policies. The Douglasses liken their train to those that carried the Jews to the gas ovens. Even Bishop Hunthausen has remarked: 'I say with a deep consciousness of these words, that Trident is the Auschwitz of Puget Sound.'

Watching the trains to hell has become a way of life today for a large number of people. They see them as alive, an incarnation of evil. Evil, they say, does not like light; and so the government does its best to prevent them from catching glimpses of the cars as they move around the country. The watchers, in response, are vigilant, believing that by seeing it, by tracking it, by staging sitdowns along the tracks, by setting up a network all along the route, they can, in some way, finally overcome it. Painted white, to lower the temperature inside, the train's whiteness has come to symbolize the extinction of all life on earth, 'the white night of its contents'. Melville's *Moby Dick* is quoted frequently: 'A nameless horror which overpowered all the rest. Yet so mystical and well nigh ineffable, it was the whiteness above all things that appalled me. Is it that, by its indefiniteness, it shadows forth the heartless voids and immensities of the universe, and thus stabs us from behind with the thought of annihilation?'

At first, the Douglasses spent their time tracking the missiles as they went by road, through Utah, Idaho, Oregon and Washington. But then, in December 1982, they learned that a special all-white armoured train, carrying nuclear warheads, was on its way to the Trident base. The Agape community turned out to observe its arrival: eight white, low armoured cars, like tanks, rumbled into sight. The train, bearing the markings ATMX, moved slowly.

Now began an intense period of research. It did not take them long to put together the facts: every four or five months, from Amarillo, site of the Mason and Hanger plant, final assembly point for all US nuclear warheads in Texas, a white train, carrying somewhere between 100 and 200 hydrogen bombs, was setting off on its journey to Bangor. A friend, a railway enthusiast, came up with its most probable route. From January to March 1983, the Douglasses made contact with sympathizers along the way, in Colorado, Montana, Wyoming, Idaho and Washington, friends who would monitor the 'phantom train bound for Hades'.

The first people to see the train were in La Junta, Colorado. It was 11 o'clock at night and snowing heavily. They telephoned ahead. Soon people had climbed out of bed and were waiting along the railway tracks, in driving snow. Mostly, as the train went by, they did nothing; they just watched, in silence. In Denver two were arrested, for getting too close to the train; in Fort Collins eight more were taken away by police for kneeling on the tracks as the white train bore down on them, while at the gates of Bangor a sitdown was prevented by police. Arrests, of those who pray, squat, in any way disturb or disrupt the train's progress, have been going on ever since.

The Douglasses have been watching the train continuously. It has been rerouted, through Kansas and Nebraska, to avoid the attentions of Colorado's particularly vigilant watchers. Alternative routes are frequently tried out. The watchers do not falter; new monitoring groups are easily and hastily recruited for the new line. 'Become a railroad buff,' the Douglasses tell their supporters. 'Order a copy of Rand McNally's *Handy Railroad Atlas of the United States* as a practical guide to prayer . . . Be prepared to meet these trains at any hour of the day or night with faith, hope and love . . .' Thousands do, their silent witness a strangely potent image of faith and stubbornness. The great white train has become the world's most closely observed symbol of nuclear destruction.

As a movement, spotting the white monster is all things that Freeze Voter is not. It is passionate, dangerous, exciting and mystical. It is virile in the way a committee can never be. The same excitement can be found in the activities of the Sojourners, a community of radical evangelists to which a number of pacifists, who came to nuclear awareness through Freeze, have recently been moving in their search for a moral dimension. It was among the Sojourners, in their house in Washington, that I found most objection to the word 'pacifism'; these devout, for the most part young, Christians say the expression is pejorative, passive, smacking of flabbiness; they prefer 'non-violent activism'.

The idea for the Sojourners was born among a group of seminarians in the late 1960s, who felt that people were increasingly failing to integrate their faith with the political realities that surrounded them. They drew inspiration from Dorothy Day, the Christian pacifist and social worker, and today group themselves around a gentle, stocky former member of the Plymouth Brethren called Jim Wallis, a man in his late thirties. Wallis spends much of his time reading the Bible and praying; he is also a highly efficient organizer, in the new style of resistance politics, and runs his group with lucidity and shrewdness. Neither exactly of the Left nor of the Right, the Sojourners take a conservative stand on matters of personal morality and maintain total obedience to Biblical authority; at the same time, they insist on disarmament, an end to the death penalty, and a change in society in order to help the people they believe God favours: the poor.

As a Christian community, the Sojourners began life in Chicago. A group of some 35 adults and seven children now live in Columbia Heights, a primarily black area of Washington DC, where they run neighbourhood programmes and practise their own kind of radical evangelism. The spirit is less that of commune than religious house; a period of novitiate is regarded seriously, and commitment, when it is made, is expected to be total. The Sojourners have only reached any degree of prominence in the last few years, and that they have done so with tactics and stunts used repeatedly by pacifists throughout the country is revealing. Though the weapons have changed, the means to oppose them have not. In 1983 Jim Wallis travelled to the Nicaragua–Honduras border, where the Contras were currently active; observing the effect their presence had on the soldiers, and seeing themselves as 'protective shields' interposing their bodies between aggressors and Nicaraguan victims, they concluded that a 'peace witness' — Dr. Maude Royden's Peace Army, in a modern form — was needed. Under the aegis of the Sojourners, groups of pacifists now travel regularly to and around Nicaragua. At home, during a retreat held in Bangor, near the Trident base, in November of the same year, the idea of a Pledge of Resistance was put up, something along the lines of Dick Sheppard's pledge in the thirties: to date, some 80,000 Americans have signed statements to say that for the time being they will protest against the war in Nicaragua by legal means, but that should it escalate they will turn to acts of non-violent civil disobedience. In the event of an American invasion, steps have been laid down: non-violent vigils, gatherings at churches, the occupation of congressional field offices. 'If the armies of the United States are mobilized to wage war on Nicaragua,' Jim Wallis has written, 'may a mighty non-violent army of UN citizens also be mobilized to wage peace.'

More recently, the Sojourners have gathered behind a movement to smuggle refugees from Central America across the borders of Arizona and Texas, and to hide them, often in the churches of sympathetic priests. The trials of those caught doing so, like the trials of the draft file mutilators, are occasions for bringing the state to book.

Nothing perhaps, certainly outside America and possibly nowhere else within it, has quite the purity of the Jonah community, a very small, very extreme group of pacifists who live in a red-brick house on a sloping street in a poor area of Baltimore. They number barely two dozen people but they have had a quite extraordinary influence over modern pacifists. They are not always approved of; some find their manner too obdurate, their commitment too absolute for comfort. But they are admired, even revered, for their courage, and for the sternness of their self-discipline. They are, people say, like soldiers, prepared to give their lives. This is the hard edge of pacifism; in its most challenging, even violent colours.

Park Avenue, Baltimore, for all the grandeur of its name, is a dingy, cobbled street on the south side of the city, beyond the railway station and far away from the parks. The two-storey houses look enclosed; shuttered. No. 1,993, unlike its neighbours, has a brightly-lit window, somewhat like a small Swiss pension, with lattice wood trellis and green plants supporting a flashing red neon sign which might read 'rooms to let' but instead says 'Nuclear Free Zone'.

Inside, the long open room that is sitting room, dining room and larder is cluttered, hospitable. There are mats on the wooden floor and a wood-burning stove; a piano; a rocking chair; a bed covered in a soft rug. It was Christmas when I went to see the house, which was warm and rather festive. A two-week-old baby was asleep in a shawl and a ginger cat sat near the stove. Someone said, pointing, laughing: 'This is a non-violent cat.' Life is communal and gregarious. Scripture is read at seven

280

each evening, but not all are Catholics; there are Jews, Protestants, a Buddhist as well. The residents at Jonah change all the time: as some come out of prison, others go in. Prison is part of the community's life. No one there has not served at least one sentence and all expect to pass a great part of their lives behind bars. They accept that the acts of radical witness they engage in are never likely to be acceptable.

Philip Berrigan, around whom the community formed some 12 years ago to focus on non-violent resistance to the arms race, and his brother Daniel were both priests, up to and beyond the Vietnam years, and it was as Jesuit priests that their voices were heard in the celebrated first actions of the draft raiders. In October 1967, Philip was one of the Baltimore Four who defiled 600 draft records with blood; six months later, Daniel joined him for the Catonsville Nine action. Philip was the first priest to become a prisoner of his kind in Lewisburg Penitentiary, where he went to serve a six-year sentence for the destruction of draft files. Daniel, who briefly went underground, escaping from Cornell where police had come to get him, dressed up as a puppet before also going to prison, wrote later . . . 'No one declares to the American mandarins — executive, military, judicial or legislative — how far is too far? . . . Moreover no one . . . no one offers to power a vision or a new way. Those of us who are powerless must literally make do with . . . a few resisters, a few draft-file burners, with semi-heroes and anti-heroes. Our profitless task is our "No" uttered at the shabby door of a civilization where today and tomorrow the rape of the innocent is in progress and murder is the hourly outcome.' The Berrigan brothers have become pacifism's most eloquent spokesmen.

It was while Philip was in Danbury, having been moved there from Lewisburg, that he started a smuggled correspondence with a nun, Sister Elizabeth McAlister, child of Irish immigrants and member of the Religious of the Sacred House of Mary. Sister Elizabeth McAlister was one of the women religious to be brought to politics by the turbulence of the sixties. Only her sense of duty to her order prevented her from joining the Catonsville Nine on the night of their Maryland raid. Their trial — for planning to blow up government heating systems and kidnap a high-ranking government official — was one of the more absurd of the Edgar Hoover and Vietnam era, in which common sense and an acquittal finally prevailed. Later, Philip and Elizabeth left their orders and married. They have three children; the smallest, Kate, is four.

In the years since the pacifist protest has again come to the fore in the United States, Philip Berrigan has been six times to prison. He is tall, a striking, loose-limbed man, with very blue eyes and heavy, grey-white hair. He talks little, but with authority; he has a prophet's voice and a prophet's manner. The other members of Jonah are younger, men and women reared on pacifism after Vietnam, but who share something of his purity and dedication, and of his vision of the future. There is John Heit, who as a boy marched with his mother for civil rights, and whose large family of brothers and sisters are harshly divided by this black sheep, seen by some as no better than a Libyan terrorist. John was once a seminarian; he has served one prison sentence; he expects another soon. There is Brian Barrett, a willowy, fair man, owner of the pacifist cat, who wears his long hair in a pony tail; Suzanne Schmidt, a solid, almost masculine woman, with a wary look; Peter de Motte, the longest resident, who came east from Des Moines from a hospice for the homeless and spent a year in Vietnam with the Marines; and Ellen Grady, quiet and very blond, the baby's mother, who was terrified when she first went to prison. Her new child entitles her to a period of rest from the actions and possible prison sentences.

For all of them, the future is the same: a new action, when the spirit and will come to them; a new trial, at which to speak out, accuse the government, bring to light the illegalities of the system, stand as witness and then, invariably, a return to prison. Members of the Jonah community have become somewhat celebrated in the federal penitentiaries, their faces familiar to inmates from television. These are, indeed, the places to which they are frequently sent. 'If the world is to survive,' says de Motte, 'we are going to have to act again and again and again.' There is little room for ambiguity: the world must disarm, radically and unilaterally, or mankind will die.

In the last five years, the Jonah community has acted 14 times. All occasions have led to arrest and trials. They have entered the General Electric Plant at King of Prussia,

Pennsylvania, and 'disarmed Mark 12A warheads'; they have rammed the nuclear Trident *USS Florida* at the Electric Boat Shipyard in Groton, Connecticut, and started dismantling the component equipment for nuclear cruise, Pershing II and MX missiles at the AVCO plant in Wilmington, Maryland. They have stood outside countless government buildings, held innumerable vigils and wandered through the White House, with tickets, as tourists, on Hiroshima Day and chanted; and they have dug graves in the lawn of James Schlesinger, former Secretary of Defense. They call these actions 'Plowshares', and like the Vietnam draft file raids they have numbers. They themselves are the Plowsharers, from Micah 4:6. 'They shall beat swords into plowshares, and spears into pruning hooks; nation shall not lift sword against nation nor ever again be trained to war . . .' 'Judeo Christians, Biblical people, seeking in our lives to be faithful to God's law,' they trace their roots to A. J. Muste, to Vietnam, to what they consider the victory of the non-violent protesters in stopping Nixon's pursuit of the war.

More than the train-watchers, with whom the Jonah community is in close contact, their language is heavy with Old Testament echoes, the prophecies and warnings of the Church's founding fathers, with the rituals and symbols of retribution and annihilation. The images are powerful; the language incantatory and awesome. 'We hammer these missiles which symbolize the deeper violence of national pride, greed and militarism and express the fear and insecurity deep within us all . . . that with our blood we rename these weapons and beg that no more blood be shed.' The Plowsharers carry ordinary hammers with them, as they set off in their serviceable and somewhat homespun clothes, bound for a furtive break-in at some distant base and a jubilant celebration of defiance and life, before the police come and lead them away to prison. The blood is their own, drawn by a nurse and stored in babies' bottles to symbolize the loss of innocent lives. The aim is both to shock, to waken people to the reality of the weapons, and to 'convert the heart'.

The actions have taken their toll. Of the flourishing community, when I went to see them, only six adults and four children were free. Twenty-four people were in prison. Greg

Boertje, the 'little farmer', was in a state prison in Rhode Island, awaiting trial for entering a base where Trident is assembled; he faced a 12-year sentence. Jim Perkins was in Danbury Federal Penitentiary serving three years for pouring his blood over documents at the Martin Marietta Plant, which makes launching pads for Pershing II missiles. Helen Woodson, mother of nine adopted children, and Carl Kabal were serving 18 years for using a jack hammer on missiles in a Kansas City base. And Elizabeth McAlister, Philip Berrigan's wife, was in Alderson Women's Prison, for her part in the Griffiss Plowshare action, when early on Thanksgiving morning, 1983, she travelled to the Griffiss Air Force base in Rome, New York, and entered Building 101, which housed a B-52 bomber the military were in the process of outfitting to carry cruise missiles. There she hammered on the bomb bay doors of the B-52; poured her own blood over the fuselage; spray-painted the words '320 Hiroshimas', 'Thou shalt not kill' and 'If I had a hammer', and taped on to one side of the plane photographs of her three children and a 'people's indictment' of what was taking place at the base. Nearby, others were doing much the same to a storage area dealing with engines for the B-52s. Indicted for sabotage, she faced a possible sentence of 25 years. In the event, she was given two and a half. Before leaving Baltimore, before saying goodbye to her three children, she wrote: 'We seek, above all, to enunciate hope, to announce that, as well as being a time when death appears to reign supreme, it is a time of hope, a time when the promise of new life is at hand for our world, if people can reach out and grasp for it, if people will in solidarity and with one another, reach out and dismantle the weapons that block our access to life.'

11

West Germany: another start

Ferdi Hülser was in his office in Cologne one morning in May in the early eighties when the telephone rang. As he picked it up he realized from the tinny and reverberating echoes that he was about to hear a taped recording; after a few seconds a ranting voice, the sounds of which were still familiar to him from the thirties, began rasping out in a series of jerky exclamations: 'Attention. Attention to all Jews. The SS inform you filthy Jewish pig that you partisans will not be forgotten. We, the very embodiment of the German Reich, we remember you. It has taken a long time, but now the moment is here for the final purge . . . You are the first. We watch all your steps. We will come to fetch you for another Auschwitz.' The next two sentences were blurred. Then, unmistakable, 'Heil Hitler'. Herr Hülser keeps a copy of the tape, automatically recorded by his office telephone system since he deals in electronics; he plays it to visitors who ask him what he did during the war.

Ferdi Hülser is not Jewish, and he was not in Auschwitz. He was, and is, a pacifist, a war resister, one of an extremely small number of thirties pacifists who survived the Nazi years. For his activities during the war Hülser was sent to Buchenwald, where he was repeatedly tortured and on three occasions sentenced to death, the last on Himmler's specific orders for what was to have been the final show trial of war resisters, a lesson to the few who remained. He was saved only by the arrival of the Americans, and went on to protest against the remilitarization of Germany, and, in recent years, the stationing in Germany of Pershing and cruise missiles.

Police and sound experts from the local radio station, who have broadcast the threatening message, have listened hard to the tape; they know that two voices made it, an older man with a somewhat shrill tone, and a throaty, coarse, younger man. They even believe they now know who the callers are, two members of a Cologne neo-Nazi group, but they can do nothing without more proof. Ferdi Hülser will be 80 next year; he is a stooped, angular man with the long sad face of a bloodhound. He is philosophical about what they may do to him; he has had special locks fitted to his front door and to his car, and in the hall, on the steps leading up to the bedrooms, he keeps a small cannister of tear gas.

Hülser was not a pacifist until the early thirties. His father, a Catholic minor civil servant, died at the end of the First War. In the late twenties, he read about Bertha von Suttner, *Friedensbertha*, Bertha of peace, founder of the Austrian peace society and the woman who inspired Nobel to create a peace prize in his will. After that, he says, he simply 'knew that I was against the right wing elites and militarism'. It was a lonely conviction; none of his friends appeared to feel the way he did. Today he refers to his two brothers, who early and enthusiastically joined the Hitler youth, as 'fascist murderers'. He never saw them again after the war.

The Hülser house is on the edge of Cologne, on what was until not long ago allotment land. From the garden, on the nights that matches are played, you can see the floodlights of the nearby football stadium, and hear the crowd shouting. Inside, the lights are kept immensely bright; the sitting room, a large, crowded, spotless room, with heavy mahogany furniture and a lot of white lace, is hung with mementoes of the peace world, embroidered messages, doves in terra-cotta, a medallion from Chile, some panels from Japan. An artist from Düsseldorf has painted an enormous poster of a blue and red vulture, standing on a red, desiccated corpse.

Throughout the thirties, Hülser listened; he sat in on evening gatherings in his wife's parents' house and followed their conversations as they talked about the First War, about the League of Nations and the Deutsche Friedensgesellschaft, the German Peace Society of which they were members. After the invasion of Poland, forced labourers began arriving in Cologne from the East, to work in the factories of the Ruhr valley. Hülser met others like himself, confused pacifists, but daily drawn to minor acts of protest; they began to produce illegal posters and raised money for young Jews and other 'undesirables', forced to the edges of society. Working in a reserved occupation in his electronics firm, he was able to defer call-up until 1942; by then, however, despite his pacifism, he had become a member of a small group of opponents to Hitler in Cologne. There were, he says, about 200 of these in the area, communists mainly, but a few, like himself, pacifists. As war intensified, they did what they could for the forced labourers, for the Jews in hiding, for the young Catholic resisters who called themselves the Edelweiss Pirates. During the intensive bombing of the Ruhr, he went with other young resisters to the roof of one of their houses and, under cover of the shelling, practised with guns they had stolen.

He was fortunate when his call-up papers came. He was kept in Cologne, working in the administration of the Luftwaffe, where he was able to falsify passes and permits for the Jews and for those on the run. On leave, he came back to a basement in a suburb of the city, kept by the group as a safe house, until the day he gave the agreed password and the door was opened by a man in the green uniform of the customs police. The Gestapo were not far away. That was 1944. Four prisons, torture and Buchenwald filled the remaining months of war; the first were spent in the jail where the Jews and the captured Edelweiss Pirates had been hanged.

Speaking of those days to me, Hülser suddenly stopped talking and left the table where we had been sitting. He was crying. Frau Hülser, a small, tidy woman with tightly-permed white hair, who said little, nodded to indicate that it was all right, that he would return when he had had a little brandy. What he minded most, he explained when he joined us again, was not the torture, though he would rather not discuss it. What hurt most was that he had always promised his wife and her family that whatever else happened he would always remain a pacifist, refusing to use violence whatever the provocation, and that he had gone back on his word. Early in 1942, returning with a cache of weapons stolen from the Luftwaffe, he and a fellow partisan had been stopped by four men in SS uniform. He had shot them all. Something of his identity as a pacifist has never been recovered.

Hülser came home from Buchenwald 30 kilos lighter, his back permanently dislocated by torture. The last 40 years have been spent in 'fighting fascism: but without violence'. He has opposed the remilitarization of West Germany and upheld the

287

rights of conscientious objectors; marched with the anti-nuclear protestors and talked to school children about the thirties and about what war can do. At 80, he is still treasurer of Cologne's 30 active peace groups.

I was lucky to find him. During the months leading up to my visit to Germany I had been writing to contacts in the peace movement and to modern historians who, I knew, had written on these subjects, to ask for introductions to pacifists who had survived the Nazi years. There were, I was told, none left; the few who were still alive were too ill or too old to talk. In the 1920s there are thought to have been some 100,000 people, calling themselves in one sense or another pacifist, but these numbers had been gradually reduced by doctrinal and political differences. Of the 35,000 members who remained in the German Peace Society in 1933, the year that Hitler made it the first organization of its kind to be officially banned, 12,000 to 15,000 were known to have vanished, either dead in concentration or work camps, or still living abroad, having emigrated as soon as the society was proscribed. What was more, I was told, it would be hard to find many traces of that pre-Second World War pacifism, or even of anything much before 1960. The records of the First War resisters had all been destroyed by the Nazis, while the country was too busy with other problems to dwell much on pacifism once peace came in 1945. Too busy, and too disinclined. As Alfred Grosser, the historian, wrote: 'Embittered and inclined to feel that they had been punished merely for their opinions, they often turned against politics of any kind for fear of being hauled before other tribunals in the future.' So much had gone: over 1,500,000 men dead, 2,000,000 made prisoner, 1,600,000 missing, 12,000,000 people homeless.

Kassel, in the centre of West Germany, is a peaceful town, with agreeable wooded suburbs overlooking a commercial city centre. During the war, 40,000 foreign workers, Poles, Russian prisoners of war, and later Italians and French were brought here to work in the 200 armaments work camps that fringed the city. Jorg Kammler is a lecturer in the department of political sciences at the university; in the seventies, he decided to make a study of local resisters during the Second World War. 'In 1930,' he said, talking in a study crammed with books, with a long dormer window overlooking woods, with the city beyond, 'Kassel had 60 members of various peace societies. Most were social democrats; a few were communists. They all emigrated. Then there were Jehovah's Witnesses and these were sentenced to jail for their pacifist views after their order was banned in 1934. They went to the camps. The men I found, 114 soldiers who resisted the war after conscription, were mostly young workers who came from families with a tradition of pacifism.' It was Kammler who told me that there was virtually no material left on the early pacifists. His resisters, he said, had been court-martialled, allowed no defence, forbidden to make statements of their own. Twenty-six had been sentenced to death; others had died in camps or been shot as deserters. One was hanged on May 10, 1945, two days after the war ended, sent to his death by the court of the German Marines.

Kammler collected his material from talking to the few surviving Kassel resisters. Of the First World War, he says, very little remains; such was the spirit of nationalism that by the time war broke out in 1914 few pacifists chose to oppose war. Records show that between 1914 and 1918 only 47 men were sentenced to death by the German army as resisters. 'It was clear,' says Kammler, 'that the punishment was not as hard as in World War Two. The Nazi judges had one enormous fear: to prevent the breakdown in military discipline that had been seen in the last stages of the First War from happening again. So from 1938 they were instructed to hand out extremely harsh sentences for anything that looked like resistance or desertion.' By the end of the Second War, however, 16,000 soldiers had been sentenced to death on the same charges that took 47 men before the firing squad 20 years before. About 14,000 of these sentences were carried out. Kammler himself was a conscientious objector in the 1960s. His father had been a high-ranking Nazi official, who died in 1945. He can barely remember him; as a teenager, he says, he found it very hard to reconcile a picture of his father as a loving family man on one side, and as a mass murderer on the other.

Germany's pacifist spirit, crushed by World War Two, reborn with remilitarization and consciousness of the all important border with the Soviet Union, has taken three separate paths in recent years: opposition to national service, religious pacifism, and ecological and anti-nuclear protest, much like that found in the United States and Britain, though with a particular intensity of its own. On important occasions, like anniversaries, these strands merge and agree; the rest of the time their supporters simply pursue their own activities. It gives modern German pacifism at the same time a feeling of great power and a complete lack of purpose, just as its lost or forgotten roots make it seem, at times, both innocent and surprisingly full of hope.

West Germany, in 1985 had 50,000 conscientious objectors to military service. A small number objected to joining the army on religious grounds, and for members of religious movements like the Jehovah's Witnesses there is a special clause, tailored to their conscience. For most of the others, objection lay in politics, in family memories of war, in fear that what they know happened in 1939 could easily happen again. Their numbers are unmatched anywhere else in Europe, though there is sometimes something rather old fashioned in the stand they take. Faithful to its 1949 constitution, West Germany, the first country to enshrine conscientious objection as an inalienable human right, does not call on them to carry arms. Instead, and for a longer period of time, they serve in hospitals and old people's homes, in hospices for the dying and among disturbed children. Their stand was not, of course, won without difficulty. As late as 1958 Franz-Joseph Strauss, Minister of Defence, was asking that soldiers of the Stalingrad generation, those born around 1922 and thus both experienced and still relatively young, be reconscripted to inject fervour and professionalism into the new army. The immense, passionate protest that followed was the first time the question of how Germans really felt about being called up again was properly aired. After that, there has never been much talk of compulsory military service.

Unlike Kassel, Hamburg is remembered for its liberal past, its history as a city open to foreigners, to foreign views and new ideas. Anarchists, communists, dissidents of every kind have found the place friendly. In between the wars Hamburg had active peace societies and many of the socialist and humanitarian organizations had their headquarters along the waterfront or in the old town. Members of the Hamburg IDK, the 'Vereinigte Kriegsdienstgegner', the German affiliate of the War Resisters' International, were regular attenders during the 1930s at the annual pacifist gatherings in Holland and Sweden and keen League of Nations supporters.

In 1946, while the city was still in ruins, a Bulgarian called Theodor Michaltseach, who spoke most Eastern European languages and acted as interpreter in court for foreigners when he was not lecturing at the university, announced that he wanted to start up the IDK once again. He was an untidy, disorganized man, greatly loved by his friends, and they came to meet in twos and threes among the muddled piles of his papers, into which he was constantly burrowing in search of lost documents. Michaltseach's passion was to prevent another war.

At night, among the papers, they talked; soon, news of their group spread to Stuttgart and Berlin; a magazine, *Peace News*, was printed, a few cyclostyled pages on rationed grey paper. One day they decided to put advertisements on local university student notice boards and in three Hamburg newspapers inviting people to come to the flat and hear about a society whose pledge was 'I will never work for war again'.

Gunther Kahl was one of the young men who read the advertisement. His mother was Jewish; married to a Gentile, she had avoided the early purges, though most of her family had died in the concentration camps. Kahl was a teenager in 1945 but he knew perfectly well that, had there been sufficient trains, his mother would have gone to the camps too. Today Kahl is in his mid-fifties, a slight man with a broad face and greying woolly hair kept long. 'As a child,' he says, in the perfect English that comes from school, the Aldermaston marches and a love of English theatre, 'we knew what happens when people are as flies, and have no rights. I just thought we had to be sure it wouldn't happen again.'

Theodor Michaltseach died in 1968, but by then the IDK in West Germany had found its voice within the larger rebirth of the German Peace Society, especially once conscription returned in 1957 and young men were turning to the 1949 constitution, but needed help in interpreting what it said and in preparing for their Tribunals. And so, says Kahl, 'we launched conscientious objection work. We had no precedents to fall back on here, so we looked to England and the Netherlands. In the first years after conscription came back about 2,000 young men every year wanted alternative service of some kind. At the height of Vietnam and student opposition it rose to 70,000. In Hamburg, we were inundated.'

Gunther Kahl and his wife Monica live in a terrace town house on the edge of the city. Their sitting room, full of modern Scandinavian furniture and spreading indoor trees, has become the centre of the current Hamburg IDK; here, two evenings a week, young men who have resolved to take a stand for conscience, who say that on their travels around Europe they make many foreign friends and do not want ever to take up arms against them, or who have relations in East Germany, come to enact mock military Tribunals of the kind they will have to face. 'What if you are in a park with your girl friend and meet two Russian soldiers with a gun who threaten to take away your girl?' Kahl asks them. It sounds like Winchester Magistrates' Court, 1916; but Kahl knows that today this is what the court at Bremen will be asking them.

Some young men, of course, resist even alternative non-combatant service, saying that whether you serve in the army or in a lunatic asylum, it is still military service. It is hardly surprising, perhaps, that Hamburg, city of such liberal traditions, is also home to a small organization which calls itself 'Total Resisters'. The man who runs it, Karl Senge, was not a total resister himself, having requested and been given permission to serve his army months working for War Resisters' International in London. His is a wary, somewhat truculent young man, hunched and watchful, who prefers to talk of legal loopholes, rather than describe the machinery of his organization. Meetings are held in the kitchen of his flat, on the fifth floor of a house in the suburbs; black instant coffee is drunk from transparent plastic cups.

The idea for Total Resisters, Senge conceded at last, for those who, mainly on political grounds, refuse all dealings with the capitalist military machine, saying that it should not be left in the hands of the state to define the meaning of someone's conscience, came when in 1974 a group of young Europeans went to Strasbourg and handed their call-up papers in to the European Parliament. Soon, young men about to be called up in

Italy, France, Switzerland and Austria were doing the same. 'Conscientious objectors,' says Senge, 'found this exciting. They saw for the first time a new way of expressing their objection.'

Senge refused to say how many Total Resisters there are today in West Germany. He said the question was absurd, irrelevant. What happens to them still depends very much on the part of Germany they come from, the South by tradition handing out stiffer penalties than the North. Officially, their prison sentence, served in a civilian jail, can run from a month to five years. More often, says Senge, the authorities decide on a game of cat and mouse, reminiscent of the First World War sentences in England. A ruling issued in December 1983 laid down that no Total Resister can be expelled from the army, unless he has been sentenced to 12 months in prison. Many, therefore, are sentenced to eight or nine months, which they serve and are then freed. This means that at any point, up to the age of 45, they can be called up again and, if they again refuse military service, they can be charged with desertion or disobedience.

There is, however, an escape. Because of West Berlin's special status, no conscription exists within the city. Today, about a thousand total resisters, knowing their call-up papers were on the way to them, are living in Berlin. Most are studying. No one can touch them, providing they stay within the city's confines, but should they be picked up while on a visit home, they can be sent to prison. After the age of 28, they can return home with impunity.

The Berlin office of the IDK is a room in a rambling, wooden house in Dahlem, one of Berlin's more expensive suburbs. It was here that in the early thirties Pastor Martin Niemöller, the most respected and remembered of all German pacifists, lived and, in a pink-wash and mullioned church alongside, set among tidy graves and yew and box hedges, preached. Niemöller himself died only in March 1984, but since the sixties his house has been home to some 20 pacifist and civil rights organizations, from European Nuclear Disarmament (END), to Amnesty International, whose members share the rather cosy chaos of informal meeting rooms and stick their announcements on to a communal and overcrowded notice board. The house, all bare boards and ramshackle furniture, is presided over by a small caretaker commune of religious young non-violent resisters, who call themselves 'living without arms'. The feeling is affable, collegiate. Chickens are kept in a wired-off corner of the large garden and from every wall Pastor Niemöller peers down from vast posters, his glasses slipping down his nose, an old man with a quizzical, kindly smile. It is from this house that the second strand in West German pacifism, the one inspired by religious belief, seems to radiate outwards.

Niemöller was not always a pacifist. In the 1914–18 War he commanded a submarine and right up until 1933, the last free German elections of the decade, he voted National Socialist. Even after he became a priest in the Evangelical Church, he, like most other young pastors in his Church, went on supporting Hitler's programme for a stronger Germany. But something changed. Hitler's control began to extend even to the Churches: a unified *Reichskirche* was set up, embracing the 29 German Protestant Churches and placed under a 'Reichbishop', a fervent Nazi; and Niemöller and other young theologians like Hans Lilje became active in starting an opposition movement, the Confessing Church, *Bekennende Kirche*, protesting against both the Nazis and the 'German Christians' they sponsored. Niemöller met Hitler; he pleaded for tolerance. He was a brave man and a tenacious one. By the mid-thirties he was regarded by the authorities as too radical a leader to be allowed in a dissenting church , especially since he objected to Hitler's policies on religious and theological grounds as well as on those of Church organization.

In the summer of 1937 he was arrested and the following year he became a 'personal prisoner' of the Führer, who ordered him held after a court had acquitted him of charges of fomenting a 'rebellion'. He was sent to the concentration camp at Sachsenhausen and then to Dachau, where he became a symbol of the resistance to Hitler, and was saved from death only by his eminence and the fact that the Nazis were reluctant to cut all links with the organized Church. Niemöller spent eight years in prison.

He emerged saying that the moment had come for the Germans to speak out loudly about their guilt towards the Jews.

Niemöller and others among the young theologians of the Confessing Church, who had fought in the thirties against the
'German Christians' and the Nazis, assembled at Treysa in
Hesse in 1945 to form a new unified body which they called the
Evangelical Church in Germany, the EKD (to distinguish it
from the earlier, German Evangelical Church with its suggestion of a specifically German type of Protestantism). At Stuttgart, in October, the leaders greeted delegates with the words:
'We accuse ourselves for not having confessed our faith with
more courage, prayed with more devotion, believed with more
joy and loved with more fervour.' The EKD formed itself as a
federation of 27 autonomous *Landkirchen* each under a bishop or
president; the tradition of blind obedience to authority was to be
replaced by better understanding of political and social
realities.

While, for many years, no social problem so concerned EKD
as its own unity, and the unity of Germany itself, from the
autumn of 1950 onwards Pastor Niemöller, by now head of the
Protestant Church in Hesse, was leading a campaign against
rearmament. He was impetuous and not always popular, a fact
he disregarded, saying that the only thing that mattered was to
avoid a repetition of 1933, when silence had led to disaster.
Soon, he concentrated his attention on nuclear weapons. 'To
become a soldier today,' he declared, 'is to become a mass
murderer.' He turned back to the New Testament and told his
congregation in Hesse that Christians must always look for non-
violent ways to resolve conflicts.

In the Kirchentag, in April 1958, the huge annual gathering
of the faithful, discussions centred on the question of how, now
Germany was politically and economically stable once more,
should ordinary Germans think through and live with their
1933–45 period of Nazi history? Niemöller argued that only by
serving those people who had been most brutalized by the Nazis
would young Germans find a future. Within a few weeks of the
Kirchentag, *Aktion Sühnezeichen*, literally 'sign of atonement',
was formed, a scheme to send young German volunteers to
places and people where some of the national guilt could be
redeemed. It is doing well today; it has an entire floor of a large
office block behind Berlin Zoo station, from where it controls
160 volunteers, working for up to two years in Holland, France,

Poland, the United States and Britain. After Eichmann's trial, volunteers were invited into Israel. The note is on 'reparation'.

The position of the churches today in West Germany is not an easy one. Officially, 90 per cent of Germans say that they belong to a church, with Catholics and Protestants dividing about evenly. In practice, only some three per cent of Protestants actually attend church regularly and the Evangelical Church, Niemöller's church, today by far the clearest voice in many of the pacifist issues, is deeply divided over the peace movement. The split over nuclear weapons, for instance, divides church leaders as it does their congregations. Even when a recent poll showed that 70 per cent of churchgoers opposed them, many pastors continued to worry more about unity than any stand on peace. Where pastors or superintendents, senior figures in the church hierarchy, take strongly pacifist views, however, their parishes become umbrellas for the many local peace groups, who feel their message to be enhanced by the dignity of the Church. In many places, the links between Christianity and the pacifists is growing stronger.

In East Germany, too, these links are growing. Within the unofficial peace movement, that is; the official body, vast, hierarchical, organized, arranger of mass meetings of factory workers and school children, at which the role of socialism in a world-wide peace movement is discussed, follows President Honneker's espousal of the line taken by Olaf Palme, the late Prime Minister of Sweden, that there should exist a central European area free of chemical and nuclear weapons. In this sense, and this sense alone, East Germany has a vigorous and all-embracing peace movement; but it is peace as in Japan, a slogan meaning something quite different. Those who worry about peace, and ask what they should do, are told: 'Work. The better you work, the stronger the system will be, and the more you will help peace.'

It is not difficult for a foreigner to visit the real pacifists of East Germany. Officially, their groups, perhaps 20 in East Berlin, possibly several times that number throughout East Germany, mainly in the larger towns where anonymity makes them safer, are tolerated, watched and on the whole ignored. Their existence, say members, is itself a form of acceptance, because they could be so quickly destroyed any day the authorities choose. It is also a source of official respectability, since it permits the government to claim that it is, after all, a tolerant and reasonable regime.

No one prevents a foreign visitor from taking a taxi to an address, given by a friend in the West, where one or two local pacifists will be waiting to see you; the understanding is simply that someone will know that you are there. Usually nothing is said. Last year, however, two young pacifist women spent six weeks in prison after a visit from a foreign journalist. But it is not this that makes them wary about meeting foreigners: 'Peace work here is for us,' one young man, who, together with his wife, cares for some 70 East Berlin pacifists, said to me. 'We aim to work for us, not to attract the attention of the Western press.' His words were like those of the IDK organizer for the war resisters not five miles away, the other side of the Wall, who, in reply to a question about links with the East, said: 'No, we can't afford to have them or all our work is branded as communist-led. It is best that we all work for ourselves.'

I crossed into East Berlin on an early evening in November 1985, and I met two members of the unofficial peace movement. One was a young pastor, with a small, soft beard and a brilliantly-coloured sweater; the other, the superintendent of a section of East Berlin's Evangelical Churches, widely recognized now as a protector of the pacifists, a holder of otherwise unacceptable views, occasionally summoned before the authorities and told to keep closer control over his groups. Werner Krätschell is in his mid-forties, and smokes an ornate, highly-carved dark wood pipe.

In the East, almost all pacifists shelter under the umbrella of the Evangelical Church; those outside seldom survive, their members exiled or intimidated. It was all right, said Krätschell, to give his name; the authorities feel safer when they can see what he is doing.

I met them in the superintendent's house, a cavernous and austere building in a wide and architecturally uniform street on the edge of the city, some way from the short strip of restaurants and hotels that cater for foreigners. There was tea, under a knitted tea-cosy; a pink fizzy drink in unmarked bottles; a 1950s gramophone. It is impossible, as a new visitor from the West, not to be disconcerted: the sudden change from shops and advertisements to ill-lit streets and apparent sameness; the queues and soldiers at the checkpoint; the move through a series of doors, Alice in Wonderland fashion, from a world in which all is muddle, colour, movement, to one where bulb wattage is low, the predominant colour is grey, where there are few cars and no traffic jams and people move and speak quietly, with restraint. Outside the superintendent's house, on the corner of an immense thoroughfare, only an occasional car passed.

The unofficial group in East Berlin started in 1981. It went on its way for a while without noticeable control. But then a number of things happened at much the same time. In Dresden, that summer, a group of young men requested that they be allowed to do alternative military service not within the army, where it is permitted, but outside it, out of uniform. The request was turned down. (There are thought to be very few Total Resisters; at any one time, according to the Evangelical Church which keeps lists of its own conscientious objectors, probably some 15 to 20 young men are in prison.) At about the same moment, young people round East Germany were seen wearing a badge with a Plowshare on it, the symbol used by the Berrigan brothers in America. They were stopped by the police and told to take them off, but since they were sewn on, this took time. Some were told that they would lose their jobs.

Quite quickly, the badges vanished. Their existence in the first place had been made possible only through an idiosyncrasy in the law, which permitted stamped bookmarks to appear without due inspection by the authorities. All other printed matter is checked before publication. The law has now been amended to include bookmarks.

These two events made the authorities uneasy. And when, in the middle of 1983, the missile issue was being debated, the pacifists became conscious that a new sort of person was coming to join in their meetings, an apparently eager stranger with forceful and rather manipulating views of his own. Today it is widely accepted that pacifists are kept under close watch; harassment is casual, an occasional summons by a party secretary, seldom a measurable punishment. However, since the

Solidarity movement in Poland, official anxiety has increased; there is, says Krätschell, no similarity between the two, Polish Solidarity and East German unofficial pacifism, but this is what the authorities fear, that pacifism will spread to the people and become a popular movement.

In the superintendent's corner of East Berlin, in the parish of the 'secret elite' as he calls the 70 pacifists, monthly meetings are held in the parish house. Ecology, pacifism, disarmament, education are all discussed. How many of the 70 are actually infiltrators, says the pastor, no one quite knows. Who are the regular attenders, supporters from the outset? 'The slightly older ones,' he says. 'Those over 25. They are the ones who came and have stayed.'

Their common concern, in the early days, was fear of the times, fear of life in an age of nuclear war. But this has changed. What distinguishes pacifism in Eastern Europe to-day, says Krätschell, is its new sense of responsibility, one born not out of aping the West, but out of the extremely lonely and confused personal experience an East German must pass through as he rejects the dogma of the state and moves towards a private commitment of his own. Western European and American peace movements are not widely admired; there is, feels Krätschell, a sameness to their style and views that sounds strange to people who have reached this commitment on their own, one by one, without help. 'It is this,' says the superintendent, 'that makes us different. There have always been dissidents here. But this sense of responsibility is new. The peace movement has brought a new melody into the Church. It is important now that the Church should be dis-. turbed by these songs, important for them and important for us. Many people are now going to want to continue exploring this new feeling that it is not senseless to fight for goals. They know it will bring them into conflict, but they sense that if they are supported by the Church they can succeed.' Our meeting took place on a Sunday night. The superintendent and the pastor were going to a christening party. It was very foggy. There was nothing on the street when I left, neither people nor cars, but eventually an unmarked taxi stopped. There had been some discussion about my notes: would it be better to leave them behind? If asked, where was I going to say I had been? At the border, in the queue of West Germans returning from one of their permitted 44 days in the East, no one asked.

November is the month to visit the West German peace movement. It is then that the conscientious objectors, the peace pastors, the nuclear protesters, the non-violence activists and the Greens start travelling for peace, to speak, to re-enact, to link hands, to march, to stand silent, to remember. Peace week, called somewhat confusingly Peace *decade*, is a Church-inspired occasion, first designated in the early eighties and now a much-heralded moment in the peace year. It is, for the pacifists, a moment of reckoning, a time to count numbers and make contacts. Without an umbrella like CND, no one quite knows what is happening. The vigour of the autumn turn-out is their barometer.

Protest of this kind, intensely local, articulate, highly imaginative and frequently quarrelsome, is a relatively recent phenomenon. In the North, it is said to draw its inspiration from détente, the Cold War and relations with the East; in the South it comes from the missile bases. It has its roots in the Vietnam War, in feminism, in war guilt and in ecology. One young lawyer I met in Berlin said that he had put his television on one evening and seen Reagan talking about Star Wars; it made him cry. Now he is a lawyer with the Greens. Everywhere, people talk of their parents, of the Nazi past, of the vulnerability of Germany's geographical position, of Nicaragua and of their fear of dying. The protest sometimes looks smaller than it is, because it is so entirely fragmented; but a call can rally thousands with banners of bewildering diversity.

The history of this third strand in modern German pacifism, alongside the conscientious objector movement and the Evangelical Churches, goes back to 1961 when the SPD, for ten years campaigning against NATO and nuclear weapons, with their slogan 'Fight nuclear death', turned direction. The unions, too, champions like them of demilitarization and the rights of conscientious objectors, shifted to a more military stance. As a result, very small groups of people, sometimes no more than twos and threes, many previously active in the conscientious objector movement and now feeling betrayed, began to see themselves as custodians of some purer Germany. And when, in the early sixties, the Protestant Churches gave them some small measure of support, they grew a little stronger. There were never very many of them, talking, producing leaflets, campaigning in the West German cities, and most of their concerns were not about military matters at all, but the environment and the nature of civil liberties, but they laid down some foundations for the vast anti-nuclear movement that was to come.

These were just seeds. Protest itself took a different form. Helga Weber and Wolfgang Zucht met 20 years ago, in 1965, at a conference of the War Resisters' International. His past lay in a Nazi father and a family split apart when Germany was divided; he was 16 when the war ended, a member of the Hitler Youth so unenthusiastic about its bombastic language that he had been relegated to special meetings for those less than perfectly keen. A teacher at school, a member of the international socialist movement, had inspired him to think differently. After an exhibition of photographs of the concentration camps he went home and had a row with his father. A chance to go to England came up; he took it and joined the National Council for Civil Liberties. Helga, when he met her in London, was working for CND for the Easter marches, paid for by a West German group called Friends of Nature. She saw herself then, she says, not as a pacifist, but as a socialist youth worker, the daughter of a man arrested in the thirties for distributing posters with messages about ethical socialism, later taken prisoner by the Americans. Her job, as a woman, was to type and listen; feminism had not reached the pacifists. In 1971 the Zuchts grew interested in the nuclear power stations.

There were not all that many with them at first. The Left, their natural allies, regarded them as lunatics. But in the summer of 1974, to repeated sneers that citizens' initiatives of this kind were bourgeois, not revolutionary gestures, they ran a summer camp in Wiel. For 18 months they had been protesting against the nuclear power stations. Now, they felt, the moment had come to regroup, to study the technicalities more seriously, assess the influence of certain forms of protest. To their camp on the slopes of a sunny hillside, tents set among the vineyards, came 50 participants; some were dissidents from conscientious objector groups who felt that what they were doing was not enough; others were simply curious. The Zuchts invited a young man from another group, successful in having a power station resited, to come and talk to them. Together they re-enacted the event. Some took the parts of lawyers, others of protesters. When they were not acting, they learnt about non-violent resistance, about sitdowns and silent protest. When it was all over, they felt ready for more.

The seventies were good years for these kinds of rallies. Vietnam brought a great influx of students into all forms of social protest, and the anti-nuclear power station protesters benefited. In Augsburg, 'Graswürzelrevolution', or Grassroots Revolution, a non-violent action group, had been formed and round the country the idea of a peaceful protest united people who now began to read Martin Luther King and Gandhi. One of the Zucht's Wiel group, a man called Wolfgang Kromer, went to Spain and chained himself to the top of a telephone booth, from where he threw down leaflets saying that because of their treatment of conscientious objectors the Spaniards had no right to join the European community. It was not exactly pacifism, but it was exciting. Early in 1974 the Zuchts, by now publishers of pacifist books and pamphlets, became the headquarters for a Federation of 'Graswürzelrevolution'.

By the late seventies, however, the energy that had gone into ecology and anti-Apartheid activity was shifting still more strongly towards the anti-nuclear power station work. The site occupations began. If many still regarded these protesters as cranks, they had their admirers too. To Brogdorf in 1982 came 100,000 people to demonstrate against a proposed power station.

By the end of the seventies, the Zuchts say with some pride, Germany had reduced its demand for wattage from nuclear power stations by two-thirds. The Greens, who entered the Bundestag for the first time in the elections of 1983, though they had been elected to the legislature of several Länder much earlier, on an anti-NATO and environmental platform, claim victory for this, and ambivalent as most West German pacifists are about the party as a true, coherent and forceful political grouping, there is admiration for a manifesto which proclaims in terms unmatched for clarity by any mainstream party anywhere. 'We are aspiring to a society free from violence, where oppression of man by man and violence to man by man is abolished . . . The principle of non-violence is valid, without restriction or exception, between all men . . . Active peace politics mean that we stand up against the occupation of any state and against the suppression of ethnic groups . . . We call for world-wide disarmament . . . the destruction of nuclear, chemical and biological weapons and the withdrawal of foreign troops from foreign territories . . .' For the Zuchts, however, real protest was born, not among the politically astute, but with them, and people like them, grassroots revolutionaries.

The Zuchts live in Kassel, not far from Jorg Kammler, in a house built on what was once a one-room shack belonging to Helga's socialist father. Wolfgang is a slender, heavily-bearded man, very bald on top; Helga is round, with straight black hair chopped in a fringe like a Dutch doll. Their publishing business is run from the front house, separated from theirs by a flourishing vegetable garden: they are strict vegetarians and grow herbs for tea as well as many different varieties of lettuce. At the Frankfurt book fair each year they take one corner of a stand. There is now, they say, a feeling of frustration in the non-violent protest movement in West Germany. It has lost the excitement of the days when they were occupying sites and when, after even a routine day of protest, a group used to having ten members found 100 jostling for room. They ask themselves where, now, it will all be going. As they were walking with me to the bus, Helga suddenly said that a number of old ladies in their suburb had recently been mugged. 'I ask myself,' she said, 'is it right to be a member of a non-violent group and not do something?'

Travelling round Germany, their disappointment seems misplaced. The anti-nuclear power station movement did not slide naturally, as it might have done, into protest against the bombs. But as it was shrinking, having accomplished what it could, elsewhere other protesters were coming alive: where nuclear energy left off, nuclear weapons began. November 21, 1983, was the day all West German pacifists remember. It was then, while a huge demonstration gathered outside in the streets, while the Green deputies came out to join them and returned to vote doused in water from police hoses, that the Bundestag voted to deploy Pershing and cruise missiles. All that year, all over the country, groups had been intensifying their campaigns to prevent it happening. They had marched and signed and sat down and called rallies and formed themselves into a human chain that stretched from Ulm to Stuttgart. There had never been protest quite like it.

Their absolute failure to influence the vote might well have killed the spirit in the movement altogether, particularly given its fragmented nature. An office in Bonn, the peace coordinating body, has become better known for its divisions than for any unity that it can bring to groups so obviously far apart in interest and ideology as 'Babies for peace' and the communist-run local *Initiative*. But it did not. What has happened instead is that, after a brief period of collapse, the groups rallied, devised new strategies, new gimmicks, new techniques, and set off again. Their vigour, now, is remarkable — the fact that 6,000 prosecutions of nuclear protesters are currently pending or going through the courts gives some idea of their activities — even if, at times, it seems that the gusto with which the movement is run serves to conceal the fact that there are very few pauses for real thought. In Berlin, a young woman who has been working without break for the European peace movement for the last eight years put it somewhat sourly: 'Sometimes I feel that what we do is to take one step forwards, then six back. It's become the standard cliché: we didn't stop Pershing, but we achieved a change of consciousness.'

All West German cities today possess their range of peace groups, and even those who regret that there is no unifying umbrella, like CND in Britain, are satisfied by the variety they see around them. Düsseldorf, in the Ruhr valley, has a population of some 650,000. Once a city of fine classical buildings, birthplace of Heinrich Heine, it was destroyed by the bombing and is now a modern town of office blocks. Between 1,500 and 2,000 people are said to support the work of the city's 40 peace groups, willing, when called upon, to link hands through the city centre and to sign petitions, while leaving daily organization to the 250 or so fully committed peace workers. One complained to me, with pride but some exasperation, that the peace movement was like a cannibal: it ate you up, 24 hours each day.

There are at least eight women's peace groups in the city, and the same number among the non-violent protesters. There are the highly disciplined communist-controlled collectives, 'Düsseldorf against Nuclear Weapons' and many single interest groups, like 'Peace Initiatives in the Health Service'. Then there are the solitary objectors. There is one man in Düsseldorf, who never speaks to anyone, who walks around the streets with a sandwich board. 'This is mother's day,' it says every day of the year. 'The best present for your mother and your enemy's mother is to become a conscientious objector.'

Placards, posters, postcards, street art have all become important tools in the peace movement's particular war, as have all kinds of play-acting. One, mainly feminist, group has taken to hiring billboards, arriving with ladders and painting vast, multicoloured questions. 'Go and see your doctor: has *he* a cure for atomic death?' To commemorate November 1985 Peace Week pacifist artists gave every group in Düsseldorf a blank piece of puzzle, and told them to write on it whatever they wanted from the local government: at the end of the week the puzzle, fully assembled, was laid against the front of the Town Hall. Completed, it formed the shape of a dove.

'Mothers for Peace' is one of the more consistent of the groups, many of the others having metamorphosed from existence to existence and concern to concern. Early in December 1981 a teacher called Barbara Gladysch, the mother of two children, put an advertisement in three Düsseldorf papers, taking the words of Wolfgang Borchert's war poem 'If you don't say no . . .' and calling on like-minded anti-war mothers to write to her. Uschi Fuchs, a freelance radio journalist in her early forties, had watched the October demonstrations in Bonn against nuclear weapons on television, felt guilty that she had not been there herself, and was looking for a group to join. She saw the advertisement and looked up Barbara Gladysch's telephone number in the book. Twenty-five women met, agreed they felt responsible for the world their children were in the process of inheriting and founded 'Mothers for Peace'. Today, four years later, it meets every Tuesday evening for two and a half hours in a room in a cultural hall in Düsseldorf. The women have sewn themselves plain black calico robes; over the years they have become familiar figures at

305

local rallies, carrying tall white crosses and singing peace songs.

Uschi Fuchs is a busy, restless woman. She is married to a magazine publisher, who puts out the most successful dress collection catalogue in Northern Europe; the hall and staircases of their house are lined with copies of a forthcoming edition. Where there are no magazines, there are cats: either real, long-haired tortoise-shells, or made out of ceramic, wood or stuffed, in glass cabinets or along shelves. Alive or false, they peer, disconcertingly, around the long room, which has a greenhouse-like kitchen at one end, with a murky aquarium of turtles. Like other women's groups which began with feminism in the late seventies, the concerns have broadened: 'Mothers for Peace' have turned to ecology, to considering the links between a pacifist outlook and the clothes they wear. They are, says Uschi Fuchs, 'vegetarians of the mind'. Talking, week after week, learning about new topics, has, she says, done something to the way she now thinks. 'It is almost,' she said, 'as if I have lost some sort of innocence. We are not political and we are not church-led. Sometimes we find it hard to believe that we grew on our own. It can be dangerous, you can lose your friends, people who haven't changed with you.' In the house, these contradictions seem everywhere: tea came in porcelain tea cups, with a scalloped raised biscuit plate, white lace cloth and petits fours; Uschi Fuchs, presiding over it, wore an enormous white boiler suit and heavy boots.

Because there has been so much to oppose, West German pacifists have been conducting their own particular wars of words and gestures ever since the country was able to put the devastation of 1945 behind them. Their battles have not been, on the whole, victorious. West Germany has reacquired an army, joined NATO and has deployed its Pershings. Furthermore, there are surprisingly few ties with anti-military and anti-nuclear forces elsewhere, so that the movement, though often frenetic, appears directionless.

Yet the protesters, anarchist, religious or feminist in inspiration, who joined the movement out of opposition to the big parties, remain buoyant. It is no longer, as Pastor Linz, Superintendant of the Evangelical Church in Düsseldorf, put it, relevant to ask whether the pacifist movement is strong and organized: 'The question is: could it be suppressed?' What matters now, he said, apparently unaware that he was echoing the words of all pacifists, at all times, is to find a way of creating a political pacifism stronger than a military mentality. 'We must emphasize not the dark side, that nuclear war is death, but the bright side, that a nuclear-free world is full of hope.'

12

Witness

Jean Hutchinson was on a pilgrimage of peace, bicycling with two friends from the island of Iona in Scotland to Canterbury, 1,100 miles there and back, 45 days of meetings, gatherings in church halls, overnight stays with Quaker families, when she heard that a camp of nuclear pacifists was being set up outside the American Air Force base at Greenham Common in Berkshire. Her first thought was one of annoyance; pedalling along, the three women had often talked of the need for some permanent witness against the missiles, some enduring presence of protest. After that, she was pleased; others were clearly thinking as she did: a merger of forces could only be good. Jean is a secondary school teacher of history and religious education, former development secretary for the Fellowship of Reconciliation, Muriel Lester's old position, a solid, sensible Methodist Yorkshirewoman who, over years as a peace camp protester, has become rounder and more unkempt. Once soberly, if idiosyncratically dressed, she now wears ill-assorted boiler suits, and keeps her fair hair frizzy. She speaks articulately and pleasantly, as one imagines a teacher should; but then she suddenly giggles, unexpected levity in a woman so rational and so forthright.

Before hearing of Greenham Common, Jean was most of her way through a Master's Degree in Philosophy at King's College in London. She never returned to it. Her last five years have revolved around the life of the peace camps, first at Greenham, later at other camps, as they have opened and grown. Today, having evolved, like most of the women at Greenham, a routine to her protest, she spends Monday to Friday at the base, sleeping in a plastic bag, returning home to her husband in his Cambridgeshire art gallery for a weekend of baths, warmth and comfort, to sit at her desk and paste up press cuttings, and scan her diary for the dates of forthcoming peace events. Her approach in this as in all things is pragmatic; her protest against what she believes is inevitable world annihilation must be treated seriously, much like any other highly demanding job. There have to be strategies and campaigns and gains. Her daughter Jill, a teacher in physical education, is based at Molesworth, at the smaller and more recent peace camp by the base: Jean will visit her in response to any urgent calls for assistance. A former Methodist preacher, the years of protest have seen a troubling erosion of her Christian faith, but an equally steady growth in pacifist commitment, a belief in anti-militarism that goes well beyond any simple weapon of destruction, but that regards the ridding of the world of bombs as a first, imperative step.

The idea for setting up a peace camp at Greenham was born early in 1981 among a group of Welsh women excited by reports they had heard of a gathering of women marching in the name of peace from Paris to the Scandinavian countries. There had been, during the seventies, many marches and rallies but there was something about this one that seemed special, that seemed, perhaps, to promise more. Why not organize a march of British women, to visit Greenham, the site for the new American cruise missiles? CND, whom they approached first, were not enthusiastic. Such marches were tactics of the past. It hardly mattered. It was August, superb weather, a good time to be on the road. The women called themselves 'Women for life on earth', and had some leaflets printed, to hand out along the way: 'Why are we walking 120 miles from a nuclear weapons factory in Cardiff to a site for cruise missiles in Berkshire?' On the back, there was a photograph of a baby born dead and deformed in Hiroshima.

On August 27, the caravan set forth: 36 women, four men, a few children. Among them was an organic market gardener, in her late seventies, called Effie Leah; a midwife, Helen John; a social worker, an artist, and a woman who simply described herself as working class. From Cardiff they walked to Newport, Caerwent, where they visited the US army munitions depot, on to Chepstow, over the Severn Bridge to Bristol, Bath, Devizes, Marlborough and Hungerford. Before reaching Newbury, they paused briefly at the RAF weapons store at Welford. It was an essentially good-humoured expedition, more holiday than cause. The marchers had brought sleeping bags but they rarely needed them, being drawn into people's spare rooms and empty barns along the way. The weather remained hot and dry; in the

309

middle of the day the women and children picnicked near the river and swam. At night, they held vigils and sang. 'It should,' wrote one woman later, 'have looked all ragged, a long straggling line of women and children trampling through the dusty Berkshire lanes with leaves in their hair. It should have seemed absurd, ineffectual. It didn't. There was too much energy and too much triumph . . .'

The peace walkers reached the United States Air Force base at Greenham Common on Friday, September 4. They had chosen their target with care: the former wartime airfield from which the bombers had left for the invasion of Normandy had been leased to the Americans in 1968 and was now to take cruise missiles and some 2–4,000 front line American troops. As they neared the base, four women, remembering the suffragettes, decided to chain themselves to the fence by the main gate. Other women, hearing what was going on, soon turned up, walking along the busy A339 to find a sunny summer scene, a very ordinary gate house, short cropped privet hedges and flowering gorse, behind which lay concealed the missile silos, the watchtowers and the many layers of fence. It was too festive to seem threatening. Soon, alerted by the women, newspaper reporters and cameras arrived.

It could very easily have fizzled out. The women had only planned a short stay. If they discussed it at all it was to say that by October, by the annual CND rally, they would be packing up and setting off back home. After a couple of weeks, the weather changed and incessant rain made the nights wretched. But there was something happening that was unlike the usual run of events, unlike the American 'actions' and the German *Initiative*. The older women, at night around the camp fires, talked of their war memories; the younger felt invigorated by the sense that they were at last doing something. Supplies arrived; water, firewood, chemical lavatories, blankets, even a blue Portakabin. A tent went up, and teepees. 'As far as I'm concerned, you can stay here as long as you like,' the commander of the base had said, in the smooth, amicable, first days. And why not? Messages of support and donations trickled in from the unions, and from individual women around the country, who wrote to say that they would be coming to join in, soon, when they had parked their babies, taken leave from jobs, persuaded husbands and relations to rally.

There was still something not quite right, however, something to do with the way the women perceived their gesture; it was to do with the feeling of their own sacrifice, the fact, as they said to each other, that, like the men who had left their homes to go to war, women were now leaving theirs for peace. When two men were arrested for painting designs on one of the gates leading to the base, it all became clear. The protest, initiated by women, was to be by women and for women, not just a protest against cruise, but a visible proof of women's ability to bring about change. There was an uproar, bitterness, a few nasty rows. Then the men left.

It was, of course, exhilarating to be doing so much and to be seen doing it. The newspaper reporters, in those early days, were often admiring, and certainly respectful. Women journalists, rather self-consciously, turned up from the more serious newspapers to peer and question; they felt nervous, in their city coats and their heated cars, and guilty, to be doing so little, and the women, in return, were scornful, smug, occasionally dismissive. As the weather worsened, what umbrellas there were at the camp were used to shelter the children: the women slept out on the heather. It grew wetter and very muddy and very cold. The peace campers referred to their condition as a 'loose truce between women and water'.

And if the events, the spectacular confrontations, blossomed, so did the arrests. Triumphant gatherings came first: 30,000 women decorating the fence with banners, photographs of their children, toys, locks of hair, and joining hands in a nine-mile chain; a break-in along six miles of fence; 'blockades' of the American vehicles; constant forays to 'liberate' documents. Skirmishes and arrests followed. In terrible weather, the women were dragged limp through the mud. Often, they felt low; they missed their families, they worried about money and longed for baths. Those who could not bear it, or had to return to jobs, left. A nucleus remained, and others arrived and by the fireside at night or in the great tent that acted as headquarters until finally and permanently removed by the police, they talked about how very free and very powerful they felt. The protest could be whimsical — 'wymen' — but it was full of ingenuity

311

and imagination: a four-mile dragon stitched in cotton, a long cloth snake, a furry animal disguise, the planting of snowdrops, the building of a peace memorial.

There is today no longer quite as much talk as there used to be, at night, around the fire, nor quite so much questioning about the nature of civil disobedience, about whether damage to property could be said to be violent, and how not to feel violent when there is violence all around you. Nowadays the women tend to arrive at the base in what they call, in the language of the eighties, 'affinity groups', their particular acts of defiance and protest carefully planned in advance and executed without consultation. Talk tends to be about wider issues; about women's freedom; about the way the cause has been traduced by the media. There is a marked underlying feeling of embattlement.

The portaloos and tents have gone, and there is an air of impermanence to the huddle of women perched on their ill-assorted folding chairs over the kettle by the gate; impermanence but not dejection. On the contrary, they may feel embattled and often hostile, their feminism barbed, but they are also exuberant. Like runners in a relay race, any woman at the base, however brief her stay, feels herself to be the custodian of the entire women's protest. She sees herself as representing victories, as they are seen, the way that since the women managed to monitor the cruise convoy so effectively — like the white train in America, the convoy has taken on the animate guise of a monster — the Americans have not taken it out as often as they promised; the way that the fence has been moved a couple of times in keeping with their legal battles. Their aim remains exactly what it was when the camp began: to prove that the base is foolish, incompetent, dangerous, unnecessary, and that it cannot endure.

Whether they succeed or not, the women themselves intend to endure. They have, as Jean repeatedly says, no intention of leaving; their presence, their witness, is undefeatable. Furthermore there are few surprises left: pigheaded, perhaps, but also courageous, the women have survived four winters; they have been cold, hungry and frightened; repeatedly manhandled by police, they know exactly what it is like to be dragged through mud when you have no change of clothes, to tear your only skirt on wire and stones, to be kept in a stifling police van for hours, then taken to court, to be charged and sent to prison, then to a punishment cell, for refusing to work. What else that is worse can happen to them now? Even 'zapping', the microwaves the women have been convinced are being beamed on them from the base, so that they have fallen sick, become sleepy and confused, suffered disruption in their cycle of menstruation, has now simply become part of the world at the Greenham base, to be borne alongside the mud. Life for these women, like Jean for whom the camp is now life in its entirety, is now reduced as in a prison to a very small round of details: who has been arrested; how many vehicles have left the base; what time the bailiffs come round; these, now, are the questions that matter. It is, as she says, very hard to go away, even for a few days. It takes so long to catch up on it all, when you come back.

Before Greenham Common, there had been no other permanent peace camp at the door of any military base, anywhere. There have been many since. None as big, nor as newsworthy, nor as long-lasting as Greenham, they have started up in America, in Seattle, Seneca and Tucson, in Canada, in Australia, in Holland, and across Britain. Jean Hutchinson and her two friends had paused for a while at Molesworth on their first peace pilgrimage, looked at the sheep grazing and the old runway, and sensed they would be back. A few years later, she was helping her daughter Jill move into a caravan along the edge of the new Molesworth base, where three miles of fencing have grown up to prepare for the arrival of more cruise missiles. Molesworth has been the site of particularly violent confrontations between police and peace activists. It is strange, then, to see just fencing and the open flatness of East Anglia beyond; no buildings yet.

Like her mother, Jill is a trained teacher; before leaving her job to come to the camp, she worked with handicapped children. She is a fair-haired, lanky girl, tall and somewhat shy, who came into the peace game as much despite her mother as because of her. Jean and her art gallery owner husband John, a quiet, bearded man who seems to accept his family's absences without resentment, took their three very small children on the Aldermaston marches in the early sixties, but took care not to get arrested. They made the decision early to give their children as long a childhood as they could organize 'without worry and without nightmares'. 'How,' says Jean, daughter and grand-daughter of Methodists and pacifists, who remembers the shame of not being allowed to take pennies to school for the Spitfires, so that while all the other girls earned gold stars, she never got one, 'is a pacifist born? I don't know.'

Not coerced; but impressed: Jill became a natural recruit. Like her mother, she is rational, somewhat phlegmatic. 'Some-times I wake up and think: what *am* I doing here? I cope either by saying I know I'm right, or by taking a break. I go home for a bath.' The two women talk tactics together; they are cosy, lov-ing. They might be discussing holiday arrangements. One day, regretting the fact that the peace campers were finding it hard to breach the fence at Molesworth, Jill suggested getting a ladder and a carpet and going over the barbed wire that way. 'No,' said Jean, thoughtfully. 'It looks so inefficient.'

There is, in the daily muted battle against the soldiers and policemen who patrol the base, a sense both of camaraderie and intense hostility; the air is volatile, as if at any moment the watchful Alsatians might be released and set upon the women as they plait ribbons into the wire or potter through the mud in their Wellington boots and brightly-coloured knitted scarves, while the withdrawn but not unfriendly soldiers might draw guns and set off in pursuit. It is a scene from the theatre, artificial but real.

I visited Molesworth one day late in November: a freezing, frosty, sunny day, with ice forming over the mud and the few peace caravans, with their stickers and slogans, a little steamy from repeated cups of tea and smelling strongly of wet wool. It was very still and very bright. Behind the fence, a few soldiers, in greatcoats, patrolled in a desultory, chilled manner. In com-parison with the cheer among the peace people they seemed solitary. Outside the tall double fence, with its rows of whirled barbed wire, there was talk among the 20 or so permanent peace campers about a forthcoming trial, about how painful it was weaving on the wire in the intense cold, about the two Quakers leaving that night for another camp. Jean and Jill were discuss-ing Christmas; they agreed that Jill should go home to be with her father, since Jean was certain she would be back in prison, a sixth sentence and the fifth in Holloway, this time for failing to

314

pay her most recent fine. Prison had lost its terrors for her; like the mud, it is inconvenient.

A man who had driven up in a minibus full of supporters approached to say that he was from the Sheffield Peace Group, and to offer £5 as a donation towards the Molesworth campers. A tall, spindly woman, with grey pigtails, and brightly-knitted woollen leggings over her jeans, joined the group to say that she had taken a fortnight off from her library in the North to come and decorate the fence, but had decided on her way down that the moment had really come to get arrested. Could they suggest a suitably provocative gesture? She had brought a small red trowel with her, in a large basket, but when she tried it out on the frozen mud, thinking to forge a hole underneath the wire and into the base, it made no impression. Jill went to find a spade. That did no better. Resigned, the woman foraged again in her basket and produced skeins of coloured wools; deftly, she began to weave a web, a surrealist sculpture in wools, exotic, a little dotty, growing at a prodigious pace. From inside, a few feet away, a policemen, holding his dog on a lead, looked on with irritation. No one arrested her; evidently it was not a day for arrests.

It is not always so. In the four years of peace camp confrontations some 4–7,000 people, most of them women, have been arrested. Many have been to prison again and again, and now face seventh or eighth sentences. Even among the sceptics, there is admiration for their tenacity. Sentences average two weeks; they can last as long as six months. Charges range from trespass to criminal damage; given the alternative of paying a fine, those arrested nearly always refuse, though other commitments — children, jobs — sometimes take precedence.

The women of Greenham have been the most arrested. Over the years, they have gained savvy, become court-wise; they know the legal jargon, the penalties, the rituals. By-laws, mitigating circumstances, failure to produce proper evidence, are so much part of daily life that they seem at times more familiar with the law than their judges. The magistrates and the police, for their part, have grown bored; they have heard these speeches before and fear they will hear them often again, and they do not believe in them. It is for the sake of British justice that they go on. The boredom, at times, is almost tangible.

There are no longer any reporters; they, too, have grown bored.

The court most used for the Greenham Common hearings is in Newbury, less than two miles from the base, a sober, conservative city better known for its race course than for the radicalness of its citizens. It is a two-storey modern building, all wood and concrete and white paint. In the corridor, on the benches outside the courtrooms, sit those women who are waiting for their hearings, and their friends come with them to lend support. They are colourful, almost exotic, and extremely companionable: because evicted so often from wherever they come to perch around the base, they carry all their belongings with them, rucksacks, sleeping bags, mittens, books, perhaps an anorak or a blanket. Tinkers, holidaymakers, they are hard to place. In age, as in voice, they are an improbable group. Some of the sweaters under the anoraks are cashmere, some of the voices unmistakably middle class. They smell of wood smoke and their hands and nails are grimy. Their mood is excited, bold.

The courtrooms, by contrast, are drab. At the high bench in the middle sit three magistrates long exhausted by procedures whose outcomes now contain no variety; these are Newbury people, embarrassed, absolutely unwilling or unable to find entertainment in this garish and lively crowd which throngs the few spectators' seats, with their guitars and sense of mission, encumbered like gypsies with paraphernalia but very courteous towards one another. Do the magistrates even listen still? Their faces reveal nothing.

The procedures, by now, are worn smooth by familiarity, and are despatched at a quickened pace, as if any hope of something new emerging had long since faded. A woman is called to the dock, sworn in and charged; the police give their evidence; the clerk officiates. Then, for a brief moment, comes the occasion the women wait for, the chance to make a speech of protest. In the dock, against the clear acoustics, their voices sound thin, initially uncertain. Soon, gathering courage, they become sharp, accusatory. They talk about their feelings, their sense of outrage, well versed in the facts and figures they need, they skip easily from opinion to statistic. They are international, mindful of other women, other protesters elsewhere, and the women

316

behind them cheer, or sing, clear soprano voices suddenly altering the heavy air of the courtroom. 'We accuse you of murder,' they say, pointing their fingers at the three impassive people who stare back. 'We don't know how you sleep at night. You can send us to prison and you can do what you like with us, but what's the point? It's not going to make any difference. It's a farce. You're going to go out of this room and then you're going to come back, and we know you're going to say we're guilty.'

The women on their benches behind them, in their badges and dirty sneakers, their pink gauze scarves and pink-dyed hair and turquoise sweaters, clap; the magistrates do not stir. The accusation dies away. The magistrates leave the room, silently, in single file. When they come back, perhaps two minutes later, it is to pronounce the woman in the dock, a little grubby, defiant, smiling, guilty.

Not very long ago, CND put out a poster: 'In the next war,' it read, 'there will be no conscientious objectors.' The War Resisters' International was outraged: it seemed to them, a body as intensively pacifist as it was at its foundation in 1921, that all militarization is wrong and all wars, whether nuclear or not, are to be opposed. To reduce it all to a bomb has always seemed to them foolish.

The WRI lives on today largely unchanged, in tone at least, from its crusading days when Fenner Brockway as its first and celebrated president carried its message of no more war into the pacifist and acquiescing twenties. The WRI office in London is a modest house, in South London, behind a street market and alongside a derelict site, but its voice is still vigorous and its affiliates meet regularly in most countries to discuss the state of the modern world's conscientious objectors, and the campaigns against a wider militarization.

What they have to say, when they meet, is not reassuring. In the mid-1980s at least 80 countries still have conscription, and in only 20 of those is there any form of legislation, however discriminatory, which recognizes the right to an objection of conscience to war. No one knows precisely how many young men at any one moment are in prison for this belief. What is clear, though, is that countries are split between those who regard certain grounds as acceptable — like Cyprus, where policemen, priests, and men of the Armenian, Greek Orthodox, Catholic and Maronite Churches can get exemption (but not Jehovah's Witnesses, who are regarded as deserters) — and those nations which send all who object, whatever their grounds or status, to prison.

On the specific question of conscientious objection little has altered. States are as threatened by individual conscience today as they were on that morning in January 1916 when Asquith moved to bring in conscription. It seems at times as if the voices of a thousand imprisoned objectors had never been heard.

The only British soldier in recent times to have challenged the state in such a way, and to have won the right to resign his commission from the British army, is a tall, black-haired, gypsy-looking man, with a long bony face and a pointed nose called Michael Biggs; he is in his thirties, a man whom it is easier to imagine in a uniform than out of it. As Captain Biggs, RAOC, he fought a prolonged battle to leave a career that had become to him, on grounds of a conscience he describes as spiritual but not religious, abhorrent. His case is exceptional only in that it is timeless; it belongs to the eighties, but might as easily fit in any pacifist trial of the 20th century.

Biggs is the son of a soldier, a cobbler's apprentice who rose to the ranks of Lieutenant-Colonel, contracting civilians for the army, and is still a serving soldier. Michael's boyhood, as the son of a family frequently posted abroad, was in boarding school, where he excelled at games and soon learnt to treat academic work with wariness. His three good A levels surprised him, but not enough to change his mind about following his father into the army which promised security and a great deal of desirable sport.

Sandhurst, after his own grammar school, appalled him. He arrived there in 1970. Quick, and something of a mimic, he rapidly adapted to the thin vowels of his middle class peers, but not so quickly to the bayonets he could never imagine sinking into a man's flesh, or to the slaughter of 'Fantasias', Sandhurst's name for the all-purpose enemy. 'I had grown up playing soldiers,' he says. 'It was scary to think of training to kill men.'

On leaving Sandhurst, passing out with the others as an

318

officer with an expectation of some 30 years of military life, he joined the Royal Army Ordnance Corps and was posted to West Germany, where he found mess life banal and distasteful and sought distraction playing chess with an unorthodox accountant in the Pay Corps. It was not until he reached Northern Ireland that military reluctance turned to revulsion. Asked to search houses and expected like the other soldiers to browbeat, in the name of peace-keeping on the border, he felt sickened; he hated the enforced distance from civilians his own age and the way they looked on his uniform with such loathing.

Michael Biggs had won a place at university; the army sent him there. It completed his alienation. On graduating he tried to find a way out from his army oaths; the military authorities were reluctant to listen, but began what proved a long and remarkably conciliatory period in which they went to great lengths to keep their dissident officer. Biggs skied, organised the Royal Tournament and married. He kept on asking for his release, but not very forcefully. 'I felt afraid I would be considered a sissy, a strange man. The army's a macho world: if you don't like killing people, you're not a man.'

Unhappy, but uncertain; it was only in London where, as another concession from the army, he was given a staff appointment at the Ministry of Defence in which he did not have to wear a uniform, that his discontent began to crystallize into a conscience against war. The signs had been there, since boyhood, but Biggs was the son of a soldier and his instincts were to obey; it took a counsellor with At Ease, the military advice service, to pinpoint its nature.

The last days of his army service were not distinguished. To get out of the army, Biggs needed a Tribunal hearing. That could not be arranged until there was proof of his discontent, but the insubordination that would prove it led only to a court martial, and not a Tribunal. It was Catch-22. Biggs is a gregarious, affable man, not prone to sulk. It took him months to win the court martial, sitting awkward and sullen at his desk, disobeying the order to work, reading Gandhi's autobiography and listening to the taunts of his superior officer; weeks more to reach a Tribunal. Then he was free. 'If ordered to bear arms I would find it impossible to comply,' he told the military men assembled to listen to him. 'If ordered to perform any form of military service I could not comply. Given my stated beliefs I can no longer be an effective member of an army and my continued presence in the British army poses for me a dilemma I can no longer live with.'

The army let him go. In the first euphoric months of liberation he trained to be a social worker, then went off to work for the borough of Lambeth. His marriage has broken up, and his job come to an end, and he now avoids the publicity and showmanship that followed his Tribunal. He needs time, he says, after 17 years of regimented life, time to work out what he needs to do. His family find it difficult to talk about what he did, but they are not unfriendly. His own position is clear. 'I cannot be convinced,' he says 'and being in the army only made this plainer, that you can bring about any kind of happiness, prevent trouble or solve disputes through force. History has shown that, if anything, it makes others more efficient at killing next time. I know, I know that violence only legitimizes further violence.'

In the autumn of 1981, ten major European cities saw demonstrations against nuclear weapons of a size the world was not accustomed to. Each numbered over 100,000 people. In Athens, Madrid and Rome, those protesting were put at 500,000; in Amsterdam, 400,000; in Bucharest, 300,000; in Palermo, 20,000; in The Hague, 10,000, and these were nearly all women. In response to the increase of nuclear weapons, to hawkish governments and in particular to President Reagan, marchers, expressing their profound sense of vulnerability, turned out in a way they have never done before. No one was quite prepared for the display. This resurgence of nuclear pacifism was mirrored in Britain, where CND had for some months been taking shape again, winning back those who had marched to Aldermaston in the sixties, in the belief that they could influence policies and had stopped marching when they felt they had, and now realized that they had been wrong, and finding new support in a generation born long after the bomb fell on Hiroshima.

Its strength, since then, has lain in its cohesion around one simple idea — getting rid of nuclear weapons — and in the extraordinary diversity of its supporters and the range of their other concerns. Before the tactics changed, and emphasis moved from massed demonstrations to more local and enduring grassroots pressure, there were several last great assemblies. One took place, in the autumn of 1984, at Barrow-in-Furness, near the Vickers' armaments works in Yorkshire.

Some 50,000 people were expected; no one knows precisely how many came, but it was a brilliant and clear autumn day and during several hours, in orderly groups, under banners and pennants stitched with different peace themes, with doves and flowers and messages, many like the splendid trade union banners, marched the individual small groups of peace. Those who walked were scruffy, colourfully dressed; most wore badges, not only about nuclear bombs, but about ecology and nuclear power and Latin America; babies had their prams covered in stickers. 'I want to grow up, not blow up.' And when the whistle went, the signal that a symbolic bomb had fallen, the marchers crumbled to the ground, in one great sprawling blanket of crushed people, their banners fallen where they lay, a confusion of bags and clothes and colours, so that no bit of pavement or road was visible, and the only sound, apart from a small plane high above, were the gulls flying over the water. In the dockyards, and along the dry docks for the submarines, the men in their overalls stopped working and watched. One by one, the cars and buses, entangled with the marchers, turned off their engines and sat waiting. For two minutes, while the gulls whirled and screeched, in the very blowy clear and sunny day, Barrow-in-Furness stood as still and silent as after a final bomb.

In the eighties, CND, which is exceptional in the world peace movements for being so homogeneous and so large, has drawn its members more widely. As an organization, it is less hierarchical and less exclusive than it was in the 1950s, more tolerant, more conscious of its supporters' wishes, as if determined to make none of the errors of the early sixties. It has grown more international, and more moral. J. B. Priestley's early concern with the lunacy of nuclear weapons has been strengthened, as in America, by a desire for a spiritual and ethical dimension. More supporters, possibly now as many as a quarter of the entire membership, would say that their motives were religious, while strong encouragement comes from the pacifist religious bodies that have sprung up within each of the churches. No church has given the same lead as the American bishops, although all have made statements against nuclear war. 'Any act of war,' says the Catholic Church, 'which aims indiscriminately at the destruction of entire cities or wide areas with their inhabitants is a crime against God and man, to be firmly and unhesitatingly condemned.' There is widespread disappointment at such pusillanimity, but also acceptance of the political realities. 'We are,' said one Church leader, 'waiting for the new theology that must logically follow the move from conventional to nuclear weapons. It is being a long time coming.'

Those who join CND and wear its badge are not all, or even very many of them, pacifists. They do not reject, as true pacifists do, violence and militarism in all and every form. Many of its leaders, however, are. Bruce Kent, enthusiastic private in the British army in 1947, chairman of CND between 1977 and 1985, defines his pacifism with care, as an intention to look for a more just and more stable world and as an inability to see how Christians can conceivably tally violence with their faith. Meg Beresford, elected chairman in 1985, came to her similar pacifism long ago, through reading Bertrand Russell, and observing for herself the nuclear catastrophe at Three Mile Island.

A rift exists, now as in the sixties, between the pure pacifists, those who came to their conviction in the thirties, schooled by the words of Gandhi and Dick Sheppard, fired by Muriel Lester and the great outdoor pacifist orators in Victoria Park and on the soap boxes at Hyde Park Corner, who hold violence to be wrong, and fear that by concentrating on nuclear weapons the peace protesters are missing the point; and the nuclear protesters, who see in the members of the now small Peace Pledge Union and the Fellowship of Reconciliation sterile passivity. Those who bridge the gap most effectively are the Christian pacifists, such as the Quaker Peace and Service Fellowship, who support CND but reflect that survival will mean living with the enemy, even if the enemy triumphs. To CND's conviction that protest has now reached such world-wide dimensions that it can never again be silenced or ignored, who point to the Labour Party's adherence to their position, to the views of social democrats and Labour parties throughout the world, they add only Bertrand Russell's words. 'It is not enough,' said Russell, 'to ban nuclear weapons, for nuclear weapons can always be manufactured again. The thing you have to ban is war.'

What the peace movement has not done this century is show itself capable of thwarting militarism. On this level, it is a story of almost pure failure. Thousands of men and women have gone to prison to uphold their opposition to war and armaments and they have altered virtually nothing. As an influence on military decisions, the women of Greenham, the Graswürzelrevolution, the Berrigan community in Baltimore and those who track the great white train across America have been powerless. The world in 1986 is a more militant and a more dangerous place than it was in 1916.

Forty countries currently have armed conflicts within their borders. World military spending, which has increased four-fold since World War Two, now stands at $1,000 billion. Seventy million people are directly or indirectly engaged in military matters. Five countries have, and acknowledge having, nuclear weapons; five others may also possess them. Civilians, who in World War One made up only five per cent of the casualties, have in recent wars accounted for between 80 and 90 per cent. The great part of these have been women and children.

The pacifists, then, have not checked conventional war, which remains, as they always feared it would, and the Falklands proved all over again, more exciting and more politically attractive than peace. The nagging uncertainty that plagued them in 1916 plagues them today: that pacifism is essentially a negative philosophy, and that unless it can be harnessed to a positive programme must lack the full bloodedness of aggression. No one has yet achieved anything to challenge seriously 'the big wars that made ambition virtue', nor convinced the world as Bertrand Russell hoped they might at the end of the First War that 'Life, not Death, however heroic, is the source of all good'. Nor, as the religious and humanitarian peace makers who gathered under Bilthoven's pines in 1919 so fondly dreamed, has the movement become a seriously international one: numerous and active at home, war protesters have found no really effective way of merging their voices on a world stage. Even the many international gatherings of the peace bodies remain curiously insular.

The passion that has gone into preventing violence this century has not however been entirely in vain. The presence in prison of so many articulate and troublesome people has led to reforms within the prisons themselves; the work of war resisters has produced enduring social experiments; while the tactics of pacifism — civil disobedience — have brought about some of the most fundamental improvements in human rights this century. What is more, the movement against weapons of mass destruction, the nuclear bombs, born with Hiroshima, has been so persistent that the debate has never gone away; nor is it likely to do so now. If anything, protest is growing, and arguably, in small ways at least, having an effect. Its concerns are also spreading, so that today fears about nuclear power have become almost indivisible from fears about nuclear weapons in people's minds. It is improbable that governments will ever again be able to ignore this feeling entirely.

There is another area in which pacifism has neither changed nor failed. As a profession of individual belief, defined so eloquently by Thoreau in 1849, it has not been altered by the events of the 20th century. The stand taken not long ago in a small English country town, by a librarian called Arthur Windsor, could have happened at any moment, in any place.

Windsor was brought up a Baptist, son of a soldier killed in the First War, whom he never knew. Working in a library in Croydon, he was called up in 1940 and went to the war, a dutiful but unenthusiastic soldier, never rising from the ranks but not doubting the legitimacy of war until he heard that an atom bomb had fallen on Hiroshima. He wondered then what he was doing. Real pacifist conviction came after visiting a Quaker meeting and resolving to refuse to do his ex-serviceman's two weeks' reserve each year. What he found appealing was the fact that the pacifist commitment was individual, not compulsory, based ultimately as the Quaker writer Neave Bradshaw put it, 'on the conception of that of God in every man to which the Christian in the presence of Evil is called on to make appeal'.

Windsor is not a demonstrative or an assertive man; he is now in his seventies, courteous and somewhat anxious, with wispy white hair and solid glasses. His clothes are brown. He speaks earnestly, as if needing to convince himself that what he is saying is right.

In 1962, he and his wife Ursula, a refugee from Nazi Germany, moved to Gloucester, to a Georgian house in a pretty square in the middle of the city, where he hoped to become part of a loose community of people under the teachings of the Quakers. Over and above their pacifist views they pooled some of their resources. In 1982, after two decades of gentle commitment to war resistance, members of many bodies and active in local causes from time to time, Windsor heard of a Quaker family in Birmingham who had decided to withhold that portion of their taxes from the Inland Revenue which they believed was going in military spending. It seemed to him such an obvious thing to do.

Windsor has been summonsed three times in the last four years. The occasions overlap, the income tax request crossing over with his repeated letters of explanation that what he is doing and intends to go on doing, is to keep back that part of what he owes which he believes is being wrongfully spent on weapons. The sums are small; £139.76, £78.70, £94.05. But they are symbolic, and with his letters Windsor sends a cheque for the money he owes, made out, not to the Inland Revenue, but to the Overseas Development Administration, of which he approves. Each time, the cheques are sent back.

In October 1983, the bailiffs came to get his car. It was sold at auction for £300, and the difference between his debt and the car money was returned to him. Bidding was low because he had had the idea of writing out a leaflet explaining what was happening and passing it around the auction house. A friend bought the car back for him. In July 1984, the bailiffs came again. This time they went away with a kitchen table, two other smaller tables, a desk and a washing machine. The kitchen table, the first to be auctioned, fetched enough to cover the debt; the other furniture, after costs had been deducted, was returned to him.

The third time, Arthur Windsor went to prison, for contempt of the court which had ordered him to pay his taxes. He is the first man in Britain to take his case all the way to jail. Three hundred other tax resisters are thought to be waiting to follow him there. In the spring of 1986 he spent three weeks in Gloucester

325

Jail, folding the proverbial mailbags that conscientious objectors have always folded and stitched. He came out to find over 500 letters from strangers. They were all approving. Many said they understood exactly what he was doing: he was going to prison for them, as an act of witness. The principle, he says, is moral: should any individual be forced to pay for others to kill? Windsor is not sanguine about the future of the world, but about his own position and his own behaviour he is absolutely clear. It is all, he explains, a question of faith. While not wanting to waste the rest of his life on this matter of tax, he knows that for him personally he has no choice. His protest must go on, even if he sees no result in his lifetime.

In 1916, pacifism was about preventing war; and it failed. In the mid-eighties, it turns out to be less about war than about the relationship between man and the power of the state. The pacifists, the nuclear protesters, all those who take their own individual stand against the machinery of war, are keeping alive that tradition of individual freedom; their importance can only grow. Conscience has not been altered by violence. 'It costs me less in every sense to incur the penalty of disobedience to the state,' wrote Thoreau, well over a hundred years ago, 'than it would to obey. I should feel as if I were worth less in that case.' No one has put it better.

Notes

Foreword

p. xv   'In 314 . . .' Peter Brock: *Pacifism in Europe to 1914*, Princetown University Press, 1972.

p. xvi   'In England . . .' For an account of British Quaker pacifists, Margaret E. Hirst: *The Quakers in Peace and War*, London 1923.

p. xvii   'It was in America . . .' For detailed writings of early pacifists, ed. Staughton Lynd, *Non-violence in America*, N.Y. 1966.

p. xviii   'The authority of . . .' Henry Thoreau: *On the Duty of Civil Disobedience*, London 1849.

p. xix   'It was also . . .' Tolstoy on peace. *What I believe*, London 1985. *The Kingdom of God is Within You*, London 1936.

Chapter 1

p. 3   'January 5 . . .' For debates in the House of Commons, *Hansard*, January– February 1916.

p. 5   'How hot . . .' John W. Graham: *Conscription and Conscience*, London 1922.

p. 6   'In its own . . .' Supplement to the *Labour Leader*, April 13, 1916.

p. 8   'only mild faced . . .' *Daily Mail*, April 10, 1916.

p. 9   'Coming away from . . .' Quoted in Jo Vellacott: *Bertrand Russell and the Pacifists of the First World War*, London 1980.

p. 11   'To stand out . . .' Quoted in *We Did Not Fight*, ed. Julian Bell, London 1935.

p. 12   'Isn't it luck . . .' Nicholas Mosley: *Julian Grenfell: His Life and Times*, London 1976.

p. 12   'By October . . .' Paul Fussell: *The Great War and Modern Memory*, London 1975. A. J. P. Taylor: *English History 1914–1945*, London 1965.

p. 13   For full account of Parliament and conscription, John Rae: *Conscience and Politics*, London 1970.

p. 16   'Fenner Brockway was . . .' Interview, June 24, 1984.

p. 23   'A wonderful . . .' *Daily Express*, June 19, 1985.

p. 24   'These women peacemakers . . .' For detailed account, Anne Wiltsher: *Most Dangerous Women*, London 1985.

Chapter 2

p. 29   'Dorothy Bing . . .' Interview, April 10, 1984.

p. 31   'On paper . . .' *Troublesome People 1914–1919*, Central Board for Conscientious Objectors.

p. 33   'Eva Gore-Booth . . .' Quoted in John W. Graham: *Conscription and Conscience*, London 1922.

p. 35   'One of the imprisoned . . .' Interview, Mark Hayler, April 26, 1984.

p. 40   'Looking out . . .' Mrs. Henry Hobhouse: *'I Appeal Unto Caesar'*, London 1917.

p. 41   'Frederick Dutch . . .' Imperial War Museum, department of sound records, 000356/10.

p. 45   'After a while . . .' Interviews with Mark Hayler and other World War One conscientious objectors.

p. 47   'There is no . . .' *The Word*, March 1940, Vol. 1, No 8.

p. 48   'Archibald Baxter . . .' *We Will Not Cease*, London 1939.

Chapter 3

p. 58   'Ramsay MacDonald . . .' *Hansard*, October 19, 1916.

p. 62   'In the House . . .' *Hansard*, April 23, 1917.

p. 63   'Though his speeches . . .' *Western Morning News*, October 9, 1917.

p. 66   'The change . . .' H. C. Peterson and Gilbert Fite: *Opponents of War 1917–1919*, University of Wisconsin, 1957.

p. 68   'Ernest Meyer . . .' *'Hey! Yellowbacks!'*, New York 1930.

p. 72   'On May 12 . . .' Quoted in Martin Gilbert: *Plough My Own Furrow*, London 1965.

p. 77   'Signed by . . .' *Manchester Guardian*, January 14, 1919.

Chapter 4

p. 81   'I went out . . .' Letter in Mark Hayler collection, Imperial War Museum.

p. 82   'By the financial . . .' *Towards Peace and Freedom: Report of the International Congress of Women*, Zurich 1919, Fawcett Library, London.

p. 87   'What'll we do . . .' Papers in the possession of Chris Judge Smith.

p. 94   'It was . . .' *The Bulletin*, (Journal of the War Resisters' International), May 1924.

p. 95   'Early the previous . . .' For full account, Martin Ceadel: *Pacifism in Britain 1914–1945*, London 1980.

p. 98   'Her style . . .' Letters in the possession of Sydney Russell.

p. 103   'If I am . . .' Quoted in James D. Hunt: *Gandhi in London*, New Delhi 1978.

Chapter 5

p. 109   'Do you remember . . .' Siegfried Sassoon: *Collected Poems*, London 1961.

p. 110   'In 1932 . . .' Beverley Nichols: *All I Could Never Be*, London 1949.

p. 114   'Before the First . . .' Quoted in Ronald Clark: *Einstein: The Life and Times*, London 1973.

p. 117   'Once again . . .' *Manchester Guardian*, February 15, 1933.

p. 122   'When he comes . . .' *Peace News*, November 6, 1937.

p. 128   'He worked himself . . .' Quoted in Carolyn Scott: *Dick Sheppard*, London 1977.

p. 129   'It was through . . .' For detailed account, Sybille Bedford: *Aldous Huxley*, London 1973.

p. 133   'I came to see . . .' Fenner Brockway: *Inside the Left*, London 1942.

p. 134   'Although the world . . .' George Lansbury: *My Quest for Peace*, London 1938.

p. 139   'The nations . . .' Max Plowman: *The Faith Called Pacifism*, London 1936.

Chapter 6

p. 142   'William Heard . . .' Interview, July 7, 1984.

p. 147   'In the First . . .' For detailed account, Denis Hayes: *Challenge of Conscience*, London 1949.

p. 158 'Ted Milligan . . .' Interview, June 20, 1984.

p. 161 'In London . . .' Interview, Doris Nicholls, February 17, 1986.

p. 164 'Arthur McMillan . . .' Interview, Muriel McMillan, July 7, 1984.

p. 169 'Much of the . . .' For detailed accounts, *Peace News*, 1939, 1940, 1941.

p. 172 'Public feeling . . .' Interview, Frances Partridge. July 9, 1984.

Chapter 7

p. 179 'In keeping with . . .' Community Service Committee reports, London 1943.

p. 181 'One of these . . .' Interview, Tom Carlisle, July 27, 1985.

p. 184 'As Gerald Heard . . .' Community Service Committee reports, London 1943.

p. 186 'No one has . . .' John Middleton Murry: *Community Farm*, London 1952.

p. 190 'Nora Page . . .' Interview, July 4, 1984.

p. 192 'Joan Layton's pacifism . . .' Interview, March 18, 1986.

p. 193 'The First War . . .' For detailed figures, Denis Hayes: *Challenge of Conscience*, London 1949.

p. 194 'I think . . .' Fenner Brockway: *Presidential Address to the 2nd Annual Conference Fellowship of Conscientious Objectors*, London 1943.

p. 196 'Jim Bristol . . .' Interview, December 5, 1985.

p. 197 'In prison . . .' For detailed account, ed. Robert Cooney & Helen Michalowski, *The Power of the People*, California 1977.

Chapter 8

p. 203 'In December . . .' For detailed account, Richard Taylor and Colin Pritchard: *The Protest Makers*, London 1980.

p. 207 'The methods . . .' *Peace News*, January 18, 1952.

p. 211 'They came from . . .' For a full account, Christopher Driver: *The Disarmers*, London 1964.

p. 212 'Canon Collins . . .' *Peace News*, February 17, 1958.

p. 213 'The DAC . . .' Interview, Michael Randle, July 10, 1985.

p. 214 '*Peace News* was . . .' *Peace News*, April 4, 1958.

p. 215 'Pat Arrowsmith . . .' Interview, May 15, 1985.

p. 220 'Bertrand Russell . . .' Ronald Clark: *Life of Bertrand Russell*, London 1975.

p. 222 'Who are . . .' *Daily Express*, April 19, 1960.

p. 226 'The fact remains . . .' *Daily Express*, September 18, 1961.

p. 226 'The trial . . .' For full account, *Peace News*, February 1962. Ed. David Boulton, *Voices from the Crowd*, London 1964.

p. 231 'I think people . . .' Quoted in J. Cox: *Overkill*, Penguin, London 1977.

Chapter 9

p. 232 'In the spring . . .' Interview, Senji Yagamuchi, September 12, 1984.

p. 234 'The facts . . .' For detailed account, *Hiroshima and Nagasaki. The Physical, Medical and Social Effects of the Atomic Bombings*, Tokyo 1979.

p. 240 'Zen Matsutani . . .' Interview, September 14, 1984.

p. 242 'The director . . .' Interview, Yoshitaka Kawamoto, September 15, 1984.

p. 249 'One of these . . .' Interview, Gyoto Sato, September 17, 1984.

Chapter 10

p. 253 'Bayard Rustin . . .' Interview, December 6, 1985.

p. 257 'There had been . . .' For a full account, ed. Robert Cooney & Helen Michalowski. *The Power of the People*, California 1977.

p. 259 'Montgomery . . .' Martin Luther King's statements on peace are to be found in *The Trumpet of Conscience*, New York 1964 and *The words of Martin Luther King*, Fount, London 1984.

p. 260 'Zohara Simmons . . .' Interview, December 11, 1985.

p. 263 'Randy Kehler . . .' Interview, December 13, 1985.

p. 265 'The war . . .' For detailed coverage, 'Trials of Resistance', *New York Review of Books*, New York 1980. Francine du Plessix Grey, *NYRB*, June 1, June 15, 1972 and September 25, 1969.

p. 270 'Catholic nuns . . .' *Sojourners*, April 1985.

Bibliography

Much of the material for this book came from unpublished letters and diaries, and from conversations with pacifists and former conscientious objectors in Britain, the United States, Japan and West Germany. I have also borrowed a great deal from the various newsletters and publications of the pacifist organizations — *Peace News*, *The Pacifist*, the *Bulletin* of the War Resisters' International, and *Sojourners* — and daily newspapers, as well as from taped interviews recorded by the Imperial War Museum with surviving conscientious objectors of both wars. Of published works, I owe most to the following:

Foreword:

Brock, Peter: *Pacifism in Europe to 1914*, Princetown University Press, 1972.

Hirst, Margaret E: *The Quakers in Peace and War*, Swarthmore Press, London 1923.

Lynd, Staughton (ed.): *Non-violence in America: A Documentary History*, The Bobbs-Merrill Co. 1966.

Thoreau, Henry David: *On the Duty of Civil Disobedience*, London 1849.

Tolstoy, Lev Nicholaevitch: *What I Believe*, Elliot Stick 1985.

Tolstoy, Lev Nicholaevitch: *The Kingdom of God is Within You*, Oxford University Press 1936.

Chapters 1, 2 and 3

Baxter, Archibald: *We Will Not Cease: The Autobiography of a Conscientious Objector*, Gollancz 1939.

Bell, Julian (ed.): *We Did Not Fight: 1914–1918*, Cobden-Sanderson 1935

Bell, Quentin: *Bloomsbury*, Weidenfeld and Nicolson 1968.

Boulton, David: *Objection Overruled*, MacGibbon and Kee 1967.

Brock, Peter: *Twentieth Century Pacifism*, (*New Perspectives in Political Science*), Von Nostrand Reinhold 1970.

Brockway, Fenner: *Bermondsey Story: The Life of Alfred Salter*, George Allen and Unwin 1949.

Brockway, Fenner: *Inside the Left*, George Allen and Unwin 1942.

Ceadel, Martin: *Pacifism in Britain 1914–1945*, Clarendon Press 1980.

Childs, Major-General Sir Wyndham: *Episodes and Reflections*, Cassell 1930.

Cross, Colin: *Philip Snowden*, Barrie & Rockliff 1966.

Forster, E. M: *Selected Letters*, edited by Mary Lago and P. N. Furbank, Collins 1983.

Fussell, Paul: *The Great War and Modern Memory*, Oxford University Press 1975.

Gilbert, Martin: *Plough My Own Furrow: The Story of Lord Allen of Hurtwood*, Longman 1965.

Graham, John W: *Conscription and Conscience. A History: 1916–1919*, George Allen and Unwin 1922.

Hobhouse, Mrs Henry: *'I Appeal Unto Caesar': The Cases of the Conscientious Objectors*, George Allen and Unwin 1917.

Johnstone, J. K: *The Bloomsbury Group*, Secker and Warburg 1954.

Marwick, Arthur: *Clifford Allen: The Open Conspirator*, Oliver & Boyd 1964.

Mayer, Peter (ed.): *The Pacifist Conscience*, Rupert Hart-Davis 1966.

Meyer, Ernest L: *'Hey! Yellowbacks!' The War Diary of a Conscientious Objector*, John Day 1930.

Mitchell, David: *Women on the Warpath: The Story of the Women of the First World War*, Jonathan Cape 1966.

Mosley, Nicholas: *Julian Grenfell: His Life and Times*, Weidenfeld and Nicolson 1976.

Peterson, H. C. and Fite, Gilbert: *Opponents of War 1917–1918*, University of Wisconsin 1957.

Rae, John: *Conscience and Politics: The British Government and the Conscientious Objector to Military Service, 1916–1919*, Oxford University Press 1970.

Postgate, Raymond: *The Life of George Lansbury*, Longman 1951.

Taylor, A. J. P: *English History 1914–1945*, Oxford University Press 1965.

Tims, Margaret: *Jane Addams of Hull House 1860–1935*, George Allen and Unwin 1961.

Troublesome People. A reprint of the NCF Souvenir describing its work during the years 1914–1919, Central Board for Conscientious Objectors, 1940.

Vellacott, Jo: *Bertrand Russell and the Pacifists of the First World War*, Harvester Press 1980.

Vansittart, Peter: *Voices from the Great War*, Jonathan Cape 1981.

Webb, Beatrice: *The Power to Alter Things. Diaries 1905–1924* (Volume Three), Virago and London School of Economics 1984.

Wiltshire, Anne: *Most Dangerous Women: Feminist Peace Campaigners of the Great War*, Pandora Press 1985.

Chapters 4 and 5

Aragon, Louis; Cunard, Nancy, etc: *Authors Take Sides on the Spanish Civil War*, The Left Review 1937.

Bedford, Sybille: *Aldous Huxley: A Biography*, Chatto and Windus 1973.

Blunden, Edmund: *A Booklist on the War 1914–1918*, Pamphlet 1929.

Brittain, Vera: *The Rebel Passion: A Short History of Some Pioneer Peace-Makers*, George Allen and Unwin 1964.

Bussey, Gertrude, and Tims, Margaret: *Women's International League for Peace and Freedom 1915–1965*, George Allen and Unwin 1965.

Clark, Ronald W: *Einstein: The Life and Times*, Hodder and Stoughton 1973.

Day Lewis, C: 'We're not going to do nothing', *The Left Review* 1936.

Goldring, Douglas: *The Nineteen Twenties*, Nicholson and Watson 1945.

Hargrave, John: *Confession of the Kibbo Kift*, Duckworth 1927.

Hargrave, John: *The Great War Brings It Home*, Constable 1919.

Hunt, James D: *Gandhi in London*, Promill, New Delhi 1978.

Huxley, Aldous: *Encyclopaedia of Pacifism*, Chatto and Windus 1937.

Joad, C. E. M: *Under the Fifth Rib: A Belligerent Autobiography*, Faber and Faber 1932.

Lansbury, Edgar: *George Lansbury: My Father*, Sampson, Low Marston 1934.

Lansbury, George: *My Quest for Peace*, Michael Joseph 1938.

Lester, Muriel: *Entertaining Gandhi*, Nicholson and Watson 1932.

Lester, Muriel: *It Occurred to Me*, Student Christian Movement Press 1939.

Lester, Muriel: *It So Happened*, Harper and Brothers 1947.

Milne, A. A: *It's Too Late Now: Autobiography of a Writer*, Methuen 1939.

Milne, A. A: *War with Honour*, Macmillan 1940.

Milne, A. A: *Peace with Honour*, Methuen 1934.

Nichols, Beverley: *Avalanche* (published in *Failures: Three Plays*), Jonathan Cape 1933.

Nichols, Beverley: *All I Could Never Be*, Jonathan Cape 1949.

Nichols, Beverley: *Cry Havoc!* Jonathan Cape 1933.

Orr, E. W: *The Quakers in Peace and War 1920–1967*, W. J. Offord 1974.

Plowman, Max: *The Faith Called Pacifism*, J. M. Dent 1936.

Russell, Bertrand: *Autobiography*, Volumes 1, 2 and 3, George Allen and Unwin 1967–1969.

Scott, Carolyn: *Dick Sheppard*, Hodder and Stoughton 1977.

Symons, J: *The Thirties*, Cresset Press 1960.

Thompson, Douglas: *Donald Soper: A Biography*, Denholm House Press 1971.

Who Was for Munich? The Role of the Peace Movements in the 1930s. Pamphlet no. 1, University Group on Defence Policy 1958.

Chapters 6 and 7

Armytage, W. H. G: *Heavens Below: Utopian Experiments in England 1560–1960*, Routledge and Kegan Paul 1961.

Barker, Rachel: *Conscience, Government and War 1939–1945*, Routledge and Kegan Paul 1982.

Blishen, Edward: *A Cackhanded War*, Hamish Hamilton 1972.

Hayes, Denis: *Challenge of Conscience: the Story of the Conscientious Objectors, 1939–49*. George Allen and Unwin 1949.

Lea, F. A: *The Life of John Middleton Murry*, Methuen 1959.

Mellanby, Kenneth: *Human Guinea Pigs*, Gollancz 1945.

Middleton Murry, John: *Community Farm*, Peter Nevill 1952.

Morrison, Sybil: *I Renounce War: The Story of the Peace Pledge Union*, Sheppard Press 1962.

Partridge, Frances: *A Pacifist's War*, Hogarth Press 1978.

Simmons, Clifford (ed.): *The Objectors*, Times Press 1965.

Chapter 8

Boulton, David (ed.): *Voices from the Crowd against the H-Bomb*, Peter Owen 1964.

Clark, Ronald W: *Life of Bertrand Russell*, Jonathan Cape and Weidenfeld and Nicolson 1975.

Driver, Christopher: *The Disarmers: A Study in Protest*, Hodder and Stoughton 1964.

Greer, Herb: *Mud Pie: The CND Story*, Max Parrish 1964.

Minnion, John and Bolsover, Philip (eds.): *The CND Story*, Allison and Busby 1983.

Taylor, Richard and Pritchard, Colin: *The Protest Makers: The British Nuclear Disarmament Movement of 1958–1965, Twenty Years On*, Pergamon Press 1980.

Chapter 9

Hiroshima and Nagasaki. The Physical, Medical and Social Effects of the Atomic Bombings (The Committee for the compilation of materials on damage caused by the Atomic bombs in Hiroshima and Nagasaki), Iwanami Shoten, Tokyo.

Nobuya Bamba and Howes, John F: *Pacifism in Japan*, Minerva Press, Kyoto 1978.

Chapter 10

Berrigan, Daniel (ed.): *For Swords into Plowshares*, Piscataway 1985.

Berrigan, Daniel: *America Is Hard to Find*, SPCK 1973.

Cooney, Robert and Michalowski, Helen (eds.): *The Power of the People: Active Non-violence in the United States*, cooperatively published 1977.

Luther King, Martin: *The Trumpet of Conscience*, Harper and Row 1964.

Trials of Resistance (a collection of essays), *New York Review of Books* 1970.

Sibley, Mulford and Jacob, Philip E: *Conscription or Conscience 1940–1947*, Cornell University Press 1962.

Chapter 11

Bentley, James: *Martin Niemöller*, Oxford University Press 1984.

Chapter 12

Harford, Barbara and Hopkins, Sarah (eds.): *Greenham Common: Women at the Wire*, The Women's Press 1984.

Index